Lecture Notes in Artificial Intellig

Edited by J. G. Carbonell and J. Siekmann

Subseries of Lecture Notes in Computer Science

Olivier Boissier   Julian Padget
Virginia Dignum   Gabriela Lindemann
Eric Matson   Sascha Ossowski
Jaime Simão Sichman
Javier Vázquez-Salceda (Eds.)

Coordination, Organizations, Institutions, and Norms in Multi-Agent Systems

AAMAS 2005 International Workshops on Agents, Norms and
Institutions for Regulated Multi-Agent Systems, ANIREM 2005
and From Organizations to Organization-Oriented Programming
in Multi-Agent Systems, OOOP 2005
Utrecht, The Netherlands, July 25-26, 2005
Revised Selected Papers

 Springer

Volume Editors

Olivier Boissier
E-mail: Olivier.Boissier@emse.fr

Julian Padget
E-mail: jap@cs.bath.ac.uk

Virginia Dignum
E-mail: virginia@cs.uu.nl

Gabriela Lindemann
E-mail: lindeman@informatik.hu-berlin.de

Eric Matson
E-mail: eric.matson@wright.edu

Sascha Ossowski
E-mail: sascha.ossowski@urjc.es

Jaime Simão Sichman
E-mail: jaime.sichman@poli.usp.br

Javier Vázquez-Salceda
E-mail: jvazquez@lsi.upc.edu

Library of Congress Control Number: 2006927157

CR Subject Classification (1998): I.2.11, D.2, F.3, D.1, C.2.4, D.3

LNCS Sublibrary: SL 7 – Artificial Intelligence

ISSN   0302-9743
ISBN-10   3-540-35173-6 Springer Berlin Heidelberg New York
ISBN-13   978-3-540-35173-3 Springer Berlin Heidelberg New York

Springer is a part of Springer Science+Business Media

springer.com

© Springer-Verlag Berlin Heidelberg 2006
Printed in Germany

Typesetting: Camera-ready by author, data conversion by Scientific Publishing Services, Chennai, India
Printed on acid-free paper   SPIN: 11775331   06/3142   5 4 3 2 1 0

Preface

This volume is the first in a planned series focussing on issues in Coordination, Organizations, Institutions and Norms (COIN) in multi-agent systems. Forthcoming events are COIN @ AAMAS 2006 and COIN @ ECIA 2006. The papers in this volume are drawn from two complementary events, ANIREM (Agents, Norms and Institutions for Regulated Multiagent Systems) and OOOP (From Organizations to Organization-Oriented Programming in MAS), that were part of the workshop program at AAMAS 2005 in Utrecht.

ANIREM: Multi-agent systems are often understood as complex entities where a multitude of agents interact, usually with some intended individual or collective purpose. Such a view usually assumes some form of structure, or set of norms or conventions that articulate or restrain interactions in order to make them more effective in attaining those goals, more certain for participants or more predictable. The engineering of effective regulatory mechanisms is a key problem for the design of open complex multi-agent systems, so that in recent years it has become a rich and challenging topic for research and development. There are many possible ways of looking at the problem of regulating multi-agent systems, and one perspective is the normative approach, based on the use of norms in artificial institutions. Lately there has been an explosion of new approaches, both theoretical and practical, exploring the use of norms as a flexible way to constrain and/or impose behavior, and these are reflected in specifications of norm languages, agent-mediated electronic institutions, contracts, protocols and policies.

OOOP: Agent organizations are an emergent area of application within multi-agent systems that pose new demands on traditional MAS models, such as the integration of organizational and individual perspectives and the dynamic adaptation of models to organizational and environmental changes, both of which are impacted by the notion of openness and heterogeneity. As systems grow to include an increasing number of agents, the view of coordination and control has to be expanded to consider both the agent-centric as well as the organization-centric views. Practical applications of agents in organizational modelling are being widely developed. All this contributes to an emerging field of research and work that could be called organization-oriented programming. However, formal theories, tools and methodologies are still very much in short supply. Even if an externally designed organizational structure is a necessary coordination device to achieve global social order there is a special tension between such imposed constraints and the agents' autonomous behavior. This leads to a focus on the trade-off between social order and agent autonomy, and on other means to achieve social order in MAS other than organizations.

ANIREM: Gabriela Lindemann, Sascha Ossowski,
Julian Padget, Javier Vázquez-Salceda
OOOP: Olivier Boissier, Virginia Dignum,
Eric Matson, Jaime Sichman

The Papers

The papers in this volume are extended, revised versions of the best papers presented at the ANIREM and the OOOP workshops at AAMAS 2005, with additionally a paper originating from an invited talk given at ANIREM. The result is a well-balanced collection of high-quality papers that really can be called representative of the field at this moment. For this volume, the papers from the two workshops have been re-grouped around the following themes:

Modelling, Analyzing and Programming Organizations: The first section contains five papers on the modelling, analysis and programming of organizations. The first paper in this section, by Sibertin-Blanc et al., proposes a basis for the design of coordination models in multi-agent systems that exploits a widely recognized sociological theory, the sociology of organized action. The paper by van den Broek et al. describes a new, formal, role-based framework for modelling and analyzing both real world and artificial organizations that considers both the dynamic properties of the organizational model and the environment. Wijngaards et al. introduce a conceptual view of realizing sustained team effectiveness, in which both the measurement of effectiveness and team management play an important role. The paper by McCallum et al. proposes a means for the formal specification, verification and analysis of agent organizations, capturing notions of role, obligation and delegation (of obligations) that furthermore allows change in the organizational structure to be modelled. The section ends with a paper by Hübner et al. describing a software implementation that aims to bridge the gap between organizational constraints and agent autonomy.

Modelling and Analyzing Institutions: The focus of the five papers in the second section is the modelling and analysis of institutions. It starts with an invited contribution from one of the pioneers of electronic institutions, Pablo Noriega, in which he surveys some of the current issues he sees in institutions research, from the perspective of three complementary case studies. The paper by Cliffe et al. describes a new approach to constructing specifications of institutional norms using answer set programming that can subsequently be used to verify properties of the institutions. Boella et al. explore the modelling of a normative system governing the production of renewable energy in the UK in which their agents map the norms into obligations represented as beliefs and goals. Rubino et al. by contrast address generic issues surrounding the engineering of normative systems and demonstrate how elements of their coordination artifacts infrastructure can capture and implement norms. The section ends with the paper by Viganò et al. in which they make the case for an event-based approach to norm specification and discuss how one institution may regulate another one.

Modelling Normative Designs: The third section is devoted to normative issues in organizations and institutions. Aldewereld et al. discuss a formal framework for the design of a protocol from a normative specification in highly regulated environments. By the use of landmarks they introduce an intermediate level in order to be able to connect descriptive norms with operational protocols. The paper by Garion and van der Torre proposes a software design language based on temporal deontic logic as a means to bridge the gap between the theory of design by contract and software engineering concepts. Additionally, they discuss the relation between the normative stance toward systems implicit in the design by contract approach and the intentional or BDI stance popular in agent theory. Kollingbaum and Norman look at norms from the perspective of the agent and how a practical reasoning agent might internalize norms, have them influence its behavior and resolve conflicts between new and existing norms. This section closes with the paper by Boella and van der Torre addressing the introduction of organizations and roles in artificial social systems using a normative system. They consider the relationship between how the behavior of an organization is determined by agents playing a roles within it and, vice versa, how an organization affects the behavior of agents. These considerations are used to explore the evolution of (artificial) organizations.

Evaluation and Regulation: The fourth and last section, on evaluation and regulation, starts with a paper by Dignum et al. who present a simulation scenario that can be used to evaluate the congruence between organizational structure and task performance. The background for their purpose is the need for reorganization that can arise when environmental conditions change. The same holds for artificial organizations in the form of open multi-agent systems that operate in dynamic environments. The second paper in this chapter by Aldewereld et al. gives a formal method, based on program verification, for checking the norm compliance of knowledge-based protocols. In achieving a goal, agents can make use of predefined protocols, which should help them avoid violating any of the norms. But it should also be guaranteed that these protocols are actually norm-compliant. The section ends with a paper by Cranefield about a rule language for defining social expectations. It is based on a metric interval temporal logic with past and future modalities and a current-time binding operator. Moreover, he presents an algorithm for run-time monitoring compliance of rules in this language based on formula progression.

The workshop organizers would like to thank the AAMAS 2005 conference and Utrecht University for hosting the workshop. We are also very grateful to all the Program Committee members, the additional reviewers, the authors and the participants for their respective contributions to the process of creating two high-quality, stimulating workshops. Finally, we are pleased to acknowledge the encouragement and support from Springer, in the person of Alfred Hofmann, for helping to bring the workshop to this concrete conclusion.

Organization

ANIREM Program Committee

Cristiano Castelfranchi	NRC Rome, Italy
Rosaria Conte	NRC Rome, Italy
Ulises Cortes	Polytechnic University of Catalonia, Spain
Paul Davidsson	BTH, Sweden
Marina De Vos	University of Bath, UK
Frank Dignum	University of Utrecht, The Netherlands
En Hong Chen	University of Science and Technology, China
Tom van Engers	Free University of Amsterdam, The Netherlands
Fabiola Lopez	Autonomous University of Puebla, Mexico
Mike Luck	University of Southampton, UK
Thomas Malsch	Tech. University Hamburg-Harburg, Germany
John-Jules Meyer	University of Utrecht, The Netherlands
Pablo Noriega	IIIA, CSIC, Spain
James Odell	Agentis, USA
Andrea Omicini	University of Bologna, Italy
Mario Paolucci	ISTC/CNR, Rome, Italy
Paolo Petta	Austrian Research Institute for AI, Austria
Juan-Antonio Rodriguez-Aguilar	IIIA, CSIC, Spain
Ingo Schulz-Schaeffer	Tech. University of Berlin, Germany
Juan-Manuel Serrano	University Rey Juan Carlos, Madrid, Spain
Phillip Sheu	University of California, USA
Jaime Sichman	University of Sao Paulo, Brazil
Carles Sierra	IIIA, CSIC, Spain
Mihaela Ulieru	University of Calgary, Canada
Wamberto Vasconcelos	University of Aberdeen, UK
Harko Verhagen	Stockholm University, Sweden

OOOP Program Committee

Guido Boella	University of Torino, Italy
Cosmin Carabelea	ENS Mines Saint-Etienne, France
Cristiano Castelfranchi	ISTC/CNR, Italy
Daniel Corkill	University of Massachusetts, USA
Ulises Cortés	UPC, Spain
Antonio Carlos da Rocha Costa	UCPEL, Brazil
Bruce Edmonds	CPM, Manchester Metropolitan University, UK
Jacques Ferber	LIRMM, France
Fabien Gandon	INRIA Sophia-Antipolis, France
Paolo Giorgini	University of Trento, Italy

Jomi Hubner	FURB, Brazil
Philippe Lamarre	LINA, France
Victor Lesser	University of Massachusetts, USA
Michael Luck	University of Southampton, UK
John-Jules Meyer	Utrecht University, The Netherlands
Steve Munroe	University of Southampton, UK
Timothy Norman	University of Aberdeen, UK
James Odell	James Odell Associates, USA
Andrea Omicini	University of Bologna, Italy
Alessandro Ricci	University of Bologna, Italy
Paul Scerri	Robotics Institute, Carnegie Mellon University, USA
Carles Sierra	IIIA, Spain
Viviane Da Silva	PUC, Brazil
Liz Sonenberg	The University of Melbourne, Australia
Catherine Tessier	ONERA, France
Luca Tummolini	ISTC-CNR Rome, Italy
Javier Vázquez-Salceda	Utrecht University, The Netherlands

Workshop Organizers

Olivier Boissier	Ecole Nationale Supérieure des Mines, Saint-Etienne, France `Olivier.Boissier@emse.fr`
Virginia Dignum	Institute for Computing and Information Sciences, Utrecht University, The Netherlands `virginia@cs.uu.nl`
Gabriela Lindemann	Department of Computer Science, Humboldt University Berlin, Germany `lindeman@informatik.hu-berlin.de`
Eric Matson	Department of Computer Science and Engineering, Wright State University, Dayton, Ohio, USA `eric.matson@wright.edu`
Sascha Ossowski	Department of Computing, University Rey Juan Carlos, Madrid, Spain `sascha.ossowski@urjc.es`
Julian Padget	Department of Computer Science, University of Bath, UK `jap@cs.bath.ac.uk`
Jaime Sichman	Computer Engineering Department, University of Sao Paulo, Brazil `jaime.sichman@poli.usp.br`
Javier Vázquez-Salceda	Polytechnic University of Catalonia, Department of Software, Barcelona, Spain `jvazquez@lsi.upc.edu`

Table of Contents

III   Modelling Normative Designs

IV   Evaluation and Regulation

Part I

Modelling, Analyzing and Programming Organizations

A Coordination Framework Based on the Sociology of Organized Action

C. Sibertin-Blanc, F. Amblard, and M. Mailliard

IRIT – Université de Toulouse 1
21, allées de Brienne, 31042 Toulouse Cedex – France
{sibertin, famblard, mmaillia}@univ-tlse1.fr

Abstract. This paper proposes a basis to design coordination models in multi-agent systems. This proposal is based on the exploitation of an in-depth exploration of a well-experienced sociological theory, the Sociology of Organized Action, also called Strategic Analysis. This theory intends to discover the functioning of any organization beyond its formal rules, especially how social actors build the organization that in return rules their behaviors, and which are the mechanisms they use to regulate their interactions. We first present the concepts developed by this theory to reveal the strategic aspects of the actors' behaviors in an organized actions framework. Then we introduce a meta-model that allows us to describe the structure of Concrete Action Systems and how social actors handle its elements. A classical case study is used to illustrate the approach.

1 Introduction

Agents' coordination mechanisms in models of organizations pose new demands compared to traditional Multi-Agent Systems models, such as the integration of organizational and individual objectives with possible problems of compatibility, the dynamic adaptation of agents' behaviors to organizational changes, or conversely the way agents' behavior lead to organizational changes. As systems grow to include increasing number and heterogeneity of agents, the coordination has to be improved in order to consider both the agent-centric, as well as the organization-centric views. However, formal theories, tools and methodologies are still very much in short supply. Even if an externally designed organizational structure is necessary as a coordination device to achieve global social order, there is a possibly inefficient and ineffective tension between such imposed constraints and the agents' autonomous behavior.

In order to enrich this field, we think that a controlled metaphor based upon well founded sociological theories could enable to devise and design high-quality models for coordination in agents' organizations. Some works similar to the Agent-Group-Role paradigm [1] showed the limits of approaches, which, inspired from metaphors with the fields of psychology or cognitive sciences, are exclusively centered on the structure and the abilities of the agents (e.g. architectures like Belief-Desire-Intention [2]). The focus on the organizational level is actually at play in many works in Multi-Agent or Component-based Systems. Our work follows the line of works like the ones

O. Boissier et al. (Eds.): ANIREM and OOOP 2005, LNCS 3913, pp. 3–17, 2006.

of Malone and Crowston [3], of Castelfranchi [4] or Hermann [5], who research in the sociology a pertinent and well-grounded metaphor for a coordination model allowing to root the definition of the organizational level in MAS. The *Sociology of the Organized Action* [6], also known as the *Strategic Analysis*, has defined emergent coordination mechanisms. Based upon very abstract concepts, they are susceptible to serve as a suggestive source of inspiration and to be used in several application domains. Despite its notoriety, its wide use by enterprise sociologists and organization consultants, and its generalized teaching, the Strategic Analysis had never been taken as a subject for modeling.

We then first present the sociological theory that is the basis for our proposal, namely the Sociology of the Organized Action (SOA), insisting on the major concepts we retained to build up a meta-model of this theory. We therefore present in the third section our framework based on the concepts of Actors and Resources-Relations, the things in the Actors' organizational environment they use to establish control and dependency links between them – in fact power relationships. This is the static aspects of the meta-model, e.g. the objects present in the model as well as the objects manipulated by the actors, allowing to describe *the structure of a social system*. The fourth section presents the dynamics aspect of the model. We focus explicitly on the distinction between *functional dimension* and *structural dimension* of the actors' actions, and how we do manage this distinction in the current version of the SocLab simulation environment. Finally in a last part, we exemplify the approach on a concrete system that is a classical example taken from the literature in the Sociology of the Organized Action. It enables us to illustrate our model of coordination as well as pointing certain limits of our approach that are currently under investigation.

2   Sociology of the Organized Action

The Sociology of the Organized Action (SOA) aims at discovering the real functioning of an organization beyond its formal rules. The Concrete Action Systems (CAS) that it allow to study, for instance a firm, a university or a local political system, are composed of « numerous differentiated actors interacting in a non-trivial way among each others » [6]. Moreover, these actors are engaged durably in the achievement of some organization's objectives. A CAS is an interaction context precisely delimited which supplies the means and motivates the cooperation among a group of social actors. This structure is admittedly constraining but it always leaves some freedom in the way of acting. The SOA deals with structured relational contexts and it does not aim to address spontaneous effects like crowd behaviors or riots [7]. If the sociology of the organized action inherits the sociology of organizations [8, 18], its application scope spreads to all kind of « organized » action systems, whatever their level of codification or formalization. The SOA focuses on regulation phenomena which ensure both the evolution of such systems and their relative stability.

The SOA is built upon the idea that an organization is a social construct actualized by and within the relationships among its member actors. Moreover, this theory assumes that each actor behaves strategically although it has only *bounded rationality* capabilities [9].

Each actor's behavior is then neither totally conditioned by the organizational rules that constrain him, nor it is by pure individual or emotional factors. This behavior is *strategic*, that is in includes actions that aim at realizing some objectives, would it be conscious or not. Beyond the achievement of both his own objectives and those given by the organization's formal rules, each actor aims, as a meta-objective, at having enough *power* to be able to preserve or increase his autonomy and acting capacity within the organization.

This power results from the mastering of one or several *uncertainty zones* (UZ) that enable him to behave in a way that is unpredictable for other actors and consequently to set, to some extent, the *exchange rules* in the course of his relations with others. Each uncertainty zone is a resource for the action, and thus both a constraint and an opportunity. Each social actor both controls some UZs and depends on some others, so that UZs are the media of the power relationships between actors. The interactions among actors regulate those power relationships and as a consequence transform the related uncertainty zones, their control as well as their relevance, and then the rules of the social game. The four main uncertainty zones that support power relationships within a CAS are based upon: competence or expertise; the control of interactions with the environment of the organization; the control of the internal communication; and the knowledge and proper use of the organization's norms and rules.

To summarize, the Sociology of Organized Action is a theory of the action that explains the effective running of organizational processes while taking into account the double dependency between the actor and the system, by using the concepts of bounded rationality, power relationships, uncertainty zones and concrete action system. This theory and the related concepts serve as a theoretical basis as well as an analysis grid to study many cases: the introduction of the automation in a traditional firm or the decision-making process during the crisis of the Cuba's missiles [10, 6]. Interested readers can refer to [8] for a detailed analysis of ten case studies.

3   The Proposed Meta-model

A formalization of the SOA leads to consider that constitutive elements of a concrete action system are of the three different types shown in Fig. 1: Actor, Relation and Resource. We indeed adopt the term *Resource* rather than *Uncertainty Zone* from the SOA terminology because every uncertainty zone is a resource required for the system's activity, and its constitutive property is less the uncertainty on the behavior of its controller actor than the existence of other actors who need this resource for whatever reason while they don't control the conditions of its use.

To describe briefly the figure 1, a *Resource* is the support of one or more *Relations* associated to *Actors* who either *control* the Relation or *depend* on it. Each actor puts *stakes* for each one of the Relations he is implied in and receives in return a *pay-off*. The actor who *masters* a Resource (by the mean of a Relation he controls) decides of the distribution of the pay-offs to the actors who depend on this Relation.

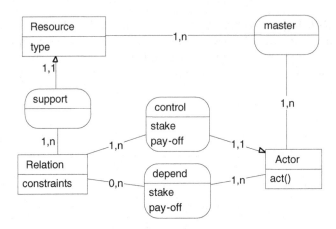

Fig. 1. Model of the structure of a CAS (using the Entity/Association formalism)

3.1 Actor, Resource and Relation

The *Resources* of a CAS are the things necessary for the organized action, their availability being required in order to make some action.

Every Resource is *mastered* by one or more Actors who decide about its availability and therefore influence the action capability of the Actors who need it. Each Resource leads to the introduction of one or several *Relations*. A Relation corresponds to a certain type of transaction, or bargaining concerning the use of this Resource. A Relation is unbalanced as a unique Actor (among the ones who master the Resource) *controls* this Relation while other Actors *depend* on this Relation because they need this Resource to achieve their goals. The controller of the Relation determines the conditions of the access to the Resource and so controls the possibility for the depending Actors to achieve their objectives.

Every *Actor* masters one or more Resources and then possesses some freedom to act that he exerts by means of the Resources he controls. As a result, the SOA denies the status of social actor to a person who would not master any Resource. The concepts of Resource and Actor are then defined one from the other: a Resource is such only if some Actors depend on it while it is controlled by another Actor; conversely, a social Actor is somebody who controls at least one Resource.

3.2 Stakes and Pay-Offs

Each Actor distributes his *stakes* on the Relations he participates to, either by controlling them or depending on them. He makes this repartition depending on the importance of the Resource in regard to his objectives. The more necessary this use of the Resource to achieve an important objective, the higher the stake he places on this Relation. Figure 2 shows how to introduce explicitly the concept of *Objective* in the model of a CAS: for a given Actor and a given Relation, the value of the *stake* property in the associations *control* and *depend* is determined by the value of the properties *importance* and *necessity*. This repartition of an Actor's stakes is in proportion with the impact of these objectives on his behavior. For the understanding of the functioning of a CAS, the very identification of the objectives of an Actor does not matter, much more important is what they lead the Actor to do. The stakes enable to link causally the Actor's behavior with his objectives. The stakes take their value on a qualitative scale such as *null, negligible, ..., important, ..., vital* that can be therefore translated on a numerical scale; we take for the example below from 0 to 10.

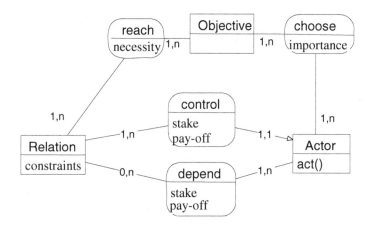

Fig. 2. Place of the *Objective* concept in the formalization of a CAS

The Actor controlling a Relation is the one who determines the *exchange rules,* that is the conditions governing transactions concerning the access to the Resource. We also use the term *pay-off,* which evokes the result of the transaction, while "exchange rules" refers to the modalities of its processing. The pay-off corresponds to the quality of the Resource availability; more or better the usability of the Resource by an Actor, higher his pay-off for this Relation. The distribution criterion of the pay-offs between the different participants of a Relation is specific to each Relation. We are expecting Relations where the pay-offs are a « zero sum game »: if the usability of the Resource is good for some actors, it will be as bad for the others. Other Relations for which the pay-offs of the controller and depending Actors vary in the same direction could be qualified of *win-win,* or *loose-loose* whether the pay-offs tend to be favorable or not. Pay-offs take their value on a scale like: *awful, ..., bad, ..., neutral, ..., good, ..., optimal* and therefore can be translated on a numerical scale, e.g. from −10 to +10.

3.3 The Constraints on a Relation

We now have to give the meaning of the *constraints* property of Relations. The Actor who controls a Relation has not the possibility to give any value to the pay-off property of the participating Actors. He has to respect organizational constraints, the « rules of the social game », that regulate the interactions among the actors within the organization and determine the range of value he may give to the pay-offs. These constraints originate either from formal rules of the organization or rules imposed by the environment, either from technical or feasibility restrictions that result from the very nature of the Resource, or from social norms that determine the socially acceptable behaviors. (The sociology of organized action does not include such a classification of constraints, but a deeper analysis of the various types of Resources and associated constraints could ease the modeling of the structure of CASs). In addition, we have to deal with the fact mentioned in the previous section that the values of pay-offs attributed to the different Actors are in relation. So we propose to formalize the constraints associated to a Relation as the following items:

- two boundary values b_min and b_max, such that $-1 \leq b\_min < b\_max \leq 1$;
- for each actor A participant in the relation, a function $Effect_A : [-1, 1] \longrightarrow [-10, 10]$.

The interval $[-1, 1]$ corresponds to the whole *space of choice* of the controller Actor when he has a full control upon the Relation: choosing a value within this interval is to set the exchange rules, it corresponds to choosing a way to manage the relation and so what kind of access is given to other Actors concerned by the relation. The choice (by the controller Actor) of a value $\alpha \in [-1, 1]$ produces the $Effect_A(\alpha)$ value for the pay-off to Actor A. It is clear that any number could be used instead of -1 and $+1$ as the boundaries of the space of choice, and only the relationships between the different functions $Effect_X$, X being the Actors participant in the Relation, is of matter. (In order to chose an interval $[a, b]$ as the space of choice instead of $[-1, 1]$, you just have to compose the $Effect_X$ function with the function $x : \longrightarrow 2/(b-a)*x - (a+b)/(b-a)$; The convenience of the $[-1, 1]$ interval as spaces of choice relies upon its similarity with the range of pay-off values, that is $[-10, 10]$).

As for the b_min and b_max boundaries, they are intended to account the fact that the Actor controlling the relation is possibly in a situation where he cannot select whatever value in the space of choice. For any reason, his *effective space of choice* is more limited and then he can only chose a value within the $[b\_min, b\_max]$ interval. So the range of this interval (that is the number $b\_max - b\_min$) measures the extent of the control on the Relation by the controller Actor.

Such a formalization describes the specificities of each Relation as a tool to exercise some power on actors dependent on it. It enables to give a quantitative value to social features of a CAS and thus to compare the respective position of Actors and Relations. We just propose some illustrative examples that would require a deep discussion to get a well-founded semantics [17]. Let us consider the *influence* that the Actor controlling a Relation R is able to exert on another Actor A participating in the Relation. If you consider:

$$influence_R(A) = max \{Effect_A(\alpha) - Effect_A(\beta) ; \alpha, \beta \in [b\_min, b\_max]\},$$

you have the maximum difference between the pay-offs that he can attribute to Actor A, that is the greatest amplitude of the effect of his choice in the management of the Relation.

The global influence of the Actor controlling the Relation R can then be defined as the greatest influence subjected by one of the Actors:

$$influence_R = max \{influence_R(A) ; A \text{ Actor concerned by the relation } R\}.$$

Indeed, the Actor subject to the greatest influence will behave accordingly and thus pass the effect of this influence to other Actors. So, one can consider that this highest level of influence is the one that will spread over the whole organization.

The following quantity

$$max\{Effect_A(\alpha) - Effect_A(\beta); A \text{ Actor concerned by the relation } R, \alpha \text{ and } \beta \in [-1, 1]\}$$

may be considered as the *strength* of the Relation R as a tool for exercising the power. Then the *influence$_R$* of the controller of Relation R is a weighting of this strength by his level of mastering of R (that is b_max – b_min, the range of his effective space of choice), and thus corresponds to the actual usability of this relation as a support for his power.

4   Actors' Behaviors and Organization's Dynamics

The modeling formalism we exposed enables to distinguish, within a CAS, what corresponds to its structure – its constitutive elements and their relations –, and what corresponds to its state which changes to pursue the achievement of the system goals. The *CAS's structure* can be described in terms of Actors, constrained Relations based on Resources, and stakes placed by Actors on Relations; as for the *CAS's state*, it can be described in terms of the pay-offs put by Actors on the Relations they participate to, that is their available means for action.

4.1   Structural and Functional Dimensions of the Actors' Behavior

This allows to distinguish two dimensions in the actions of an Actor who searches to comfort his power: a structural dimension which acts on the system structure, and a functional dimension which acts on the system state (Cf. Figure 3). The action's *structural dimension* contributes to the building of the CAS organization, to the establishment of the social game rules and then consists in, following our formalization, acting on the elements which constitute its structure: the Resources, the Relations, the constraints and the stakes. Concerning the action's *functional dimension* of an Actor, it is the one which insures the regular operating of the system and makes its state to evolve in a synchronic way. It participates in the achievement of the Actors' immediate objectives. This functional dimension of Actors' activity complies with the current rules of the game, without regard for possible changes concerning the mission and objectives (i.e. the stakes) or the means for action (i.e. the Relations and the associated constraints). In the behavior of a human being social actor, each concrete action comprises a structural and a functional component in a proportion specific to the circumstances of the action achievement. When modeling a CAS, we are not trying to account for the practical modalities of the actions, instead we only focus on their effects. These effects on the structure and on the state of a CAS being disjoint, we have the possibility, concerning simulation issues, to model the actors' behavior by mean of mechanisms specific for each one of these two dimensions.

Within the structural dimension of actors' behavior, actions deal with the Resources, the Relations, the constraints and the stakes. Concerning Resources, an

Actor may introduce a new Resource supporting a Relation that he will master by using his proper capacities, or rather introduce a new Relation based on a Resource that he is yet mastering. An Actor may also neutralize the possibility of another Actor to control a relation, for instance by giving a free open access to the Resource or conversely to make it definitely inaccessible whatever the circumstances. Another possible structural action is to transform a Resource in such a way that some $Effect_X()$ functions become modified. Concerning the constraints which apply on the pay-offs of Relations, an Actor may decrease their severity for a Relation he controls by enlarging the effective space of choice (decreasing b_min or increasing b_max), or conversely reinforce the severity of constraints applied to a Relation controlled by another Actor. Finally, concerning the stakes, Actors may move their own stakes to reinforce their autonomy, but also and above all they may influence other Actors in the distribution of their stakes.

Within the functional dimension of the actor's behavior, every action consists in exerting control on a mastered Relation, e.g. manipulating the pay-offs value attributed to the participating Actors, while staying inside the limits imposed by the constraints on this Relation. This manipulation can be absolute, then it modifies the pay-offs value without care to their current value, or relative if it increases or decreases regularly this value. This latter case corresponds to a management of the control, without sudden shift, which seems to be the norm in most social structures.

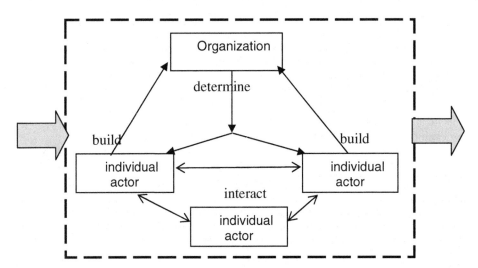

Fig. 3. The structural behavior of Actors builds the organization that in return constraints their functional behavior

4.2 Actor's Satisfaction and Strategic Behavior

The distribution of pay-offs and stakes on numerical scales enables, applying simple operations, to aggregate those values in synthetic and significant values. One can graduate the stakes on a scale *null = 0, negligible = 1, important = 5, vital = 10*, and the pay-offs with the correspondence *awful = -10, bad = -5, neutral = 0, good = 5, optimal* = *10*. As evidence, these numerical values do not correspond to something; they just enable to perform comparison among them. To do so, we have to normalize the sum of the Actors' stakes and then to attribute to each one the same amount of stake points to be distributed on the relations he participates to. This normalization comes down to grant the same investment to each actor, the same possibility of personal implication in the social interactions game.

It becomes therefore possible to quantify several concepts of the SOA by numerical values belonging to the same scale of values, and thus to compare them. For instance, the *relevance of a Resource* could be estimated as the sum of the stakes placed by the whole population of Actors on the Relation supported by this Resource, as those stakes reflect the importance of these Relations for the Actors. The *power of an Actor* can be also estimated as the sum, over all the relations he controls, of a combination between the relevance of this Relation and the influence of this Relation. The *autonomy of an Actor* can be evaluated as the sum of the stakes he places on the Relations he controls. It corresponds to the possibility to achieve his objectives independently from other Actors, the *actor's dependency* being evaluated conversely as the sum of the stakes he places on the Relations he depends on. Other notions like the power of an Actor on another one or the dependency network among Actors could be defined also.

A particularly significant value for an actor is the sum, on the whole set of Relation he is involved in, of a combination between his stake and the pay-off he receives. We name this value the actor's *satisfaction* (rather than utility because it is more linked to a bounded rationality context). It expresses the possibility for an actor to access the resources he needs in order to achieve his objectives, and then the means available for him to achieve these objectives. A linear version consists in considering the sum, on every relation he is involved in, of the stake by the pay-off:

$$Satis(a) = \sum_{r/\, a\ participates\ to\ r} stake(a,\ r) * pay\text{-}off(a,\ r) \tag{1}$$

As far as the satisfaction of an Actor is a measure of his possibility to achieve his concrete objectives, to obtain or preserve a high level for this satisfaction is a *meta-objective* for every actor. Abstracting the objectives of each particular Actor at the level of the stakes he puts on the common Resources allow to consider that each Actor has his own version of the same meta-objective.

The strategic characteristic of an actor's behavior leads him, by definition, to aim to achieve his objectives and then to obtain an acceptable level (if not the optimum) for his satisfaction. The rationality hypothesis implies to ground this behavior on the standard three steps cycle:

1. perception of his own state and of the environment;
2. selection of an action to perform, according to its expected effect on the gap between the current state and the goal state;
3. execution of this action.

We have implemented a simulation environment, SocLab [11], that allows to describe the structure of a CAS according to the meta-model introduced in section 3 and to simulate the functional dimension of Actors' behaviors, that is the mutual adjustment of the payoffs they give the ones to the others. This "social behavior engine" uses the classifiers mechanism [12] for the selection of the action; a classifier system is based upon the learning of behavioral rules by test-errors and reinforcement of the rules depending on the results they produce. This approach presents two advantages compared to a cognitive approach [13]: we only need a global model of the CAS, while the cognitive approach requires to make explicit the own representation of the CAS by each one of the Actors; it brings little hypothesis on the required abilities to act as a social actor within a CAS, and it not need to explicit the rules governing the social behavior of the actors.

5   The Trouville Case

To illustrate how the SOA analyses a concrete action system and how we formalize this analysis, we consider a classical example from the strategic analysis (the other name for the SOA) [14]. The Travel-tours firm is a tour operator having two agencies, TRO1 and TRO2, situated in the Trouville city. These last months, the results of the TRO1 agency increase, as the ones of TRO2 agency stay stable, or even decrease. The regional director decides to reward the TRO1 agency for its merits. He proposes then to regularize the position of Agnès, the secretary of the agency and to allocate her exclusively to TRO1. As she is temporary employed for several months, and even if she is attached to TRO1, she works half time in each one of the TRO1 and TRO2 agencies and this obliges her to move between two jobs.

Both Agnès and the TRO1 agency's director, Paul, should be glad with this proposal. Agnès will have a permanent job contract and will be relieved to split her work in two parts, while Paul will have a full-time secretary at his disposal in the agency. But each one of them refuses vigorously the proposal. How to understand this matter of fact? The strategic analysis by identifying the uncertainty zones shows that both of them are rationally right to be opposed to this organizational change, because it would decrease their respective power. Indeed, a more attentive analysis of the case reveals that:

- The TRO2 agency is more inventive than TRO1 in designing travel packages, while the TRO1 agency includes a very efficient commercial staff; being aware of the TRO2 agency's activity, the secretary provides information to the director so that the TRO1 agency takes full advantage of finalizing the TRO2's ideas.
- For personal reasons, to get a steady job is not a short-time objective of the secretary. On the other hand, she is very cool in her working relations with the other employees of TRO1, and she greatly appreciates that none of the TRO1 and TRO2 directors has the possibility to exert a precise control on her work.

Thus the situation shift would increase the control of the director on the secretary's activities (that is what she does not want), and the director would loose the information given by the secretary on TRO2 (that is what he does not want).

5.1   Model of the Concrete Action System

The purpose of the analysis is to understand the behavior of the director and the secretary, so both of them are Actors to be considered, and it appears that other employees of the TRO1 or TRO2 agencies do not play a significant role is this affair.

Concerning the uncertainty zones or Resources, *Information about TRO2* is the one mastered by the secretary while the director masters *the secretary's job*. This latter Resource gives raise to two different Relations between the director and the secretary: the stability of the job and the content of the work she has to achieve. Table 1 shows the values given to the different parameters of the model. The value of stakes results straight from the observations below about the wishes of the director and the secretary. Both of them have ten points to distribute over the three Relations, and the relevance of each Relation is just the sum of the stakes.

The value of the *b_min* and *b_max* bounds and the definition of the Effect functions require more explanations. Concerning the stability of the job, the director has only a partial mastering of this Relation; on one side he may renew the contract of the secretary each week without discussion, although he may not set a firm contract to on his own, only the regional director can do this, so $b\_max \approx 0.4$; on the other side, he has to respect the job legislation, to justify his decision to the regional director, and to account for the reaction of other employees in case of unfairness, so $b\_min \approx -0.4$. Having a steady job produces a full effect for the secretary and thus $Effect_{secretary}(1) = 10$, $Effect_{secretary}(-1) = -10$, -10 and 10 being the extreme values of a pay-off. As for the director, his worry about this job is in proportion with its stability, but this worry is quite low, that is $Effect_{director}(x) = 3 * x$.

Concerning the content of the job, the agency director has a larger room of manoeuvre. We consider positive values in the space of choice as a strict control on the quantity and the quality of the secretary's work and on the organization of this work, and negative values as the lack of such a control. The $b\_min \approx -0.3$ value results from a high concern of the director for having friendly relationships with the employees; nevertheless, he has to ensure the production of the agency and thus to have a look at the work achieved by each employee, so the $b\_max \approx 0.7$ value. The effect on the secretary is in proportion with the level of control, because the convenience of any employee is to suffer a low level of control on his/her work. As for the director, the proposed effect function is based upon the ideas that any excess or lack of control could rapidly bring difficulties and that his interest is to exercise a moderate control.

Table 1. Parameters of a formal model for the Travel-tours case study

		Stability of the job	Content of the job	Information about TRO2
Controller Actor		Director	Director	Secretary
Stake	Director	1	2	7
	Secretary	2	7	1
Relevance		3	9	8
Effect	Director	$3 * x$	$-3 * x^2$	$10 * x$
	Secretary	$10 * x$	$7 * x$	$-2 * \lvert x \rvert$
b_min , b_max		$-0.4 , 0.4$	$-0.3 , 0.7$	$-0.3 , 0.8$
Influence		$0.8 * 10 = 8$	$1 * 7 = 7$	$1.1 * 10 = 11$

For the information about the TRO2 agency Relation, positive values in the space of choice correspond to give information about the projects of TRO2, negative values to give false information, and the zero to give no information. The b_min and b_max proposed values correspond to the amount of information on TRO2 that the secretary can obtain and make to be credible by the TRO1's director. The effect function for the director models his full use of this information; as for the secretary, her own tranquility would be to give no information, neither real nor false.

Table 2. Satisfaction of Actors in notable cases, and their respective power

		Secretary's satisfaction		Director's satisfaction		global satisfaction		Autonomy	Power
		min	max	min	max	min	max		
Value in the space of choice	Stability of the job	-0.4	0.4	-0.4	0.4	-0.4	0.4		
	Content of the job	-0.3	0.7	-0.3	0	-0.3	0.7		
	Info on TRO2	0.8	0	-0.3	0.8	-0.3	0.8		
Satisfaction	Director	54.3	-1.7	**-22.7**	**57.2**	-22.7	54.3	3	87
	Secretary	**-24.3**	**42.3**	-23.3	6.4	-23.3	40.7	1	88
	Global	30	40.5	-46	63.5	**-46**	**95**		

5.2 Behavior of Actors

The columns of table 2 correspond to typical states of the system resulting from an analysis providing the values given in table 1. The three last rows show the satisfaction of the director, the secretary and the whole system, while the three first ones show the values in the spaces of choice of the relations that lead to these satisfactions. The cases where the secretary or the director get their extremum satisfaction are not socially feasible; considering the Secretary's maximum satisfaction as an example, the director has no reason to be especially indulgent with her if she does not bring any specific advantage to the agency. More generally, no Actor will accept to relinquish the power given by the control of a Resource if this renouncement leads to a situation that is too far from an acceptable satisfaction. We observe that the maximal global satisfaction, that is the Pareto optimum, is reached with each Actor having the most cooperative behavior; but this fact is specific to the Travel-tour case study and can not considered as a general property of CAS. Figures 4 shows one simulation of this case study with the *SocLab* environment. In almost simulations of this case, the satisfactions of both Actors stabilize at a level that is near the Pareto optimum. The gap between the satisfactions of the secretary and the director is about 20%; it allows to conclude some thing like "the director has at least as much means to act as the secretary has", that is: the informal (and effective) power relationships among the secretary and the director are not inconsistent with the formal rules of the organization (organizations where the *authority* granted by formal rules is in opposition with the *power* resulting from informal behaviors are not safe). Considering the two last columns, it appears that the secretary and the director are highly dependent since they have a low level of autonomy, and this can be related to the fact that their worst (minimum) satisfaction is very low. They have the same power one on the other, and since they can get a acceptable satisfaction, they have rational reasons for refusing the proposition of the regional director of Travel-Tour.

All these numerical results must be considered very carefully when they are used to provide a social interpretation that is meaningful. First, the scales of values are arbitrary, so that each value considered in isolation has no meaning; only the relative values of parameters make sense, and the results are given for comparison only. Second, the gap between two values must be important – e.g. 20 or 30 per cent – to be considered as significant. Indeed, the values of the stakes and other parameters provided by the empirical sociological analysis are rough in nature. Moreover, the formulas proposed to evaluate the power or satisfaction of Actors are not the result of a formal argument; they are grounded in a firm sociological theory but intend only to be an approximation of these concepts. Finally, we agree with the bounded rationality paradigm that considers errors as a constitutive properties of affairs.

Concerning the Travel-tour case, a sensitivity analysis shows that the model summed up in table 1 is quite robust. But a better use of the numeric values introduced by our meta-model would be to process and interpret them within a fuzzy calculus [15].

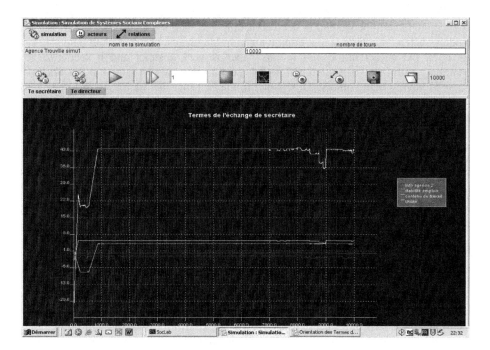

Fig. 4. Evolution of the satisfaction (sum of the pay-offs weighted by the stakes) of the secretary during one 10000 steps simulation

6 Conclusion

From the viewpoint of the Sociology, this project could appreciably transform both the practice and the teaching of the SOA thanks to possibilities offered by a tool which objectifies the hypothesizes and results of a sociological analysis. Such an attempt to formalize an inherently discursive theory goes with questions about this theory; and this project has already proved to impact the theoretical corpus of the SOA [17], by the mean of investigations that can be done in using a virtual experimental framework, a radically new approach in sociology [16]. In this respect, the work presented in this paper differs of the very interesting socionik German project (see [19, 20] as representative papers) that mainly proposes straight translations of sociologic theories into computer science formalisms. Concepts and models in social and human sciences are often not well defined, not formalized and thus can support inconsistent and ambiguous discourses. AI and MAS are sciences that produces new concepts, new models, new experimental evidences by simulation, and also new theories of mental and social phenomena that can benefit to sociology. In accordance with an (anonymous) referee of this paper, "Artificial modeling and computer simulation will change the social sciences at least as much as cybernetics, information theory, logic, IA, … has changed the behavioral sciences, giving origin to 'cognitive sciences'".

From the viewpoint of computer science, it could be the case that the SOA provides a *coordination model* for MASs, and more generally for computer applications including a lot of heterogeneous components that collaborate to some ends. The specific properties of such a coordination model and its domain of application have to be studied in deep and compared with the other main coordination models such as planning, agent communication languages, protocols and games [21]. As it is, the model introduced in this paper is very abstract and it seems to be compliant with most organizational models such as the ones presented in this bock or [1, 4, 5] among many others. This is due to the fact that the Sociology of Organized Action does not account for the formal dimension of organizations: the hierarchical positions of actors, their roles, missions and duties, etc. These aspects need to be re-introduced in the theory in order to lead to an organizational model allowing to define the global structure of a system, independent of the micro-level architecture and properties of its populating computational components (agents).

The model presented in this paper raises many questions that must be answered for it becomes operational, either for sociologist, or as a powerful coordination model for MASs and distributed systems, or for providing virtual creatures with a plausible human-like social behavior. Among these questions we can cite the followings. Coalition-actors, who have their own stakes related to the objective of the coalition, but whose satisfaction relies upon the satisfaction of the coalition member actors; a typology of resources and relations to ease their identification and the definition of the Effect function in analyzing the structure of CASs; the resources dynamics: how to characterize resources and relations which can be removed or conversely introduced in a CAS in the course of its regular operating; the circumstances that lead an Actor to try to make the structure of a CAS to evolve, the kind of changes he will prefer, and the means he could use to achieve this change. This last question, which is nothing else than the auto-evolution and adaptation of social systems, is probably one of the most difficult, but also one of the most interesting if we focus on the expressive power of this coordination model.

References

1. Ferber, J., Gutknecht, O.: A Meta-Model for the Analysis and Design of Organizations in Multi-Agent Systems. Proceedings of the *3rd International Conference on Multi-Agents Systems* (ICMAS), IEEE CS Press , 1998.
2. Cohen, P.R., Levesque, H.J. : Intention is Choice with Commitment. *Artificial Intelligence*, vol. 42, 213-261, 1990.
3. Malone, T.W., Crowston, K. : The interdisciplinary study of coordination. *ACM Computing Survey* 26, 1, 1994.
4. Castelfranchi, C.: Modeling social action for AI Agents. *Artificial Intelligence*, 103, 157–182, 1998.
5. Hermann, T., Jahnke, I., Loser K-U.: The Role Concept as a Basis for Designing Community Systems . In *Cooperative Systems Design*, M. Zacklad & al Eds, IOS Press, 2004.
6. Crozier, M., Friedberg, E. : *L'acteur et le système : les contraintes de l'action collective*. Edition du Seuil, Paris, 1977.
6. Crozier, M., Friedberg, E. : Organizations and Collective Action: our Contribution to Organizational Analysis. In S.B. Bacharrach, P. Gagliardi and B. Mundel (Eds), *Studies of Organiszations in the European Tradition*. Series « Research in the Sociology of Organizations » Greenwich Corn. jay-Press, vol 13, p. 71-93, 1995.
7. Granovetter, M.: Threshold models of collective behavior. *American Journal of Sociology*, vol. 83, 1360–1380 (1978).
8. Bernoux, P.: *La sociologie des organisations,* Edition du Seuil, Paris, (1985).
9. Simon, H.: *The sciences of the artificial*, MIT Press, 3rd edition (1996).
10. Crozier, M. *The Bureaucratic Phenomenon*. University of Chicago Press, *Le phénomène bureaucratique*, Edition du Seuil, Paris, 1964.
11. Mailliard, M., Audras, S., Casula, M. : Multi Agents Systems based on Classifiers for the Simulation of Concrete Action Systems. In Proceedings of the *1st EUropean Workshop on Multi-Agent Systems* (EUMAS), Oxford University, (2003).
12. Holland, J., Booker, L.B., Colombetti, M., Dorigo, M., Godberg, D.E., Forrest, S., Riolo, R., Smith, R.E., Lanzi, P.L., Soltzmann, W., Wilson, S.W.: What Is a Learning Classifier System?. *LCS'99*, LNAI 1813, 3-32, 2000.
13. Sichman, J., Conte, R., Demazeau Y., Castelfranchi, C.: Reasonning about others using dependence networks. Proc. of the *3rd italian Workshop on Distributed Artificial Intelligence*, Rome, 1993.
14. Smets P.: The Travel-Tours Agency. http://homepages.ulb.ac.be/~psmets1/travel.pdf.
15. Slowinski, R., Teghem, J.: *Optimization models using fuzzy sets and possibility theory.* Theory and decision library; Kluwer Academic Publishers, 1990.
16. Gilbert, N., Troitzsch, K.: *Simulation for the social scientist*. Open University Press, Londres, 1999.
17. Sibertin-Blanc C.: Pour une formalisation de la Sociologie de l'Action Organisée. Communication au *XVIème* congrès de l'*Association International des Sociologues de Langue Française*, 5-9 juillet, Tours (F), 2004.
18. Clegg S.R., Hardy C., Nord W. R.: *Handbook of organization studies*. Sage, 1996.
19. Michael Köhler M., Langer R., Moldt D., Rölke H.: Combining the Sociological Theory Bourdieu's with Multi Agent Systems. *Sozionikaktuell* vol. 1, http://www.sozionik-aktuell.de, University Hamburg, 2001.
20. Köhler M., Martens M., Rölke H.: Modelling Social Behaviour with Petri net based Multi-Agent Systems. *Sozionikaktuell* 4, http://www.sozionik-aktuell.de, Univ. Hamburg, 2003.
21. Wooldridge M. : *An Introduction to MutiAgent Systems*. Wiley, 2002.

Formal Modeling and Analysis of Organizations

Egon L. van den Broek[1], Catholijn M. Jonker[2], Alexei Sharpanskykh[1],
Jan Treur[1], and pInar Yolum[3]

[1] Department of Artificial Intelligence, Vrije Universiteit Amsterdam,
De Boelelaan 1081a, NL-1081 HV Amsterdam, The Netherlands
{egon, sharp, treur}@few.vu.nl
[2] NICI, Radboud University Nijmegen
Montessorilaan 3, 6525 HR Nijmegen, The Netherlands
C.Jonker@nici.ru.nl
[3] Department of Computer Engineering, Bogazici University,
TR-34342 Bebek, Istanbul, Turkey
pyolum@cmpe.boun.edu.tr

Abstract. A new, formal, role-based, framework for modeling and analyzing both real world and artificial organizations is introduced. It exploits static and dynamic properties of the organizational model and includes the (frequently ignored) environment. The transition is described from a generic framework of an organization to its deployed model and to the actual agent allocation. For verification and validation purposes, a set of dedicated techniques is introduced. Moreover, where most models can handle only two or three layered organizational structures, our framework can handle any arbitrary number of organizational layers. Henceforth, real-world organizations can be modeled and analyzed, as illustrated by a case study, within the DEAL project line.

1 Introduction

Organizations have proven to be a useful paradigm for analyzing and designing multi-agent systems (MAS) [5, 21, 22]. Representation of MAS as an organization consisting of roles and groups can tackle major drawbacks concerned with traditional multi-agent models; e.g., high complexity and poor predictability of dynamics in a system [5, 21]. We adopt a generic representation of organizations, abstracted from instances of real agents. As has been shown in [9], organizational structure can be used to limit the scope of interactions between agents, reduce or explicitly increase redundancy of a system, or formalize high-level system goals, of which a single agent may be not aware. Moreover, organizational research has recognized the advantages of agent-based models; e.g., for analysis of structure and dynamics of real organizations. However, formal theories, approaches, and tools for designing such models are rare. In this paper, we propose a new modeling approach for analyzing and formal modeling of real or artificial organizations (e.g., MAS).

In the next Section, main principles for modeling and analyzing organizations are discussed and related with the new modeling approach. In Section 3, the basic concepts used for specifying an organization model are introduced. Section 4 discusses how an organization model can be specified in a formal manner. In Section 5, a set of

O. Boissier et al. (Eds.): ANIREM and OOOP 2005, LNCS 3913, pp. 18–34, 2006.

dedicated validation and verification techniques are described. Section 6 presents a case study, which explains how the proposed approach can be applied for analyzing an organization from the area of logistics. It includes the introduction of a new technique for the graphical representation of organization models. The paper ends with a discussion in Section 7.

2 Principles for Modeling and Analyzing Organizations

Modern organizations are characterized by their complex structure, dense information flows, and incorporation of information technology. To a large extent, the underlying organization model is responsible for how efficiently and effectively organizations carry out their tasks. In literature, a range of theories and guidelines concerning the design of organizations are present [15, 17]. However, almost no operational theories or formal models exist. Scott [20] even stated that there are no general principles applicable to organizational design. In contrast, Minzberg proposed a set of guidelines for modeling any arbitrary organization [15]. These guidelines are applicable to mechanistic types of organizations, which represent systems of hierarchically linked job positions with clear responsibilities that use standard well-understood technology and operate in a relatively stable (possibly complex) environment. However, many modern organizations are characterized by a highly dynamic, constantly changing, organic structure and show a hardly identified, not formalized, non-linear behavior [16].

2.1 Two Perspectives

In this subsection, we will briefly discuss two perspectives from which organizations are analyzed. The first perspective emerges from social sciences and the second originates from computational organization theory and artificial intelligence.

In social science theories, the structure of organizations is frequently specified as informal or semi-formal graphical representations [15, 17]. They can provide a detailed organization structure at an abstract level. However, such approaches lack the means to represent the more detailed dynamics and to relate them to the structures present.

From computational organization theory and artificial intelligence, approaches have been developed that are able to capture both structural and dynamic aspects of organizations. However, usually they describe organization models, using only two or three levels of abstraction; i.e., the level of an individual role, the level of a group composed of roles, and the overall organization level, as in GAIA [22], MOISE [7] (extended to S-MOISE+ [11]), MOCA [1], and OperA [3]. In contrast, multiple levels and relations need to be described for the representation of complex hierarchical structures of modern organizations; e.g., mechanistic type of organizations [17].

Some models (e.g., ISLANDER [4], OperA [3]) consider organizations as electronic institutions; i.e., norms and global rules that govern an organization are explicitly defined. However, in many modern organic organizations with much individual autonomy, the normative aspects do not play a central role and are of minor importance for the prosperity of an organization.

Independent of the previous distinction in approaches, the importance of explicit modeling of interactions between agents and the environment is recognized [3, 18]. This is of importance since the environment plays a crucial role in the functioning of organizations. Moreover, for modeling in general, verification and validation of the models used or generated is of the utmost importance. This is no different for modeling organizations. However, this aspect of modeling organizations is frequently ignored; two of the exceptions are TROPOS [2] and ISLANDER [4].

2.2 A New Perspective

In this paper, we propose an approach for formal specification of organizations. To this end, it is highly suitable for specifying mechanistic types of organizations; i.e., machine and professional bureaucracy and divisionalized forms of organizations. Furthermore, this approach can also be applied for modeling organic types of organizations, when extended with organizational change techniques.

The proposed, formal approach can capture both structural and dynamic aspects of the organization and, subsequently, has four advantages:

(1) Representation of organization structure (including specifications of actors (or roles), relations between them, and information flows).
(2) The means for simulations of different scenarios on the basis of a model and observing their results.
(3) Organization analysis by means of verifying static and dynamic properties against (formalized) empirical data, taken from real organizations, or against simulated scenarios.
(4) Diagnosis of inconsistencies, redundancies, and errors in structure and functioning (e.g., with regard to organizational performance indicators) of real organizations and providing recommendations for their improvement.

In the proposed model, organizations are specified as composite roles that can be refined. The refined structures consist of (interacting) roles, representing as many aggregation levels as needed. Moreover, global normative aspects of an organization are considered as static and dynamic properties of the role, defined at the highest abstraction level, which represents the whole organization, without recognizing them as special notions and placing them on top of an organization. In addition, the environment is considered as a special component of an organization model.

The modeling method introduced in this paper incorporates two types of verification and validation techniques: role-centered and agent-centered, as will be discussed in Section 5. However, the introduction of these techniques is preceded by the introduction of the model itself in the next section and its formal specification in Section 4.

3 Organization Modeling Concepts

In this section, the concepts are introduced on which the organization modeling approach is founded. First, the specification of the organizational structure is described. A template model is generated, which encapsulates the structure of the organization. On all existing levels of aggregation, the behavior of an organization can be described.

Taken together, this provides description of the behavior of an organization. In Section 3.2, will be explained how such dynamic behavior can be specified. In Section 3.3, the transition from template model to deployed model will be discussed.

3.1 Organization Structure

An organization structure is described by relationships between roles at the same and at adjoining aggregation levels and between parts of the conceptualized environment and roles. The specification of an organization structure uses the following elements:

(1) A role represents a subset of functionalities, performed by an organization, abstracted from specific agents who fulfill them.

Each role can be composed by several other roles, until the necessary detailed level of aggregation is achieved, where a role that is composed of (interacting) subroles, is called a composite role. Each role has an input and an output interface, which facilitate in the interaction (communication) with other roles. The interfaces are described in terms of interaction (input and output) ontologies: a vocabulary or a signature specified in order-sorted logic. At the highest aggregation level, the whole organization can be represented as one role. Such representation is useful both for specifying general organizational properties and further utilizing an organization as a component for more complex organizations. Graphically, a role is represented as an ellipse with white dots (the input interfaces) and black dots (the output interfaces). Roles and relations between them are specified using sorts and predicates from the structure ontology (see Table 1).

(2) An interaction link represents an information channel between two roles at the same aggregation level. Graphically, it is depicted as a solid arrow, which denotes the direction of possible information transfer.

(3) The conceptualized environment represents a special component of an organization model. Similarly to roles, the environment has input and output interfaces, which facilitate in the interaction with roles of an organization. The interfaces are conceptualized by the environment interaction (input and output) ontologies. These ontologies are defined using three types of predicates: to_be_observed, observation_result, and to_be_performed (see Table 1).

The internal specification for the environment can be conceptualized using one of the existing world ontologies (e.g., CYC, SUMO, TOVE). It can be defined by a set of objects with certain properties and states and with causal relations between objects. Graphically, the environment is depicted as a rectangle with rounded corners.

(4) An environment interaction link represents an information channel between a role and the conceptualized environment. Graphically, it is depicted as a dotted arrow, which denotes the direction of possible information transfer.

(5) An interlevel link connects a composite role with one of its subroles. It represents a transition between two adjacent aggregation levels. It may describe an ontology mapping for representing mechanisms of information abstraction. Graphically, it is depicted as a dashed arrow, which shows the direction of the interlevel transition.

Table 1. Ontology for formalizing organizational structure

Sort	Description
ROLE	Sort for a role
AGENT	Sort for an agent
ENVIRONMENT	Sort for the conceptualized environment
INTERACTION_LINK	Sort for an interaction link between two roles at the same aggregation level
INTERLEVEL_LINK	Sort for an interlevel link between two roles at two adjacent aggregation levels
ENVIRONMENT_INTERACTION_LINK	Sort for an environment interaction link between a role and the conceptualized environment
ONTOLOGY	Sort for an ontology
ONTO_MAPPING	Sort for an ontology mapping
STATE_PROPERTY	Sort for a state property expressed using some ontology
ACTION	Sort for an action performed in the environment

Predicate	Description
is_role: ROLE	Specifies a role in an organization
has_subrole: ROLE x ROLE	For a subrole of a composite role
source_of_interaction: ROLE x INTERACTION_LINK	Specifies a source role of an interaction
destination_of_interaction: ROLE x INTERACTION_LINK	Specifies a destination role of interaction
interlevel_connection_from: ROLE x INTERLEVEL_LINK	Identifies a source role of an interlevel link
interlevel_connection_to: ROLE x INTERLEVEL_LINK	Identifies a destination role of an interlevel link
initiator_env_interaction: ROLE x ENVIRONMENT_INTERACTION_LINK	Specifies a role-initiator in interaction with the environment
recipient_env_information: ROLE x ENVIRONMENT_INTERACTION_LINK	Identifies a role-recipient of information from the environment
part_of_env_in_interaction: ENVIRONMENT x ENVIRONMENT_INTERACTION_LINK	Identifies the conceptualized part of the environment involved in interaction with a role
has_input_ontology: ROLE x ONTOLOGY	Specifies an input ontology for a role
has_output_ontology: ROLE x ONTOLOGY	Specifies an output ontology for a role
has_input_ontology: ENVIRONMENT x ONTOLOGY	Specifies an input ontology for the environment
has_output_ontology: ENVIRONMENT x ONTOLOGY	Specifies an output ontology for the environment
has_interaction_ontology: ROLE x ONTOLOGY	Specifies an interaction ontology for a role
has_interaction_ontology: ENVIRONMENT x ONTOLOGY	Specifies an interaction ontology for the environment
has_onto_mapping: INTERACTION_LINK x ONTO_MAPPING	Identifies an ontology mapping
to_be_observed: STATE_PROPERTY	Describes a state property that will be observed in the environment
observation_result: STATE_PROPERTY x BOOLEAN_VALUE	Determines if a certain state property holds in the environment
to_be_performed: ACTION	Specifies an action that will be performed in the environment

3.2 Organizational Dynamics

At each aggregation level, it can be specified how the organization's behavior is assumed to be. To this end, organization dynamics are described by a dynamic representation, for each of the elements in an organization structure. The level of detail for specifying dynamics of an organization depends on its organizational type. Since the behavior of most mechanistic organizations is deterministic, dynamics for such organizations can only be modeled by a set of dynamic properties with high level of detail. In contrast, behavior of many organic organizations is defined loosely. Consequently, the dynamics of models for such organizations can be specified only partially; hence, actors (agents) can act autonomously.

The dynamics of each structural element are defined by the specification of a set of dynamic properties, formalized using the dynamic ontology (see Table 2).

Table 2. Dynamics ontology for formalizing properties of an organization

Sort	Description
DYNPROP	Sort for the name of a dynamic property
DPEXPR	Sort for the expression of a dynamic property
Predicate	**Description**
has_dynamic_property: ROLE x DYNPROP	Specifies a role dynamic property
has_dynamic_property: INTERACTION_LINK x DYNPROP	Identifies a dynamic property for an interaction link
has_dynamic_property: ENVIRONMENT x DYNPROP	Identifies a dynamic property for the conceptualized part of the environment
has_dynamic_property: ENVIRONMENT_INTERACTION_LINK x DYNPROP	Identifies a dynamic property for an environment interaction link
has_expression: DYNPROP x DPEXPR	Specifies an expression for a dynamic property

We define five types of dynamic properties:

(1) *A role property* (**RP**) describes the relationship between input and output states of a role, over time. The input and output states are represented as an assignment of truth-values to the set of ground atoms, expressed in terms of a role interaction (input or output) ontology.

For example, in the settings of a typical logistics company, a role property of a truck driver would be: if role Truck Driver receives a request from his manager to provide his coordinates, then role Truck Driver will generate this data for his manager.

(2) *A transfer property* (**TP**) describes the relationship of the output state of the source role of an interaction link to the input state of the destination role. Again, in the settings of a logistic company an example of a transfer company would be: if role Customer generates an order to role Transport Company, then Transport Company will receive this order.

(3) *An interlevel link property* (**ILP**) describes the relationship between the input or output state of a composite role and the input or output state of its subrole. Note that an interlevel link is considered to be instantaneous: it does not represent a temporal process, but gives a different view (using a different ontology) on the same information state. An interlevel transition is specified by an ontology mapping, which can include information abstraction.

(4) *An environment property* (**EP**) describes a temporal relationship between states or properties of objects of interest in the environment.

(5) *An environment interaction property* (**EIP**) describes a relation either between the output state of the environment and the input state of a role (or an agent) or between the output state of a role (or an agent) and the input state of the environment. On one hand, roles (or agents) are capable of observing states and properties of objects in the environment; on the other hand, they can act or react and, thus, affect the environment. We distinguish passive and active observation processes. For example, when some object is observable by a role (or an agent) and the role (or the agent) continuously keeps track of its state, changing its internal representation of the object if necessary, passive observation occurs. For passive observation, no initiative of the role or agent is needed. Active observation is always concerned with the role or agent's initiative.

3.3 Deployed Model and Agent Allocation

The generic or template model of an organization provides abstracted information concerning its structure and functioning. However, for a more detailed analysis, a deployed model is needed. It should be based on both unfolded generic relations between roles, as defined in the template model, and on creating new role instances. Moreover, the environment (or scenario) influences the specification of a deployed model considerably. Subsequently, different deployed models can be specified for different scenarios, using the same template model of an organization. For formalizing the structure and behavior of a deployed model, the same ontologies are used as for formalizing a template model.

The deployed model abstracts from the actual agent allocation but provides the detailed specifications for the behavior of role instances. Based on these specifications, a set of requirements is formulated for each role instance. These requirements (restricting and defining behavior) are imposed onto the agents, who will eventually enact these roles. The formalization of the allocation principles is performed in line with the formalization of the template and the deployed models, using the predicate allocate_to. In some scenarios, a complex role can act as a single aggregated role and, thus, representing its constituting subroles. In such cases, an agent(s) can be assigned to the complex role. If, for some reason, an allocated agent is not anymore capable of enacting a certain role, dynamic reallocation of another agent will take place, as described in Section 6.

4   Formal Specification of the Organization Model

In the previous section, the elements of the methodology were introduced. The current section provides the formal specification of them.

4.1 Structural Properties

Structural properties represent relations between structural elements of the organiza-tion. They are specified in a sorted first-order predicate logic, based on the structure ontology. For example, in the settings of a logistics company, subroles Fleet Manager (FM) and Load Manager (LM) belong to the same composite role Operational de-partment (OP). Formally:

has_subrole(OP, FM) ∧ has_subrole(OP, LM)

Often, structural properties are valid during the whole period of organization exis-tence and can be considered as static. But in rapidly developing and adapting organi-zations, structural change processes gain special importance. Structural properties for such organizations get a temporal dimension and can be considered as a subclass of dynamic properties.

4.2 State and Dynamic Properties

A dynamic property represents a relation in time either between (input or output) states of roles or a (input or output) state of a role and a (input or output) state of the environment. To achieve this, every role as well as the conceptualized part of the environment has assigned state ontologies for input and output states. A state for ontology Ont is an assignment of truth-values to the set At(Ont) of ground atoms ex-pressed in terms of Ont. The set of all possible states for state ontology Ont is denoted by STATES(Ont). A state property is defined by a formula over a state ontology.

Role or environment states are related to state properties via the formally defined satisfaction relation ⊨, comparable to the Holds-predicate in situation calculus: state(γ, t, output(r)) ⊨ p, which denotes that state property p holds in trace γ at time t in the output state of role r.

For a fixed, linearly ordered, time frame TIME (e.g., natural or real numbers), a trace γ over a state ontology Ont is defined as a mapping γ : TIME → STATES(Ont) or, in other words, a sequence of states γ_t (t ∈ TIME) in STATES(Ont). The set of all traces over state ontology Ont is denoted by TRACES(Ont).

Dynamic properties (e.g., for roles, environment, and links) are specified in the language Temporal Trace Language (TTL) [12], based on a sorted first-order predi-cate logic with sorts TIME for time points and TRACE for traces, using quantifiers over time and logical connectives. The specification of properties in TTL is supported by a dedicated editor [13]. For examples of dynamic properties in formal form, see Sections 6.

5 Verification and Validation

The model as introduced in this paper offers the means for both role-centered and agent-centered verification and validation. This section briefly discusses these.

Role-centered verification techniques may be used for analysis of both template and deployed models of organizations. Subsequently, inconsistencies and bottlenecks in an organization can be detected. Agent-centered verification techniques are used for analyzing scenarios with roles of an organization model, allocated to (human) agents.

For those cases where empirical traces (i.e., sequences of states) of the processes within an organization are (partially) available, it is possible to validate properties against such a trace. For example, a trace can be obtained from log-files of a company. If an empirical trace is given informally, the first step is to formalize it (by hand), using formal state ontologies. If it is already given in a formal form, the first step is to translate (e.g., automatically) the formal representation into one based on ontologies used in the organization model. For the trace that has been generated by simulation, translation into the right formal format can be automated as an interface between the simulation environment and the checking environment. Once such a trace is in the right formal form, it is possible to verify dynamic properties of the organization (including structural properties), using dedicated checking software.

As input for the verification software, a formalized trace and a formalized property have to be provided. Given such input, after automatic verification of the given property against the given trace, the software will generate a decision (positive or negative). The positive decision denotes that the property holds with respect to the given trace. In case of a negative decision, the software explains why the property does not hold. This type of verification is shown in the case study in Section 6.

Another verification method uses a simulation model based on the specification of the dynamic properties of the lower aggregation level for checking the properties of the higher aggregation level. This verification method is supported by the dedicated checking software [13].

When an organization model is specified including dynamic properties at different aggregation levels, it is not automatically guaranteed that these properties at different levels fit to each other. A verification process that relates properties at one aggregation level to those of another level (e.g., as in compositional verification) can reveal incompleteness or inconsistencies. In the case study presented in the next section, it is shown how such a mutual verification process can be performed.

6 Case study

In this section, a case study is described. In parallel, the newly developed graphical representation of organization models is introduced. This case study was done within the project DEAL (Distributed Engine for Advanced Logistics). For the project description, we refer to *http://www.almende.com/deal/*. A template organizational model was created, based on the informal description of the structure and functioning of the large Dutch logistics company. To secure anonymity of the company, the real names of the organizational units were substituted by general ones,.

At the highest level (abstraction level 0) we represent the whole organization as one role. At abstraction level 1, the organization consists of two interacting roles: TC and CI (see Fig.1). Note, that the organizational model is depicted in a modular way; i.e., components of every aggregation level can be visualized and analyzed both separately and in relation to each other. Consequently, scalability of graphical representation of an organizational model is achieved.

Fig. 1. Representation of the organization at abstraction level 1, which consists of role Transport Company (TC) and role Customer Interaction (CI)

At abstraction level 2 role TC can be refined into three interacting roles: ST, CR, and OP (see Fig.2). All interactions with a customer are conducted within CI role. At abstraction level 2 it consists of two roles: TCR and C (see Fig. 2). Role TCR produces at its output messages from CR and ST departments of the transport company, i.e., CR and ST roles stand as company representatives in certain interactions with a customer. Therefore, the input state of role TCR has influence on the output state of role CR and vice versa. The same holds for role ST.

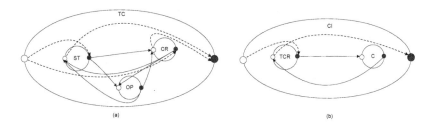

Fig. 2. Representation of (a) the Transport Company (TC) and (b) the Customer Interaction role (CI) at abstraction level 2

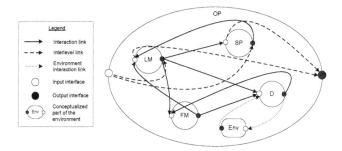

Fig. 3. Representation of the operational department at abstraction level 3

The corresponding dynamic properties may be specified at abstraction level 0 and can be further refined into basic properties at lower abstraction levels. In our case study, we particularly concentrate on the structure and functioning of the OP (see Fig. 3), part of the TC.

Table 3. Role names, abbreviations, and descriptions for the organizational model in the case study

Role name	Abbreviation	Description
Transport Company	TC	Provides logistic services to customers
Customer Interaction	CI	Identifies interaction rules between a customer and the transport company
Strategy and Tactical Department	ST	Performs analysis and planning of company activities; considers complaints from customers; analyses the satisfaction level of a customer by means of surveys and questionnaires
Custom Relations Department	CR	Handles requests from customers
Operational Department	OP	Responsible for direct fulfillment of the order from a customer
Transport Company Representative	TCR	Mediator role between a customer and the transport company
Customer	C	Generates an order for the transport company; sends inquiries about the delivery status
Sales Person	SP	Assigns an order to a certain load manager, based on the type and the region of a delivery
Load Manager	LM	Assigns orders to suitable trucks and available drivers; assigns fleet managers to drivers; provides CR department with up-to-date information about delivery; provides a driver with instructions in case of a severe problem; informs CR department about possible delays with delivery
Fleet Manager	FM	Keeps constant contact with the assigned drivers; updates automatic support system with actual data on the delivery status; provides consultations for drivers in case of minor problems in transit
Driver	D	Delivers goods; informs a superior fleet manager about the delivery status; interacts (by means of observations and actions) with the conceptualized part of the environment
Environment	Env	Represents the conceptualized environment; in this case study only a driver interacts with it

The static aspects of the considered organization have been formally described in the organization structure specification. The sets of dynamic properties for the components of the organization structure have been identified at different abstraction levels. For example, consider the information distribution property of role OP called RP1(OP), specified at abstraction level 2. Informally, when a severe problem with some delivery occurs, OP should generate a message to CR about possible delay. Formally specified:

$\forall \gamma$:TRACE $\forall$t1:TIME $\exists$T:TRUCK_TYPE $\exists$D:DRIVER $\exists$ON:ORDER_NUM state(γ, t1, environment))|= truck_state(T, incident, severe_incident) $\wedge$ truck_property(T, operated_by, D) $\wedge$ order_property(ON, assigned_to, D)$\Rightarrow$ $\exists$t2:TIME t2>t1 state(γ, t2, output(OP))|=communicate_from_to(OP, CR, inform, order_state(ON, delay, severe_incident)),

where Table 4 provides the description of the predicates.

Table 4. Predicates for formalizing the dynamic properties used in the examples

Predicate	Description
communication_from_to(r1:ROLE, r2:ROLE, s_act:SPEECH_ACT, message:STRING)	Specifies the speech act *s_act* (e.g., inform, request, ask) from role-source *r1* to role-destination *r2* with the content *message*
deliverable_object(on: ORDER_NUM, desc:STRING)	Assigns the order number *on* with the description *desc* to the object that has to be delivered
truck_property(trt:TRUCK_TYPE, operated_by, d:DRIVER)	Assigns the driver *d* to a truck of the type *trt*
order_property(on:ORDER_NUM, assigned_to, d:DRIVER)	Assignes the order *on* to the driver *d*
order_property(on:ORDER_NUM, deadline, d_value:INTEGER)	Identifies the deadline *d_value* for the order *on*
truck_state(trt:TRUCK_TYPE, st:STATE, descr:STATE_DESCRIPTION)	Denotes the state *st* with the state description *descr* of a truck of the type *trt*
order_state(on:ORDER_NUM, st:STATE, descr:STATE_DESCRIPTION)	Specifies the state *st* with the state description *descr* of the order with the number *on*

This property can be logically related to the conjunction of dynamic properties at a lower abstraction level 3 in the following way:

EP1(Env, T, severe_incident) ∧ EIP1(Env, D) ∧ RP1(D) ∧ TP1(D, FM) ∧ RP2(FM) ∧ TP2(FM, LM) ∧ RP3(LM) ∧ ILP1(LM, OP) ⇒ RP1(OP)

Using the verification technique, as described in Section 5, can be shown that the latter logical relation indeed holds. Between brackets, the abbreviations of the dynamic properties, are provided, conform the specification provided in Section 3.2. In the environment occurs an event: a severe incident with the truck T, for which role D is responsible (EP1). D observes this incident (EIP1) and reacts by generating a request for advice to FM (RP1). FM receives this request (TP1). FM is not empowered of making decisions in such situations; therefore s/he propagates the request further to LM (RP2). LM receives the request (TP2). LM officially identifies the incident as severe (RP3) and outputs the notification about a possible delay from role OP to CR (ILP1). Thus, by a manually conducted, mathematical proof, the previously identified logical relation between two adjoining aggregation level spaces indeed holds. In general, attempting to set up such a manually conducted, mathematical proof can reveal missing premises or other shortcomings such as inconsistencies.

In the deployed model for the considered case study, all roles specified at abstraction levels 1 and 2 have one-to-one mapping to the role instances. While roles LM, FM, and D (defined at abstraction level 3) have multiple instances; e.g., LM and FM are represented differently in different geographical regions and, subsequently, different types of trucks and professional skills of drivers are required for different kinds of deliveries. The deployed model for our case study (see Fig. 4) is based on the assignment relation. For example, assigned_to(D2, FM1) denotes that a middle-size truck and his driver are assigned to the fleet manager in eastern Europe and the region belonging relation in_region(D1, LM1) specifies that both a big-size truck driver and a load manager should belong to the same region in eastern Europe).

When a template and a deployed organizational model are specified, agent allocation principles should be formulated. The capabilities of agents, essential for this case study were identified. For example, a driver-agent can drive a truck; hence, he has a driver license of a certain type, has acceptable results of medical tests etc. In addition, the allocation requirements for role instances were formulated; e.g., in order to enact role LM, an agent should have working experience as a senior manager in logistics for at least 3 years.

Let us briefly consider the scenario reconstructed from empirical data of the transport company, using specified organizational model:

(1) A Customer places an order by means of a contact with TCR (CR department in this case) in CI.
(2) Inside TC this order is being transmitted from CR to OP.
(3) Within OP the order is distributed by SP to LM1.
(4) LM1 assigns the order to D1, D1 is associated with FM1 (see Fig. 4).
(5) D1 starts delivery, then after some time a severe incident occurs with his truck.
(6) D1 asks for help FM1, who incapable of making a decision in this case.
(7) FM asks for a solution LM1, who decides to send another truck to proceed with delivery.
(8) Now D1 is reallocated to another truck and driver, who picks up goods and continues delivery.
(9) At the same time LM1 informs CR about possible delay with delivery.
(10) CR, who shares the same knowledge with TCR, informs the Customer about possible delay.
(11) D1 successfully finishes delivery and the Customer is being informed about that.

Using formal state ontologies (see Tables 1 and 2), we formalized this trace in the LEADSTO environment [13]. A formalized empirical trace is useful for analysis of organizational functioning. For the case study, we identified several properties of interest that can be automatically verified against the trace. Let us consider some of these properties.

(1) Delivery successfulness
Informally: the order has been fulfilled. Formally:

$\exists$t:TIME $\exists$O:ORDER_NUM state(γ, t, environment)|= order_state(O, delivered, final_report)

An automatic verification, as mentioned in Section 5, confirmed that this property holds against the formalized empirical trace.

(2) Customer notification
Informally: always if a severe problem occurs with the truck and the driver, who was fulfilling the order of some customer, then this customer should be notified about possible delay with delivery. Formally:

$\forall\gamma$:TRACE $\forall$t1:TIME $\exists$T:TRUCK_TYPE $\exists$D:DRIVER $\exists$ON:ORDER_NUM state(γ, t1, environment))|= truck_state(T, incident, severe_incident) $\wedge$ truck_property(T, operated_by, D) $\wedge$ order_property(ON, assigned_to, D) $\Rightarrow$ $\exists$t2:TIME t2>t1 $\exists$TCR:ROLE state(γ, t2, input(customer))|=communicate_from_to(TCR, customer, inform, order_state(ON, delay, customer_report))

Again automatic verification confirmed that this property holds against the trace.
(3) Delivery accuracy
Informally: the order has been fulfilled on time. Formally:

$\exists$t:TIME $\exists$O:ORDER_NUM $\exists$d_value:integer state(γ, t, environment)|= order_state(O, delivered, final_report) $\wedge$ order_details(O, deadline, d_value) $\wedge$ d_value $\geq$ t

This property does not hold with respect to the trace. The next logical step in analysis of the causes for property failing would be to check if some incident occurred in transit. In case that a severe incident happened with the truck and the agent (a truck driver) was incapable of performing his role any more, the next step would be to verify whether or not enough time is available for a role reallocation. Subsequently, analysis of organization functioning can be continued until all inquiries about delivery are satisfied.

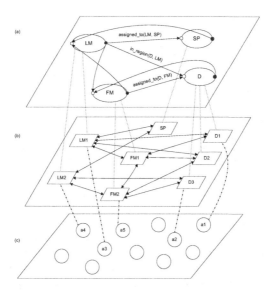

Fig. 4. The operational department of the transport company represented at abstraction level 3, with (a) the template model (b) the deployed model, and (c) agent allocation

7 Discussion

Both in human society and for software agents, organizational structure provides the means to make complex, composite dynamics manageable. To understand and formalize how exactly organization structure constrains composite dynamics is a fundamental challenge in the area of organizational modeling. The modeling approach presented in this paper addresses this challenge. It concerns a method for formal specification of organizations, which can capture both structural and dynamic aspects of organizations and provides the means for (i) representation of organization structure, (ii) simulations of different scenarios, (iii) analysis of organization, verifying static and dynamic properties against (formalized) empirical data or simulated scenarios, (iv) diagnosis of inconsistencies, redundancies, and errors in structure and functioning. Additionally, the environment is integrated as a special component within the organization model.

Specification of organization structure usually takes the form of pictorial descriptions, in a graph-like framework. These descriptions often abstract from detailed dynamics within an organization. Specification of the dynamic properties of organizations, on the other hand, usually takes place in a completely different conceptual framework; these dynamic properties are often specified in the form of a set of logical formulae in some temporal language. The logical relationships express the kind of relations between dynamics of parts of an organization, their interaction, and dynamic properties of the organization as a whole, which were indicated as crucial by Lomi and Larsen [14] in their introduction.

This paper shows how pictorial descriptions, in a graph-like framework, and a set of logical formulae in some temporal language can be combined in one agent-based modeling approach. Inspection can be done on the abstraction level preferred and both the pictorial and formal specifications of the dynamic properties can be inspected. Five essential types of dynamic properties characterizing behavior of main structural components of an organization model (including environment) are identified. So far, more complex cases of organizational behavior (e.g., the synchronization problem for joint action) were not discussed. For example, in the case of joint lifting by roles or agents more sophisticated types of dynamic properties are needed; e.g., combined role properties that define temporal relations between a number of states for some set of roles and a number of states of another set of roles. Furthermore, the approach proposed here supports formal specification and verification for both static and dynamic properties. This possibility is especially useful for diagnosis of inconsistencies, redundancies, and errors in structure and functioning of real organizations and providing recommendations for their improvement (e.g., by way of evaluating of performance indicators).

Compared to most organization-oriented, multi-agent system, design approaches [1, 4, 5, 22], our model allows any number of aggregation levels in the organization model, which makes it more suitable for modeling and analyzing real organizations. While a role aggregation relation is considered to be crucial for representing an organizational model, other types of relations between roles should also be taken into account. For example, a role specified in a template model and its corresponding role instances defined in a deployed model are related by means of a generalization relation. Furthermore, it would be interesting to investigate how role hierarchies, based on generalization, and other types of relations can be used in the specification of a template model.

Let us now consider a case in which agents show autonomous behavior, independent of (or sometimes conflicting to) organizational rules and goals. In this case, an agent behavior can be specified from the positions of sociological theories, which take into account an individual behavior of social actors. One of such theories, the Sociology of Organized Action studies an organization functioning beyond its formal rules and is used for specifying informal coordination mechanisms in agent organizations [21]. To tackle the forthcoming compatibility problems from the relationships between formally predefined organizational model and agent autonomous behavior, further investigation will be undertaken. When the latter would be accomplished, many types of modern organizations could be modeled.

In the case of highly dynamic organizations (e.g., self-organizing and organic organizations), organizational change is a crucial and frequent process. Due to their high complexity, such organizations are difficult to investigate. However, different simulation techniques can help in providing further insights into mechanisms of functioning of such organizations. For the latter purpose, research has been conducted based on the introduced formal model [8]. In [6] a simulation technique is suggested that can be used for evaluation of different alternatives of an organizational structure with respect to the task performance and reorganization when necessary.

In addition, the different types of modern organizations should be taken in consideration, as organization theory [15, 20] classifies and describes them. It would be useful to develop and formally specify the templates capturing essential structural and dynamic aspects of most frequently encountered types of organizations. Such templates would be of great help for organization designers and analysts.

In conclusion, this paper introduced a new, formal, fully traceable method on modeling and analyzing (multi-agent) organizations. It comprises both static and dynamic aspects as well as environment representation. Hence, it provides the basis of a formal framework, which provides the means for both the design and for the automatic validation and verification of organizations.

Acknowledgments

This research was partially supported by the Netherlands Organization for Scientific Research (NWO) under project number 612.062.006. SenterNovem is gratefully acknowledged for funding the projects Cybernetic Incident Management (CIM) and Distributed Engine for Advanced Logistics (DEAL) that also funded this research partially. Further, we thank the reviewers for their detailed comments on the original manuscript.

References

1. Amiguet, M., Müller, J.P., B'aez-Barranco, J.A., Nagy, A.: The MOCA platform. Lecture Notes in Computer Science (Multi-Agent-Based Simulation) 2581 (2003) 70-88
2. Bresciani, P., Giorgini, P., Giunchiglia, F., Mylopoulos, J., Perini, A.: Tropos: An agent-oriented software development methodology. Autonomous Agents and Multi-Agent Sytems 8 (2004) 203-236
3. Dastani, M., Hulstijn, J., Dignum, F., Meyer, J.J.Ch.: Issues in multiagent system development. In Jennings, N.R., Sierra, C., Sonenberg, L., Tambe, M., eds.: Proceedings of the third International Joint Conference on Autonomous Agents and Multiagent Systems (AAMAS 2004). Volume 2, IEEE Computer Society (2004) 922-929
4. Esteva, M., de la Cruz, D., Sierra, C.: ISLANDER: An electronic institutions editor. In Gini, M., Ishida, T., Castelfranchi, C., Johnson, W.L., eds.: The First International Joint Conference on Autonomous Agents and Multiagent Systems (AAMAS 2002). Volume 3, ACM (2002) 1045-1052
5. Ferber, J., Gutknecht, O., Michel, F.: From agents to organizations: An organizational view of multi-agent systems. Lecture Notes in Computer Science (AOSE) 2935 (2003) 214-230
6. Furtado, V., Melo, A., Dignum, V., Dignum, F., Sonenberg, L.: Exploring congruence between organizational structure and task performance: A simulation approach. Lecture Notes in Computer Science [in the same volume]
7. Hannoun, M., Sichman, J.S., Boissier, O., Sayettat, C.: Dependence relations between roles in a multi-agent system: Towards the detection of inconsistencies in organization. Lecture Notes in Computer Science (Multi-Agent-Based Simulation) 1534 (1998) 169-182
8. Hoogendoorn, M., Jonker, C.M., Schut,M.C., Treur, J.: Modelling the organisation of organizational change. In Giorgini, P., Winikoff, M., eds.: Proceedings of the Sixth International Workshop on Agent-Oriented Information Systems (AOIS'04). (2004) 26-46
9. Horling, B., Lesser, V.: A survey of multi-agent organizational paradigms. The Knowledge Engineering Review 9 (2005) 281-316
10. Hübner, J.F., Sichman, J.S., Boissier, O.: A model for the structural, functional, and deontic specification of organizations in multiagent systems. Lecture Notes in Computer Science (Advances in Artificial Intelligence) 2507 (2002) 118-128

11. Hübner, J.F., Sichman, J.S., Boissier, O.: S-MOISE+: A Middleware for developing Organized Multi-Agent Systems. Lecture Notes in Computer Science [in the same volume]
12. Jonker, C.M., Treur, J.: A temporal-interactivist perspective on the dynamics of mental states. Cognitive Systems Research Journal 4 (2003) 137-155
13. Jonker, C.M., Treur J., Wijngaards W.C.A.: A temporal-modelling environment for internally grounded beliefs, desires, and intentions. Cognitive Systems Research Journal 4(3) (2003) 191-210
14. Lomi, A., Larsen, E.R. (eds.): Dynamics of Organizations: Computational Modeling and Organization Theories. Cambridge, MA: The M.I.T. Press (2001)
15. Mintzberg, H.: The Structuring of Organizations. Prentice Hall, Englewood Cliffs (1979)
16. Miles, R.E., Snow, C.C., Mathews, J.A., Miles, G., and Coleman, H.J.: Organizing in the Knowledge Age: Anticipating the Cellular Form. Academy of Management Executive 11 (1997) 7-20
17. Morgan, G.: Images of organizations. SAGE Publications, Thousand Oaks London New Delhi (1996)
18. Omicini, A.: SODA: Societies and infrastructures in the analysis and design of agent-based systems. Lecture Notes in Computer Science (AOSE) 1957 (2001) 185-193
19. Prietula, M., Gasser, L., Carley, K.: Simulating Organizations. MIT Press (1997)
20. Scott, W.R.: Institutions and organizations. 2nd ed. SAGE Publications, Thousand Oaks London New Delhi (2001)
21. Sibertin-Blanc, C., Amblard, F., Mailliard, M.: A coordination framework based on the Sociology of the Organized Action. Lecture Notes in Computer Science [in the same volume]
22. Zambonelli, F., Jennings, N. R., Wooldridge, M.: Developing multiagent systems: the Gaia Methodology. ACM Transactions on Software Engineering and Methodology (TOSEM) 12(3) (2003) 317-370

Towards Sustained Team Effectiveness

Niek Wijngaards, Masja Kempen, Annika Smit, and Kees Nieuwenhuis

Delft Co-operation in Intelligent Systems Laboratory –
Thales Research and Technology Nederland
P.O. box 90, NL-2600 AB, Delft, The Netherlands
Telephone: +31-15-2517867; Fax.: +31-15-2517801
{niek.wijngaards, masja.kempen, annika.smit,
kees.nieuwenhuis}@icis.decis.nl

Abstract. Collaboration environments impose high demands on humans and artificial systems. Especially during critical tasks team members, including humans, artificial systems and other (sub-) teams, require support to guarantee their continued effectiveness. Effectiveness of individuals and teams is an important ingredient for organizational effectiveness, managerial decision quality, as well as for maintaining organizational awareness. In this position paper we introduce our conceptual view on realizing sustained team effectiveness, in which both the measurement of effectiveness and team management play an important role. A unified, interdisciplinary approach facilitates measuring effectiveness in more complex organizations.

1 Introduction

Highly dynamic, or even chaotic, environments are often encountered when a disruptive event occurs; such as a car-crash in a tunnel involving a fuel-truck. Suddenly the (tunnel) environment becomes unpredictable, normal courses of action may not yield expected results, and performance of teams as well as individuals is affected. Nevertheless, individuals and teams are expected to effectively address crisis situations over a period of time. In our view, it is a collection of teams and individuals that make up an organization, in which effectiveness plays a crucial role (for an overview, see e.g. [1]). We loosely define the term effectiveness as the degree to which a team is successful in reaching its goals/objectives. In this paper we focus mostly on individuals and teams, as they provide us with insights which can be translated to organizations.

Teams are often considered to consist of humans, e.g. [2, pp. 126-127] defines a team as "a distinguishable set of two or more people who interact dynamically, inter-dependently, and adaptively toward a common and valued goal/object/mission, who have each been assigned specific roles or functions to perform, and who have a limited life span of membership". In our opinion, intelligent systems such as agents and robots can also be team-members, equivalent in status to humans. This is in contrast to a large amount of system-level teams and agent research, which concentrates on agent-based support for individual human team members, see e.g. [3], [4] and [5]. In our view, agents (whether software entities on a network or robots) may also take the initiative and give orders to human (and other agent) team members. In essence, we approach a 'team' as an actor-agent community.

O. Boissier et al. (Eds.): ANIREM and OOOP 2005, LNCS 3913, pp. 35–47, 2006.
© Springer-Verlag Berlin Heidelberg 2006

An *actor-agent community* is a particular type of organization that involves collaboration of multiple participants, including humans and artificial systems, for the realization of a common mission or for the support of a shared process [6]. Within a community there are social rules that members adhere to, and there is communication, sharing of responsibility and a certain distinct identity among the community members. From a human perspective, an actor-agent community is not unlike any conventional human community – the same traits apply. From a technical perspective an actor-agent community contains distributed systems and processes that have autonomous and anticipatory capabilities – software systems that can be referred to as agents or agent systems. Actor-agent communities are typically involved in complex collaborative decision making processes, such as the day-to-day air traffic management. These are characteristic settings where humans and artificial systems are foreseen to collaborate in the near future.

In our view actor-agent communities need to be able to operate in the real world. This requires the ability to adapt to changes and unforeseen events. There is a need to be able to operate in highly dynamic situations under high degrees of uncertainty. Such a realistic domain is *crisis management*, in which both humans and artificial systems are involved, such as victims, rescuers, observers, and decision makers, all working together to mitigate the situation as quickly as possible [6]. This implies that a team consists of heterogeneous team members of potentially equal status (cf. 'mixed initiative taking').

In crisis situations normal operational conditions change radically. A crisis cannot be predicted (otherwise it is not a 'crisis'), yet preparations can be made (e.g., [7] and see the SEVESO II Directive of the European Community). Although the exact crisis is unknown, certain aspects of a crisis can be identified, e.g. constraints regarding the location of the incident, including availability of resources, victims, geographical setting; team structure, including team members and their skills, team resources such as tools and team norms; culture, as team members may originate from different 'host' organizations with different cultural identities, social norms, etc.

Crisis management involves addressing a number of interrelated issues:

- Time-criticality: time is a critical factor in decision-making, de-escalation of incidents, treatment of victims, restoration of normal operating conditions, etc.
- Performance fluctuations: during a crisis, performance of teams and machines changes (usually: degrades), e.g. due to (mental) fatigue, reduced alertness, resource depletion, etc.
- Incomplete situation awareness: dispersed, partial, information about (parts of) the situation, unreliable and faulty observations, etc.
- Changes in courses of action: chaotic environments or situations yield (unpredictable) changes to current goals, plans, schedules, problems at hand, etc.
- Team-(re)composition: during a crisis, teams may be formed, changed, and disbanded.
- Alignment: choreography and coordination of teams require understanding time-critical issues, performance, shared awareness, changes in courses of action and composition of teams.

- Organizational sustainability: organizations need support for their evolution and adaptation at multiple levels of abstraction to address chaotic environments such as crisis situations, while still adhering to necessary levels of coherence and coordination to retain levels of effectiveness.

In this position paper we briefly explore how to support sustained effectiveness of (organizations consisting of) teams consisting of heterogeneous team members, including humans, artificial systems and other (sub-) teams, in crisis situations. Section 2 addresses our view on sustained team effectiveness. Section 3 describes our view on team management, which is a key element in realizing team sustainability. Section 4 proposes a number of future research directions.

2 Sustained Team Effectiveness

Sustained team effectiveness is, from our perspective, a basic team property, which plays an important role in the usefulness, robustness, employability and composition of teams over a period of time. Effectiveness can be viewed as a utility, which is useful for planning and scheduling algorithms, for example. We explicitly assume that the effectiveness of individuals, teams and organizations changes over time; this evolving process may be manageable to a certain extent. In this section we describe our views on effectiveness and sustained effectiveness.

A good source for research on effectiveness stems from Psychology, in which an individual's effectiveness is often termed 'performance'. The level of performance is stated in terms of behavioral measures such as reaction times and errors (false positives and false negatives). Of major importance is the individual fitness level, which is often labeled 'vigilance' [8]. With respect to vigilance, it is not only important to measure general performance levels (e.g. average performance), but also the changes in performance over time are critical. That is, a decrement in performance (even when the average performance level is not very low) is indicative of declining vigilance of an individual [9], [10]. Whenever a vigilance decrement sets in, the deterioration is bound to get worse in the near future. So, for an individual, vigilance is determined in the following manner: performance (reaction times, errors) and performance change over time.

Interestingly enough, independence between physical and mental aspects of vigilance has been demonstrated [11]. That is, after demanding mental tasks, the mental component of vigilance is declined. Hence, subsequent mental task performance is decreased. However, purely physical tasks can still be performed adequately. The opposite also holds true: After strenuous physical tasks, performance on subsequent physical tasks is worse, but performance on mental tasks is generally not affected.

Besides the more basic issue of vigilance, other individual human variables also determine performance to a certain extent. Skills and expertise are known to have a considerable impact on performance [12]. Even when a person is highly vigilant, he or she may not be able to perform well if faced with a totally unfamiliar situation. For example, a skilled air-traffic operator would probably not know how to extinguish a fire, not even in a vigilant state.

Furthermore, especially in a crisis situation, performance is not only dependent on intrinsic aspects, but is also dependent on other aspects such as tools and external resources. For example, a firefighter may be both mentally fit (good and stable performance on mental tasks) and physically fit (good and stable performance on physical tasks), but if he does not have a proper suit or a full fire extinguisher, he will not perform as expected. Related to both aspects is whether the individual is in a relevant situational context: Is the right person at the right place at the right time? A vigilant, highly skilled and fully equipped fire fighter still needs to be near a fire in order to be able to extinguish it.

As stated above, there is a separation of physical and mental tasks. This is not so surprising, because physical systems, such as a human, operate within different dynamical regimes under normal conditions. Physical tasks, such as scrolling, and mental tasks, such as writing a paper, are assigned to different subsystems of the brain. In this case one could argue that the subsystems are most likely completely independent, meaning that the performance of one subsystem carrying out the mental task is not affected by the subsystem carrying out the physical task. In sum, these tasks do not interfere with one another. However, in real, more complex settings such as air traffic control operation, this independence of subsystems in the brain that carry out physical and mental tasks might not be plausible, due to the complexity of the cognitive tasks that need to be performed. Here, the physical and mental components might actually be coupled.

An example of coupling is the writing of a research paper, where the physical effort of clicking, scrolling and moving your head to read comments in the margin of a research paper interferes with the high-level mental activity of creating a nice piece of text that aims at getting your message across. Moving your head from the text field to the margin field – a physical task – involves a mental task, namely that of conscious motor control of neck and eye muscles. This places a burden on the other ongoing mental task: the creative process of writing the paper. Both physical and mental subsystems obstruct each other in such cases, due to their (un)fortunate coupling. Concluding, mental and physical task alignment, ensuring the highest possible independence of both subsystems, is first of all a pre-requisite for avoiding stress and strain, as well as mental and physical overload. Secondly, optimal alignment should sustain good task performance, as both sub-systems will minimally interfere with each other. From a cognitive ergonomic perspective it is a challenge to provide an empirical account of when, why and how such alignment is achieved for which subsystems. Furthermore, it is interesting to embody psycho-physical findings in future applications, systems and teams [13].

In short, effectiveness is dependent on physical and mental aspects of an individual, its tools and resources, cognitive ergonomic design factors, and situational context. Part of our future research is to investigate whether it is possible to measure and maintain effectiveness of teams of humans, software agents and robots. Our initial stance is that these constituents of (human) effectiveness are applicable to artificial entities. For example, consider vigilance; although vigilance may not seem directly applicable to a software agent, its processing capacity and supportive resources (e.g., memory, electricity, fuel, and bandwidth) may deplete over time. This corresponds with one of the definitions of human vigilance, which refers to the availability of capacity or resources [8]. The use of vigilance as one of the effectiveness parameters thus appears justified for both actors and agents. Despite the fact that similar principles apply, there of course remain structural differences between actors and agents. They will differ in actual task performance; quality and speed of performance will not be identical on all tasks. However, this will not interfere with our statement that their effectiveness can be *measured* in a similar manner.

We suggest that the fitness level of human *teams* can be measured in a similar manner as on the individual human level. That is, we intend to apply the same criteria for the team level as defined for the individual level. A unified approach facilitates measuring effectiveness in more complex organizations, including teams consisting of individuals and (sub-)teams. Determining the fitness of individuals and teams also requires a mechanism that monitors the actions/progress of individuals and teams in relation to their joint goals. E.g., in [14, p. 1] "Team situation awareness involves the team's assessment (i.e., perception, comprehension, and projection) of the current situation, which can include the surrounding environment (including any equipment or systems), the task, and the team itself." We would like to extend this approach from human teams to 'hybrid' teams (consisting of actors and agents (software and/or robots), which can be monitored in a similar fashion to measure effectiveness.

An important issue concerning measurements is that sustained team effectiveness is a desired high-level emergent property of a (possibly ad-hoc or changing) team or organization. This implies that the effectiveness of individuals and teams needs to be *measured* in time-critical circumstances. The measurements of effectiveness need to be such that they can be used in time by the right actors, agents or teams to manage themselves and others. Being able to measure effectiveness implies both attaching values to 'effectiveness', as well as having methods to determine these values. In addition, a number of 'levels' of effectiveness need to be distinguished in order to guarantee a specific level of effectiveness,. The relationship between required (minimal) effectiveness and coping with a certain class of problems in specific situations needs to become explicit as well.

Sustained effectiveness basically entails managing team effectiveness over time according to some criteria. Unfortunately, changes to team effectiveness are neither easily planned nor predicted, as the environment is essentially unpredictable and the criteria are not easily determined. In addition, time-criticality requires pragmatic approaches to measuring effectiveness of individual humans and agents as well as teams, and establishing pragmatic criteria (including a desired minimal level of effectiveness). Nevertheless, methods and techniques are required to positively influence effectiveness of individuals and teams. In the next section we elaborate on effectively managing ad-hoc and dynamic teams.

3 Sustained Team Management

Sustained effectiveness, by nature, is an emergent property (which may or may not manifest itself), of both individuals and teams. Sustained effectiveness even shows at the organizational level. The Aisin crisis in the Toyota Group [15] illustrates the possibility that without direct high management control, sustained effectiveness is feasible, even in a large crisis situation. Sustained effectiveness may be measured, to some extent, but cannot be directly controlled; it is not a simple 'parameter' of any human or artificial system. In organizational literature, 'management' is responsible for organization effectiveness, e.g. see [1]. We currently assume that at each level in the organization, team management is concerned with measuring and influencing effectiveness. In this section our initial model for sustained team management is described. First, a conceptual model is introduced, after which team management and its relation to sustained effectiveness is elaborated in some detail. This section is concluded by a discussion regarding measuring sustained effectiveness.

3.1 Towards a Model

To study sustained team effectiveness, a model is needed which represents teams, their composition, and the role of sustaining effectiveness. Our initial view is shown in Figure 1, in which team composition and team context are outlined. A team is a compositional construct, which can be composed of any combination of specific individuals (actors and/or agents) and sub-teams. In this compositional approach, *no* strict hierarchy is enforced: A team may be sub-team of multiple other teams, and similarly an individual may be a team-member of multiple teams. With this approach we intend to model dynamic organizational structures – although this needs further research to understand the limitations. The work by [16] and [17] are examples of a formal approach to model organizations and their dynamics.

We currently assume that it is not necessary to have a 'top-most' team which has a compositional relation with every individual in the entire organization. Similarly, we do not enforce that, at the 'bottom' of composition relations, teams can only consist of individuals; we leave open the possibility that a team 'believes' that it has a sub-team as a team-member, but this sub-team is not (yet) populated with individuals. How a sub-team is represented as a team-member is also part of future research.

In Figure 1, the composition of one team is shown. The team consists of two individuals (an agent and a human actor) and two sub-teams (which may again consist of actors, agents, and/or sub-sub-teams). A team has an associated 'team management' process, which is shared by all team-members. At this point, it is not important how this management process is realized by specific team-members; multiple options exist and will be explored in future research. On the one hand, team management is responsible for real-time dynamic (re)scheduling of allocation of tasks to humans and agents in order to solve problems given certain goals. On the other hand, there is the responsibility for acquiring and analyzing relevant status information of all members including their effectiveness, and changes of their effectiveness over time. These two responsibilities overlap; effectiveness is also a basis for (re)scheduling task allocations. For example, the fitness or vigilance that is determined of individuals and sub-teams serves as a basis for task allocation. An air-traffic operator who is very tired (i.e. not vigilant) will not be allocated a task that requires high vigilance. Likewise, a highly effective sub-team will be required to take the responsibility of a high-priority, demanding set of tasks.

A team operates in a specific environment. Goals and issues that are relevant for the situation at hand are common to all team members: the well-known joint or shared goals, commitments, intentions, etc. The shared environment, in turn, is part of the entire (global) environment. Within the global environment resides an entity

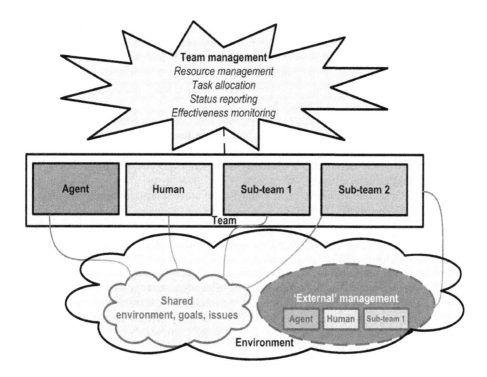

Fig. 1. A conceptual view on sustained team effectiveness

(or multiple entities) that fulfill(s) the role of 'external manager(s)'; this is explicitly separated from the (internally shared) team management process. It is assumed that each team and each individual is capable of understanding and reacting to internal and external management directives and needs for reports. Each individual or team may also fulfill the role of 'manager' for another individual or team, possibly external to its own team. So the management-relationships do not have to adhere to a specific team-composition structure. In addition, note that team management processes need not be heavy-weight; it may be virtually non-existent – which places a burden on external managers to manage the internals of those teams.

3.2 Management Scenarios

In this sub-section three example scenarios illustrate the application of our view on sustained effectiveness of individuals and teams. In these examples, the management process related to a team is shown to involve sub-processes for strategic deliberation, task allocation, team-composition, choreography and coordination, dealing with external managers and maintaining organizational synergy. In essence, a (team) management process entails a feedback loop, in the simplest form involving team and situation monitoring, deliberation and action effectuation (e.g., compare with the well-known OODA loop of decision making cycles: observe-orient-decide-act). The team as a whole follows specific strategies to deal with issues arising from the current crisis within their shared environment. The initial strategy can be an arbitrary choice, but is nevertheless constrained by the resources available and possible rules and regulations imposed by the host organization(s) of the team-members. Team management keeps track of the available resources, task allocations and continually monitors the status of individual entities' performance, team goals, and information from and reports to external management.

For all scenarios, assume that a team has already been formed and currently addresses (part of) a crisis situation. The focus is on team management deliberations, irrespective of how the team management process is realized (by one or more team members). All team-members are currently assumed to be cooperative, reliable, and have non-conflicting norms, etc.

In the first example scenario, team management aims at sustaining effectiveness of its own team members. The crisis situation places a heavy burden on all team members, and the overall effectiveness is slowly but surely decreasing. A simple, opportunistic management strategy to maintain an overall acceptable level of effectiveness within the team is to allocate new tasks directly to those team members that have the most suitable vigilance level, without any explicit negotiations or inquiries about status. This opportunistic task allocation strategy may be particularly appropriate in time-critical circumstances. In addition, the effectiveness of team members may be (in)directly influenced. For example, current measurement information shows that one human team member in particular is showing signs of decreased vigilance. It is a matter of strategic deliberation when the right moment arises to give this human team member a 'bogus' high priority task which involves taking a rest break, and the human's other tasks can be postponed or delegated to other team members. Another predictable decline in team effectiveness caused by resource depletion is addressed by charging a team member with an extra task to acquire additional resources. As an illustration of differences between humans and artificial team members, consider an (artificial) agent team member, whose effectiveness in the current situation is too low to be acceptable. As its skill set is deemed insufficient for the current task and problem, this software agent team member is required to update its knowledge-bases and acquire additional functionality to increase its effectiveness immediately, as other team members depend on the performance of this specific team member.

In the second example scenario, team management addresses the issue that team effectiveness cannot be increased by influencing its current team members; other team members need to be acquired, and possibly a number of current team members need to be removed to prevent unnecessary complexity in the team's organizational structure. Prospective team members may for example be found by means of brokers (specialized actors or agents who trade in team members, e.g. external managers may fulfill this role as they may have more complete organizational awareness), by proximity in the environment (an opportunistic approach), or by searching in databases (yellow pages) and by 'word of mouth'.

In the third example scenario, an external manager coordinates collective actions of multiple teams. For example, the team management of the current team (team 1) considers its team to be sufficiently effective, and reports this to its external manager. However, the external manager (which may be a team by itself) is also informed by another team (team 2) that team 2 is currently significantly reduced in effectiveness because of a skill-set deficiency. Based on information concerning the locations of teams 1 and 2, the external manager decides that team 1 may be in a favorable position to fulfill the request of team 2. Team 1 is contacted by the external manager, and is provided with information on team 2, its predicament, and is ordered to select a suitable team member to move to team 2.

Each of these example scenarios involves a monitoring process. Maintaining current and accurate information on the local, intra-team situation as well as on (relevant parts of) the environment, is a non-trivial issue. This issue is compounded by the need of external management for reports on the effectiveness and other aspects of teams and individuals. Criteria need to be established for information distribution, e.g. on a 'need to know basis', to prevent both information overload and a higher likelihood of timely arrival of task-relevant information. In [18] an information distribution system is proposed which is capable of providing an actor or an agent with task-relevant information. With such a system in place, necessary information and/or knowledge are reported back and the team's strategy is adapted accordingly.

In addition, sustaining team effectiveness ultimately implies measuring the effectiveness of the entire organization involved in the crisis resolution. Measuring effectiveness on an organizational scale means that an external manager is aware of the entire organization. The design of an information system that supports the exchange of organizational information is presented in [19]. With our view we intend to provide a scalable approach to time-critical monitoring and control in ad-hoc, dynamic, organizations.

3.3 Measurement of Sustained Effectiveness

The above examples illustrate the role of measuring effectiveness of individuals and teams over time. Although time can be measured to a certain degree of accuracy in a distributed system, measuring effectiveness remains a challenge, especially when the measurement techniques need to be applicable in time-critical, resource-sparse organizations. A major challenge is how to come up with the right indicators that determine whether the performance of the individuals, teams, and the overall organization is optimal. A first step is to devise performance measurement techniques at the individual and team level. In addition, the contextual sensitivity of effectiveness needs to be addressed; measuring effectiveness is dependent on tasks, goals, situation at hand, available individuals, teams, tools and resources, etc. Note that this is in contrast with vigilance, which can be measured out of context as it reflects, for humans, a basic energetic level of information processing capacity [8]. However, the impact a certain level of vigilance will have on performance, depends on the actual task that needs to be performed. It is to be expected that the more specific the context becomes, the more accurate the measurement of effectiveness will be.

The techniques for measurement should have a minimal impact on the effectiveness of individuals and teams, otherwise they defy their purpose. An example technique to determine the fitness or vigilance level of an actor involves measuring behavior. This may be accomplished on an objective task performance level, but also on a subjective scale by means of (short) alertness questionnaires. It has been shown that these subjective measures can be remarkably accurate as they correlate highly with sensitive vigilance measures such as brain responses measured in the EEG and they distinguish between mental and physical components of vigilance [8]. Although vigilance can thus be determined with a short alertness questionnaire and with performance measures on tasks, these tasks should not be intrusive and should be naturally integrated in the work environment (such as checking incoming mail for an operator or answering the mobile phone for a police officer). An open question remains how to measure "team or organizational vigilance" in chaotic and dynamic environments.

We explore the practical uses of measuring effectiveness in time-critical, chaotic situations. Merely measuring the time it takes before a police officer answers his mobile phone does not yield sufficient information. An officer who responds rather slowly might still be vigilant, but busy aiding civilians. Of equal importance is the fact that a police officer may not be able to answer to a questionnaire in a full-blown crisis situation. It is probably necessary to develop two (or more) styles or modes of measurement. The first mode entails performance and subjective measures that may include tasks that are not strictly part of the work environment itself (such as questionnaires). The second mode involves an aggregation of 'naturalistic' work-related tasks.

With respect to effectiveness of individuals and teams, it is important to distinguish levels of effectiveness on different dimensions. There are various facets of effectiveness (fitness of the individual, of a team, (higher-order) goal satisfaction, etc.) and these facets together determine the overall effectiveness. That is, effectiveness should be determined in a sensitive manner (not just high or low). These different aspects or dimensions should be explored and determined in order to gain proper insight into why and how overall team effectiveness may be lacking.

Moreover, effectiveness should not be expressed as a single value; it is a multi-facetted concept, which looses expressiveness (and comparative usage) when used as a single value. This is similar to valuations of the 'trust' concept. Trust as a single-value does not help to differentiate between e.g. the belief in an agent's competence versus willingness: important aspects for decision making [20]. To continue the comparison with 'trust': The trust in another agent's capacity to fulfill a certain task is based on aspects of the task and the other agent. Similarly, we expect effectiveness to consist of a number of aspects, which can also be determined (perhaps to some extent) for individuals, teams, problems, situations, resources and their relations. It then becomes possible to, for example, use aspects related to a specific problem to specify necessary levels of effectiveness that have to be met by a specific team. Differentiation in aspects is also expected to facilitate prediction of change in effectiveness, e.g. by task completion or management actions.

A potential problem in using the same aspects (or concepts) to measure effectiveness of both actors and agent concerns the abstraction level of descriptions. One of the problems in the interaction of humans with computers (e.g., agents) is the fact that computers are described at a much lower level of abstraction than humans, who are supposed to work with them [21]. In order to realize actual collaboration between actors and agents within a community, it is necessary to describe their behavior in a situational context dependent manner and on related levels of abstraction – even if this involves additional antropomorphisation of agents. Another problem is that there is no a priori reason to suppose that the interaction between actors and agents can be abstracted to a similar enough level, because of their inherently different technological make-up.

4   Future Research

This position paper outlines our progress towards sustained team effectiveness – in our opinion a basic element in managing team performance over time. The approach and issues presented manifest in at least three interrelated and interdisciplinary research projects regarding possible influences of the emergent aspect of sustained team effectiveness. These three research projects are intended to further refine our model for human-agent team management within the domain of crisis management in the context of the interdisciplinary ICIS research program on interactive collaborative information systems.

The first research project concerns instruments for enhancing effectiveness within one team. An example is task allocation on the basis of vigilance levels of human actors and artificial agents. The second research project involves instruments for enhancing effectiveness of teams on the level of team formation. This project involves team formation and re-composition, with many types of entities (actors, artificial agents) and roles. The third research project focuses on increasing effectiveness on an 'inter-team' level that is sustaining effectiveness over multiple teams distributed in the environment. A major challenge is to address the combination of increasing scale of organization size and crisis escalation together with the need for time-critical information flows.

Our approach to modeling and analyzing team management in dynamic organizations needs to be related to other, existing, approaches in literature and practice: a major component of our future research. For example, the well-known model for agents and teams [22], STEAM and it successor Machinette, provide support for communication and coordination within a team, where agents support humans and intend to maximize overall team utility. Our approach is an extension, both in the autonomy of the agents (from supportive to equivalent team member) and in the management of effectiveness of individuals and teams. Another model for organizational oriented programming, S-MOISE$^+$ [23], proposes a means to provide agents with 'organisational managers', thereby reducing the agent's complexity. How and to what extent this can be used to support humans in an organization is a research issue. Another research issue concerns the relation between team management and reorganization [e.g. 24], including issues such as team re-formation and intra- & inter-team task (re)allocation. In addition, our approach needs to be compared to other research disciplines regarding sustaining effectiveness (or utility) of teaming of humans and artificial systems; example research areas include cybernetics [e.g. 25], psychology [e.g. 26], cognitive ergonomics [e.g. 27] and robots [e.g. 28].

In addition, the impact of a number of important aspects in the design of distributed systems needs to be investigated. For example, the role of trust in relation to measuring effectiveness in specific, and management processes in general; interoperability in terms of communication, understanding, norms and culture; and security, privacy and malicious intent.

Acknowledgements

This work is supported by the Dutch Ministry of Economic Affairs, grant nr: BSIK03024. The ICIS project (http://www.icis.decis.nl/) is hosted by the DECIS Lab (http://www.decis.nl), the open research partnership of Thales Nederland, the Delft University of Technology, the University of Amsterdam and the Netherlands Foundation of Applied Scientific Research (TNO).

References

1. Baker, K. A. and Branch, K. M. (2002). Concepts Underlying Organizational Effectiveness: Trends in the Organization and Management Science Literature, In: *Management Benchmark Study*, Chapter 1, Office of Planning & Analysis, Department of Energy, USA, http://www.sc.doe.gov/sc-5/whatwedo/com-benchmark.html.
2. Salas, E. Dickinson, T. L., Converse, S. A., and Tannenbaum, S. I. (1992). Toward an understanding of team performance and training. In: Swezey, R.W. and Salas, E. (Eds.), *Teams: Their training and performance* (pp. 3-29). Norwood, NJ: Ablex.
3. Sycara, K. and Lewis, M. (2004). Integrating intelligent agents into human teams. In: Salas, E. and. Fiore, S. (Eds.) *Team Cognition: Understanding the Factors that Drive Process and Performance*, Washington, DC: American Psychological Association.
4. Lenox, T., Lewis, M., Roth, E., Roberts, L., Shern, R. and Rafalski, T. (1998). Support of Teamwork in Human-Agent Teams. In: *Proceedings of the 1998 IEEE International Conference on Systems, Man, and Cybernetics*, Oct 12-14, San Diego, CA, pp. 1341-1346.
5. Lewis, M. and Sycara, K. and Payne, T. (2003). Agent Roles in Human Teams. In: *Proceedings of AAMAS-03 Workshop on Humans and Multi-Agent Systems*.
6. Wijngaards, N., Nieuwenhuis, K. and Burghardt, P. (2004). Actor-Agent Communities in Dynamic Environments. In: *Proceedings of the workshop ICT Agents*, November 2004, TNO Defence, Security and Safety, The Hague, The Netherlands.
7. Lin, Z. and Carley, K. (2001), Organizational Design and Adaptation in Response to Crises: Theory and Practice, In: *2001 Academy of Management Best Papers Proceedings*, 2001: B1-B7, Washington, D.C.
8. Smit, A. S. (2004). *Vigilance or availability of processing resources: A study on cognitive energetics.* PhD thesis, Radboud University Nijmegen.
9. Smit, A. S., Eling, P. A. T. M., and Coenen, A. M. L. (2004). Mental effort causes vigilance decrease due to resource depletion. In: *Acta Psychologica, 115*, 35-42.
10. Parasuraman, R. (1985). Sustained attention: a multifactorial approach. In: Posner, M. J. and Marin, O. S. M. (Eds.), *Attention and performance* (492-511). New York: Erlbaum.
11. Smit, A. S., Eling, P. A. T. M., Hopman, M. T., & Coenen, A. M. L. (2005). Mental and physical effort affect vigilance differently. In: *Int.Jnl. of Psychophysiology, 57*, 211-217.
12. Parasuraman, R., and Davies, D. R. (Eds.) (1984). *Varieties of attention.* Academic Press, Inc, Florida.
13. Salden, A. H, and Kempen, M. H. (2004). Sustainable Cybernetics Systems - Backbones of Ambient Intelligent Environments, In: Remagnino, P, Foresti, G. L. and Ellis, T. (Eds.), *Ambient Intelligence- A Novel Paradigm*, Springer, November 2004.
14. Cooke, N. J., Stout, R. and Salas, E. (2001). A Knowledge Elicitation Approach To The Measurement Of Team Situation Awareness. In: McNeese, M., Endsley, M. and Salas, E. (Eds.). *New Trends in Cooperative Activities: System Dynamics in Complex Settings*, pp. 114-139. Santa Monica, CA: Human Factors.

15. Nishiguchi, T. and Beaudet, A. (1997). Self-Organization and Clustered Control in the Toyota Group: Lessons from the Aisin Fire. *Report #w-0167a, Massachusetts Institute of Technology International Motor vehicle Program.*

16. van den Broek, E.L., Jonker, C.M., Sharpanskykh, A., Treur, J., and Yolum, P. (2006), Formal Modeling and Analysis of Organizations. In: *Proceedings of the OOOP and ANIREM workshops of AAMAS 2005.* In this volume.

17. McCallum, M., Vasconcelos, W.W., and Norman, T.J. (2006). Verification and Analysis of Organisational Change. In: *Proceedings of the OOOP and ANIREM workshops of AAMAS 2005.* In this volume.

18. van Someren, M., Netten, N., Evers, V., Cramer, H., de Hoog, R. and Bruinsma, G. (2005). A trainable information distribution system to support crisis management. In: Carle, B. & Van de Walle, B. (Eds.) *Proceedings of the Second International ISCRAM Conference*, Brussels, Belgium, April 2005.

19. Oomes, A. H. J. and Neef, R. M. (2005). Scaling-up support for emergency response organizations. In: Carle, B. and Van de Walle, B. (Eds.) *Proceedings of the Second International ISCRAM Conference*, Brussels, Belgium, April 2005.

20. Wijngaards, N.J.E., Boonstra, H.M. and Brazier, F.M.T. (2004). The Role of Trust in Distributed Design, In: Brazier, F.M.T. and Gero, J.S. (Eds.), *Artificial Intelligence for Engineering Design, Analysis and Manufacturing*, volume 18, Special Issue on Intelligent Agents in Design, pp. 199-209.

21. Wilpert, B., and Qvale, T. (1993). *Reliability and Safety in Hazardous Work Systems: Approaches to Analysis and Design*, Lawrence Erlbaum Associates: East Sussex, UK.

22. Schurr, N., Okamoto, S., Maheswaran, R. T., Scerri, P. and Tambe, M. (2004). Evolution of a Teamwork Model. In: *Cognition and Multi-Agent Interaction: From Cognitive Modeling to Social Simulation*, Cambridge University Press.

23. Hübner, J.F., Sichman, J.S., and Boissier, O. (2006). S-MOISE+: A Middleware for developing Organised Multi-Agent Systems. In: *Proceedings of the OOOP and ANIREM workshops of AAMAS 2005.* In this volume.

24. Furtado, V., Melo, A., Dignum, V., Dignum, F., and Sonenberg, L. (2006). Exploring congruence between organizational structure and task performance: a simulation approach. In: *Proceedings of the OOOP and ANIREM workshops of AAMAS 2005.* In this volume.

25. Wolpert, D. and Tumer, K. (1999). An Introduction to Collective Intelligence. In: *Handbook of Agent Technology*, AAAI Press/MIT Press.

26. Rasker, P. (2002), *Communication and Performance in Teams*, PhD Thesis, University of Amsterdam

27. Klein, G. Woods, D. D., Bradshaw, J. M., Hoffman, R. R., and Feltovich, P. J. (2004). Ten Challenges for Making Automation a "team player" in Joint Human-Agent Activity, In: *IEEE Intelligent Systems,* Vol. 19, No. 6, November/December 2004.

28. Nourbakhsh, I., Sycara, K., Koes, M., Yong, M., Lewis, M. and Burion, S. (2005). Human-Robot Teaming for Search and Rescue, *IEEE Pervasive Computing: Mobile and Ubiquitous Systems*, January, 2005, pp. 72-78.

Verification and Analysis of Organisational Change

Mairi McCallum, Wamberto W. Vasconcelos, and Timothy J. Norman

Department of Computing Science, University of Aberdeen, Aberdeen, AB24 3UE, UK
{mmccallu, wvasconc, tnorman}@csd.abdn.ac.uk

Abstract. In the engineering of multi-agent systems both the analyst and architect may benefit by thinking about the solution in terms of the roles that agents
may enact and the relationships between them. The organisational structure thus
produced provides an effective way to capture medium- to long-term associations
and dependencies between agents. In this paper we propose a means to formally
specify, verify and analyse agent organisations, capturing notions of role, obligation and delegation (of obligations). Furthermore, our framework allows change
in the organisational structure to be modelled and alternative organisation specifications to be developed in order to handle the consequences of change. Our model
gives rise to a suite of tools and functionalities with which engineers can specify,
verify and analyse organisations, the roles of their components, their obligations
and the relationships among these roles.

1 Introduction

When engineering multi-agent systems, both the analyst and architect may benefit by
thinking about the solution in terms of the roles that agents may enact and the relationships that exist between them.

In this paper we propose a means to formally specify, verify and analyse agent organisations. Ours is a flexible and expressive approach that contemplates agents taking
part in multiple organisations with distinct roles and disparate obligations. Furthermore,
our framework allows change in the organisational structure to be modelled and alternative organisation specifications to be developed in order to handle the consequences
of change. We adopt a normative view of organisations, and capture the notion of social influence through relationships between roles. Our model gives rise to a suite of
tools and functionalities with which engineers can specify, verify and analyse organisations, the roles of their components, their obligations and the relationships among these
roles.

Our principal contributions are:

- A formal model of organisational structure that captures both (aspects of) the normative state of a role and the influences that agents may have due to their organisational position (or role).
- Mechanisms to model changes in agents' organisational positions. These mechanisms enable an engineer to pose questions such as "what if agent a took on role
  r?" and "can agent b transfer a responsibility to some other agent temporarily?".
- Machinery for the analysis and verification of organisational structures specified
  using our formal model.

O. Boissier et al. (Eds.): ANIREM and OOOP 2005, LNCS 3913, pp. 48–63, 2006.

The structure of this document is as follows. In section 2 we present and justify our notation. The social phenomena of influence in our model and the corresponding implementation is described in section 3. The automation of verification and analysis is discussed in section 5, as is the value of providing an additional representation of the organisational model for the engineer. In section 4 we describe the types of change we intend to model and how this will be done. Finally we examine how this approach relates to existing work and discuss possible directions for future work.

2   Organisational Model

An organisation is not necessarily an independent entity, and its components may overlap with or be a subset of a larger organisation. Within an organisation such as a university department, for example, many other organisations will exist for research groups, the teaching of specific courses and so on. Some of these organisations may include components from outside the department organisation – there may be, for example, staff from other departments involved in teaching a course – and the department as a whole will be a subsidiary of the larger organisations of faculties and the university.

In our formalism we choose not to consider issues such as the capabilities and mental states of agents, and some of the details of actions. This is not to say that these are not important features of a multi-agent system, but we choose to make this simplification in order to focus on the organisational structure (cf. Panzarasa *et al.* [20]).

Prior to presenting our model of organisational structure, we need to define a number of sets of labels to refer to the components of our model. We state that the sets be disjoint for clarity, although the usage of a label in the formalism implies the type of component represented.

Definition 1. *Let there be a finite and non-empty set* $labels = (labels^{Agents} \cup labels^{Orgs} \cup labels^{Roles} \cup labels^{Actions})$ *where:*

- $labels^{Agents} = \{label^{Agent_1}, \ldots, label^{Agent_n}\}$ *of agent identifiers,*
- $labels^{Orgs} = \{label^{Org_1}, \ldots label^{Org_n}\}$ *of organisation names,*
- $labels^{Roles} = \{label^{Role_1}, \ldots, label^{Role_n}\}$ *of role labels,*
- $labels^{Actions} = \{label^{Act_1}, \ldots, label^{Act_n}\}$ *of action labels.*

The rest of this section details the formal framework for specifying an organisation. A syntactical variant of this formalism is presented in more detail in [16].

2.1   Agents

Each agent in the model is described by an agent label and a set of role allocation tuples. The agent label uniquely identifies the agent, and each role allocation tuple consists of an organisation label, a role label and a set of attitudes. The organisation and role labels identify each role that the agent holds, and in which organisation it applies. The attitudes determine the agent's attitude to delegation in the role, the effects of which are discussed in section 3. Note that organisations can also be considered agents in the model. They can take on roles within other organisations in exactly the same way that individual agents do. The consequences of this are discussed further in section 2.2.

Definition 2. *An agent is the pair* $A = \langle label^{Actor}, Alloc \rangle$ *where:*

- *$label^{Actor} \in (labels^{Agents} \cup labels^{Orgs})$ is the unique identifier of the agent.*
- *Alloc is a set of organisation, role and attitude allocations of the form $\langle label^{Org}, label^{Role}, Attitudes \rangle$ where:*
  - *$label^{Org} \in labels^{Orgs}$, $label^{Org} \neq label^{Actor}$ is the name of the organisation in which the role allocation holds.*
  - *$label^{Role} \in labels^{Roles}$ is the label of the role held,*
  - *Attitudes are the agent's attitudes to delegation in this role, detailed further in section 3.1.*

At this stage we should emphasis that *attitude* is a property of an agent and as such is not part of the organisational structure. An organisation can be populated with any number of different societies of agents which may have different attitudes.

2.2   Roles

Roles are a key component of our organisational model. In its simplest form a role may specify a single task or action to carry out, or a certain state of the world to bring about (cf. the notion of *RoleGoal* in [4]). However, it is more useful if these activities can be associated with norms – we would like to be able to express statements such as 'It is obligatory for all students to complete this assignment' and 'Students are prohibited from sitting the exam if they have not completed the assignment'. To simplify our representation we currently choose to include only obligations. Our definition and use of obligations is in keeping with the work of Jones and Sergot [12], and as such obligations can be violated by agents – our model describes the 'ideal' not necessarily the 'actual'. For an analysis of the anatomy of normative positions see, for example, [22].

As obligations are generally held by one party to another, we also require a set of predecessor roles to whom these obligations are held.

We also want to capture the idea that one member of an organisation may influence the behaviour of another because of the relationship that exists between them. This adds an additional element of non-determinism to the formalism, as the agents who have the potential to influence others may not always choose to exert it [20].

As the formalism allows organisations as well as individuals to hold roles, some or all of the predecessor roles may be held by organisations. This flexibility adds not only the concept of group responsibility for obligations (see [17]), but also the possibility of organisations influencing agents, which can be compared to Jones and Sergot's *counts as* operator [12].

These notions are incorporated in the following definition of a role.

Definition 3. *A role is the tuple* $R = \langle label^{Org}, label^{Role}, Obls, Infs, labels^{Roles^P}, labels^{Roles^S} \rangle$ *where:*

- *$label^{Org} \in labels^{Orgs}$ is the name of the organisation in which this role definition applies.*
- *$label^{Role} \in labels^{Roles}$ is the label of the role.*
- *Obls is the set of obligations associated with the role, described further in section 2.4.*
- *Infs is the set of influences associated with the role, described further in section 2.4.*
- *$labels^{Roles^P} \subseteq labels^{Roles}$ is the set of labels of predecessor roles to the role. This set is the union of all the sets of predecessors in the obligations and influences of the role. (See section 2.4.)*

- $labels^{Roles^S} \subseteq labels^{Roles}$ is the set of labels of successor roles to the role. This set is the set of all roles in the organisation, $label^{Org}$, in which $label^{Role}$ appears in the predecessor set.

In addition to identifying the organisation to which a role belongs, the organisation label can be considered a context for the role. This distinction is necessary in the role definition because the same role may have different responsibilities associated with it in different organisations. For example, the role *lecturer* will have different obligations within the organisation representing a computing science department to those associated with the same role within an organisation representing a specific course.

The set of obligations, *Obls*, are the obligations of this role. The holders of predecessor roles within the same organisation are also able to call upon the holders of this role to adopt obligations in the set of influences, *Infs*. Influences are in exactly the same form as obligations, but only apply when a predecessor has made a request for them to be adopted. Even if a role has no influences, the predecessor set must be non-empty as long as there are obligations associated with the role, as an obligation must have at least one predecessor. The exact nature of an obligation is described in section 2.4. Note that our definition of a role does not state that the sets *Obls* and *Infs* be non-empty. We acknowledge, however, that if a role has neither obligations nor influences it is essentially inactive in that organisation.

The set of successors, $labels^{Roles^S}$, is the set of roles within the same organisation that hold an obligation to a role or that a role can request to adopt obligations. The obligations that can be requested are those in the successor role's set of influences. Holders of successor roles can only be affected by predecessors in the same organisation – that is, the role definitions must have the same organisational label. Note that the sets $labels^{Roles^S}$ and $labels^{Roles^P}$ can be computed from the sets of obligations and influences. Their explicit specification by the engineer may therefore not be necessary but may be used to check consistency.

Predecessors and successors may be considered analogous to superiors and subordinates, but we have avoided the use of these terms as they imply a hierarchical system that may not necessarily be the nature of the organisation being modelled.

2.3 Actions

The set of all possible actions in the model consists of tuples of an action label, a duration and an expression describing the constituents of the action. The action label is simply the name of the action and the duration is a natural number signifying the length of time that action will take to perform. The constituents are the other actions, if there are any, that make up the action being described.

Definition 4. *An action is the tuple $A = \langle label^{Act}, n, Constituents \rangle$ where:*

- $label^{Act} \in labels^{Actions}$ *is a label uniquely identifying the action.*
- $n \in \mathbb{N}$ *is the duration of the action,*
- *Constituents is an expression of action labels identifying the actions that make up this action. If Constituents is empty then the action is a primitive action, as opposed to a composite action.*

The time or duration of an action is simply a resource requirement and as such could be used to represent other kinds of resources such as cost or energy.

The *Constituents* expression is a disjunction of conjunctions of action labels. The execution of all the actions in any one of these conjunctions equates to the execution of the action being defined. Example 1 gives a simple example of constituents in an action definition.

Example 1. An action definition with two alternative ways to achieve it.

$$Action = \langle\ doChores, 100,$$
$$(vacuum \wedge dust \wedge washDishes \wedge buyGroceries) \vee$$
$$(hireCleaningStaff \wedge buyGroceries)\ \rangle$$

The use of disjunctive normal form allows us to express more complex situations than simply, for example, an ordered list. When a composite action is prohibited, for example, rather than prohibiting every action in the conjunctions we can express that there must only remain one action in a conjunction that is not executed to ensure that the prohibition against the composite action is not violated.

The resulting action hierarchy can be used as a plan database, allowing agents to select from different plans to achieve the same result. This allows us to model some interesting aspects of real world problems without having to include a more sophisticated planning approach. The hierarchy can also be automatically checked for loops and undefined actions as part of the verification process described in section 5.

2.4 Obligations

Obligations in the model are defined by an action label, conditions and a set of predecessors. The conditions on an obligation determine when that obligation holds, or is active and the predecessors are the roles to which this obligation is held:

Definition 5. *An obligation is the tuple $O = \langle label^{Act}, C, labels^{Roles^{P'}}\rangle$ where:*

- *$label^{Act} \in labels^{Actions}$ is the name of the action to which the obligation refers.*
- *C is an expression determining the conditions under which the obligation holds, described below.*
- *$labels^{Roles^{P'}} \subseteq labels^{Roles^{P}}$, $labels^{Roles^{P'}} \neq \emptyset$, is the set of labels of predecessor roles within this organisation to whom the obligation is held.*

Our model does not take into account the preconditions and effects of actions. This is not to say that these are not important, but we make a simplification in only dealing with conditions on obligations, not on the actions themselves. Nor are we concerned with applying sanctions or penalties when violations are detected, although this will be considered for future work, as it would allow for more sophisticated resolution of conflicts of obligations.

Each obligation has conditions that denote when the obligation is active and should be fulfilled. In our model these conditions are restricted to temporal ones, and are expressed in simple arithmetic expressions, as described in definition 6.

Definition 6. *In obligation,* $O = \langle label^{Act}, \mathcal{C}, labels^{Roles^{P'}} \rangle$, *the conditions* $\mathcal{C}$ *are of the form* $x : Exprs$. *Exprs is defined below, where* $c \in \mathbb{N}$ *and* x, y *are variables.*

$Exprs ::= Expr, Exprs \mid Expr$
$Expr \ ::= Term \ Op \ Term$
$Term \ ::= y \mid c \mid f(Terms)$
$Terms ::= Term, Terms \mid Term$
$Op \quad ::= < \mid \leq \mid = \mid > \mid \geq$

The use of variables throughout the conditions means that obligations can be specified that force a partial ordering of actions. For example, an assessment has to be written by the lecturer before it can be issued to students. Students are required to have at least a certain amount of time to attempt the assessment (in this example, 2000 units of time) before it is collected by the lecturer and marked. The *lecturer* role may contain the obligations detailed in example 2.

Example 2. Interdependent variables in obligations.

Obls = { $\langle$ *writeAssessment*, $w : w > 0$, {*courseCoordinator*} $\rangle$
$\langle issueAssessments, x : x > w, x < (y - 2000), \{courseCoordinator\} \rangle$
$\langle collectAssessments, y : y < z, \{courseCoordinator\} \rangle$
$\langle markAssessments, z : z = 5000, \{courseCoordinator\} \rangle$ }

As mentioned in section 2.2, an influence takes exactly the same form as a obligation but only applies when a predecessor has successfully exerted the influence. The conditions on influences refer to when that influence can be exerted by a predecessor – outside of the specified times the power of influence does not hold.

Whilst there is no reason why this language should not be used to express conditionals relating to world states, there is a practical problem in detecting violation of conditions such as these, as the agent concerned may not believe the condition has been satisfied. We assume that the belief in the passage of time is universally held by all agents who share a global clock, and the eventual arrival at any specified time is inevitable, but beliefs about the state of the world are subjective. Similarly, whilst we only have obligations to carry out actions it would be desirable to include obligations to maintain certain states of the world.

We can now give our definition of an organisation. Note that we do not include the population of agents when defining the organisational structure.

Definition 7. *An organisation is the tuple* $Org = \langle label^{Org}, Roles, Actions \rangle$ *where:*

- $label^{Org} \in labels^{Orgs}$ *is the name of the organisation,*
- $Roles = \{R_1, \ldots, R_n\}$ *such that* $R_i = \langle \ label^{Org}, label^{Role_i}, Obls_i, Infs_i, labels^{Roles_i^P}$, $labels^{Roles_i^S} \rangle$, $1 \leq i \leq n$, *that is, all the roles have the same* $label^{Org}$ *label,*
- $Actions = \{Act_0, \ldots, Act_m\}$ *such that:*
    - $Act_j = \langle \ label^{Act_j}, Duration_j, Constituents_j \ \rangle$, $0 \leq j \leq m$,
    - $\langle Act_j, \mathcal{C}, labels^{Roles^P} \ \rangle \in (Obls_i \cup Infs_i)$.
    That is, every action is part of either an obligation or influence in atleast one of the roles in the organisation.

3   Organisational Change Through Influencing

In this section we examine changes in the organisational state; that is, changes in the distribution of obligations in the organisation. Such changes come about through the phenomena of influencing captured by our model. In this section we begin by discussing the motivation for agents attempting to influence one another. We then describes how we can then establish a set of rules that determine the outcome of attempts to delegate depending on the roles and attitudes held by the agents involved, and these rules can be encoded to create a system which can predict the attempts to influence and ultimately the actions carried out by every agent in an organisation.

3.1   Motivation for Delegation

In our model obligations are the only motivators for action, and as a result they are the only motivators for social influence; influencing only occurs when the agent attempting to influence has an existing obligation related to the action concerned.

When we use the term delegation in relation to our model we are referring to an agent's attempt to exert influence in order to have another achieve an obligation (or part of an obligation) that it is responsible for.

Delegation requires one agent to have influence over another in regard to the action to be delegated, and that the temporal conditions associated with the influence are satisfied. When an agent will choose to exert influence over a successor is determined by its attitude to delegation, which in its turn is determined in the definition of an agent. In our definition of an agent (definition 2) we do not restrict the members of the set of attitudes. We feel that any attitudes could be included providing the required associated behaviour was also defined. For the time being we have chosen to restrict ourselves to two delegator attitudes and two delegatee attitudes.

If an agent has a delegator attitude which is *Keen* it will attempt to carry out it's obligation itself, only delegating when necessary to relieve a conflict. A *Lazy* delegator will attempt to delegate as many of its obligations as possible, regardless of its own ability to schedule them.

Similarly, an agent's response to an attempt to delegate to it is dependent to some degree on its delegatee attitude. If an agent is *Cautious* it will only accept a delegated obligation if it can fulfil the obligation itself without causing conflict with any of its existing obligations. A *Bold* delegatee, however, will accept an obligation it can't fulfill itself as long as it believes it can influence a third agent to do so. A *Bold* agent may still refuse to accept an obligation delegated to it if there is no way it could fulfil it.

If an attempt to influence is successful the delegator can remove the obligation delegated from the set of obligations it is required to fulfil and the delegatee must add it to their own obligation set.

If it is unsuccessful the delegator may have a number of other options. It may attempt to influence a different agent to accept the obligation, or it may influence any agent to take on an obligation concerning an action of which the original obligation action is a constituent. If this is not possible it may attempt to influence one or more agents to take on the constituent actions of the obligation and fulfil the original obligation that way. Finally, if the delegate is unable to fulfill the obligation itself or delegate it with any of the above approaches it will fail to complete the obligation.

We want to use our model to ask questions such as "if all agents attempt to satisfy all obligations whenever possible – if they comply with the ideal – is the organisation feasible?" or "if agent x has an attitude such that it does not comply with the ideal, is the organisation sufficiently robust?".

3.2   Rules of Influence

In our investigations into describing the semantics of our representation we have been influenced by rewrite rules to describe changes in state. In particular, the phenomena of influence in our formalism lends itself well to expression in rewrite rules. On the lefthand side of the rule we can describe the agents involved and the task the delegator is attempting to delegate and on the righthand side the consequences of the attempt to influence, either successful or unsuccessful.

It is necessary to record the attempts to influence so they can be included in the delegatee's schedule. However, we cannot modify a role definition when an influence is accepted because this would affect all agents in all organisations who hold this role. Similarly, we cannot actually remove an obligation that has been delegated from the delegator's obligations in the role definition. All attempts to influence must be recorded, along with whether or not they were successful so that an agent is not repeatedly asked to do the same thing and obligations that have been delegated are not delegated again. So, a new structure *AttemptsToInfluence* is introduced.

Definition 8. *The influences that have already been attempted are described by a set of tuples*
$Attempt = \langle A_1, Alloc_1, A_2, Alloc_2, Obl, Inf, DelObl, Status \rangle$ *where:*

- $A_1 \in labels^{Agents}$ *identifies the delegator agent,*
- $Alloc_1$ *is the allocation held by A_1, $\langle Org, R_1, Attitudes_1 \rangle$ that permits the attempt to influence, where $Org \in labels^{Orgs}$ and $R_1 \in labels^{Roles}$.*
- $A_2 \in labels^{Agents}$ *identifies the delegatee agent,*
- $Alloc_2$ *is the allocation $\langle Org, R_2, Attitudes_2 \rangle$ that permits the attempt to influence, where $R_2 \in labels^{Roles}$.*
- Obl *is the obligation, $\langle ActionName, C_1, P_1 \rangle$ which the attempt is concerned with, held by the delegator agent, where $ActionName \in labels^{Actions}$.*
- Inf *is the influence $\langle ActionName, C_2, P_2 \rangle$ that allows the delegator to attempt to influence, where $R_1 \in P_2$*
- $DelObl$ *is the new obligation $\langle ActionName, C_3, \{R_1\} \rangle$ that the delegatee will take on if the attempt is successful, where $C_3 = C_1 \cap C_2$.*
- $Status \in \{accepted, refused\}$ *records whether or not the delegatee accepted the attempt to influence and took on the obligation.*

We can create a set of rules that describe all possible occasions for delegation, and all possible results of it. These rules modify the state of the organisation and their repeated application creates a sequence of states that record how the distribution of obligations has changed due to delegation. The rules, which can be expressed in our existing notation, check details such as the roles of the participating agents and the influences they contain, types of conflict between obligations and the attitudes of the agents as well as the current state.

$$Agent_1 = \langle A_1, Alloc_1 \rangle \wedge$$
$$\langle O, R_1, Attitudes \rangle \in Alloc_1 \wedge$$
$$Lazy \in Attitudes \wedge$$
$$Role_1 = \langle O, R_1, Obls_1, Infs_1, R_1^P, R_1^S \rangle \wedge$$

$$\langle X, C_{X_1}, P \rangle \in Obls_1 \wedge$$

$$Agent_2 = \langle A_2, Alloc_2 \rangle \wedge$$
$$\langle O, R_2, Attitude \rangle \in Alloc_2 \wedge$$
$$R_2 \in R_1^S \wedge$$
$$Role_2 = \langle O, R_2, Obls_2, Infs_2, R_2^P, R_2^S \rangle \wedge$$
$$\langle X, C_X', R_X^P \rangle \in Infs_2 \wedge$$
$$R_1 \in R_X^P \wedge$$
$$C_X \cap C_X' \neq \emptyset \wedge$$

$$\langle A_1, Alloc_1, \_, \_, \langle X, C_{X_1}, \_ \rangle, \_, \_, Status \rangle \notin AttemptsToInfluence \wedge$$
$$\langle A_1, Alloc_1, A_2, Alloc_2, \langle X, C_{X_1}, \_ \rangle, \langle X, C_X', R_X^P \rangle,$$
$$\quad \langle X, C_X \cap C_X', R_X^P \rangle, Status \rangle \notin AttemptsToInfluence \wedge$$
$$getAllObls(A_2, AllObls_2) \wedge$$
$$NewAttempts = \{AttemptsToInfluence \cup$$
$$\quad \langle A_1, Alloc_1, A_2, Alloc_2, \langle X, C_{X_1}, \_ \rangle, \langle X, C_X', R_X^P \rangle,$$
$$\quad \langle X, C_X \cap C_X', R_X^P \rangle, accepted \rangle \} \wedge$$
$$schedule(S, A_2, NewAttempts)$$
$$\longrightarrow$$

$$\oplus \langle A_1, Alloc_1, A_2, Alloc_2, \langle X, C_{X_1}, P \rangle, \langle X, C_X', R_X^P \rangle,$$
$$\quad \langle X, C_X \cap C_X', R_X^P \rangle, accepted \rangle$$

Details of delegator agent	
Details of obligation to be delegated	
Details of delegatee agent	
Delegation has not already been attempted	
Delegatee is able to fulfill the obligation	
Add *attempt* to record result	

Fig. 1. A sample rule template

The specific rules for an organisation and population are automatically generated from the organisation and population definitions using a set of rule templates. An annotated sample rule template is given in figure 1. The template describes the case of an agent whose has no conflict, but has the attitude *Lazy* in regard to a particular obligation and as a result will attempt to delegate. In the example we introduce three new operators. The $\cap$ operator captures the overlap between the conditions of the obligation, C_X, and the conditions of the influence, C_X'. This subset is the conditions under which both sets will be satisfied. If there was no overlap then it would not be possible to satisfy this obligation by delegating using this influence. The *schedule()* predicate attempts to find a schedule where all the obligations of an agent are satisfied. This includes all the obligations of each role, taking into account all the previously accepted attempts to influence and (depending on the agent's attitudes) possible future delegations. The operator $\oplus$ is used to add an attempt to influence to record the application of the rule – this is the only structure that is changed; the organisation and population specification remain unchanged.

A full set of templates detailing all possible variations of attitude types, conflict types and so on are provided to the engineer and can be re-used within different organisations. By finding all possible instantiations of the role, agent and action variables the templates can be used to extract specific rules for any organisation.

We define a populated organisation as both the organisation and all the agents who hold one or more roles in that organisation, as detailed below.

Definition 9. *A populated organisation is the pair* $\langle Org, Agents \rangle$ *where:*

- $Org = \langle label^{Org}, Roles, Actions \rangle$, $label^{Org} \in labels^{Orgs}$,
- $Agents = \{Agent_0, \ldots, Agent_n\}$ *such that* $Agent_i = \langle label^{Actor_i}, Alloc_i \rangle$, $0 \leq i \leq n$, $\exists\, alloc \in Alloc_i$ *such that* $alloc = \langle label^{Org}, label^{Role}, Attitudes \rangle$.

We can automatically generate a set of rules $\mathcal{R}^{\langle Org, Agents\rangle}$ that describe all possibilities for delegation in a populated organisation:

$$\langle Org, Agents\rangle \longrightarrow \{\ Rule_0, \ldots, Rule_n\} = \mathcal{R}^{\langle Org, Agents\rangle}$$

We can also generate the intial state of the organisation $\mathcal{S}_0^{\langle Org, Agents\rangle}$ before there has been any attempts to delegate:

$$\langle Org, Agents\rangle \longrightarrow \{\ Atf_0, \ldots, Atf_n\ \} = \mathcal{S}_0^{\langle Org, Agents\rangle}$$

By exhaustively applying the rules $\mathcal{R}^{\langle Org, Agents\rangle}$ to $\mathcal{S}_0^{\langle Org, Agents\rangle}$ we can find the next state of the organisation, $\mathcal{S}_1^{\langle Org, Agents\rangle}$. The process is repeated on $\mathcal{S}_1^{\langle Org, Agents\rangle}$ and so on:

$$\mathcal{S}_0^{\langle Org, Agents\rangle} \quad\overset{\mathcal{R}^{\langle Org, Agents\rangle}}{\longrightarrow}\quad \mathcal{S}_1^{\langle Org, Agents\rangle} \quad\overset{\mathcal{R}^{\langle Org, Agents\rangle}}{\longrightarrow}\quad \mathcal{S}_2^{\langle Org, Agents\rangle} \quad\overset{\mathcal{R}^{\langle Org, Agents\rangle}}{\longrightarrow}\ldots$$

Intuitively, the lefthand side of a rule describes the conditions on the organisational structure and distribution of obligations required for the rule to apply. The righthand side depicts the updates to components of the organisation as a result of the attempted delegation.

The specific rules for an organisation and population are automatically generated from the organisation and population definitions using a set of rule templates. By finding all possible instantiations of the role, agent and action variables the templates can be used to extract specific rules for any organisation. A full set of templates detailing all possible variations of attitude types, conflict types and so on are provided to the engineer and can be re-used within different organisations. In practice, the 'instantiated' rules need not be explicitly generated; the templates themselves can be used to find future states of the organisation.

3.3   Implementation

When combined with a constraint solver the rules described above can be used to check a model and determine if the entire organisation is viable – that is, whether all obligations can be fulfilled. We can find a 'solution' by finding a set of schedules, one for each agent in the organisation. Each schedule details the actions the agent should carry out to fulfil its obligations, allowing it to delegate actions according to the rules above and taking into account the actions other agents have delegated to it. This allows us to

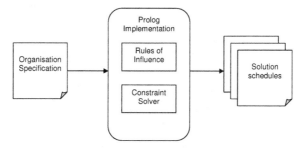

Fig. 2. The system

use the static model to create multiple sets of schedules that determine how the organisation would operate without actually having to run it, as illustrated in figure 2. If no set of schedules in which all agents fulfil their obligations can be found then the organisation is not viable. The engineer may wish to consider the mechanisms described in section 5.2 at this stage, such as examining the population of the organisation.

We have chosen to implement the rules in Sicstus Prolog [18], using the clp(FD) library [15] to handle the scheduling. Our notation lends itself well to conversion into Prolog syntax, allowing us to keep the Prolog representation of an organisation very close to the original mathematical notation.

The implementation of these rules will also form the basis of a system that can be used to answer many of our potential questions about change (*i.e.* "what happens when agent *a* is removed?" "what is the smallest set of agents that could successfully populate this organisation?"). This is discussed further in the next section.

4   Further Organisational Change

There are three main types of change that we have addressed with our approach. The first is simply a change in the organisational state; that is, a change in the distribution of obligations as captured by our rules of influence described in section 3.

The second is a change in the population of an organisation. We automatically generate a population for an organisation with a set of user-specified properties. We may wish to restrict the number of agents holding particular roles, for example, or find the mimimum set of agents that can populate an organisation whilst still fulfilling all obligations. The analysis of this type of change is supported by the strategies discussed in section 5.2.

Finally, we are interested in changes in the organisational structure, such as reassigning obligations of an existing role to other roles in the organisation. For example, if a lecturer is away from work for some time some of his duties may be taken on by another member of staff. We may not necessarily wish the individual providing cover to take on the *lecturer* role as a whole, however, but just parts of it – they may be required to give lectures, for example, but not to prepare and mark assessments and exam papers.

This process is more complex to automate that the previous types of change described due to the vast numbers of possible alternatives. As a result, this type of change is currently manual but supported by the tools for analysis described below. That automation of this type of change is a valuable addition for future work.

5   Verification and Analysis of Models

Once engineers prepare their formal specifications of organisations, they will be able to perform a number of automatic checks to guarantee the existence of desirable properties (or the absence of undesirable ones). The formal specification of our model allows for a number of checks to be carried out on the static model which should aid the engineer in fine-tuning a specification.

5.1   Verification

A preliminary verification concerns the *well-formedness* of the specifications to ensure that the constructs conform to the syntax of our notation and that the components (labels) referred to are indeed defined.

There are many properties of an organisation that can be checked for statically. One of the most important checks concerns whether the organisation is actually workable, in that it is possible for all the agents to fulfil all their obligations. If it is not, the designer may wish to identify whether the conflicts arise from how the roles are assigned, or whether it is the organisation specification itself that is unworkable.

It is also important that an organisation does not concentrate too many responsibilities on one role: in this case we can perform a check whereby any role with more than n obligations is flagged to engineers. Another automatic analysis aims to detect those roles concentrating too many responsibilities: roles with a large set of obligations as well as the potential to have more obligations delegated to them ought to be flagged for they may cause catastrophic malfunctioning if agents incorporating these roles go out of action. We can formally define how we can go about checking for properties in our model and an example of such a definition is given in [16].

5.2   Analysis

It may also be useful to analyse the specification of an organisation in such a way that a new specification is produced. For example, analysis could determine the minimum number of agents of each role required to populate an organisation. Similarly, it may be possible to generate a modified specification in which a specific role has been removed, without losing any of the capabilities of the organisation. A specification may be presented in different ways for more detailed analysis. For example, the engineer may be concerned with parts of an organisation concerning a specific action or may wish to view the organisation from the perspective of a particular agent.

In addition to checking properties of the static model, the engineer may wish to examine the simulation of the organisational model defined. This is particularly useful for examining the effect of populating the model with different societies of agents with different attitudes. In our implementation the output of the system described in section 3 can, to some extent, replace a true distributed simulation, as it consists of a set of possible *run specifications* for the organisation. These 'solutions' include the details of all attempts to influence, both failed and successful, and each agent's schedule to fulfill their obligations.

As large, complex organisations are likely to be difficult for the engineer to examine in either the formalism defined above or its complementary Prolog representation, we feel there is a need to provide a third representation that can be easily manipulated for human consumption. We will provide an XML description of an organisation specification that can be automatically generated from the other representations. The data can then be displayed according to the needs of the engineer. For example, the network of relationships between agents or the action hierarchy in a specific organisation could be extracted and displayed. Similarly, the 'solution' schedules for an organisation could also be described in XML, allowing the engineer to examine the state of the organisation at a specified time.

6   Related Work

There are a number of methods that use role models to design deployable applications. The general approach is to study existing organisations and fully describe the organisational structure before implementation. As a result, there is usually little opportunity or motivation for change within the organisations modelled. In GAIA [26] organisations are viewed as collections of roles, which have a similar interpretation to our own. Zambonelli *et al* [27] extend the role model concept used in GAIA with organisational rules, structures and patterns which can describe organisations, including their roles, in more detail. In Agent UML [2], an extension of the Unified Modelling Language (UML), agents hold roles and their behaviour within these roles is defined by interaction protocols. In Esteva's [10] description of an electronic institution roles determine the actions that can be carried out by the agent holding the role – where the actions are illocutions.

The general problem with these approaches to modelling organisations is that the role model is fixed at the design stage – there is no support for investigating alternative role models for the same organisation. In addition, these approaches are intended to provide tailor-made organisational models for specific domains, and do not lend themselves well to creating or optimising more generic models. Skarmeas [24] presents one of the few frameworks for organisational modelling in which roles can be changed. This framework, however, is specific to the office automation domain and cannot be used to rapidly model the effects of change in the way we intend to. Some of the reasons for reorganization in agent societies and the issues involved are discussed in [9].

There are a number of approaches to producing mechanisms to govern agents' social behaviour, some of which are discussed in depth by Conte and Castelfranchi [5, 3]. Influenced by Castelfranchi's notion of social commitment, Cavedon and Sonenberg [4] present teamwork and collaborative action models for determining how social commitments arise and how roles and relationships are determined. In the many-sorted first order logic notation defined, goals are associated with roles using the modality *RoleGoal*. This notion is extended by Panzarasa *et al.* [20], who allow roles to include beliefs and intentions, as well as goals – a role is essentially a set of mental attitudes that is adopted when an agent takes on that role. The notion of influence is concerned with agents exerting influence over one another to change their mental states. Although our concept of a role is also a mechanism for governing social behaviour and allowing agents to influence one another, it differs in that we are only concerned with obligations, and no other aspect of an agent's mental state. It is, therefore, comparable to the approach taken by Barbuceanu [1] in which obligations and interdictions are associated with roles.

Concerning our use of obligations, this work can be compared to several other norm-based systems. Our decision to attach obligations to roles is informed by the work of Pacheco and Carmo [19]. They adopt a normative perspective of organisations influenced by Jones and Sergot [12], as we have done, and define a logic for expressing roles with deontic notions attached. Roles are distinct from the set of deontic notions that they consist of in that the notions of a role can change and it is still the same role. The formal semantics of obligations described by Dignum *et al* [8] fits in with the approach used in our model. Each obligation applies within a particular society or organisation, and has conditions that specify when it applies. Further, it is necessary to specify between whom an obligation is held; in our model, an obligation is always held by a successor to a predecessor. Although it is not an area of the system we intend to explore to great depth, the structure of dependency created by the obligations is comparable to existing work in the area of dependency networks [3, 5, 23]. López and Luck [14] examine the incorporation of norms in agent societies using a set-based theoretic not dissimilar to ours, however, they do not provide a clear organisational model. Neither López and Luck nor Dignum *et al* provide a computational realisation.

Dastani *et al* [6] examine when an agent is able to adopt a role without being in conflict or violating a norm. Their property of *consistency* between the goals of an agent and the goals of the role it wishes to adopt is similar to the conflict-free state we try to achieve between the obligations of the roles of each agent when any change in the organisational structure occurs. Esteva *et al.* [11] present a computational approach to determining whether or not an electronic institution is normatively consistent. The NoA agent architecture [13] also includes the notion of consistency between norms. The detection of conflicts between norms concerning actions requires checking the effects of the action against other norms, and also checking the *activation* and *expiration* conditions of potentially conflicting norms. Whilst we are not concerned with the effects of actions, this approach is comparable to ours in that we do check the actions and temporal conditions of obligations to detect conflicts between roles.

Regarding our rules of influence, our approach is a kind of *production system* [21] whose rules are exhaustively applied to a database of facts. Our institutional rules differ from rewrite rules (also called term rewriting systems) [7] in that they do not automatically remove the elements that triggered the rule (*i.e.*, those elements that matched the left-hand side of the rule). Our institutional rules give rise to a rule-based programming language [25] to support the management of a distributed information model, our institutional states.

7 Discussion and Future Work

There are several additions to the model that we are considering that will allow for the specification of more sophisticated organisations. Our use of only obligations is somewhat restrictive and it would be desirable to include additional norms and social concepts in the notation. Jones and Sergot [12] discuss some of the many subtleties in this area, such as the difference between *permission* and *right*. In particular, their *counts as* operator would give us a possible way of expressing an agent acting as a representative for an organisation in situations where the organisation holds a role.

If we are to extend the formalism to bring our model closer to reality we must consider developing our use of conditions on obligations. Although we acknowledge the complications this would introduce, we would like to consider allowing obligations to become active given certain world states or the execution of certain actions.

We currently make no mention of cardinality of roles in our notation. It is feasible that a designer may wish to specify the actual number of agents that can hold any one role. For example, it may be the case that a particular role must be taken on by at least one agent for the organisation to be valid, or similarly that a role cannot be held by more than one agent within the same organisation. We feel that this issue has been overlooked in most role-based modelling systems to date and warrants further investigation.

Beyond the notation itself, we intend to extend and refine our implemention of the mechanisms for change (section 4) and further develop the tools for analysis and visualisation described in section 5.

8   Conclusions

We have described means to formally specify and analyse agent organisations based on the roles of individual components. Ours is a flexible and expressive approach that contemplates agents taking part in multiple organisations with distinct roles and disparate obligations. Our framework allows change in the organisational structure to be modelled and alternative organisation specifications to be developed in order to handle the consequences of change. Our model gives rise to a suite of tools and functionalities with which engineers can specify, verify and analyse organisations, the roles of their components, their obligations and the relationships among these roles. This is the first recorded attempt to provide a toolkit that not only allows an engineer to develop flexible organisations of agents but also enables the engineer to investigate issues of change.

References

[1] M. Barbuceanu. Coordinating agents by role based social constraints and conversation plans. In *Proceedings of the 14th National Conference on Artificial Intelligence*, pages 16–21, 1997.
[2] B. Bauer, J. P. Muller, and J. Odell. Agent UML: A formalism for specifying multiagent interaction. In P. Ciancarini and M. Wooldridge, editors, *Agent-Oriented Software Engineering*, pages 91–103. Springer-Verlag, 2001.
[3] C. Castelfranchi. Modelling social action for AI agents. *Artificial Intelligence*, 103:157–182, 1998.
[4] L. Cavedon and L. Sonenberg. On social commitment, roles and preferred goals. In *Proceedings of the Third International Conference on Multi-Agent Systems*, pages 80–87, 1998.
[5] R. Conte and C. Castelfranchi. *Cognitive and Social Action*. UCL Press, 1995.
[6] M. Dastani, V. Dignum, and F. Dignum. Role-assignment in open agent societies. In *Proceedings of the Second International Joint Conference on Autonomous Agents and Multiagent Systems*, pages 489–496, 2003.
[7] N. Dershowitz and J.-P. Jouannaud. Rewrite Systems. In J. van Leeuwen, editor, *Handbook of Theoretical Computer Science*, volume B. MIT Press, 1990.
[8] F. Dignum, D. Morley, E. Sonenberg, and L. Cavedon. Towards socially sophisticated BDI agents. In *Proceedings of the Fourth International Conference on MultiAgent Systems*, pages 111–118, 2000.
[9] V. Dignum, F. Dignum, and L. Sonenberg. Towards dynamic reorganization of agent societies. In *ECAI Workshop on Coordinating Emergent Agent Societies*, 2004.
[10] M. Esteva. *Electronic Institutions: from specification to development*. PhD thesis, Universitat Politècnica de Catalunya (UPC), 2003. IIIA monography Vol. 19.
[11] M. Esteva, W. Vasconcelos, C. Sierra, and J. A. Rodríguez-Aguilar. Verifying Norm Consistency in Electronic Institutions. In *Proceedings of AAAI 2004 Workshop on Agent Organizations: Theory and Practice*, San Jose, California, U.S.A., 2004. AAAI Press.
[12] A. J. I. Jones and M. Sergot. A formal characterisation of institutionalised power. *Journal of the Interest Group in Pure and Applied Logic*, 4(3):427–443, 1996.

[13] M. J. Kollingbaum and T. J. Norman. Norm consistency in practical reasoning agents. In *PROMAS Workshop on Programming Multiagent Systems*, 2003.

[14] F. López y López and M. Luck. Towards a model of the dynamics of normative multi-agent systems. In *Proceedings of the International Workshop on Regulated Agent-Based Social Systems: Theories and Applications at AAMAS 2002*, pages 175–193, 2002.

[15] Carlsson M., Ottosson G., and Carlson B. An open-ended finite domain constraint solver. In *Proc. Programming Languages: Implementations, Logics, and Programs*, 1997.

[16] M. McCallum, T. J. Norman, and W. W. Vasconcelos. A formal model of organisations for engineering multi-agent systems. In *ECAI Workshop on Coordinating Emergent Agent Societies*, 2004.

[17] T. J. Norman and C. A. Reed. Group delegation and responsibility. In *In Proceedings of the First International Joint Conference on Autonomous Agents and Multi-Agent Systems*, pages 491–498, 2002.

[18] Swedish Institute of Computer Science. SICStus prolog. http://www.sics.se/isl/sicstuswww/site/index.html.

[19] O. Pacheco and J. Carmo. A role based model for the normative specification of organized collective agency and agents interaction. *Autonomous Agents and Multi-Agent Systems*, 6(6):145–184, 2003.

[20] P. Panzarasa, N. R. Jennings, and T. J. Norman. Social mental shaping: Modelling the impact of sociality on the mental states of autonomous agents. *Computational Intelligence*, 17(4):738–782, 2001.

[21] S. J. Russell and P. Norvig. *Artificial Intelligence: A Modern Approach*. Prentice Hall, Inc., U.S.A., 2 edition, 2003.

[22] M. Sergot. Normative positions. In Henry Prakken and Paul McNamara, editors, *Norms, Logics and Information Systems. New Studies in Deontic Logic and Computer Science*, pages 289–310. IOS Press, 1998.

[23] J. S. Sichman and Y. Demazeau. On social reasoning in multi-agent systems. In *Revista Ibero-Americana de Inteligncia Artificial*, volume 13, pages 68–84, 2001.

[24] N. Skarmeas. Organizations through roles and agents. citeseer.nj.nec.com/174774.html.

[25] Victor Vianu. Rule-Based Languages. *Annals of Mathematics and Artificial Intelligence*, 19(1–2):215–259, March 1997.

[26] M. Wooldridge, N. R. Jennings, and D. Kinny. The GAIA methodology for agent-oriented analysis and design. *Autonomous Agents and Multi-Agent Systems*, 3(3):285–312, 2000.

[27] F. Zambonelli, N. R. Jennings, and M. Wooldridge. Organisational rules as an abstraction for the analysis and design of multi-agent systems. *International Journal of Software Engineering and Knowledge Engineering*, 11(3):303–328, 2001.

S-Moise+: A Middleware for Developing Organised Multi-agent Systems

Jomi Fred Hübner[1], Jaime Simão Sichman[2], and Olivier Boissier[3]

[1] GIA / DSC / FURB
Braz Wanka, 238
89035-160, Blumenau, Brazil
jomi@inf.furb.br
[2] LTI / EP / USP
Av. Prof. Luciano Gualberto, 158, trav. 3
05508-900 São Paulo, SP, Brazil
jaime.sichman@poli.usp.br
[3] SMA / G2I / ENSM.SE
158 Cours Fauriel
42023 Saint-Etienne Cedex, France
Olivier.Boissier@emse.fr

Abstract. The Multi-agent Systems (MAS) area, while concerning heterogeneous and open systems, has evolved towards the specification of global constraints that agents are supposed to follow. A subset of these constraints are known as organisation of the MAS. This paper describes a software implementation, called S-Moise+, that tries to fill the gap between the organisational constraints and the agents autonomy. This software ensures that all agents will follow the organisation without requiring that they are developed in a specific language or architecture.

Keywords: Multi-agent Systems, MAS organisations, Engineering organisations for MAS.

1 Introduction

The assignment of an organisation to a Multi-Agent System (MAS) is useful to deal with the problems that could arise from the agents' autonomy, specially in *open* MAS [12] where we do not know what kind of agent will enter into the system (this motivation for organised MAS is well described in [21, 4]). In this context, the organisation is a set of behavioural constraints that a group of agents adopts in order to control the agent's autonomy and easily achieve their global purposes [5]. This approach is based on human societies that are successfully using organisation (e.g. social roles) to have a global coherent behaviour. The definition of a proper organisation for a MAS is not an easy task, once the organisation could be too flexible (the organisation does not help the achievement

O. Boissier et al. (Eds.): ANIREM and OOOP 2005, LNCS 3913, pp. 64–77, 2006.

of the global purpose) or too stiff (the organisation extinguishes the agent's autonomy). A initial good organisation is normally set up by the MAS designer, however it may become not suitable in dynamic environments. In these cases the system must support dynamic changes on its organisation [17].

The precise concept of constraint that will be used to describe an organisation is defined by the underlying organisational model. These models may be divided in two points of view: *agent* centered or *organisation* centered [18]. While the former takes the agents as the engine for the organisation formation, the latter sees the opposite direction: the organisation exists *a priori* (defined by the designer or by the agents themselves) and the agents ought to follow it. In addition to this classification, we propose to group these organisational models in (*i*) those that stress the society's *global plans* and their execution coordination (e.g. TÆMS [19], STEAM [22]); (*ii*) those that have their focus on the society's *roles* and groups (e.g. AGR [8], TOVE [9]); and (*iii*) the models based on a deontic approach where *norm*, among others, is the main concept (e.g. ISLANDER [6], OPERA [4]). Thus we should state that organisation models usually take into account the functional (the first group), the structural (second group), and/or the deontic (the third group) dimension of the organisation. The MOISE$^+$ organisational model is an attempt to join these three dimensions into an unified model suitable for the reorganisation process [15, 16]. The MOISE$^+$ main property concerning the reorganisation problem is to be an organizational centered (OC) model where the first two dimensions can be specified almost *independently* of each other and after properly linked by the deontic dimension. This linkage allows the MAS to change the structure without changing the functioning, and vice versa, the system only needs to adjust its deontic relation.

In order to implement a system that follows organisational constraints we can also take either an agent centered or an organisational centered point of view (in [23] these points of view are called agent and institutional perspectives). In the former point of view, the focus is on how to develop an agent reasoning mechanism that follows the organisation. The implementation approach is endogenous to the agent. In the latter, the main concern is how to develop a MAS framework that ensures the satisfaction of the organisational constraints. This point of view is more suitable for heterogeneous and open systems, since, as an exogenous approach, the agent implementation, architecture, and programming language do not matter. Of course the agents probably need to have access to an organisational specification that enable them to eventually reason about it. However, the agents will follow the organisation despite their organisational reasoning abilities. As far as we know, the following implementations of such a kind of framework are available: AMELI [7] (based on ISLANDER), MadKit [11] (based on AGR), and KARMA [20] (based on STEAM). Hence we are concerned with dynamic organisation, the MOISE$^+$ should be used as the underlying organisational model. In this paper we describe an MAS framework called $\mathcal{S}$-MOISE$^+$ (Sec. 3) which ensures that agents running on it will follow the constraints specified using the MOISE$^+$ model (Sec. 2).

2   The $\mathcal{M}$oise$^+$ Organisational Model

The $\mathcal{M}$OISE$^+$ (Model of Organisation for multI-agent SystEms) considers the organisational structure and functioning. However, this model adds an explicit deontic relation among these first two dimensions to better explain how an MAS's organisation collaborates for the global purpose and makes the agents able to reason on the fulfillment of their obligations or not [16]. These three dimensions form the Organisational Specification (OS). When a set of agents adopts an OS they form an Organisational Entity (OE) and, once created, its history starts and runs by events like other agents entering and/or leaving the OE, group creation, role adoption, mission commitment, etc.

The $\mathcal{M}$OISE$^+$ Structural Specification (SS) is built in three levels: (*i*) the behaviours that an agent is responsible for when it adopts a role (*individual* level), (*ii*) the acquaintance, communication, and authority links between roles (*social* level), and (*iii*) the aggregation of roles in groups (*collective* level). The $\mathcal{M}$OISE$^+$'s SS also allows us to ascribe the well formed attribute to a group in case the roles of the agents are compatible among them, the minimum and maximum number of role players are satisfied inside a group, etc.

Throughout the text, a soccer team is used as an example to describe the model (a formal definition is found in [15]). A soccer team that we will specify is formed by players with roles like goalkeeper, back player, leader, attacker, coach, etc. These role players are distributed in two groups (defense and attack) which form the main group (the team group). This team structure is specified, using the $\mathcal{M}$OISE$^+$ notation, in the Fig. 1. For instance, in the defense group specification, three roles are allowed and any defense group will be well formed if there is one, and only one, agent playing the role goalkeeper, exactly three agents playing backs, and, optionally, one agent playing the leader role (see the composition relation in Fig. 1). The goalkeeper has authority on the backs. The leader player is also allowed to be a back since these roles are compatible. Due to the role specialization (see the inheritance relation in Fig. 1), the leader also can play the goalkeeper role. In the same example, a team is well formed if it has one defense sub-group, one attack sub-group, one or two agents playing the coach role, one agent playing the leader role, and the two sub-groups are also well formed. In this structure, the coach has authority on all players by an authority link. The players, in any group, can communicate with each other and are allowed to represent the coach (since they have an acquaintance link). There must be a leader either in the defense or attack group. The leader has authority on all players on all groups, since s/he has an authority link on the player role. For every authority link there is an implicit communication link and for every communication link there is an implicit acquaintance link.

A $\mathcal{M}$OISE$^+$ group can have intra-group and inter-group links. The intra-group links state that an agent playing the link source role in a group *gr* is linked to all agents playing the destination role in the *same* group *gr* or in a *gr* sub-group. The inter-group links state that an agent playing the source role is linked to all agents playing the destination role despite the groups these agents belong to. For example, the coach authority on player is an inter-group link (the coach and

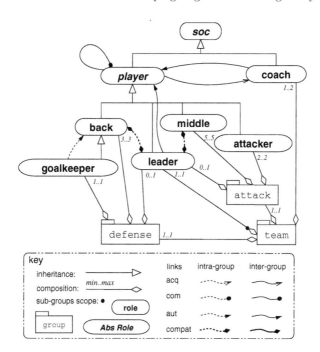

Fig. 1. The structure of the soccer team

the player agents do not need to belong to the same group), while the goalkeeper authority on backs is an intra-group link (both agents must belong to the same group to "use" this link).

The Functional Specification (FS) describes how an MAS usually achieves its *global* (collective) goals [2] stating how these goals are decomposed (by plans) and distributed to the agents (by missions). The scheme can be seen as a goal decomposition tree where the root is a global goal and the leaves are goals that can be achieved by one agent. Such decompositions may be set either by the MAS designer who specifies its expertise in the scheme or by the agents that store their past (best) solutions. In the soccer example, suppose the team has a rehearsed play as the one specified in the Fig. 2. This scheme has three missions (m_1, m_2, and m_3) — a mission is a set of coherent goal that an agent can commit to. When an agent commits to a mission, it is responsible for all this missions' goals. For example, an agent committed to the mission m_3 has the goals "be placed in the opponent goal area", "shot at the opponent's goal", and, a common goal, "score a goal".

In a scheme, each goal $g_i \in \mathcal{G}$ (where $\mathcal{G}$ is the set of global goals) may be decomposed in sub-goals through plans using three operators:

- sequence ",": the plan "$g_1 = g_2, g_3$" means that the goal g_1 will be achieved if the goal g_2 is achieved and after that also the goal g_3 is achieved;
- choice "|": the plan "$g_1 = g_2 \mid g_3$" means that the goal g_1 will be achieved if one, and only one, of the goals g_2 or g_3 is achieved; and

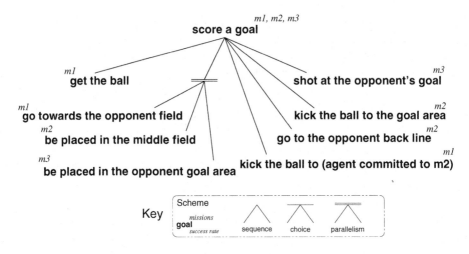

Fig. 2. A "side attack" scheme of the soccer team

– parallelism "∥": the plan "$g_1 = g_2 \parallel g_3$" means that the goal g_1 will be achieved if both g_2 and g_3 are achieved, but they can be achieved in parallel.

The Deontic Specification (DS) describes the roles' permissions and obligations for missions. A permission $permission(\rho, m)$ states that an agent playing the role ρ is allowed to commit to the mission m. Furthermore, an obligation $obligation(\rho, m)$ states that an agent playing ρ ought to commit to m. For example, in the soccer team DS (Tab. 1), three roles have the right to start the scheme of the Fig. 2 because they have the permission for this scheme's root missions. Once the scheme is created, the other agents (playing back, middle, ...) are obligated by their roles' deontic relations to participate in this scheme. These other agents ought to pursue their mission's goals just in the order allowed by this scheme. For instance, when a middle agent accepts the mission m_2, it will try to achieve its goal "be placed in the middle field" only after the goal "get the ball" is already satisfied by a back agent committed to the mission m_1.

Table 1. Partial view of the soccer team deontic relations

role	deontic relation	mission
back	*permission*	m_1
middle	*obligation*	m_2
attacker	*obligation*	m_3

3   𝒮-ℳoise⁺ Organisational Middleware

𝒮-ℳoise⁺ is an open source implementation of an *organisational middleware* that follows the ℳoise⁺ model. This middleware is the interface between the agents and the overall system, providing access to the communication layer (see

Fig. 3), information about the current state of the organisation (created groups, schemes, roles assignments, etc.), and allowing the agents to change the organisation entity and specification. Of course these changes are constrained to ensure that the agents respect the organisational specification.

$\mathcal{S}$-$\mathcal{M}$OISE$^+$ has two main components: an OrgBox API that agents use to access the organisational layer (this component is detailed in Sec. 3.2) and a special agent called OrgManager. This agent has the current state of the OE and maintains it consistent. The OrgManager receives messages from the agents' OrgBox asking for changes in the OE state (e.g. role adoption, group creation, mission commitment). This OrgManager changes the OE only if it does not violate an organisational constraint. For example, if an agent wants to adopt a role ρ_1 but it already has a role ρ_2 and these two roles are not compatible, the adoption of ρ_1 must be denied.

The state of an OE is represented by the following tuple:

$$\langle os, \mathcal{A}, \mathcal{GI}, grType, subGr, agRole, \mathcal{SI}, scType, agMis, gState \rangle \tag{1}$$

where:

- os is the initial organisational specification (in $\mathcal{S}$-$\mathcal{M}$OISE$^+$, OrgManager reads this OS from an XML file);
- $\mathcal{A}$ is the set of agents in the MAS;
- $\mathcal{GI}$ is the set of created groups;
- $grType : \mathcal{GI} \to \mathcal{GT}$ maps the group specification for each group in $\mathcal{GI}$ ($\mathcal{GT}$ is the set of group specifications defined in os);
- $subGr : \mathcal{GI} \to \mathbb{P}(\mathcal{GI})$ maps the sub-groups of each group;
- $agRole : \mathcal{A} \twoheadrightarrow \mathbb{P}(\mathcal{R} \times \mathcal{GI})$ maps the roles of the agents ($\mathcal{R}$ is the set of roles defined in os);
- $\mathcal{SI}$ is the set of scheme instances;
- $scType : \mathcal{SI} \to \mathcal{ST} \times \mathbb{P}(\mathcal{GI})$ maps the specification and the responsible groups for each scheme instance ($\mathcal{ST}$ is the set of scheme specifications defined in os)[1];
- $agMis : \mathcal{A} \twoheadrightarrow \mathbb{P}(\mathcal{M} \times \mathcal{SI})$ maps the missions of the agents ($\mathcal{M}$ is the set of missions defined in os);
- $gState : \mathcal{SI} \times \mathcal{G} \twoheadrightarrow \{unsatisfied, satisfied, impossible\}$ maps the state of each goal ($\mathcal{G}$ is the set of global goals defined in os).

3.1 Organisational Entity Dynamics

The OE is changed by *organisational events* created by messages that OrgManager receives from the agents. Each event has arguments, preconditions and effects (Tab. 2 summarises these events). In this paper we describe only some of the events using our soccer example, a full formalization can be found in [13] and http://www.lti.usp.br/moise.

---

[1] The current version of $\mathcal{M}$OISE$^+$ does not constrain the type of the groups that are allowed to be responsible for a scheme instance.

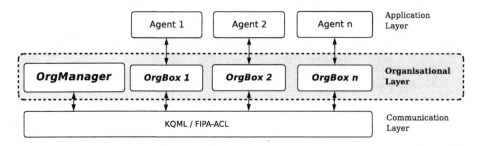

Fig. 3. $\mathcal{S}$-$\mathcal{M}$OISE$^+$ Components

As an example, suppose we have an OE where the following events happened:

- `createGroup('team')`: a group, identified hereafter by gr_t, was created from the team group specification defined in Fig. 1;
- `createSubGroup('defense', `gr_t`)`: a group, identified hereafter by gr_d, was created from the defense group specification as gr_t sub-group;
- `createSubGroup('attack', `gr_t`)`: a group, identified hereafter by gr_a, was created from the attack group specification as a gr_t sub-group;
- `createScheme('side_attack', `$\{gr_t\}$`)`: an instance of the side attack scheme specification (Fig. 2), identified by sch_{sa}, was created, the agents of the group gr_t are responsible for these scheme missions.

After these events, the groups are not well formed, since there is no agents engaged with their roles (see Fig. 4). The defense group, for instance, needs one agent playing goalkeeper. If an agent α wants to adopt the role ρ in the group gr, it must create the event `roleAdoption(`α`, `ρ`, `gr`)`. Notice that a role is always adopted inside a group of agents, since role is a relational concept [1]. The reasons for an agent to adopt a role is not covered by the $\mathcal{M}$OISE$^+$ model, for more details regarding motivations for role adoption, the reader is referred to [10, 8, 3]. The role adoption event in $\mathcal{S}$-$\mathcal{M}$OISE$^+$ has the following preconditions:

1. the role ρ must belong to gr's group specification;
2. the number of ρ players in gr must be lesser or equals to the maximum number of ρ players defined in the gr's compositional specification;
3. for all roles ρ_i that α already plays, the roles ρ and ρ_i must be intra-group compatible in the gr's group specification;
4. for all roles ρ_i that α already plays in groups other than gr, the roles ρ and ρ_i must be inter-group compatible.

In our example, suppose that eleven agents have adopted roles such as the three groups are well formed and the goal "get the ball" of the scheme sch_{sa} is already satisfied. Among these agents, 'Lucio' has adopted the role middle in the gr_d group (once gr_d is a sub-group of gr_t, Lucio also belongs to gr_t). Is this agent following its organisational obligations? No, because he plays a middle role, there is a side attack scheme created by his group, and his role is obligated to commit to mission m_2 (the Alg. 1 describes the algorithm that gets all missions an agent is obligated to). To be organisationally well behaved, Lucio commits to

Table 2. $\mathcal{S}$-$\mathcal{M}$OISE$^+$ main Organisational Events

Event	Description (some preconditions)
createGroup(gt)	Creates a new group from specification gt ($gt \in \mathcal{GT}$).
createSubGroup(gt, gi)	Creates a new gi sub-group based on specification gt (gi identifies an instance group).
removeGroup(gi)	Removes the group identified by gi (the group must be empty — no player, no sub-groups, and no schemes).
createScheme(st, gis)	Creates a new scheme instance from specification st ($st \in \mathcal{ST}$), gis ($gis \preceq \mathcal{GI}$) is a set of groups that are responsible for the new scheme execution.
finishScheme(si)	The scheme si is finished.
setSatified(α, si, g)	The goal g of the scheme si is satisfied by the agent α (α must be committed to a mission that includes g).
setImpossible(α, si, g)	The goal g of the scheme si is impossible (α must be committed to a mission that includes g).
enterOrg(α)	The agent α enters in the system.
leaveOrg(α)	the agent α leaves the system (it must have neither roles nor missions).
roleAdoption(α, ρ, gr)	The agent α adopts the role ρ in the group gr.
giveRoleUp(α, ρ, gr)	The agent α gives up the role ρ in the group gr (this role missions must be finished).
commitMission(α, m, si)	The agent α commits to the mission m in the scheme si.
finishMission(α, m, si)	The agent α finishes its mission m in the scheme si (all the mission's goal must be satisfied or declared impossible).

the m_2 mission through the event commitMission('Lucio', m_2, sch_{sa}). From the OrgManager point of view, this event also has some preconditions:

1. the scheme must not be finished yet;
2. the agent must play a role in the scheme's responsible groups;
3. this role must be permitted or obligated to the mission, as defined in the DS.

After his commitment, Lucio will likely pose the question: what are the global goal I have to achieve? In the case of his m_2 goals, only the goal "be placed in the middle field" is permitted (see Fig. 2). His second goal "go to the opponent back line" is not permitted by the current state of sch_{sa}. This second goal should be pursued only after another global goal is satisfied, since it depends on "kick the ball to" achievement. The Alg. 2 is used in the OrgManager implementation to identify permitted global goals. Thus, while some goals are becoming satisfied (event setSatified), others become permitted. When a goal becomes permitted, the agents committed to it are informed by the OrgManager. This mechanism is very useful to *coordinate* the agents in the scheme execution. The agent developer does not need to program messages that synchronize the agents in the schema execution.

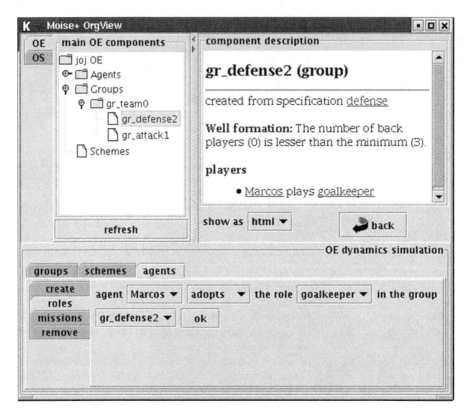

Fig. 4. Example of organisational entity not well formed

The OrgManager ensures that every organisational events generated by the agents will not violate the following organisational constraints specified in $\mathcal{M}$OISE$^+$:

- the maximum number of role players in a group;
- the roles compatibility;
- an agent will commit only to missions it is permitted or obligated by its roles;
- only specified groups, schemes, and roles can be created.

Moreover, OrgManager provides useful information for the agents' organisational reasoning and coordination, for example: missions they are forced to commit to and goals it can pursue. The agents can get this information through their OrgBox API.

Among the $\mathcal{M}$OISE$^+$ specification elements, only the authority link is not ensured in the current implementation. We probably need to change the agent reasoning mechanism to ensure authority, and it is out of the focus of this paper.

```
 1  function getObligatedMissions(agent α)
 2
 3  all ← empty list // list of obligated missions
 4  forall role ρ the agent α plays do
 5      gr ← the group where ρ is being played;
 6      forall scheme si that gr is responsible to do
 7          if si is not finished then
 8              forall mission m in the scheme si do
 9                  if obligated(ρ, m) is in the deontic specification then
10                      all ← append(all, m);

11  return all;
```

Algorithm 1. Algorithm to compute the missions an agent is obligated to

```
 1  function isPermitted(scheme sch, goal g)
 2
 3  if g is the sch root then
 4      return true;
 5  else
 6      g is in a plan that match "g₀ = · · · g · · ·";
 7      if g is in a plan that match "g₀ = · · · gᵢ , g · · ·" then
 8          if gᵢ is already satisfied then
 9              return true;
10          else
11              return false;
12      else
13          return isPermitted(sch, g₀);
```

Algorithm 2. Algorithm to verify permitted goals

3.2 Agents' OrgBox

The OrgBox is the interface the agents use to access the organisational layer and thus the communication layer. When an agent desires to (i) change the organisational entity (adopt a role, for instance), (ii) send a message to another agent, or (iii) get the organisational entity state it has to ask this service for its OrgBox. The OrgBox will therefore interact with the OrgManager or another agent using the communication layer. In the $\mathcal{S}$-$\mathcal{M}$OISE$^+$ current implementation, the communication layer is implemented by SACI (http://www.lti.pcs.usp.br/saci) — a KQML compliant multi-agent communication infrastructure. We have developed a protocol in the communication layer that OrgManager and OrgBox follow to exchange information and organisational events. We can see the OrgBox as a component that encapsulates this protocol.

When an agent asks OrgManager for a "copy" of the current state of the OE, it will not receive exactly what is in the OrgManager's memory. In the $\mathcal{M}$OISE$^+$, an agent is allowed to know another agent α only in case it plays a role ρ_1, α plays ρ_2 and these roles are linked by an acquaintance relation. For example the player role of the Fig. 1 has an acquaintance link to the coach role, thus an agent playing this role is allowed to know the agents playing coach. Indeed, since player is an abstract role, no agent will adopt it, however other roles (like back, leader, etc.) will inherit this acquaintance link from the player role. OrgBox also ensures that an agent will send messages only to agents it has a communication link with.

While the OrgBox is invoked by the agent (to send messages, ask for information, change the organisation), it is also invoked by the OrgManager. When the state of a scheme that some agent is committed to changes, OrgManager informs this agent's OrgBox about its new obligations and goals it can pursue. The OrgBox then notifies the agent about this event. Of course the OrgBox only informs the agent about its permitted goals, it is a matter of the agent to achieve them (by plans, behaviours, etc.). What is stated in the organisational model is that the agent is responsible for such a goal. However, in case the agent does not achieve its organisational responsibilities, the current implementation of the middleware does nothing. It is a future work to propose a solution for this drawback.

An important feature of our proposal is that it does not require any specific type of agent architecture, since we are concerned with open system. The only requirement is that agents use the OrgBox API to interact with the system. An agent could even interact with the OrgManager directly using KQML or FIPA-ACL. However, in this case the communication link constraint will not be guaranteed, since in this case agents are getting direct access to the communication layer.

4   Contributions and Future Work

In this paper we described a proposal towards declarative organisation programming. In our proposal, a middleware called $\mathcal{S}$-$\mathcal{M}$OISE$^+$ ensures that the agents will follow the organisational constraints. These constraints are declared by the developer (or even by the agents themselves) according to an organisational model. The organisational model used in our proposal enables the declaration of MAS organisational structure (role, groups, links), functioning (global goals, global plans, missions), obligations, and permission. The main features of $\mathcal{S}$-$\mathcal{M}$OISE$^+$ are:

- $\mathcal{S}$-$\mathcal{M}$OISE$^+$ follows an organisational centred point of view where the organisational specification is interpreted at runtime, it is not hardwired in the agents' code.
- It provides a synchronization mechanism for scheme execution.
- It is suitable for heterogeneous and open system, since $\mathcal{S}$-$\mathcal{M}$OISE$^+$ is an exogenous approach and therefore does not require a special agent architecture or programming language.

– It is suitable for reorganisation where the declaration of the organisation can dynamically change. We have successfully used this framework in a soccer team that change its $\mathcal{M}$OISE$^+$ organisational at runtime [17] and to specify contract dynamics in an electronic business alliance [14]. Like the organisational events described in Sec. 3.1, the $\mathcal{S}$-$\mathcal{M}$OISE$^+$ also has reorganisational events that changes the current specification. However, these events are controlled by a special group of agents responsible for the reorganisation process.

Regarding related frameworks, $\mathcal{S}$-$\mathcal{M}$OISE$^+$ is quite complementary to AMELI[7], MadKit [11], and KARMA[20]. Many implementation solutions proposed by these frameworks were adopted in $\mathcal{S}$-$\mathcal{M}$OISE$^+$ (like the OrgBox which is very similar to Teamcore proxy from KARMA and governor from AMELI). AMELI has a good support for communication and protocols that $\mathcal{S}$-$\mathcal{M}$OISE$^+$ does not have. However, it does not stress the structural and deontic dimensions like $\mathcal{S}$-$\mathcal{M}$OISE$^+$. MadKit is focused on the structural dimension and does not include functional and deontic dimension. KARMA is concerned with both the structure and the functioning and has an excellent support for coordination of global plan execution, however it lacks an explicit deontic dimension.

As a future development, we intend to extends $\mathcal{S}$-$\mathcal{M}$OISE$^+$ with new features like communication dimension, detection of violation of an agent obligation, and a sanction system. We also plan to define an organisational meta level, independently of the adopted organisational model, to create a (i) generic ontology of organisational terms and (ii) to provide translation to and from a particular organisational model to other.

Although we have adopted an organisational point of view, a complete solution towards an organisational oriented programming demands answers to some questions related to an agent point of view. For instance, how organisational information, obligations, and permissions are used inside the agent reasoning cycle? How to conciliate the agent autonomy with organisational responsibilities?

References

1. Cristiano Castelfranchi. Commitments: From individual intentions to groups and organizations. In Toru Ishida, editor, *Proceedings of the 2nd International Conference on Multi-Agent Systems (ICMAS'96)*, pages 41–48. AAAI Press, 1996.
2. Cristiano Castelfranchi. Modeling social action for AI agents. *Artificial Intelligence*, (103):157–182, 1998.
3. Mehdi Dastani, Virginia Dignum, and Frank Dignum. Role-assignment in open agent societies. In Jeffrey S. Rosenschein, Tuomas Sandholm, Wooldridge Michael, and Makoto Yokoo, editors, *Proceedings of the Second International Joint Conference on Autonomous Agents and Multi-Agent Systems (AAMAS'2003)*, pages 489–496. ACM Press, 2003.
4. Maria Virgínia Ferreira de Almeida Júdice Gamito Dignum. *A model for organizational interaction: based on agents, founded in logic.* PhD thesis, Universiteit Utrecht, 2003.

5. Virginia Dignum and Frank Dignum. Modelling agent societies: Co-ordination frameworks and institutions. In Pavel Brazdil and Alípio Jorge, editors, *Proceedings of the 10th Portuguese Conference on Artificial Intelligence (EPIA'01)*, LNAI 2258, pages 191–204, Berlin, 2001. Springer.

6. Marc Esteva, Juan A. Rodriguez-Aguiar, Carles Sierra, Pere Garcia, and Josep L. Arcos. On the formal specification of electronic institutions. In Frank Dignum and Carles Sierra, editors, *Proceedings of the Agent-mediated Electronic Commerce*, LNAI 1191, pages 126–147, Berlin, 2001. Springer.

7. Marc Esteva, Juan A. Rodríguez-Aguilar, Bruno Rosell, and Josep L. AMELI: An agent-based middleware for electronic institutions. In Nicholas R. Jennings, Carles Sierra, Liz Sonenberg, and Milind Tambe, editors, *Proceedings of the Third International Joint Conference on Autonomous Agents and Multi-Agent Systems (AAMAS'2004)*, pages 236–243, New York, 2004. ACM.

8. Jacques Ferber and Olivier Gutknecht. A meta-model for the analysis and design of organizations in multi-agents systems. In Yves Demazeau, editor, *Proceedings of the 3rd International Conference on Multi-Agent Systems (ICMAS'98)*, pages 128–135. IEEE Press, 1998.

9. Mark S. Fox, Mihai Barbuceanu, Michael Gruninger, and Jinxin Lon. An organizational ontology for enterprise modeling. In Michael J. Prietula, Kathleen M. Carley, and Les Gasser, editors, *Simulating Organizations: Computational Models of Institutions and Groups*, chapter 7, pages 131–152. AAAI Press / MIT Press, Menlo Park, 1998.

10. Norbert Glaser and Philippe Morignot. The reorganization of societies of autonomous agents. In Magnus Boman and Walter Van de Velde, editors, *Multi-Agent Rationality*, LNAI 1237, pages 98–111, Berlin, 1997. Springer.

11. Olivier Gutknecht and Jacques Ferber. The MadKit agent platform architecture. In *Agents Workshop on Infrastructure for Multi-Agent Systems*, pages 48–55, 2000.

12. Carl Hewitt. Open information system semantics for distributed artificial intelligence. *Artificial Intelligence*, (47):79–106, 1991.

13. Jomi Fred Hübner. *Um Modelo de Reorganização de Sistemas Multiagentes*. PhD thesis, Universidade de São Paulo, Escola Politécnica, 2003. http://www.inf.furb.br/~jomi/pubs/2003/Hubner-tese.pdf.

14. Jomi Fred Hübner, Jaime Simão Sichman, and Olivier Boissier. Specifying E-Alliance contract dynamics through the MOISE+ reorganisation process. In *V Encontro Nacional de Inteligência Artificial (ENIA'2005)*, 2005.

15. Jomi Fred Hübner, Jaime Simão Sichman, and Olivier Boissier. $\mathcal{M}$OISE$^+$: Towards a structural, functional, and deontic model for MAS organization. In Cristiano Castelfranchi and W. Lewis Johnson, editors, *Proceedings of the First International Joint Conference on Autonomous Agents and Multi-Agent Systems (AAMAS'2002)*, pages 501–502. ACM Press, 2002. http://www.inf.furb.br/~jomi/pubs/2002/Hubner-aamas2002.pdf.

16. Jomi Fred Hübner, Jaime Simão Sichman, and Olivier Boissier. A model for the structural, functional, and deontic specification of organizations in multiagent systems. In Guilherme Bittencourt and Geber L. Ramalho, editors, *Proceedings of the 16th Brazilian Symposium on Artificial Intelligence (SBIA'02)*, LNAI 2507, pages 118–128, Berlin, 2002. Springer. http://www.inf.furb.br/~jomi/pubs/2002/Hubner-sbia2002.pdf.

17. Jomi Fred Hübner, Jaime Simão Sichman, and Olivier Boissier. Using the $\mathcal{M}$OISE$^+$ for a cooperative framework of MAS reorganisation. In Ana L. C. Bazzan and Sofiane Labidi, editors, *Proceedings of the 17th Brazilian Symposium on Artificial Intelligence (SBIA'04)*, LNAI 3171, pages 506–515, Berlin, 2004. Springer. http://www.inf.furb.br/~jomi/pubs/2004/Hubner-sbia2004.pdf.
18. Christian Lemaître and Cora B. Excelente. Multi-agent organization approach. In Francisco J. Garijo and Christian Lemaître, editors, *Proceedings of II Iberoamerican Workshop on DAI and MAS*, 1998.
19. M.V. Nagendra Prasad, Keith Decker, Alan Garvey, and Victor Lesser. Exploring organizational design with TÆMS: A case study of distributed data processing. In Toru Ishida, editor, *Proceedings of the 2nd International Conference on Multi-Agent Systems (ICMAS'96)*, pages 283–290. AAAI Press, 1996.
20. David V. Pynadath and Milind Tambe. An automated teamwork infrastructure for heterogeneous software agents and humans. *Autonomous Agents and Multi-Agent Systems*, 7(1–2):71–100, 2003.
21. Carles Sierra, Juan Antonio Rodríguez-Aguilar, Pablo Noriega, Marc Esteva, and Josep Lluís Arcos. Engineering multi-agent systems as electronic institutions. *European Journal for the Informatics Professional*, V(4), August 2004.
22. Milind Tambe. Towards flexible teamwork. *Journal of Artificial Intelligence Reseearch*, 7:83–124, 1997.
23. J. Vázquez-Salceda, H. Aldewereld, and F. Dignum. Norms in multiagent systems: some implementation guidelines. In *Proceedings of the Second European Workshop on Multi-Agent Systems (EUMAS 2004)*, 2004.

Part II

Modelling and Analyzing Institutions

Fencing the Open Fields:
Empirical Concerns on Electronic Institutions
(Invited Paper)

Pablo Noriega

Institut d'Investigació en Intel.ligència Artificial
IIIA-CSIC. Bellaterra, Barcelona, Spain

Abstract. The regulation of multiagent systems may be approached from different stand-points. In this paper I will take the perspective of using a certain type of devices, electronic institutions, to regulate agent interactions. Furthermore, in this paper I am concerned with the tasks of design and construction of actual electronic institutions and I will explore some of the empirical aspects that one may encounter in such activities. More specifically, I will focus on those empirical aspects that are characteristic of electronic institutions rather than those that may be typical of multi–agent systems development in general or other types of software engineering. I use three examples of actual electronic institutions that show different and complementary features in order to motivate a number of distinctions that may be used to treat empirical features in a systematic way.

1   Introduction

Social interaction in everyday life is structured in many ways. When I buy fruit in the local market I exchange information with the fruit lady to find out what is today's price of the best fruit available and, if I like the options she offers me, I pay her and I get my apples. That simple interaction entailed conventions for simple bargaining and payment which in turn involved a common understanding of fruit features, money and the delivery of goods. Other interactions may involve conventions that are far more complex that the ones my fruit lady and I need to share. Traveling by bus, getting medical attention or passing a law through Parliament would be impossible if we didn't share with those with whom we interact some conventions that guide our individual behavior and facilitate us to achieve our intended goals; Society has developed organizations, contracts, standard procedures, markets, laws and many other such devices to *regulate* human interactions and make them effective.

In multiagent systems interactions may need to be structured as well. Generally the structuring is part of the design of the multiagent system because the participating agents are built by the same designer that builds the environment where the agents interact or because the rational components of agents are in some way accessible to the system. However, when the multiagent system is open to the participation of unknown agents or when the autonomy of participating

O. Boissier et al. (Eds.): ANIREM and OOOP 2005, LNCS 3913, pp. 81–98, 2006.

agents may have undesirable social consequences, the structuring of agent interactions may need to resort to regulation devices analogous to those that are practical in human affairs.

MAS literature has addressed the problem of structuring agent interactions from different approaches: coordination, agent communication languages, communication and interaction protocols, teams and coalitions, negotiation, institutions, organizations and norms. Sometimes these efforts have taken an agent-centric perspective in which the prevalent issues are how the agent receives, adopts or contravenes the conventions, while other works have taken a social perspective where the objective is the design of conventions that provoke the intended aggregate behavior of agents and the prevalent issues are those that affect the system components that are shared or used by participants, like the expressiveness of languages, effectiveness of interaction protocols, enforcement of commitments. The motivation of much of the MAS community's work along these lines has been theoretical, inspired by Logic, Game-Theory, (Economics) Mechanism Design or Sociology and Social Psychology. Nevertheless there has also been considerable work derived from applications of multiagent systems to domains like supply networks, auctions, virtual organizations or conflict resolution that address different forms of structuring or regulating agent interactions.

In this paper I will address the subject of regulating interactions in multiagent systems. I will look into the problem from a social perspective and will focus my discussion around one particular approach: electronic institutions. I will concern myself only with the empirical aspects involved in the development and use of electronic institutions, motivated by the real-world application of these devices. Although in this paper I will merely test the waters, my purpose is to throw some light on a significant but elusive subject that, I believe, deserves a systematic treatment.

In the next section I outline the generic notion of an electronic institution and then make explicit some compromises adopted to make such generic view operational. Next, I discuss three examples of actual electronic institutions whose features will allow me to outline, in Sec. 4, some empirical aspects involved in the development of electronic institutions.

2 Institutional Intuitions

The easiest way to describe electronic institutions is as the computational counterpart of traditional institutions. Traditional institutions are conventions that a group of agents follows in order to accomplish some socially agreed upon objective. Although we take institutions to be distinct from the agents that interact within them, it is not unusual to abuse language and identify an institution —the set of conventions— with an entity —a firm, company, organization— which is the warrant of those conventions ([5], p.5).[1] We can picture an institution as a nicely fenced plot in an open field. Things in the open field may be confuse and unpredictable, but inside the institution agents are able to play on a safe level ground.

---

[1] In keeping with this abuse of language we refer to the implementation of an electronic institution as an electronic institution.

Traditional —and electronic institutions— are used to regulate interactions where participants establish commitments and to facilitate that these commitments are upheld. It makes sense to institute some conventions if the establishment of commitments between participants is a process that is repeated with the same or different participants, but always under those same conventions. In that way participants are liberated of devising a process for establishing the commitments and concentrate on the decision-making tasks. The institutional conventions are devised so that those commitments can be established and fulfilled in an effective fashion and therefore participants be willing to submit to those conventions.

Institutions, in general terms, are established to facilitate effective interactions, and in order to do so they are devised to deal with a few complementary concerns, the most salient are:

- Establish the institutional conventions. So that these conventions have an objective reference that participants may invoke to understand the conventions, follow them, be accountable for their satisfaction and contend the wrongdoing of other participants.
- Assure permanence and stability of the conventions. In order that participant may hold sufficient certainty of the requirements and outcomes of their interactions and that they may expect and choose to participate on different opportunities without undue adjustment of their participation requirements.
- Enforce satisfaction of institutional commitments. So that all participants may rely and be held responsible for their institutional actions as far as the institutional conventions state.
- Guarantee accountability of institutional interactions. Be able to allocate risk and blame in an objective and effective manner. In most institutions, participants may be liable when they establish a commitment and if these participants are unreliable or even malevolent, there is risk involved that the institution is intended to allocate properly and limit damage effectively.
- Manage access and identity of participants. Validate that they satisfy the requirements of capability, resources of entitlement as long as they act within the institution, in order to be held accountable for their institutional actions.

From this intuitive description, it is not difficult to conceive electronic institutions as devices that facilitate on–line interactions: *coordination artifacts* that constitute —in Herbert Simon's engineering design image [8]— an interface between the internal rational decision-making capabilities of agents and the social effect of their interactions.

Two features of that description are readily apprehended and I will take for granted from now on: the fact that participants are willing and able to *interact* and that these participants may be *human or software agents*. However, two more aspects of that description need further discussion because they may be operationalized in different ways and give ground to electronic institutions of different flavors. The first subtle issue is what constitutes an interaction, the other is the way interactions are structured to achieve the shared or common social purpose.

Institutional Interactions and Constitutive Rules. What would a bare-bones interaction within an institution may be? I take it that if we think of humans interacting with software agents, or software agents interacting amongst themselves, in any significant way, the least one requires of any two participants that interact is that they exchange some sort of a *message* that is mutually *intelligible* to both of them.[2] Intelligible messages is all we need, provided intelligibility involves some communication conventions that entail syntactic compatibility and some ontology alignment so that, in particular, the message could satisfy presumable conditions and have foreseeable effects that are acknowledged by the speaker and the receiver of the message. To achieve intelligibility, electronic institutions ought to be virtual entities that *establish* –define and uphold– the shared communication conventions. In this sense the electronic institution will then be not only the set of communication conventions that regulate agent interactions, but also the warrant of the conventions that make messages intelligible.

In order to fulfill these functions electronic institutions need to institute a connection with the real world through some *constitutive rules*. Constitutive rules fix the socially shared meaning of messages by linking the utterance of illocutions within the institution with conditions and effects those messages have in the real world. Hence, institutional interactions are messages that comply with the conventions for interactions of the institution, but institutional interactions *count as* real–world interactions when participants are bound to their meaning and effects by the constitutive rules of the electronic institution where they participate.

Notice that in the previous paragraphs I have taken a strong dialogical stance by assuming that all institutional interactions are messages and only messages, however these messages do have a connection with the real world through the constitutive rules that make them count as true actions[3]. So, from now on, I will assume electronic institutions to contain a set of constitutive rules on one hand and, on the other, a set of interaction conventions that regulate institutional actions properly.

We may think of interaction conventions as a way of establishing the pragmatics of institutional illocutions, that is, what are the admissible messages, what their proper sequencing and, in general, what their pre and post–conditions are. We can also look at interaction conventions as sets of norms that institutional illocutions are bound to satisfy. In the first approach we may think of the institution as commitment-based interaction protocols, as structured dialogues or as some sort of workflow. In this case, the interaction conventions constrain the class of potential interactions to an acceptable subclass and determine how a

---

[2] Here I take "message" to be an ostensible manifestation (a string of characters, a coded signal, or movements) with an ostensible effect (a change of state in the systems or their environment).

[3] Nothing extraordinary here. Recall, for example, that a trial involves merely an exchange of statements that are linked to the purported criminal action, evidence, and derived actions. A death sentence, for example, is based on an institutionally valid sequence of illocutions and the prisoner's life ended by force of a constitutive rule

given interaction forces or prevents certain future interactions. From the normative perspective, an institution may be formally construed as some logical system whose components involve all the meta-normal resources involved in the issuance, adoption, compliance and enforcement of norms. In both cases we need to express a mixture of declarative and procedural requirements that may be expressed in different ways. The choice is made on pragmatic and formal factors like the ease of specification, the ease of communication and adoption of the conventions by participating agents, the completeness of the specification, its enforceability or the computational complexity of the formalism, or, of particular relevance for this paper, the implementation constraints.

3   Three Examples

The following three examples illustrate various empirical features that are pertinent for regulated MAS development.

3.1   Example 1: Compranet, a Public Procurement Institution

Compranet is the on-line public procurement system developed and managed by the Comptrollers Office –now part of the Ministry for Public Administration– of the Mexican Federal Government.[4] All Federal Government ministries, agencies, departments and offices that are entitled to perform any contracting or acquisition on their own and the publicly owned companies –like the very large national oil (PEMEX), electricity (CFE, CLyFC)— are, by law, required to use this system for all of their purchases, service contracting as well as all building and construction of public facilities contracting.[5]

The more significant motivations for instituting Compranet were transparency of government transactions, making information on demand and contract settlements readily available to all potential and actual participants, enabling convenient access of SME and international suppliers to the large federal market, lowering transaction costs and motivating the adoption of IT technology by SMEs. The system was conceived and a prototype designed in 1995, it was gradually deployed, starting in 1996 until it reached its full functionalities around 2002.

Description of the Compranet Institution. The system runs in a centralized location managed by the Comptroller's Office. Each time a purchasing agency starts a procurement process, a new procurement thread is opened in the central site. All processes follow essentially the same interaction protocol with minor variations in requirements and sometimes also in time. The protocol is comprehensive of the whole process. The CFP is posted in a public database and RFQs made available to paying participants who then may ask for clarifications of the RFQ conditions. These requests and the procurer's responses are

---

[4] http://www.compranet.gob.mx/
[5] Ley de Adquisiciones, Arrendamientos y Servicios del Sector Público. Out of convenience, many State and Municipal governments also use this system although they are not bound to this law.

made available to all participating suppliers. Bids may then be submitted electronically. Bids are kept secret until the contract is awarded, then the winning bid (only) is posted in a public database. The awarded contract is registered in the system and landmarks are registered and audited by the Comptroller's Office. The process lasts from one to three months depending on the purchasing modality. All interactions are asynchronous but subject to deadlines enforced by the system. Appeals follow also a due process that may involve the Comptroller's Office and may even force a new enactment of the procurement process. Each buying party may activate multiple processes and suppliers may simultaneously participate in as many processes as they wish. In every step of the process, electronic documents are issued by the corresponding parties and copies of those documents are kept in the system for appeals and auditing purposes. Compranet's main functions are outlined in Figure 1 The diagram on the left shows the preparatory process of procurement, from issuance of CFPs to the purchasing of the RFQ by supplier agents. The diagram on the right shows the ensuing, electronic bidding and contract awarding phases of the process.

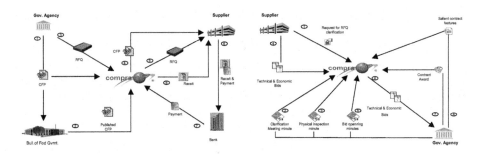

Fig. 1. The *Compranet* public procurement processes: (a) CFP and RFP cycle; (b) Electronic bid submission cycle

3.2   Example 2: MASFIT, On-line Fish Market Auctions

MASFIT (Multi Agent System for FIsh Trading) is a MAS-enabled electronic marketplace that allows buyers to bid on-line in different fish auctions simultaneously. The main motivation for the system is to expand the daily market of fresh coastal fish catches by increasing the number of potential buyers and by aggregating the offer of several local fish markets (cf. [1]).

MASFIT was a joint proposal of, on one side, a firm that provides the back–office systems to local and electromechanical technology for handling fish (weighting, labeling) and controlling the bidding clock and the the electomechanical devices for face-to-face bidding (buttons on a desk or infrared remote–control devices), AUTEC, and, on the other side, a consortium formed by the Office for Livestock and Fisheries of the Catalonian regional government and the *lonjas* (fish markets) of three different ports. The MAS technology was originally developed through an EU Take–up Action (IST-2000-28221) designed to profit from the

IIIIA's Fishmarket developments ([4, 7, 2]) and continues through a Spanish government grant involving AUTEC and the IIIA. There is a working system undergoing user adoption tests and commercial deployment is pending on AUTEC business model satisfaction.

Description of the MASFIT Institution. The MAS is subject to three design requirements:

1. That face-to-face bidding conditions of each local marketplace continue exactly as before, except for the possibility of the participation of remote buyers.
2. That on-line bidding follows exactly the same conventions —information flows, auctioneer, timing and interaction protocol— as face-to-face bidding.
3. That a remote buyer may participate simultaneously in all the fishmarkets that subscribe to MASFIT.

Because of condition 1, the auctioning protocols were already defined. All involve the same —dutch auction—conventions for bidding but have slight differences on admission and accounting procedures. The consortium creates a federation of markets but it still allows each market to have direct relations with its customers. Buyers will need to sign a contract and establish some guarantees to participate in any or all local markets. For human buyers in the actual *lonja* sites, the only difference from the current situation is that they may loose a round against a buyer that is not physically present in the auction house. . Remote buyers bid through a remote device (a PDA or some other web client), or software agents acting on their behalf. Each remote buyer may have as many buyer agents as he or she wants and these may participate in one or many *lonjas* simultaneously. Each buyer agent is activated in a virtual *lonja* where a governor (owned and controlled by the virtual *lonja*) is attached to it . That governor controls all information flows between the agent and the specific *lonjas* where the owner of that buying agent wants to bid. Buyer agents have access in real time to all the information that is institutionally becoming available and to historical market information. Figure 2 depicts the trading architecture.

The MASFIT system includes two important additional sevices for buyers: a training environment and an agent-builder toolbox. In the training environment a user may test and tailor his or her buyer agents using data from past auctions or the information that is being generated in current auctions. The agent-builder tool box facilitates the assembly of an agent shell that is capable of following the *lonja* conventions with a decision-making model developed by the owner of an agent. AUTEC also provides complete agents with different parametric decision-making models that human buyers may instantiate.

3.3 Example 3: Framework for EI-Enabled Information Systems for Organizations

This example refers to a work in progress ([6]. The general idea is to have a framework to develop and deploy corporate information systems (CIS) whose

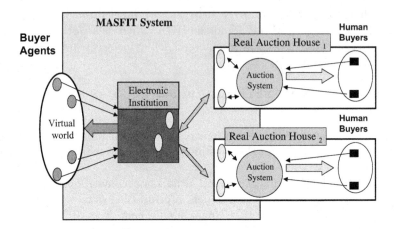

Fig. 2. MASFIT virtual auction federation. Traditional fish markets (right) allow human and software buyers to participate concurrently in simultaneous auctions.

operation is regulated by a prescriptive description of the way the organization is intended to function. The intuitions are rather simple: We take organizations to be groups of individuals that work together to achieve their shared goals the best way they can. Furthermore, we assume theses individuals should follow some *institutional* conventions that make their interactions structured and predictable. Our framework, then should allow us to connect the institutional conventions that prescribe the procedures as well as the guidelines staff members should follow in their everyday activities, with the way those activities actually happen as reflected in the organization's CIS.

The framework we are developing is outlined in Figure 3. Staff and client interactions are coordinated by an institutional convention which, in this example, is specified, enforced and enacted through the type of electronic institutions proposed by the IIIA (top layers of the diagram). Agent interactions, are mapped onto the CIS through a grounding language that establishes a correspondence between the linguistic interactions that take place in the institutional layer and actions that take place in the business domain (bottom layers).

The framework is designed for the development of actual corporate systems of significant complexity. These CIS involve the usual CIS components: data repositories, human users as well as business forms and procedures that are *agentified.* [6] Institutional conventions are captured as interaction protocols that take care of procedural conventions, and as in-house software agents whose behavior — specified and implemented by the organization— is subject to the organizational guidelines, policies or norms.

Figure 4 is an illustration of a typical organization, a hotel, whose activities are organized as a network of interrelated "business contexts". The illustration

---

[6] Simplifying things, we have conventional CIS components handled through front-end devices —that we build— that are reified as *server* agents.

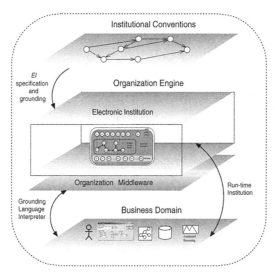

Fig. 3. EIO: An institutional description of an organization (top level) is implemented as an electronic institution that controls the operation of the organization's conventional information system (bottom level)

indicates how each business context is implemented as a standard institution that involves client and organizational agents that act on behalf of those users of the CIS, plus server agents that translate institutional illocutions in terms of the CIS components (users, forms, databases, business rules, ...) and actions (database updates, PDA messages, procedure executions, ...).

4   A Timid Proposal

I propose to look into three "dimensions" that involve the design decisions I have found most significant in the development of electronic institutions that are intended for use. The rationale for choice is that they are closely linked to the concerns of institutions and to the type of conventions electronic institutions implement that I mentioned in Section 2. Moreover, I believe these dimensions apply also to regulated multiagent systems in general and are peculiar to them in the sense that they are not equally significant for other types of MAS applications or conventional IS development.

It is worth mentioning here that the design of electronic institutions, and regulated MAS, is in practice a matter of organizational design [3], and as such involves engineering and design technologies, methodological approaches and validation assessments that are part of that discipline. My remarks will take them for granted.

4.1   Grounding

This dimension is concerned with the relation between the actions that take place within the institution and the relation they have with the real world. How

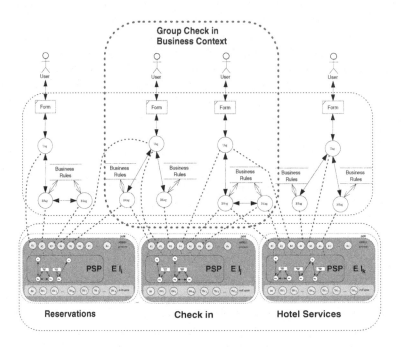

Fig. 4. EI-enabled corporate information system as a federation of electronic institutions each corresponding to the business units of the corporation

institutional actions represent, correspond and get to count as legitimate actions in the world, i.e. how to *establish* the constitutive conventions of an electronic institution

It is worth distinguishing two types of grounding, the first is legitimating the institution, i.e. making it legitimate or, more plainly, making it exist in the world. The other type of grounding is achieved by establishing a working correspondence between entities that are involved in institutional actions, within the institution, and the entities of the real world that should affect and be affected through institutional actions. The first involves, usually some constitutional act like a contract between participants, a public charter for the institution or a legal regulation that declares the achievement of a legitimate status —in the actual social world— of the institution and the commitments established therein. The second type involves the establishment of a sort of isomorphism between the language of the institution and the application domain where the institution applies.

Our three examples provide good illustration of different grounding mechanisms.

Compranet was created as an electronic institution to support the actual compliance with a law. It came to exist as an act of authority from the office in charge of enforcing and interpreting the law that regulates public procurement in the Federal Government. In fact, once Compranet became operational, the regulations that determined the procedures involved in public procurement were rewritten to be a textual description of a functional specification of the Compranet sytem. Those regulations made precise the correspondence between institutional actions and the real world, by stating, for instance, the conditions that a company needed to fulfill in order to participate in any procurement contract, how RFP should be paid, what were the requirements for a valid "electronic bid" or how to appeal an award resolution.

In MASFIT constitution comes about through a contract that binds the technology supplier and the *lonjas*, on one side and another contract between the *lonjas* and the participants on the other. The first contract makes the virtual institution become the actual regulator and enforcer of the conventions for on-site trading as well as remote on–line trading. The other contracts make the trading regulations applicable to participants. The first contract establishes the ontological and procedural grounding that translate virtual exchanges into real exchanges. The second agreement guarantees that both parties will be liable.

Notice that the MASFIT contracts need to be concerned with very concrete matters like setting up guarantees to cover misbehaviors of different sorts in order to make the grounding work. For instance, the *lonja* establishes the obligation to pay the seller every item sold in an auction and to deal with the eventuality of a defaulting buyer, the *lonja* falls back on a credit line —or some escrow mechanism— that buyers need to establish when signing their corresponding contract with the *lonja*. Likewise the technology supplier commits to a certain level of service and some penalties in case of system malfunction, that may for instance be underwritten in an insurance policy.

The case of EIO is of a different nature. The company owns the institution and "owns" the staff that is supposed to work under the institutional conventions. Grounding in this case involves the obvious constitutional act of making the system operational but the isomorphism between institutional actions and activities in the world takes a very characteristic form. First note that grounding is in fact made not in the *physical* world properly but in the *virtual* world of the corporate information system on which the company operates. The links between the CIS and the real world are the ones we are familiar with and do not require further comment, but the link between the institutional conventions and the CIS involves an ontology alignment between illocutionary language terms and CIS entities and the instrumentalization of the institutional actions catalogue into functionalities of the CIS (e.g. Database diagrams correspond to constants and relations in the EI; functions —like making a payment— correspond to table look-ups, execution of business rules and updating database registers).

An important concern in the design of an electronic institution is —as with traditional ones— to determine the interplay of interests involved in the agents' interactions and the proper allocation of responsibility and control that such interplay requires. It is essentially a matter of choosing appropriate checks and balances to make the interplay conducive to the stated objectives of the institution. It is also a matter of deciding what to make an institutional convention and how.

In EIO the company that owns the CIS that is regulated by the EI is the the same company that defines, deploys and runs the EI. The choice of conventions and their enforcement mechanisms is made by the same company that will abide by them. The choice of conventions and their enforcement mechanisms is precisely a matter of institutional design, in classical terms, that the designer of the company undertakes in order to shape everyday activities to better serve the company needs and in the case of EIO the chosen checks and balances, departmental structure, lines of authority, decision guidelines and standard procedures *are* the conventions that define the EI. The EI is just making the normative specification becoming operational.

The case of Compranet is quite different. The EI facilitates the interactions of buyers and sellers and is in fact an independent third party that guarantees fair play and ideally contributes to make the market more effective. Consequently, fairness and effectiveness are the leading design features. In Compranet, for example, the choice of having a unique centralized procurement clearinghouse over a distributed procurement mechanism –a little Compranet in every government agentcy– was to better serve the objective of guaranteeing that the public procurement market was fair and reliable. In that light, the choice of a single trading room housed at the Comptroller's Office signaled its ostensible unquestionable authority for that market. In addition, although centralization concentrated risk of technical and political failure, it greatly facilitated the adoption of the institutional practices and, in fact, their gradual deployment and uniform applicability. Both aspects make the third party strong *vis a vis* the sometimes conflictive objectives of buyers and sellers, and specially *vis a vis* a corruption-prone market culture.

MASFIT is an interesting case where the technology supplier creates a virtual institution that is a market-maker, an independent third party between buyers and sellers whose ownership is shared by the technology supplier, and a consortium of the regional government with the *lonjas* –which in turn are owned by the fishermen guilds and hence twice-removed from the sellers. However, the same technology supplier may enable buyers with *buyer agents* that perform aptly in the virtual institution thus blurring the border between the independent market-maker and the buyer. Notice then that the stakeholders in the fish trade have different relationshipos with the technology supplier who is on one hand in charge of enforcing the conventions, and on the other facilitating the participation of buyers through a technology that would be hard to develop by them but that unless the buyers have it they could hardly profit from the advantages of the virtual institution over the traditional *lonjas*.

4.2   Degree of Agentification

The fact that agents are present in one form or another in an electronic institution is again a matter of institutional design in the sense that agents are a component that is brought into the design in order to achieve certain functionalities or realize certain advantages, but that as other components the use of agents needs to be managed in order to achieve the intended benefits without undesirable side effects. The characteristic features that agents may bring into the institutional design are persistence, automated rationality and ubiquity. They need to be assessed against their effect on reliability of the interactions, identity or entitlement of the participants, and their competency as suggested before, and upon this assessment decide where, to what extent and in what capacity agents are conducive to a better articulation of interactions in the application. By degree of agentification I want to refer to those choices, the type and level of functionalities that is delegated to software agents in the system and to the way such delegation is managed in the electronic institution. I hope the examples clarify what I mean.

I have used the notion of electronic institution as a rather generic coordination artifact without committing to many specific features. In particular I have not required, nor assumed, the need of software agents anywhere. Not as a constitutive component of the institution, not as participants. Thus I am confident to talk about Compranet as an electronic institution even if it didn't involve any agents whatsoever. In fact it doesn't assume the need of software agents in its design. It was designed to support them and some care was taken in order to guarantee that all institutional interactions could be performed by software agents but that is as far as the "agentification" of Compranet went. It was only *agent–compatible*. In Compranet no agent is involved n the operation of the institution, although agents may be —are being— used by suppliers to find interesting CFPs, to analyze competitors or market behavior, and by authorities to audit contracts, keep track of incidents and to gather evidence of punishable misbehavior.

The case of MASFIT is another extreme. The federation of *lonjas* is accessible only through software agents that represent the human buyers. In MASFIT human buyers may still bid in a physical *lonja* exactly as they used too, and they may get to participate in the different physical *lonjas* in the same circumvented and limited way they used to: having a partner present in another *lonja* to bid on their behalf and using a telephone to coordinate with that partner. Notice that, from the buyers perspective, the real benefits of the virtual market are realized to their full potential when software agents are making bidding decisions autonomously for two main reasons. First, because a human user may deploy software agents that can participate simultaneously in all the *lonja* according to whatever buying strategy the buyer delegates on them –notably strategies that involve real-time information from other *lonja* and coordination of the buyer agents; second because those software agents may profit from all the information that is available in the market whose volume and speed is excessive for human users and are able to exploit it in whatever automated reasoning technology their owner puts in their decision-making strategies. On the market-maker side agents are also essential as internal "staff" to govern buyer agents, manage bidder's interactions, access to the virtual auction floors and on-line clearing of bids and keeping track of the commitments incurred by the totality of agents belonging to each buyer. MASFIT is *agent-based* in a very strong sense: it is feasible only if software agents are involved.

While in Compranet agentification is dispensable, in MASFIT it is essential. The case of EIO is still a different type of MAS agentification, it is *agent-pervasive*. You start with a human organization and a traditional CIS that supports its operation, and you end–up with agents all over: agents that mediate interactions with external users, agents that encapsulate the decision–making functions of the organization's staff, agents that mediate the interactions human staff users of the CIS still need to perform and, finally, agents that manage the resources of the CIS, that is, server agents that interact with CIS components in order to get or pass information to a data base, activate a business rule or a standard procedure.

4.3 Autonomy

In the previous subsection I purposely left autonomy out of the characteristic features of agents that need to be assessed for the design of an electronic institutions. I left autonomy out because, I believe, it deserves a more systematic treatment along two aspects that are fundamental in electronic institution design: the openness of the electronic institution and the way institutional conventions are enforced.

Openness can be understood in two ways. First, as the extent of requirements imposed on participants to join an institutions, second as an indication of how structured or rigid are the conventions the institution upholds. Evidently, both have to do with the flexibility agents may or need to have in order to participate in a given institution and to a certain extent to the type of autonomy they are entitled or forced to exercise.

MASFIT is a good example of a rather generous openness of access and highly inflexible interaction conventions. In MASFIT any potential buyer is admitted as long as he or she provides good enough guarantees to cover his or her purchases and accept other conventional contractual obligations. Once the human buyer is accepted he or she may deploy in the federated market any (external) software agent of whatever structure or composition he or she wishes. No requirements are imposed on the agent's capabilities, truthfulness, livelihood, benevolence and none is validated in the institution, thus in the first sense of the term, that electronic institution is completely open. However, the external buyer agent has no choice over the way it would go about buying fish, it has to abide strictly by the MASFIT rules. The institutional interaction conventions in MASFIT are explicit and comprehensive and the buyer agent is only allowed to utter admissible utterances at admissible moments. The contents of the buyer agent utterances are up to the agent's internals and the institution has no business in determining how or why a given utterance has such or such content. MASFIT either admits it or refuses it, but if MASFIT admits it the buyer agent is held to the commitments entailed by that utterance in a strict unavoidable manner. The autonomy of the buyer agent is limited only to its choice of parameters for the admissible illocutions it decides to make. And that is quite enough for an auction market.

In the Compranet case the situation is similar but less definite. Access to any particular procurement process is restricted to suppliers who have first documented their personality, entitlements, pertinence and competitiveness in the thorough manner dictated by the Law of Acquisitions and its associated regulations, once that process is completed the admissible suppliers need to buy their right to submit a bid by paying for the RFQ of the specific procurement event. Once these —grounding conditions— are met, the supplier may participate by following the legally established protocol. The protocol conventions are explicit but are open to adjustment and interpretation to a certain extent. Institutional actions are electronic documents that register bids, clarifications, protocol adjustments (time-schedules, updated conditions), award resolutions, signed contracts, certifications of termination and acceptance, etc. All may be performed electronically and the procedure doesn't impose any condition on the agents rationality in performing those actions, only in their preconditions and effects. Compranet as a third party in the process keeps a register of all institutional actions and as I will comment below, sees to it that commitments are satisfied. Hence, the institution is rather open to access and the statement and satisfaction of interaction conventions is not as explicit and inflexible as MASFIT.

The EIO model leans towards the opposite balance. It is mostly closed in the sense that many interactions involve agents that are owned by the organization, and it is somewhat open in the sense that the organizational staff does have contact with external agents whose motivation and worthiness are opaque to the organization. For the organization, those external agents are black boxes that are dealt with like buyer agents are dealt with in MASFIT: each external agent is governed by an internal agent that controls all information flows in and out of that agent and imposes on it the interaction conventions of the organization in a strict manner. However, having control over internal agents allows the designer to use autonomy in a rather fruitful way. The point of having a prescriptive description of the organization in the top-level of the EIO model is to govern interactions of the members or the organization in such a way that all participants are aware of what is expected of them and do what they are expected to do in *foreseeable situations*. In practice, this means that stable institutional conventions govern explicitly procedures and also some of the decision-making processes some staff agents are endowed with. Evidently there is a problem of granularity, the detail with which procedural conventions need to be expressed is related to the complexity of the process, its variability and the amount of local decision-making needed to make the conventions work. But notice that having control of the deliberative components of staff agents allows the designer to rely on their autonomy by specifying simpler standard procedures and program, in some autonomous staff agents, the decision-making capabilities to contend with non-standard situations *institutionally*, that is, according to the prescriptive definition of the organization. These individual decision-making capabilities can in fact be considerable since nothing prevents the designer from making the statement of the convention for a case —standard or not— in a way that prescribes —declaratively— the intended final outcome and leaves the —procedural— implementation up to the intervening staff agents that have been endowed with sufficient knowledge and dexterity to carry out the task in question.

Enforcement of Conventions. While the EIOs model can take advantage of the autonomy of its staff agents, inside the institution autonomy is nil for all external agents. Likewise in MASFIT. In both cases, that is a significant design decision. In both cases, the explicit definition of the interaction conventions and their strict enforcement is necessary in order to assure reliability, fairness, trust and accountability *vis a vis* their clients. Although in Compranet trust, reliability, fairness, accountability and transparency are also relevant design features, the enforcement of conventions is more discretional. The reason is the way constitutive conventions are established. MASFIT and the EIO are autarchic: Their constitutive conventions legitimize a social space where they define the rules, they control them and they let agents participate in that space if and only if those agents are willing to abide by the rules and, notably, MASFIT and the EIO are capable of strictly enforcing those rules. Strict enforcement is possible because the rules are explicit, and because of the way interaction conventions are implemented in that private space, their observance is mandatory and infractions are impossible. Through the constitutive conventions, MASFIT and the EIO have the authority, capability and power to enforce interaction conventions universally and strictly.

By contrast, Compranet is legitimized through an implementation that institutes only very basic procedural interactions, leaving participants enough leeway in their compliance of the conventions that are declaratively instituted by law and practice. Compranet as an electronic institution leaves considerable autonomy to participants at many stages of the process and its interaction conventions are not explicit enough to prevent discretional interpretation. Compranet solves this problem through two classical mechanisms self-enforcement and authority. Self-enforcement is achieved by the fact that pertinent information is made public (transparency), that supplier and buyer interests are opposed, by having checks and balances among the roles that different buyer staff agents perform and by establishing significant penalties for misbehavior. Authority is centralized and final, has access to every institutional commitment, resolves any interpretation disagreements and has power to impose sanctions swiftly.

5   Closing Remarks

The three examples I discussed are representative of a variety of applications that regulated MAS may have. In particular, the highly structured model behind MASFIT is adequate for applications that are heavy in individual agent's decision-making but light in interaction, however high the liability of participants may be. Applications of this sort are typical in electronic commerce, customer complaints management and TRAMITES, the model is also convenient for classical mechanism design. Compranet is a token of due processes, whose purpose is to channel a complex agreement or coordination process into a manageable

—potentially intricate— sequence of standardized interaction stages that facilitate fair and objective conditions for the parties involved. Common examples of these processes arise for instance in conflict resolution, judiciary and legislative practice or in the execution of publicly sponsored programs. The EIO model is being developed to apply to large corporate information systems and should be applicable to recursively decomposable complex systems (i.e. that are decomposable into a few similar subsystems of less complexity, and these decomposable in turn). Hence, hospitals, retail chains and franchises, emergency response organizations are natural applications of it.

The comments I made around the three examples show how tentative and unsystematic my understanding of the subject still is. Nevertheless I hope that they serve to facilitate the establishment of a rudimentary set of distinctions and considerations that may be beneficial for the development of applied regulated agent systems.

Although I made my remarks around the notion of electronic institution I believe that most of what I said applies to other ways of regulating MAS because the main concerns of an institution that I postulated are also in the domain of most regulation of agent interactions. Notwithstanding this intended generality, I did persist in holding to a single major bias along my discussion: I have assumed that interactions among agents are repeated and structured around rather stable processes. It is a justified bias in the sense that (as stated above) it is appropriate for a large number of applications and also in the sense that is has proven feasible to implement a set of tools that have been adequate for a variety of applications. Nevertheless, the assumption imposes regulatory features that are unnecessary in some cases and unacceptable in others. I trust it can be weakened by focusing on the essential features required for peer to peer interaction I mentioned in Section 2.

When addressing the more general problem of regulating interactions in open systems we may profit by holding another metaphor that frees us from a building a neat enclosure and allows us to regulate directly the essential communication and commitment making assumptions that permit agents to interact "in the wild". So far we have learned how to "fence the open fields" we may now consider "hanging the bell on the cat".

Acknowledgements

The research reported in this paper is partially supported by the Spanish MEC project Web-i (2) (TIC-2003-08763-C02-01).

References

1. Guifré Cuní, Marc Esteva, Pere Garcia, Eloi Puertas, Carles Sierra, and Teresa Solchaga. Masfit: Multi-agent systems for fish trading. In *16th European Conference on Artificial Intelligence (ECAI 2004)*, Valencia, Spain, August 2004.
2. Marc Esteva. *Electronic Institutions: from specification to development.* Number 19 in IIIA Monograph Series. PhD Thesis, 2003.

3. James G. March and Herbert A. Simon. *Organizations*. John Wiley and sons, New York, USA., 1958.
4. Pablo Noriega. *Agent-Mediated Auctions: The Fishmarket Metaphor*. Number 8 in IIIA Monograph Series. PhD Thesis, 1998.
5. Douglass C. North. *Institutions, Institutional change and economic performance*. Cambridge Universisy press, 40 west 20th Street, New York, NY 10011-4211, USA, 1990.
6. Armando Robles and Pablo Noriega. A framework for building EI-enabled intelligent organizations using MAS technology. In *Proceedings of the Third European Conference on Multiagent Systems. EUMAS 2005*, page 344354, 2005.
7. Juan Antonio Rodriguez-Aguilar. *On the Design and Construction of Agent-mediated Electronic Institutions*. Number 14 in IIIA Monograph Series. PhD Thesis, 2003.
8. Herbert A. Simon. *The Sciences of the Artificial*. MIT Press, Cambridge, MA, 1969.

Specifying and Analysing Agent-Based Social Institutions Using Answer Set Programming

Owen Cliffe*, Marina De Vos, and Julian Padget

Department of Computer Science
University of Bath
Bath, United Kingdom
{occ, mdv, jap}@cs.bath.ac.uk

Abstract. In this paper we discuss the use of the Answer Set Programming paradigm for representing and analysing specifications of agent-based institutions. We outline the features of institutions we model, and describe how they are translated into ASP programs which can then be used to verify properties of the specifications. We demonstrate the effectiveness of this approach through the institutions of property and exchange.

1 Introduction

Most human interactions are governed by conventions or rules of some sort, having their origin in society (emergent) or the laws (codification of emergent rules) that society has developed. Thus we find that all human societies, even the least developed ones, have some kind of social constraints upon their members in order to structure their relations and simplify their interactions. Some of these constraints are quite informal (taboos, customs, traditions) while some others are formally defined (written laws, constitutions).

The economist and Nobel laureate Douglas North has analysed the effect of this corpora of constraints, that he refers as to *institutions*, on the behaviour of human organisations (including human societies). North states in [10] that institutional constraints ease human interaction (reducing the cost of this interaction), shaping choices and making outcomes foreseeable. By the creation of these constraints, either the organisations and the interactions they require can grow in complexity while interaction costs can even be reduced. Having established these institutional constraints, every competent participant in the institution will be able to act—and expect others to act—according to a list of rights, duties, and protocols of interaction.

Within the field of multi-agent systems there is a view, which we share, that the social consequences of real-world (communicative) interactions among agents may be captured through an explicit *social semantics* [25, 17], these social semantics give an objective description of how an agents' actions in a society may necessarily lead to to the creation of *social states* which in turn may effect the consequences of agents' future interactions on other social states. We take the view that a particular social institution

---

* This work was partially supported by the European Fifth Framework Programme under the grant IST-2001-37004 (WASP).

O. Boissier et al. (Eds.): ANIREM and OOOP 2005, LNCS 3913, pp. 99–113, 2006.

can be represented through the description of the types of social state which may created by agents participating in that institution, and the social rules which cause those states to be created.

Institutions can be applied to the description of a large class of social systems, operating at varying levels of abstraction, from highly abstract notions such as that of property to more concrete ones such as exchange scenarios and protocols. Additionally institutions may be related to one another in a variety of ways, with one making reference to, or depending on another. Our intention is to make it possible to specify a variety of these institution independently and in the case that two institutions are related, to make those relationships explicit.

By encoding institutions as declarative specifications it becomes possible to computationally reason about the consequences of "real world" actions such as message exchanges on social states, allowing agents participating in an institution to take an account of events up to given point in time and to execute the specification in order to determine the social state at that time, this then allows agents to reason about the social effects of future actions.

As with any complex specification language the potential for errors in institution specifications is high, and as such it is highly desirable to have a reasoning framework in which instances of specifications can be animated, and the presence of various desirable properties verified.

In this paper we report on our initial experiments in capturing some of the concepts above using the Answer Set Programming (ASP) paradigm, we show how institution specifications may be written as answer set programs, and reasoned about using an answer set solver.

Answer set programming formalised as $AnsProlog^*$[4] is a modern logic programming system, designed for semantic clarity, efficient implementation and ease of use for knowledge representation and declarative problem solving. It has been under development for the past 15 years and as well as an extensive body of theoretical work, a number of mature implementations [11, 23] exist.

ASP has a variety of powerful and useful features supporting non-monotonic reasoning, handling of multiple possible world views, both classical and epistemic negation and the ability to characterise and reason about partial and incomplete information, it is these capabilities we aim to exploit in modelling and reasoning about institutions.

2   Why Answer Set Programming?

ASP is a powerful and intuitive non-monotonic logic programming language for modelling reasoning and verification tasks. One common question asked of researchers working on non-monotonic logic programming systems such as ASP is 'Prolog has been around for many years and is a mature technology, why not just use that?'. The short answer is that Prolog has a number of limitations both in concept and design that make it unsuitable for many knowledge representation and 'real world' reasoning tasks. As with comparing any languages or language paradigms the key issues here are suitability and ease of expression in the problem domain in question.

Negation is problematic in logic programming languages and Prolog is no exception. A variety of different mechanisms for computing when the negation of a predicate is true and a variety of different intuitions of what this means have been proposed[8]. The most common approach is to compute negation as failure, i.e. $not(p)$ is true if p cannot be proved using the current program; and to characterise this as classical negation i.e. every proposition is either true or false and cannot be both. This combination creates a problem referred to as the closed world assumption when using Prolog to model real world reasoning. By equating negation as failure with classical negation anything that cannot be proven to be true is known to be false, essentially assuming that everything that is known about the world is contained in the program.

In contrast the semantics used in ASP naturally give rise to two different forms of negation, negation as failure and constraint-based negation. Negation as failure, (i.e. we cannot prove p to be true) is characterised as epistemic negation, (i.e. we do not know p to be true). Constraint-based negation introduces constraints that prevent certain combinations of atoms from being simultaneously true in any answer set. This is characterised as classical negation as it is possible to prevent a and $\neg a$ both being simultaneously true, a sufficient condition for modelling classical negation. This is a significant advantage in some reasoning tasks as it allows reasoning about incomplete information, and is supported by the intuition that "I do not know that P is true" (auto-epistemic negation) and "I know that P is not true" (classical negation) are fundamentally different. Critically the closed world assumption is not present in ASP, as negation as failure is not associated with classical negation.

One key difference with Prolog is that the semantics of ASP clearly give rise to multiple possible world views in which the program is consistent. The number and composition of these varies with the program. Attempting to model the same ideas in Prolog can lead to confusion as the multiple possible views may manifest themselves differently dependant on the query asked. In ASP terms Prolog would answer a query on a as true if there is at least one answer set in which a is true. However there is no notion of in which answer set this is true. Thus a subsequent query on b might also return true, but without another query it would not be possible to infer if a and b could be simultaneously true.

3   Answer Set Semantics

There is a large body of literature about ASP but it is largely unknown in the agents community, for in-depth coverage see [4]. For the sake of this paper we provide a brief overview.

$AnsProlog^*$ uses a language that has *terms* which are inductively closed. A *term* is a variable or a *constant*. An *atom* is denoted $a(t_1, \ldots, t_n)$, where a is a predicate of arity n and $t_1, \ldots, t_n$, its arguments, are terms. A term or an atom is called *ground* if it does not contain any variables. A literal is an atom $a(t_1, \ldots, t_n)$ or its negation $\neg a(t_1, \ldots, t_n)$, where $\neg$ should be read in the classical sense (i.e. $a(t_1, \ldots, t_n)$ is proven to be false). An extended literal is a literal L or **not** L with **not** being negation as failure (L cannot be proven to be true).

An $AnsDatalog^*$ program is made up of a series of *rules*. Each rule has the form:
$$L_0 \leftarrow L_1, \ldots, L_n, \textbf{not } L_{n+1}, \ldots, \textbf{not } L_m .$$

Where L_0 is a *literal* or $\perp$ and L_i for $i \in [1, m]$ are literals. L_0 is the *head* of the rule, denoted $H(r)$ for rule r and $\{L_1, \ldots, L_m\}$ is the *body*, denoted $B(r)$. The intuition for this rule is that if all of $L_1, \ldots, L_n$ are known and none of $L_{n+1}, \ldots, L_m$ are known then L_0 is considered to be known (in the case that L_0 is $\perp$, this indicates a contradiction).

When speaking about the status of rules with respect to a given set of ground literals the terms *applicable* and *applied* are used. A rule is said to be applicable with respect to a set if all of $L_1, \ldots, L_n$ and none of $L_{n+1}, \ldots, L_m$ are in the set. It is applied if it is applicable and L_0 is also in the set.

In order for a program to obtain its full semantics, all variables that appear in the program need to be replaced by values. This process is called *grounding*. The values that a variable can take are defined by the ground terms in your program. Having these, a *ground instance* of a rule may be obtained by replacing each variable symbol by one of these values. The *ground version* of a program is the set of all ground instances of all the rules in the program.

In this paper we shall use the characterisation of answer set semantics given by [16]. This is divided into two sections, the semantics of ground programs that do not contain negation and a semantic criterion and reduct for removing negation. Ground programs without negation as failure (**not**)(also referred to as $AnsDatalog^{-\mathbf{not}}$) each have at most one answer set. It can be obtained from the logical closure of the rule set, i.e. starting with the facts (rules that have no body and are thus not dependent on anything), recursively build a set of anything that can be concluded using a rule who's body is in the set.

To remove negation the Gelfond-Lifschitz reduct (or transformation)[15] is used, working with respect to a set of ground literals S:

– Removing every rule that contains **not** p in the body if $p \in S$
– Removing all remaining negative literals (i.e. **not** q) from the rules

The answer sets of the program are the sets of literals S such that S is the answer set of the reduced program.

In short the answer sets of a program can be thought of as all of the possible world views that can be supported by the rules. For example, program: P:

$$\{a \leftarrow b; c \leftarrow \mathbf{not}\ d, a;\ d \leftarrow \mathbf{not}\ c; b\ ; e \leftarrow d\}$$

has two answer sets $\{a, b, c\}$ and $\{a, b, d, e\}$. When reduced with respect to $\{a, b, c\}$, only one rule is removed resulting the program:

$$\{a \leftarrow b\ ;\ c \leftarrow a\ ;\ b\ ;\ e \leftarrow d\}$$

which has the answer set $\{a, b, c\}$ (thus making it an answer set of P). Note that e is not included in the answer set of the reduced program as there is no way of concluding d and so the rule giving e cannot be used. On the other hand if P is reduced by $\{a, b, e\}$ then the following program is obtained:

$$\{a \leftarrow b\ ;\ c \leftarrow a\ ;\ d\ ;\ b\ ;\ e \leftarrow d\}$$

which has the answer set $\{a, b, c, d, e\}$, which is not the same as the set used to perform the reduct and thus not an answer set of P. Notice that each answer set is a set of literals in which every rule in a program is either applied or not applicable. The converse is not true: a set of literals that makes every rule in a program not applicable or applied is not necessarily an answer set; consider the set $\{a, b, c, e\}$ and the program P.

Algorithms and implementations for obtaining answer sets of (possibly un-ground) logic programs are referred to as *answer set solvers*. The most popular and widely used solvers are DLV[11] and Smodels[23] which we use for the development of this paper.

4 Specification of Agent-Based Social Institutions

The foundation of our approach revolves around the descriptions of *institutional states*, and how these evolve over time. We define an institutional state as a set of *institutional facts* (cf. the definition of institutional fact in philosophy [19]) which may be held to be true at given point in time. These facts may be broken down into *institutional domain facts*, which are dependant on the institution being modelled (such as "A owns something" in our example below), and *normative facts* which are common to all specifications, which may be classified as follows.

Institutional Power. We incorporate the notion of explicit institutional power (based on the formalisation in [20]) this may be summarised as the capability of an agent to bring about a change in some facts in the institutional state. We do not represent the power to change institutional facts directly, instead we allow institutional facts which describe agents' ability to perform empowered *institutional actions*, (see below). In this case power separates meaningful (empowered) actions, which may have an effect, from unempowered (meaningless) actions.

Permission. This describes an agent's ability to perform some institutional action without sanction. Each permission fact captures the property that an agent is allowed to perform a given empowered institutional action. If an agent performs an empowered institutional action, and that action is not permitted, then a violation occurs with respect to that agents behaviour.

Obligation. Obligation facts are modelled as the dual of permission and are targeted towards a particular agent. We draw on the the formalism for obligations with explicit deadlines described in [14] where each obligation is associated with a corresponding deadline (this is is similar to Singh's formalisation of conditional commitment in [25]). In this paper we limit the obligations to those of the form $O_A(done(\alpha) \preceq \delta)$ where α is some action and δ is some deadline, which may be read as "Agent A is obliged to have done action α before deadline δ".

Violation. Violation facts model the consequence of an agent either performing an action for which they did not have permission or not performing an action they were obliged to do before the deadline state of that obligation was reached. At present we do not model the effect of sanctions or an agent's ability to recover from violation.

Within our specifications we define a number of abstract *institutional action* descriptions, each of these notionally associates the satisfaction of some conditions in the current institutional and/or world state (such as the issuing of an utterance) with some consequences on the institution state. Actions are said to be have been *performed* by an agent if it caused these conditions to be met , and *validly performed* if the action was performed and the agent was empowered to do perform the action. In order to capture relationships between institutions we also allow an action's consequences to explicitly cause performance of an action in another institution.

Finally, the operational semantics of a specification are given by a set of *social constraints* which describe how institutional facts may be determined and evolve over time. Constraints may describe static declarative dependencies between institutional facts (such as "If an agent is empowered to perform an action then they are also permitted to perform that action") and causal rules which describe the effects of validly performed actions, such as "An obligation to pay before some timeout is caused by the valid performance of a buy action".

5   Expressing Institution Specifications in ASP

We express institution specifications as a set of ASP rules which describe possible values for each institutional fact at a given instance of time. The general form of these rules for determining the value of a fact of type f with parameters $Fp_1, \ldots, Fp_n$ at time I is as follows:

$$f(Fp_1, \ldots, Fp_n, I) \leftarrow cons_1(\ldots, I), \ldots cons_n(\ldots, I).$$

Where $cons_1, \ldots, cons_n$ are atoms (denoting the of state of some institutional facts at time I) which must hold true at time I. We express change in the value of institutional facts using a *frame rule* of the form:

$$f(Fp_1, \ldots, Fp_n, I + 1) \leftarrow cons_1(\ldots, I), \ldots cons_n(\ldots, I).$$

Where $cons_1 \ldots, cons_n$ are atoms which must hold in the previous state (such as the occurrence of an action or, the value of one or more institutional states). In some cases we wish the value of some institutional fact to have *inertia* that is it should stay the same in the next state, unless something causes it to stop holding, we express inertia using classical negation as follows:

$$f(Fp_1 \ldots, Fp_n, I + 1) \leftarrow f(Fp_1 \ldots, Fp_n, I), \text{not } \neg f(Fp_1 \ldots, Fp_n, I + 1).$$

Which states that f holds in the next state, if it held in the previous state and we cannot show that it does not hold in the next state. A corollary of this is that inertial facts must be terminated by causal rules of the form $\neg f(Fp_1 \ldots, Fp_n, I) \leftarrow \ldots$.

Institutional Actions: Each action description (denoting the possible performance of an institutional action) is represented in ASP by a set of atoms of the form[1]:

$iact(actType(Ap_1, \ldots, Ap_n))$

Where $actType(Ap_1, \ldots, Ap_n)$ denotes an action type and its parameters, which may refer to agents, or objects in the domain of the specification.

We represent the occurrence of an institutional action at a given time with a set of atoms of the form: $iact\_happened(Agent, IAct, I)$ meaning $Agent$ has performed

---

[1] Note that in this and subsequent examples we use the symbolic function extension to conventional ASP syntax; $iact(actType(X, Y, Z))$ is equivalent to there being a set of atoms $iact(\alpha)$ with α ranging over $X \times Y \times Z$ for all grounded values of X, Y and Z.

the necessary conditions for $IAct$ to have occurred at time I (Note that the effects of $IAct$ are not performed unless $Agent$ was also empowered to perform the action (see institutional power below)).

Institutional Power: Power is modelled through a set of atoms of the form: $pow(Agent, IAct, I)$ which state that a given agent $Agent$ has the power to enact institutional action $IAct$ at time I. Power atoms are used to determine when performance institutional action is considered to be valid (i.e. has some institutional effect), this fact is recorded through atoms of the form

$valid\_act\_happened(Agent, IAct)$

these atoms are inferred using the following rule:

$valid\_act\_happened(Agent, IAct, I) \leftarrow$
   $iact\_happened(Agent, IAct, I), pow(Agent, IAct, I).$

Which states that at a given time, if an agent causes the conditions for some institutional action $IAct$ to be met at time I, and that action was empowered for that agent, then a valid occurrence of $IAct$ action occurred.

Permission and Violation: Permission is represented in a similar way to power as a set of atoms of the form: $permi(Agent, IAct, I)$.

The presence of permission entails the possibility for violation and violations are modelled as a set of atoms of the form $viol(Agent, I)$ indicating that $Agent$ is in a state of violation at time I. Violation atoms (in the case of performing an action which is not permitted (see obligation with deadlines, below)) are determined using the following causal rule:

$viol(Agent, I + 1) \leftarrow$
   $valid\_act\_happened(Agent, IAct, I), \text{not } permi(Agent, IAct, I).$

which states that at time $I + 1$ agent is in violation if it validly performed action $IAct$ at time I and it was not permitted to do so at time I.

Obligation and Deadlines: Each deadline is declared with an atom of the form $deadline(Deadline)$. Deadlines expire when some deadline condition is satisfied, a fact which is modelled by atoms of the form $deadline\_sat(Deadline, I)$ indicating that $Deadline$ is satisfied at time I. Additionally deadlines have implicit inertia, so once they become satisfied they remain satisfied, this is modelled using a frame rule as follows:

$deadline\_sat(Deadline, I + 1) \leftarrow deadline\_sat(Deadline, I).$

The presence of an obligation on $Agent$ to have performed some institutional action $IAct$ before $Deadline$ is represented with atoms of the form $obl\_deadline(Agent, IAct, Deadline, I)$. An obligation is satisfied if there exists a previous valid occurrence of an institutional action which satisfies the obligation and the obligation deadline has not been satisfied:

$obl\_deadline\_sat(Agent, IAct, Deadline, I) \leftarrow$
   $obl\_deadline(Agent, IAct, Deadline, I), \text{not } deadline\_sat(Deadline, I),$
   $valid\_act\_happened(Agent, IAct, J), J < I.$

Once an obligation on $Agent$ is instantiated at time I, the state of the obligation persists until either the obligation is satisfied, or its deadline is satisfied:

$obl\_deadline(Agent, Obl, Deadline, I + 1) \leftarrow$
  $obl\_deadline(Agent, Obl, Deadline, I),$
  $not \neg obl\_deadline(Agent, Obl, Deadline, I + 1),$
  $not\ obl\_deadline\_sat(Agent, Obl, Deadline, I + 1),$
  $not\ deadline\_sat(Deadline, I + 1).$

The above rule also allows for the cancellation of obligations through the clause $not \neg obl\_deadline(Agent, Obl, Deadline, I + 1)$ which prevents a deadline from persisting if a rule asserts $\neg obl\_deadline(\ldots)$ in this case the obligation is neither satisfied or violated.

Finally a violation against $Agent$ occurs at time $I + 1$ if the obligation deadline is satisfied at time I and the obligation condition has not been satisfied by this time.

$viol(Agent, IAct, I + 1) \leftarrow obl\_deadline(Agent, IAct, Deadline, I),$
  $deadline\_sat(Deadline, I),$
  $not\ obl\_deadline\_sat(Agent, Obl, Deadline, I).$

5.1 Making Specifications Executable

In order to make institution specifications in ASP executable, it is necessary to define a set of "real world" actions Act_{ag} which might be performed by participating agents, such that each action in Act_{ag} corresponds to the performance of exactly one institutional action in the modelled specification (this mapping may be partial in the case of derived institutional actions, or if we are only modelling a subset of the institution). By limiting the number of action rules from Act_{ag} which may be inferred at any given time instance with an ASP constraint, we allow the definition of a labelled transition system over the institutional states, this has the effect in ASP of limiting answer sets to those containing action traces of the form:

$ag\_act\_happened(act_a, 0), ag\_act\_happened(act_b, 1), \ldots, ag\_act\_happened(act_x, n)$

and all associated inferable institutional states.

In general we assume that actions in Act_{ag} model communicative actions, and as such may be performed (albeit invalidly) by any agent at any time, this condition is necessary in the case of prediction and postdiction queries (see below) (where a chain of actions may have occurred, but due to one or more actions not being empowered no corresponding change in institutional state occurred). However in the case of planning queries where we wish to determine if a given institutional state can be obtained, we can omit meaningless actions (as they have no possible effect on the institution state) from the transition system.

5.2 Specification Queries

We identify three classes of query (from [3]):

Prediction: Where we know that a given sequence of events has occurred and we wish to determine some information about the institution state at some point along this trace.

Postdiction: In which we have some information about a final state and partial information about the initial state and the sequence of events which led us to this state and we wish to determine some additional information about the initial state.

Planning: Where given an initial state we wish to determine one or more sequences of agent actions which lead us to a desired final state.

Queries are specified in ASP by encoding a description of the initial state and then computing answer sets which include the states specified by the query. In the case of prediction and planning the initial state description is known and is asserted as a set of facts in the program. In the case of postdiction the initial state description is expressed as a set of choice rules denoting all possible initial states. If the query is satisfied then the result is one ore more answer sets describing possible traces which satisfy the query. Verification questions will in general be expressed as planning queries describing desirable or undesirable states, for example with simple validation, *"given initial state, is this outcome ever possible"*, or more complex query to determine conflicts between two institutions which regulate a common set of agents: *"is it possible for an agent to be in a state of obligation but unable or forbidden to dispense that obligation"*.

6   An Example

In order to illustrate our approach we specify a simplified institution of property (ownership of goods) and a related institution for exchanging goods with payment.

In our institution of property we wish to describe one type of institutional domain fact F_1 which captures the state of ownership of some type of object by one of a set of agents, and a single institutional action description A_1 which accounts for the transfer of ownership from one agent to another. We also wish to include the following social constraints.

C_1: After a valid transfer of ownership of an object the recipient of the transfer becomes the owner of the object.

C_2: After a valid transfer of ownership of an object the original owner ceases to be the owner of the object.

C_3: Agents are permitted to transfer ownership of objects, if they own them.

C_4: Transfers are empowered if the initiator of the transfer is the owner of the object being transferred.

The state of F_1 over time is modelled with a set of atoms of the form:

$owns(Agent, Object, I)$.

As this fact has inertia we also add the following frame rule:

$owns(Agent, Object, I + 1) \leftarrow$ not $\neg owns(Agent, Object, I + 1)$,
    $owns(Agent, Object, I)$.

The sorts of action described by A_1 are specified with a set of atoms of the form:

$iact(transfer\_ownership(FromAgent, ToAgent, Object))$.

C_1 and C_2 are encoded with the following rules:

$owns(ToAgent, Object, I + 1) \leftarrow valid\_act\_happened(FromAgent,$
    $transfer\_ownership(FromAgent, ToAgent, Object), I)$.

$\neg owns(FromAgent, Object, I + 1) \leftarrow valid\_act\_happened(FromAgent,$
    $transfer\_ownership(FromAgent, ToAgent, Object), I)$.

C_3 is encoded as follows:

$permi(FromAgent, transfer\_ownership(FromAgent, ToAgent, Object), I) \leftarrow$
    $owns(FromAgent, Object, I).$

and C_4 as follows:

$pow(FromAgent, transfer\_ownership(FromAgent, ToAgent, Object), I) \leftarrow$
    $owns(FromAgent, Object, I), ToAgent \neq FromAgent.$

The exchange institution is described below, in this institution we describe a small family of protocols where goods are exchanged for some payment, the scenario allows encodes the following five actions:

A_2 **Request Goods:** A customer sends a request for some goods to a merchant.
A_3 **Refuse Request:** The merchant refuses a request from a customer.
A_4 **Send Goods:** The merchant sends goods to the customer.
A_5 **Send Payment:** The customer sends payment for the good.
A_6 **Send Receipt:** The merchant sends a receipt to the customer.

We impose also impose the following constraints:

C_5 : Sending a request for goods (A_2) creates an obligation on the merchant to have sent the goods before the interaction ends (C_5).
C_6 : Sending a refusal (A_3) cancels the merchants obligation to send goods.
C_7 : Sending goods (A_4) creates an obligation on the customer to have payed for the goods before the interaction ends.
C_8 : Sending payment creates an obligation on the merchant to have sent a receipt for the payment before the interaction ends.
C_9 : Customers are initially empowered to perform actions of type A_2, A_5.
C_{10} : Merchants are initially empowered to actions of type A_3, A_4
C_{11} : All actions are permitted if they have not already been performed (i.e. all agents are only permitted to perform each action once).
C_{12} : Sending a receipt (A_6) is empowered only if an agent has received a valid payment (A_5) in the past.

We additionally wish to express the following relationship between the exchange scenario actions and the property institution:

C_{13} : If both a valid Send Goods (A_4) action a valid Send Payment (A_5) action take place between two agents then a transfer of ownership occurs .

Atoms for actions $A_{2,...6}$ are declared as follows:

$iact(sendRequest(Cust, Merch, Object)).iact(sendRefuse(Merch, Cust, Object)).$
$iact(sendGoods(Merch, Cust, Object)).iact(sendPayment(Cust, Merch, Object)).$
$iact(sendReceipt(Merch, Cust, Object)).$

Where $Cust, Merch$ are agent atoms, $Object$ ranges over atoms matching the domain predicate $object(Object)$ which is shared with the ownership institution.

Constraints C_5 and C_6 are written as follows (C_7 and C_8 are omitted for space reasons):

$obl\_deadline(Merch, sendGoods(Merch, Cust, Object), end\_int, I + 1) \leftarrow$
    $valid\_act\_happened(Cust, sendRequest(Cust, Merch, Object), I).$

$obl\_deadline\_sat(Merch, sendGoods(Merch, Cust, Object), end\_int, I + 1) \leftarrow$
    $obl\_deadline(Merch, sendGoods(Merch, Cust, Object), Deadline, I),$
    $valid\_act\_happened(Cust, sendRefuse(Merch, Cust, Object), I).$

The translations of $C_9, \ldots, C_{12}$ are omitted from this description. C_{13} is written using the following rules (indicating either of the orderings of A_4 and A_5.

$iact\_happened(Merch, transfer\_ownership(Merch, Cust, Object), I) \leftarrow$
    $valid\_act\_happened(Merch, sendGoods(Merch, Cust, Object), I),$
    $J < I, valid\_act\_happened(Cust, sendPayment(Cust, Merch, Object), J).$

$iact\_happened(Merch, transfer\_ownership(Merch, Cust, Object), I) \leftarrow$
    $valid\_act\_happened(Cust, sendPayment(Cust, Merch, Object), I),$
    $J < I, valid\_act\_happened(Merch, sendGoods(Merch, Cust, Object), J).$

A sample validation query is described as follows, given a merchant *alis* and a customer *bob* and one object *soft* and an initial state of *alis* owning *soft* we wish to determine if there is a valid sequence of actions after which *bob* owns *soft* during which time neither *alis* or *bob* are ever in violation. In ASP the domain, initial state and query are encoded as follows:

$agent(alis; bob).$
$merchant(alis).customer(bob).$
$time(0..3).$
$owns(alis, soft, 0).$
$compute \; all\{owns(bob, soft, 3), not \; viol(alis, 3), not \; viol(bob, 3)\}.$

```
=========== ANSWER SET 1 ===========
owns(alis,soft,0)
ag_act_happened(bob,sendPayment(bob,alis,soft),0)
iact_happened(bob,sendPayment(bob,alis,soft),0)
valid_act_happened(bob,sendPayment(bob,alis,soft),0)
owns(alis,soft,1)
obl_deadline(alis,sendReceipt(alis,bob,soft),end_i,1)
ag_act_happened(alis,sendGoods(alis,bob,soft),1)
iact_happened(alis,sendGoods(alis,bob,soft),1)
iact_happened(alis,transfer_ownership(alis,bob,soft),1)
valid_act_happened(alis,sendGoods(alis,bob,soft),1)
valid_act_happened(alis,transfer_ownership(alis,bob,soft),1)
-owns(alis,soft,2)
owns(bob,soft,2)
obl_deadline(alis,sendReceipt(alis,bob,soft),end_i,2)
obl_deadline(bob,sendPayment(bob,alis,soft),end_i,2)
obl_deadline_sat(bob,sendPayment(bob,alis,soft),end_i,2)
ag_act_happened(alis,sendReceipt(alis,bob,soft),2)
iact_happened(alis,sendReceipt(alis,bob,soft),2)
valid_act_happened(alis,sendReceipt(alis,bob,soft),2)
deadline_sat(end_i,3)
owns(bob,soft,3)
obl_deadline_sat(alis,sendReceipt(alis,bob,soft),end_i,3)
obl_deadline_sat(bob,sendPayment(bob,alis,soft),end_i,3)
```

Fig. 1. First answer set for example query

Two answer sets are produced indicating traces of actions corresponding to $< A_4, A_5, A_6 >$ and $< A_5, A_4, A_6 >$. Figure 1 shows how the social states (in bold) evolve in relation to the first trace (facts relating to permission and power have been omitted).

The above traces demonstrate how two independently specified institutions (one based on a description of communicative acts and another based on a higher-level interpretation of their institutional effects) interact to give a set of traces which represent possible conversations which fulfil particular desired requirements. By modifying the query structure the same approach can be applied to searching for conversation traces which satisfy undesirable conditions. In such a case the absence of any answer sets satisfying the query would indicate the absence of the undesirable property in the analysed model, and the presence of one or more answer sets would indicate traces in which the undesirable property was present.

7   Discussion and Related Work

Normative and institutional aspects of multi-agent systems have been studied extensively in recent years, while complete account of related work is beyond the scope of this paper, however some recent work deserves mention.

In [18] Vázquez-Salceda, Dignum et al outline the need for an *operational* system for expressing norms which allows for both their interpretation and also their efficient implementation and enforcement. In their work (including [14, 9]) they outline a language for expressing norms, their approach describes three types of deontic modality (OBLIGED, PERMITTED, FORBIDDEN) which may refer to either actions or states and which may be predicated on system states including temporal (BEFORE, AFTER) references to the occurrence of actions. As well as capturing a concise social semantics for norms they also extend their descriptions to include advisory properties which make explicit how the violation of norms should be detected by an agent responsible for the enforcement of a norm, and plans which describe how such agents should go about sanctioning violating agents. In their approach, unlike ours social states beyond those related to the deontic properties described above are not considered in the description of norms, our approach allows for the inclusion of the subset of these states which relate to the institution as institutional facts while still allowing for external states and actions, which we feel provides a better basis for the types of modelling we describe above.

Colombetti et al in [5] outline an abstract model for agent institutions based on social commitments. Their model describes institutions as being composed of a set of *registration rules* which deal with the entry and exit of agents from institutions, a set of *interaction rules* which govern how commitments are created and dispensed between agents, a set of *authorisations* which describe agents innate abilities to perform certain actions and an *internal ontology* which describes a model for the interpretation of terms relevant to the institution. A number of aspects of this approach correspond with our model for describing institutions as outlined in Section 4, in particular interaction rules correspond to our social rules, authorisations with our treatment of institutionalised power and the internal ontology with our domain specific rules. One particularly appealing aspect of their approach (further expanded in [13, 6, 26]) is the notion that institutions of this type can be applied to the specification of agent communication languages in general, with social consequences such as commitments between agents being ascribed to speech acts of a particular type. The combination of "base-level" institutions such as these with institutions capturing more general social properties such as ours provides an interesting area for further study.

The types of specification we describe are closely related to the work of Artikis et al described in [1, 2, 3, 21] from which we derive much of our specification model. In their work specifications of social systems are formalised in both the event calculus [22] and using a subset of the action language $C+$ [12]. Intuitively our approach is capable of expressing similar constraints and social properties as specifications in the above languages. However as our approach lacks a formal basis beyond its syntax in ASP at present, we are unable to make a formal comparison. In comparison to $C+$, which has similar reasoning capabilities (with similar complexity) to ASP using the CCalc tool, we feel our approach yields a more intuitive way of expressing social constraints which include temporal aspects such as C_{13} in our example (in $C+$ the program must be modified to record action histories). This also extends to the formulation of queries, where ASP makes it possible to encode queries similar to those found in (bounded) temporal logic model checking. As with $C+$, the properties we can verify using our approach are limited to those which can be found in models of specifications of a limited depth in time and with a somewhat limited number of grounded actions, states, and agents. This is partly a constraint on the grounding process used in Smodels which requires that all possible atoms be grounded and stored in memory before answer sets are computed and partly due to the implicit complexity of computing answer sets of large models. Despite this constraint, early results indicate that even for relatively complex models which ground to hundreds of thousands of rules interesting properties may still be shown in reasonable time.

$C+$ and ASP share a common heritage and both have both been used to model planning and verification problems in artificial intelligence. $C+$ offers a concise syntax for the description of problems involving the modelling of actions their effects which can be somewhat cumbersome when expressed directly in ASP as we have done, this however comes at the cost of not being able to naturally express certain properties such as conventional generation of actions and complex queries based on the temporal relationship between actions. A natural solution to this would be to extend $C+$ to include these desired properties as is proposed by Sergot in [24] where institutional properties such as permission, violation and conventional generation of action are incorporated.

In this paper we have not dealt directly with expressing sanctions on violating agents, or agents' ability to recover from violations. Intuitively these may be expressed in our framework as follows: a sanction on a violating agent may be expressed as a permission and/or obligation and/or empowerment on a third party agent or agents to perform some sanction action or actions. Recovery from sanction would then be expressed as effects of the successful application of the sanction action(s). Sanctions play an important role when considering efficacy of institutions, in order for a sanction to be effective it must both be applicable (i.e. it must be possible for the sanctioning agent to successfully perform the actions required) and effective in that the result of the sanction must be sufficient to discourage or negate the social cost of the violation which entails it. While the second issue is outside the scope of our approach (as we do not use a quantify agents' utilities in our model) the former presents interesting questions which could potentially be expressed as queries for verification using our framework.

We have not discussed a general mechanism for representing institutional roles which give a convenient way of referring to groups of permissions, obligations and empowerments in a variety of institutions, intuitively the property of an agent assuming a particular role may be expressed as an institutional fact which evolves in the same way as other normative facts which may then be used as constraints on the application or social rules according to the roles they are relevant to, the modelling of this is left to future work.

Finally, in this paper we have focussed on using ASP to reason about institutions from a design perspective. In [7] we describe an extension to ASP for reasoning within communicating agents, it would be interesting to see if these two approaches can be combined to allow agents to reason about institution descriptions online.

References

1. Alexander Artikis. *Executable Specification of Open Norm-Governed Computational Systems*. PhD thesis, Department of Electrical & Electronic Engineering, Imperial College London, September 2003.
2. A. Artikis, M. Sergot, and J. Pitt. An executable specification of an argumentation protocol. In *Proceedings of conference on artificial intelligence and law (icail)*, pages 1–11. ACM Press, 2003.
3. A. Artikis, M. Sergot, and J. Pitt. Specifying electronic societies with the Causal Calculator. In F. Giunchiglia, J. Odell, and G. Weiss, editors, *Proceedings of Workshop on Agent-Oriented Software Engineering III (AOSE)*, LNCS 2585. Springer, 2003.
4. Chitta Baral. *Knowledge Representation, Reasoning and Declarative Problem Solving*. Cambridge Press, 2003.
5. M. Colombetti, N. Fornara, and M. Verdicchio. The role of institutions in multiagent systems. In *Proceedings of the Workshop on Knowledge based and reasoning agents, VIII Convegno AI*IA 2002, Siena, Italy*, 2002.
6. Marco Colombetti and Mario Verdicchio. An analysis of agent speech acts as institutional actions. In *The First International Joint Conference on Autonomous Agents and Multiagent Systems (AAMAS '02)*, pages 1157–1164, New York, NY, USA, 2002. ACM Press.
7. Marina De Vos and Dirk Vermeir. Extending Answer Sets for Logic Programming Agents. *Annals of Mathematics and Artifical Intelligence*, 42(1–3):103–139, September 2004. Special Issue on Computational Logic in Multi-Agent Systems.
8. Mark Denecker. What's in a Model? Epistemological Analysis of Logic Programming. Ceur-WS, September 2003. online CEUR-WS.org/Vol-78/.
9. Virginia Dignum, John-Jules Meyer, Frank Dignum, and Hans Weigand. Formal Specification of Interaction in Agent Societies. In *Formal Approaches to Agent-Based Systems (FAABS-02)*, volume 2699 of *Lecture Notes in Computer Science*, pages 37–52, October 2003.
10. Douglass C. North. *Institutions, Institutional Change and Economic Performance*. Cambridge University Press, 1991.
11. Thomas Eiter, Nicola Leone, Cristinel Mateis, Gerald Pfeifer, and Francesco Scarcello. The KR system dlv: Progress report, comparisons and benchmarks. In Anthony G. Cohn, Lenhart Schubert, and Stuart C. Shapiro, editors, *KR'98: Principles of Knowledge Representation and Reasoning*, pages 406–417. Morgan Kaufmann, San Francisco, California, 1998.

12. Enrico Giunchiglia, Joohyung Lee, Vladimir Lifschitz, Norman McCain, and Hudson Turner. Nonmonotonic causal theories. *Artificial Intelligence, Vol. 153, pp. 49-104*, 2004.
13. Nicoletta Fornara and Marco Colombetti. Operational specification of a commitment-based agent communication language. In *AAMAS '02: Proceedings of the first international joint conference on Autonomous agents and multiagent systems*, pages 536–542, New York, NY, USA, 2002. ACM Press.
14. Frank Dignum, Jan Broersen, Virginia Dignum, and John-Jules Meyer. Meeting the Deadline: Why, When and How. In Michael G. Hinchey, James L. Rash, and Walter F. Truszkowski, editors, *Proceedins of the 3rd Conference on Formal Aspects of Agent-Based Systems (FAABS III), Greenbelt, Maryland, USA*, volume 3228 of *Lecture Notes in Computer Science*, pages 30–40. Springer-Verlag, 26 April 2004.
15. M. Gelfond and V. Lifschitz. The stable model semantics for logic programming. In *Proc. of fifth logic programming symposium*, pages 1070–1080. MIT PRESS, 1988.
16. Michael Gelfond and Vladimir Lifschitz. Classical negation in logic programs and disjunctive databases. *New Generation Computing*, 9(3-4):365–386, 1991.
17. Frank Guerin and Jeremy Pitt. Denotational semantics for agent communication language. In *AGENTS '01: Proceedings of the fifth international conference on Autonomous agents*, pages 497–504. ACM Press, 2001.
18. Javier Vázquez-Salceda, Huib Aldewereld, and Frank Dignum. Imlementing Norms in Multiagent Systems. In Gabriela Lindemann, Jörg Denzinger, Ingo J. Timm, and et al., editors, *Multiagent System Technologies: Second German Conference, MATES 2004, Erfurt, Germany*, volume 3187 of *Lecture Notes in Computer Science*, pages 313–327. Springer Verlag GmbH, September 2004.
19. John R. Searle. *The Construction of Social Reality*. Allen Lane, The Penguin Press, 1995.
20. Andrew J.I. Jones and Marek Sergot. A Formal Characterisation of Institutionalised Power. *ACM Computing Surveys*, 28(4es):121, 1996. Read 28/11/2004.
21. L. Kamara, A. Artikis, B. Neville, and J. Pitt. Simulating computational societies. In P. Petta, R. Tolksdorf, and F. Zambonelli, editors, *Proceedings of workshop on engineering societies in the agents world (esaw)*, LNCS 2577, pages 53–67. Springer, 2003.
22. R Kowalski and M Sergot. A logic-based calculus of events. *New Gen. Comput.*, 4(1):67–95, 1986.
23. I. Niemelä and P. Simons. Smodels: An implementation of the stable model and well-founded semantics for normal LP. In Jürgen Dix, Ulrich Furbach, and Anil Nerode, editors, *Proceedings of the 4th International Conference on Logic Programing and Nonmonotonic Reasoning*, volume 1265 of *LNAI*, pages 420–429, Berlin, July 28–31 1997. Springer.
24. Marek Sergot. $(C+)^{++}$: An action language for representing norms and institutions. Technical report, Imperial College, London, August 2004.
25. Munindar P. Singh. A social semantics for agent communication languages. In Frank Dignum and Mark Greaves, editors, *Issues in Agent Communication*, pages 31–45. Springer-Verlag: Heidelberg, Germany, 2000.
26. Mario Verdicchio and Marco Colombetti. A logical model of social commitment for agent communication. In *AAMAS '03: Proceedings of the second international joint conference on Autonomous agents and multiagent systems*, pages 528–535, New York, NY, USA, 2003. ACM Press.

Modeling Control Mechanisms with Normative Multiagent Systems: The Case of the Renewables Obligation

Guido Boella[1], Joris Hulstijn[2], Yao-Hua Tan[2], and Leendert van der Torre[3]

[1] Universitá di Torino
[2] Vrije Universiteit, Amsterdam
[3] CWI Amsterdam and Delft University of Technology

Abstract. This paper is about control mechanisms for virtual organizations. As a case study, we discuss the Renewables Obligation (RO), a control mechanism that was introduced in the United Kingdom to stimulate the production of renewable energy. We apply a conceptual model based on normative multiagent systems (NMAS). We propose to model both the participants and the normative system as autonomous agents, having beliefs and goals. Norms, which can be internalized by the agents as obligations, are translated into conditional beliefs and goals of the normative system, which concern both detection and sanctioning measures. We show that the model can handle both the regulative and the evidential aspects of the case.

1 Introduction

Recent developments in the areas of computer supported collaborative work, distributed knowledge management and 'grid' architectures for sharing resources and computational services have lead to an increasing interest in what has been termed a *virtual organization*: a collection of enterprizes or organizations that need to coordinate across organizational boundaries [23, 27, 26]. A crucial aspect of virtual organizations is that participants are autonomous: they can join and leave, and although some participants are more powerful than others, there is no central authority that can completely impose its will. Joining a virtual organization may provide benefits which participants could not achieve by themselves. On the other hand, participants must trust other participants not to behave opportunistically. To create a sustainable network, participants must therefore observe some general norms about what constitutes accepted behavior. In the case of computational coordination infrastructures, such norms will have to be enforced automatically, by means of electronic data interchange protocols or web services [21]. That means that norms will have to be encoded explicitly, in the form of some specific *control mechanism* [17, 6]. Ideally, a control mechanism is evaluated before it is implemented. To facilitate the specification and evaluation of control mechanism, we need a conceptual model that allows us to reason about the expected behavior of participants when they are subjected to norms in a virtual organization.

We discuss a case study of an actual control mechanism, the Renewables Obligation (RO), which was introduced in the United Kingdom to stimulate the production of

O. Boissier et al. (Eds.): ANIREM and OOOP 2005, LNCS 3913, pp. 114–126, 2006.

energy from renewable sources [20]. The ruling involves an obligation for energy suppliers to produce evidence of having distributed a certain minimal amount of renewable energy. In case energy producers do not comply, a buy-out fee must be paid. This is an example of a so called regulative rule. To present evidence of the amount of renewable energy produced, suppliers use so called Renewables Obligation Certificates (ROCs). This shows the use of a so called constitutive rule. The ROCs can be traded freely. The whole process is administered by a special agency, called OfGEM, with several tasks. It must monitor the amount of ROCs presented by suppliers, to detect whether the obligation has not been breached. If so, it must collect the penalty. OfGEM also accredits those renewable energy producers that are allowed to issue ROCs. This shows the use of a delegation mechanism.

Because of the inherent autonomy of participants and the lack of central control, the conceptual models used to design and reason about virtual organizations are likely to be similar to the kinds of models used in agent-oriented software engineering [9, 28, 8]. Typically, such models speak of an organizational structure involving agents that fulfill tasks on the basis of the organizational roles they play. Because agents may have conflicting tasks, or even conflicting individual goals, the possible behavior of agents is restricted by social norms. Although the RO case is not about computational agents as such, the network of energy producers does form a virtual organization. Energy producers share a network on which they have to coordinate energy distribution. There is a global objective, to produce more renewable energy, but the government is not in a position to force all energy producers to make the initial investments involved. Therefore a control mechanism is introduced, that should achieve the global objective indirectly. So in both cases we are dealing with a form of mechanism design: a control mechanism is designed in such a way, that the resulting agent society or virtual organization will uphold a general norm, and thus be able to sustain itself.

In this paper we therefore present a style of conceptual modeling based on *normative multiagent systems* (NMASs). Normative multiagent systems are "sets of agents (human or artificial) whose interactions can fruitfully be regarded as norm-governed; the norms prescribe how the agents ideally should and should not behave. [...] Importantly, the norms allow for the possibility that actual behavior may at times deviate from the ideal, i.e., that violations of obligations, or of agents' rights, may occur" [13]. The idea is to model all parties involved by *autonomous agents*: agents that are free to determine their courses of action, based on their interests (goals) and on their current information about the world (beliefs). Norms govern the behavior of agents, based on the roles they occupy in a virtual organization. A crucial aspect of our approach is that in principle any decision making entity can be modeled as an autonomous agent. In particular, the normative system itself can be viewed as an autonomous agent too, with specific beliefs and goals [5, 4]. The model has also been applied to other case studies. In particular, it has been used to explain issues of trust in electronic commerce [3].

The remainder of the paper is structured as follows. In section 2 we give a brief description of the RO case. In section 3 we define our version of normative multiagent systems, and illustrate it by two examples. In section 4 we then show how the RO case can be modeled using normative multiagent systems. The paper ends with lessons learned from this modeling exercise.

2   Case Description: Renewables Obligation

An example of an actual control mechanism is provided by the Renewables Obligation case [20, 14]. In order to comply with international environmental agreements, such as the Kyoto protocol, governments implement different incentive schemes, to stimulate the generation and supply of 'renewable energy'. Research and development of renewable energy generating technologies such as wind turbines, photovoltaic panels, hydro-electric power generators, and others, require high initial investments by energy producers. Therefore the production costs of renewable energy are higher than those of the energy produced by conventional means. The incentive scheme implemented in Great Britain, starting from April 2002, is based on the Renewables Obligation (RO) [20]. This is a legal obligation on all licensed electricity suppliers to produce evidence that they have supplied a percentage target of their electricity from renewable energy sources to customers in Great Britain. A special organization, the Office of Gas and Electricity Markets (OfGEM), a branch of the official regulator of the British Gas and Electricity markets, has been set up to manage the scheme.

Suppliers are required to produce evidence to OfGEM of their compliance with the RO. An important evidence token is the so-called Renewables Obligation Certificate (ROC). A ROC is received by the supplier when it buys electricity from an accredited renewable producer. A ROC can also be traded. Because electricity can be added, bought and sold as a commodity, it does not matter which supplier actually produces the ROCs, and which supplier buys them. This has led to the development of a market for ROCs. If the target number of ROCs increases, the total number of renewable energy in the system will increase, which was the objective of the scheme.

So suppliers can meet their Renewables Obligation in three ways. They can produce ROCs corresponding to the target level, expressed as a percentage of all electricity supplied to customers in Great Britain; they can use a so called buy-out clause which allows them to pay £30.51/Mwh for any shortfall below the target level, or they can use a combination of ROCs and buy-out fees. If a supplier fails to meet its obligation, either through ROCs or buy-out payments, the supplier is likely to be in breach of the Electricity Act, and may be liable to enforcement action. In practice this means that an additional fine has to be paid. Note that the OfGEM can manipulate the level of the buy-out fees in such a way that it becomes more beneficial for a supplier to buy the relatively expensive renewable energy with corresponding ROCs, rather than to violate the Renewable Obligation.

OfGEM has the authority to accredit electricity producers that are capable of generating electricity from renewable sources. Such renewable energy producers are subsequently allowed to issue ROCs. By modifying the accreditation criteria, the British government can make adjustments. For instance, there are plans to extend eligibility to producers that make use of biomass [16].

The efficiency of the Renewables Obligation has been evaluated and the result is largely positive: "The large majority of respondents considered that the Obligation has provided a positive stimulus for investment in renewable technologies, particularly lower cost technologies such as onshore wind and landfill gas. Most considered that the Obligation is largely working as anticipated and would deliver a significant expansion in renewable electricity generation over the coming years." [16]

3   Normative Multiagent Systems

We present the basic idea of our version of normative multiagent systems here. For a more technical exposition, please refer to [5, 4].

The model is based on mental attitudes of agents, like beliefs (information) and goals (internal motivation), that drive decisions to plan and execute actions. External motivations, such as social norms or laws, can be represented in the form of obligations, once they are known and accepted by the agent. Later we show how obligations can again be reduced to goals of the individual agent and the normative system, using violation conditions and sanctions.

Mental attitudes of agents are represented in a logical representation language. The logic allows us to derive what other mental attitudes can be inferred from the specification of the agents, and what not. When the rules of the model are implemented, we can run simulations of the decision making of various agents.

3.1   Mental Attitudes

In our logic, the mental attitudes are not represented as sets of sentences as is customary, but as sets of conditionals or production rules. This expresses the fact that mental attitudes are context dependent [12]. So each attitude Bel, $Goal$, etc., is represented by a set of rules of the form $A \rightarrow B$, where both A and B are formulas, composed of facts by means of logical operators $\wedge$ (and), $\vee$ (or), $\neg$ (not) and the constant $\top$ (always true). Here A represents the conditions under which the facts represented by B may be inferred by the agent. Moreover, B may contain special decision variables, also called actions, that will alter the state of the world. The values of decision variables are under the control of the agent. For simplicity, both facts and decision variables are represented by boolean variables, being either true or false. The decision making process of an agent is represented by a forward reasoning loop, which runs roughly as follows[1].

The agent receives input from observations, represented as a set of facts S. Alternatively, the agent may start with a set of initial goals, represented by a set of decision variables S. Now the agent tries to match each rule $A \rightarrow B$ against S. If A is contained in S, and the facts of B do not contradict a fact in S, the rule is applicable. However, there may be several rules applicable to S, from the same and from different mental attitudes, each with a different possible outcome. Using a priority ordering, the agent selects one rule – this is called conflict resolution – and applies it: the result B is now added to S. This process continues, until a stable set of facts is reached, to which no further additions can be made. Such a stable set, an extension, represents one of the possible outcomes of the decision making.

The decision making behavior of an agent crucially depends on the way the conflicts among the mental attitudes are resolved. Different priority orders may lead to different extensions, which represent sets of goals and hence lead to different behavior.

Example 1 (Beer and Smoking.). An agent has the following inclination. Whenever it finds itself at a party, it wants to drink beer. And whenever it is drinking beer, it needs a

---

[1] Technical details of the reasoning is expressed using input/output logics [18]. Their application to Normative Multiagent Systems is explained in [5, 4].

cigarette. The agent knows that smoking is bad, and therefore the agent has the intention not to smoke. What will happen?

> Belief: at_party
> Goal 1: at_party → drink_beer
> Goal 2: drink_beer → smoke_cigarette
> Goal 3: ¬ smoke_cigarette

What will happen depends on the relative strength of the agent's urge to smoke and its resolution not to. These relative strengths can be expressed by a priority ordering on sets of rules. Rules in one set are considered equally important. In general, belief rules outrank goal rules; otherwise the agent would suffer from *wishful thinking* [7]. There are two possibilities. If the urge to smoke is too strong, and the agent has already drunk a beer, it will smoke despite its resolution not to. But if the resolution outranks the urge, the agent will refrain from smoking, or refrain both from drinking and smoking.

> Priority: Belief > {Goal 1, Goal 2} > Goal 3
> Outcome: {at_party, drink_beer, smoke_cigarette}

> Priority: Belief > Goal 3 > {Goal 1, Goal 2}
> Outcomes: {at_party, drink_beer } , { at_party}

What do we observe in this example? Before trying to achieve its goals, an agent will consider the previously derived goals in the extension along with their consequences. This process is called *goal generation* [7]. Goal generation precedes the planning process. Roughly, there are two kinds of goals. Achievement goals are satisfied once some state of affairs has been realized. An example is the goal to reach some location. Maintenance goals on the other hand, are only satisfied for as long as some state of affairs continues to hold. Consider for example the goal to maintain some safety standard.

3.2   Norms and Obligations

Now what about norms and obligations? Some people have observed that the stabilizing effect of goals for individual agents, is similar to the stabilizing effects of norms on a community of agents. Norms protect long term interests of the group against individual deviators. But how can we model norms in this setting?

The general idea is to use a reduction of obligations to goals of the normative system, where the normative system itself is seen as a separate agent. This may be summarized by the slogan "Your wish is my command": the wishes of the normative system count as commands for the individual agent, provided that the normative system has authority over the individual agents.

The reduction makes use of a so called *violation predicate* [1]. Although violation predicates have been known for a long time, making a reduction to goals rather than to modal or epistemic operators, does make a difference. It expresses that the normative agent makes a conscious decision to detect or sanction a violation. Violation detection is a specific kind of goal of the normative system. It may lead to the addition of a belief in case a violation is indeed detected. Violation detection is separated from sanctioning.

Sanctioning concerns the decision to sanction an agent in case a violation has been detected, and what sanction is most appropriate.

To make sure that obligations are translated correctly, a number of conditions must be observed [4].

Definition 1 (Conditional Obligations). Agent a is obliged to bring about x under sanction s in circumstances C, with respect to a normative system n in a given model M, written as $M \models O_{a-n}(x,\ s|C)$, iff:

1. Goal of n: $C \to x$
   If agent n believes that C, then it has as a goal that x should be brought about.
2. Goal of n: $C \wedge \neg x \to Viol(\neg x)$
   If agent n believes that C and $\neg x$ is the case, then it has the goal $Viol(\neg x)$, i.e., to recognize $\neg x$ as a violation by agent a.
3. Goal of n: $\neg Viol(\neg x)$
   By itself, agent n has no goal for violations. This is to prevent arbitrary detection.
4. Goal of n: $C \wedge Viol(\neg x) \to s$
   If agent n believes that C and detects $Viol(\neg x)$, then it has as a goal to apply sanction s.
5. Goal of n: $\neg s$
   By itself, agent n does not have a goal to apply sanction s. This is to prevent arbitrary sanctions.
6. Goal of a: $\neg s$
   Agent a has a goal not be sanctioned. Without this condition, the sanction would not deter agent a from violating the obligation.

Example 2 (Common-Pool Resources). Consider the following situation. There is a group of agents $A = \{a_1, .., a_n\}$ that share access to a common pool resource R. Think for example of common fishing grounds, which may suffer from overfishing in spring [22]. Only if all fishermen have a modest spring catch, the fish stocks can be sustained. For this reason, a normative system is set up, with a norm that in spring, no fisherman is allowed to catch more than some predetermined quota[2].

The model M_{pool} is set up as follows. We use boolean variables 'spring' to represent the fact that it is now spring, 'overfish', which stands for fishing more than the quota allow, and 'fine' for the penalty that must be paid. Variable a ranges over agents $a_1, .., a_n$. Now we have an obligation of agent a towards the community, not to overfish in spring against the penalty of paying a fine. Using definition 1, this obligation can be modeled as follows.

$M_{pool} \models O_{a-n}(\neg\text{overfish}, \text{fine}|\text{spring})$, if and only if:

1. Goal of n: spring $\to \neg$ overfish
2. Goal of n: spring $\wedge$ overfish $\to Viol(\text{overfish})$
3. Goal of n: $\neg Viol(\text{overfish})$

---

[2] Such cases have been studied extensively in economics, for example using evolutionary game theory. See for example [25]. Our example is only meant for illustrative purposes.

4. Goal of n: spring $\land$ $Viol$(overfish) $\rightarrow$ fine
5. Goal of n: $\neg$ fine
6. Goal of a: $\neg$ fine

In addition to these aspects of the norm, we must also model the usual beliefs and goals of an agent. In particular, we must model the fact that without the obligation, overfishing is profitable. This aspect is modeled here by a simple goal. Moreover, for the sake of simulation, let us suppose that it is now spring and that everybody believes this.

7. Goal of a: overfish
8. Belief of a, n: spring

3.3 Recursive Modeling

How are these rules applied? Suppose it is spring and agent a has a goal to overfish. Agent a also has a goal not be fined. So we get an initial extension of the form {spring, overfish, $\neg$ fine}. Because the consequences are to a large part controlled by other agents, agent a will try and predict the goals and actions of other agents. It applies all the rules it knows that other agents possess, including those of the normative agent n. A set of rules of another agent is called a *profile*. Crucially, profiles contain rules that are affected by the actions of the agent itself. That is why we call this process *recursive modeling*. However, for most applications no infinite recursion is needed; recursive models up to three levels of embedding are quite sufficient.

In the first step, a applies n's rule 2 to its own initial extension, which will trigger a goal to detect a violation. On the other hand, n has goal 3 not to detect violations. Which of these will get priority depends on a's profile of n. Lets assume that a believes that n's conditional goal to report a violation outranks its general goal not to detect violations. That will produce an extension { spring, overfish, $Viol$(overfish), $\neg$ fine}.

In the second step, a applies n's goal 4 to sanction, weighed against n's goal 3 not to sanction. If a believes that n's goal not to sanction outweighs its goal to sanction, for example because of prohibitive costs of sanctioning, a will form the goal to overfish. But if a believes n will indeed punish detected overfishing, this would produce an extension { spring, overfish, $Viol$(overfish), fine, $\neg$ fine}, which contains a contradiction. This conflict will have to be resolved by a's own priority order. In case the goal not to be fined outweighs the goal to overfish – in practice: if the penalty is larger than the expected profits – the agent will not form a goal to overfish.

The example shows that an obligation will only work, if two conditions are met. First, the sanction must outweigh the benefits of overfishing. In our model we can express this by a priority constraint.

Goal of a: $\neg$ fine $>$ Goal of a: overfish

Second, the perceived chances of being detected and fined, must be sufficiently high. In our model we can express this by adding priority constraints to the profiles of n used by a during recursive modeling.

Goal of n: (spring $\land$ $Viol$(overfish) $\rightarrow$ fine) $>$ Goal of n: $\neg$ fine

Thus a lot depends on the enforcement mechanism. Because the normative system, embodied by the village council for example, has no physical power, violation detection and sanctioning must be delegated to specific agents, such as a police force. There are examples of self-organizing communities in which these tasks are performed by ordinary community members, who may even behave altruistically, in the sense that they are not compensated for their detection and punishing efforts [22].

3.4 Constitutive Norms

So how do we model the fish quota? Suppose there is an accepted belief among the fishing community that a catch of more than two tonnes a week 'counts as' overfishing. The idea is to use *constitutive norms* [24] to model such general beliefs of the community. A constitutive norm applies only under certain circumstances and is intimately linked to an institution. This institution can be a (legal) person or an abstract entity such as a community of users. Whether a rule applies depends on the jurisdiction of the institution. In case we have a normative system, we can re-apply index n to stand for the institution. Thus constitutive rules are of the form "x counts as y under circumstances C in institution n".

In the example, the quota for overfishing in spring can be expressed as a belief rule of the institution n, and all agents a that fall under its jurisdiction.

Belief of a, n: spring $\wedge$ (weekly catch > 2 tonnes) $\rightarrow$ overfish

Constitutive norms can create new institutional facts. The prototypical example is a declarative speech act [2]. For example, the utterance "I name this ship Johanna", uttered by a lady at an appropriate christening ceremony, will create the institutional fact of the ship bearing this name. So the right kind of utterance uttered by the right person under the right circumstances 'counts as' as the creation of an institutional fact.

3.5 Value Objects

One way to express that objects represent a value in a community of agents, is as a goal to obtain such objects, attributed to an abstract agent that represents the shared conventions in the community. Just like beliefs can capture 'counts as' rules, goals can capture value, up to a point. Note that the attribution of value need not be shared. There are conventions about what is considered valuable in a community, but the value that an individual agent attaches to an object is not modeled. In our example, the fact that overfishing is generally considered profitable, clause 7, is an example of a value expression.

Goal of a: overfish

Although we do not explicitly model value, as for example [11], the effect of the relative priority of goals in the recursive simulation and violation games that agents play with each other, is similar to that of value.

4   Case Analysis

The case hinges on several aspects. There is a penalty mechanism that creates an incentive for energy suppliers to acquire evidence of having distributed a minimal level of renewable energy to British customers. The supplier has a choice whether to buy the obligatory amount of "green" energy, to buy ROCs from other suppliers, or else to pay a buy-out fee that corresponds to the amount of ROCs missing. The penalty aspect can be modeled by violation detection and sanctioning goals, similar to the obligation in section 3.

We consider a set of suppliers $\{s_1, .., s_n\}$ and the normative system, appropriately called OfGEM. The main variables of the model M_{ROC} are 'meet_target', which represents the fact that a supplier has collected enough ROCs, either by selling renewable energy to customers, or by buying them of other suppliers, 'buy-out' which represents that a supplier must pay a buy-out fee, and 'enforcement_order' which represents the sanctioning action of OfGEM in case the Renewables Obligation has been breached.

The normative status of the buy-out fee is interesting. There are two options. On the one hand, paying a buy-out fee is a legitimate way of conforming to the Renewables Obligation. A supplier who pays a buy-out fee is not in breach of the law. This would suggest that there is one obligation, that can be fulfilled in two different ways[3]:

$$O_{s-\text{OfGEM}}(\text{meet\_target} \vee \text{buy-out}, \text{enforcement\_order}|\top)$$

On the other hand, paying a buy-out fee is not the preferred option. The buyer can choose to pay a buy-out fee, but the penalty level is set by OfGEM in such a way, that paying the fee is always more expensive than the appropriate number of ROCs would have been. Hence, we believe that the buy-out fee is better classified as a sanction for not meeting the target. That suggests that there are in fact two obligations. When the supplier is in breach of this second obligation, to buy the buy-out fee, OfGEM can call for a further sanction: an enforcement order. This will force the supplier to pay, against a penalty of further legal sanctions.

$$O_{s-\text{OfGEM}}(\text{meet\_target}, \text{buy-out}|\top)$$
$$O_{s-\text{OfGEM}}(\neg\text{buy-out}, \text{enforcement\_order}|\neg\text{meet\_target})$$

The first of these clauses is worked out in more detail.

$M_{ROC} \models O_{s-\text{OfGEM}}(\text{meet\_target}, \text{buy-out}|\top)$, if and only if:

1. Goal of OfGEM: meet_target
2. Goal of OfGEM: $\neg$ meet_target $\rightarrow Viol(\neg$ meet_target$)$
3. Goal of OfGEM: $\neg Viol(\neg$ meet_target$, a)$
4. Goal of OfGEM: $\neg$ meet_target $\wedge Viol(\neg$ meet_target$) \rightarrow$ buy_out
5. Goal of OfGEM: $\neg$ buy_out
6. Goal of s: $\neg$ buy_out

Again, we have to state that without the RO scheme, not meeting the target for renewable energy would be profitable, because of the initial investments required.

7. Goal of s: $\neg$ meet_target

---

[3] Note that the representation does not account for the fact that a partial shortfall in ROCs may also be supplemented with a corresponding partial buy-out fee.

How can we predict the behavior of an average supplier? What matters is the relative priority of goals 6 and 7. This priority is determined by economic considerations of the supplier agents. Since renewable energy is much more expensive to purchase for the supplier than non-renewable energy, the supplier will only consider purchasing renewable energy, when the level of the buy-out fee is set high enough. So, if the buy-out fee is higher than the extra cost for purchasing renewable energy, then the supplier will prefer 6 to 7. However, if the buy-out fee is less than the extra cost for purchasing renewable energy, then the supplier will prefer 7 to 6. A detailed profitability analysis to determine this preference ordering is beyond the scope of this paper. Detailed tools exist for such purposes. An example is the e^3-value tool [11]. We will investigate the links with profitability in further research.

Regulative Aspect. The Renewable Obligation will only work, in case some further conditions are met. First, the probability of being detected must be perceived to be high by the energy suppliers. Since the ROC scheme makes use of evidential documents and the burden of proof lies with the suppliers, this condition is taken care of. Second, the perceived probability of the OfGEM actually collecting buy-out fees, must be high enough. Currently, buy-out fees flow back into the system. They are used to finance the OfGEM itself and for other renewable energy stimulation. Thus, it is in the interest of OfGEM to actually collect buy-out fees. Moreover, if a supplier fails to pay the buy-out fees, a more severe sanction is invoked. In the ROC case this is called an enforcement order. The obligation $O_{s-\text{OfGEM}}(\neg\text{buy-out}, \text{enforcement\_order}|\neg\text{meet\_target})$ is modeled analogously to clause 1-7 above.

In the two years that the scheme has been up and running, OfGEM has managed to collect most buy-out fees that were due. Recently, two electricity suppliers, Atlantic Electric and Gas Ltd and Maverick Energy Ltd were fined for their likely breach of the Renewables Obligation. Because both companies went into administrative receivership (bankruptcy), OfGEM decided not to issue further enforcement orders [19]. This shows that OfGEM is willing and able to enforce the Renewables Obligation.

Evidential Aspect. The ROC documents provide *evidence* of a certain amount of energy having been produced from renewable sources. This evidence is needed for different control purposes, such as to verify that the energy is indeed from an accredited renewable generator, that suppliers meet their Renewables Obligation, and that ROCs keep their value when traded.

This use of ROC evidence documents can be modeled by specific constitutive rules of the normative system, in this case embodied by the OfGEM. So OfGEM guarantees that within the wider community of energy trade, these ROCs 'count as' evidence that renewable energy was produced, and can be traded as such. In our formalization, this comes out as a simple belief rule of the normative system, and of all relevant suppliers. Similar reasoning holds for the establishment of the target number of ROCs that a supplier must meet. Note that this target number is relative to the size of the supplier.

Belief of s,OfGEM: 1 ROC $\rightarrow$ 1 Mwh renewable electricity
Belief of s,OfGEM: x ROC $\wedge$ $(x > \text{target})$ $\rightarrow$ meet_target

OfGEM delegates authority to accredited renewable energy producers. Only accredited producers are allowed to issue ROCs. The effect of this delegation relation also shows as part of the 'counts as'-rules. Thus, only documents by accredited energy producers will count as true ROCs.

As long as the OfGEM continues to guarantee the validity of the evidence documents, these documents themselves can be traded as valuables. The identity of the holder of a ROC does not matter. For the overall objective of the scheme – to increase the amount of renewable energy produced – it does not matter whether a ROC or real renewable energy is traded, since every ROC stands for a certain quantity of renewable energy having been generated at some point. Because of the existence of a trading market, a supplier may specialize. Some, most notably in Scotland, are better at producing renewable energy; others are better at distributing it.

Other Aspects.   Regarding some of the other aspects of the case, like the total flow of value between parties, and the fact that no ROCs must disappear from the system, our approach can still benefit from insights of other formalisms. In particular, modeling the decision of a supplier whether to produce ROCs, buy them or pay the buy-out fee, and in what relative proportions, would require the use of more detailed profitability analysis tools. We refer to [14, 15] for an analysis of the case that makes use of the e^3-value method [11], which does provide such quantitative tools. In an extension to e^3-value, called e^3-value$^+$, Gordijn and Tan [10] also incorporate aspects of trust and control into the e^3-value approach. A promising direction for further research, is to investigate further combinations of value-based and normative approaches to virtual organizations.

5   Conclusions

In this paper we analyze how normative systems help create a sustainable network or virtual organization. Participants can make a choice to participate in a network or not. When there is no normative structure, participants may suffer from opportunistic behavior of others. The example of the common pool resource illustrated how this can be remedied by a normative system. On the other hand, when too severe a sanction is imposed, agents may not survive, or leave the network. Thus participants are autonomous in their decision to remain in the network. For this reason, it makes sense to apply agent-based modeling techniques. In particular, we apply Normative Multiagent Systems (NMAS) [5, 4]

We model a normative system as an autonomous agent, with explicit beliefs and goals. Norms are reduced to beliefs and goals of the subjects and the normative system, according to the slogan "My wish is your command". Having an explicit agent to represent the normative system helps in particular to deal with delegation relations, and the way norm enforcement mechanisms such as detection and sanctions are implemented. It also makes it possible to explicitly capture the objectives of a norm, namely as the goals of the normative system.

The normative multiagent systems approach is validated with a case study of the Renewables Obligation in the United Kingdom. This control mechanism was introduced to stimulate the production of energy from renewable sources. What lessons did we learn from this modeling effort?

With respect to the RO case, we learned that the status of the buy-out fee is unclear. It can either be regarded as a legitimate way of complying with the Renewables

Obligation, or as a kind of sanction. The difference comes out clearly in the model. We choose to model the Renewables Obligation as a combination of two obligations: one to meet the target, and a second one that is conditional on not meeting the target, to pay the buy-out fee. This pattern of cascading obligations, in which sanctions are themselves modeled as regulative rules, is quite common in legal texts. Another lesson is that evidential documents like ROCs are difficult to capture. They have an ambivalent meaning because they are both evidential documents and value objects that can be traded themselves.

With respect to the Normative Multiagent Systems approach, we learned that there are in fact normative systems that need the whole range of concepts to be modeled accurately: beliefs, goals, obligations, violation conditions, sanctions and 'count as'-rules. The case study shows that a complex example can be modeled consistently (internal validity), and that normative multiagent systems can analyze relevant aspects of existing control mechanisms in a virtual organization (external validity).

The model does have important limitations. First, the underlying representation of facts and events is too simple. For example, temporal or organizational relationships can not be conveniently captured. Second, the approach is only qualitative, using relative comparisons to model priorities. Many applications need a quantitative profitability analysis to set the right penalty levels, for the incentive scheme to work. But only after a qualitative analysis has shown the viability of a control mechanism, does it pay to make a detailed quantitative model.

Acknowledgements. Thanks to Vera Kartseva for providing details of the RO case.

References

1. A. Anderson. A reduction of deontic logic to alethic modal logic. *Mind*, 67:100–103, 1958.
2. J.L. Austin. *How to do things with words*. Harvard U.P., Cambridge MA, 1962.
3. G. Boella, J. Hulstijn, Y-H. Tan, and L. van der Torre. Transaction trust in normative multiagent systems. In C. Castelfranchi, S. Barber, J. Sabater, and Munindar Singh, editors, *Proceedings of AAMAS Workshop on Trust in Agent Societies, Utrecht, The Nederlands, 2005 (Trust'05)*, 2005.
4. G. Boella and L. van der Torre. A game theoretic approach to contracts in multiagent systems. *IEEE Transactions on Systems, Man and Cybernetics - Part C*, to appear 2006. Special issue on Game-theoretic Analysis and Stochastic Simulation of Negotiation Agents.
5. G. Boella and L. van der Torre. Security policies for sharing knowledge in virtual communities. *IEEE Transactions on Systems, Man and Cybernetics - Part A.*, to appear 2006. Special issue on Secure Knowledge Management.
6. Roger W.H. Bons, Frank Dignum, Ronald M. Lee, and Yao-Hua Tan. A formal analysis of auditing principles for electronic trade procedures. *International Journal of Electronic Commerce*, 5(1):57–82, 2000.
7. J. Broersen, M. Dastani, J. Hulstijn, and L. Van der Torre. Goal generation in the BOID architecture. *Cognitive Science Quarterly*, 2(3-4):431–450, 2002.
8. J. Castro, M. Kolp, and J. Mylopoulos. Towards requirements-driven information systems engineering: the TROPOS project. *Information Systems*, 27:365–389, 2002.
9. Jacques Ferber. *Multi-Agent Systems: An Introduction to Distributed Artificial Intelligence*. Addison-Wesley, 1999.

10. J. Gordijn and Y.-H. Tan. A design methodology for trust and value exchanges in business models. *International Journal of Electronic Commerce*, 9(3):31, 2005.

11. Jaap Gordijn and J.M. Akkermans. Value-based requirements engineering: Exploring innovative e-commerce ideas. *Requirements Engineering*, 8(2):114–134, 2003.

12. B. Hansson. An analysis of some deontic logics. *Noûs*, 3:373–398, 1969.

13. A. Jones and J. Carmo. Deontic logic and contrary-to-duties. In D. Gabbay, editor, *Handbook of Philosophical Logic*, pages 203–279. Kluwer, 2002.

14. Vera Kartseva, Jaap Gordijn, and Yao-Hua Tan. Value-based business modelling for network organizations: Lessons learned from the electricity sector. In Jrg Becker and Freimut Bodendorf, editors, *Proceedings of the 12th European Conference on Information Systems (ECIS'04), Turku, CD-ROM*, 2004.

15. Vera Kartseva, Jaap Gordijn, and Yao-Hua Tan. Towards a modelling tool for designing control mechanisms in network organisations. *International Journal of Electronic Commerce*, forthcoming.

16. Alex King. 2005/6 review of the renewables obligation statutory consultation. Technical Report september 2005, Department of Trade and Industry, United Kingdom, 2005.

17. R.M. Lee and R. W. H. Bons. Soft-coded trade procedures for open-edi. *International Journal of Electronic Commerce*, 1(1):27–49, 1996.

18. D. Makinson and L. van der Torre. Input/output logics. *Journal of Philosophical Logic*, 29:383–408, 2000.

19. OFGEM. Renewables Obligation - Atlantic Electric and Gas Limited and Maverick Energy Limited. Technical Report R/65, Office of Gas and Electricity Markets, United Kingdom, 2004. www.ofgas.gov.uk.

20. OFGEM. The renewables obligation: Annual report 2003-2004. Technical Report HC 786, Office of Gas and Electricity Markets, United Kingdom, 2004. www.ofgas.gov.uk.

21. Alexander Osterwalder and Yves Pigneur. An eBusiness model ontology for modeling eBusiness. In Joze Gricar, editor, *Proceedings of the 15th Bled Electronic Commerce Conference – eReality: Constructing the eEconomy (Bled'02)*, pages 75–91, 2002.

22. Elinor Ostrom. *Governing the Commons: The Evolution of Institutions for Collective Action*. Cambridge University Press, New York, 1990.

23. M. B. Sarkar and C. Butler, B. andSteinfield. Cybermediaries in electronic marketspace: Toward theory building. *Journal of Business Research*, 41:215–221, 1998.

24. J.R. Searle. *The Construction of Social Reality*. The Free Press, New York, 1995.

25. R. Sethi and E. Somanathan. The evolution of social norms in common property resource use. *American Economuic Review*, 86(4):766–789, 1996.

26. Don Tapscott, Alex Lowy, and David Ticoll. *Harnessing the Power of Business Webs*. Harvard Business School Press, Boston, MA, 2000.

27. P. Timmers. Business models for electronic markets. *Electronic Markets*, 8(2):3 – 8, 1998.

28. Michael J. Wooldridge, Nicholas R. Jennings, and David Kinny. The Gaia methodology for agent-oriented analysis and design. *Autonomous Agents and Multi-Agent Systems*, 3(3):285–312, 2000.

Computational Institutions for Modelling Norm-Regulated MAS: An Approach Based on Coordination Artifacts

Rossella Rubino[1], Andrea Omicini[2], and Enrico Denti[3]

[1] CIRSFID, Alma Mater Studiorum—Università di Bologna
Via Galliera 3, 40121 Bologna, Italy
rossella.rubino@unibo.it
[2] DEIS, Alma Mater Studiorum—Università di Bologna a Cesena
via Venezia 52, 47023 Cesena, Italy
andrea.omicini@unibo.it
[3] DEIS, Alma Mater Studiorum—Università di Bologna
viale Risorgimento 2, 40136 Bologna, Italy
enrico.denti@unibo.it

Abstract. As agent autonomy emphasises the need of norms for governing agent interactions, increasing attention is being devoted to (electronic) institutions for modelling organisations governed by norms. Moving from the concepts of role (with its normative consequences, i.e. obligations, permissions and prohibitions), norms (both regulative and constitutive), and normative agents, we first introduce the notion of *computational institution* for modelling norm-regulated MAS. Then, we discuss how infrastructural abstractions like coordination artifacts can be exploited to express norms inside computational institutions. Finally, we present an example based on the TuCSoN infrastructure.

1 Norms and Agents

Generally speaking, *norms* are rules, enforced by some (trusted) third parties, aimed at governing the individual behaviour of the members of a society. Although the most common semantics of norm recalls the idea of *imposing* a specific rule or behaviour, this is not always the case in real life. According to Searle's classification [1], norms can be classified in two categories:

- *constitutive norms*, i.e. norms that are affirmed to create (constitute) new states of affairs (example: the rules of a game, like chess);
- *regulative norms*, also called *deontic rules* [2], i.e. norms that are aimed at governing activities, by expressing the obligation or the permission to perform an action (example: "you should drive on the right").

According to Peczenik [3], a special case of constitutive norms is the case of *qualification norms*, which are defined as constituting some particular legal properties; among these, notable examples are *norms that confer competence* and *norms that*

O. Boissier et al. (Eds.): ANIREM and OOOP 2005, LNCS 3913, pp. 127–141, 2006.

confer power—i.e, norms that constitute a specific ability for some specific entity. On the other hand, regulative norms are further classified into *behavioural norms* and *aim norms*.

In the context of MAS, we will mainly refer to Searle's classification, since the basic distinction is between norms for ruling social activities (which fall inside the class of regulative norms), and norms for ascribing responsibilities and creating new concepts (which belong to the class of constitutive norms). In particular, regulative norms should both enable each agent to achieve its goal(s), and allow interactive social activities to be handled as virtual organisations or societies, somehow mediating among different exigencies.

In this paper, we introduce the concept of *computational institution* as a model to capture the notion of norm into virtual organisations, and show how computational institutions can be actually represented and effectively set up via suitable *coordination artifacts* [4] exploited as *normative abstractions*. As a concrete example, we outline a case study showing how to build a simple computational institution on top of the TuCSoN coordination infrastructure.

2   Organisations and Virtual Institutions

From an abstract viewpoint, an organisation can be defined as "a social unit or human grouping deliberately constructed to seek specific goals" [5]. Institutions, in their turn, can be introduced as "the framework within which interaction takes place" [6]: they provide a society with the structure and the rules (constraints) needed to shape interaction among its participants. Among the models defined in the literature to frame the concept of virtual institution, Noriega and Sierra introduced the notion of *electronic institution* [7, 8], later extended by Vasconcelos by introducing the notion of *logic-based e-institution* [7]. On the other hand, in the MAS context, Boella and Van der Torre defined the notion of *normative system* [9, 10, 11] as a MAS with norms. Altogether, these models introduce the key concepts of *deliberative agent*, *role*, *norm*, and *normative agent*.

Both electronic institutions and normative systems adopt a notion of agent which emphasises agent autonomy: there, agents can decide to violate a norm to achieve their goals, or to change their goals so that they match the existing norms—a property called *norm autonomy*. This is why such agents are known as *norm autonomous agents* or *deliberative normative agents* [12]—in the following, just *deliberative agents*, for short.

Each agent in the institution can play one or more *roles*, which determine what an agent can do: basically, the concept of role is common to both approaches. Roles may be shared by several agents, and may be acquired either statically or dynamically.

On the contrary, *norms* are not seen in the same way in the approaches above, since normative systems feature both regulative and constitutive norms, while electronic institutions consider regulative norms only. So, the electronic institution norms can be seen as a subset of the normative-system norms. In particular, electronic institutions define regulative norms that may be submitted to preconditions—a natural choice, since they mainly focus on communication languages and interaction protocols.

The concept of *normative agent*—i.e., a member of the institution whose goal is to enforce norms—, instead, is unique to normative systems.

Within computational systems, electronic institutions and normative systems can both be considered as institutions. Nevertheless, they take into account only some institutional aspects which are often complementary. Consequently, a more general definition of institution is required, which should also abstract from implementation details. In such way all the most common notions of institution could be captured. This is what computational institutions are introduced for.

3   Computational Institutions

A *computational institution* is a virtual organisation ruled by norms intended as in Section 1. The word "computational" means that the entities participating in the institution are not necessarily humans, but also computational virtual entities that operate in order to achieve the social shared goal(s). As in real life, according to [8], the main institutional tasks are:

- to manage the identity of the participants;
- to define and validate the requirements on participant capabilities;
- to establish some conventions for the interaction among agents;
- to enforce the possible obligations.

With respect to the first issue, each member of the institution is characterised by its identity, and by the role played in the institution. Of course, participant identity management is essential, for both social and legal reasons: on the one hand, knowing participants' identities might be necessary to perform some tasks, or just to facilitate their collaboration; on the other, knowing their identities also simplifies the task of creating and enforcing norms.

As regards the second issue, every agent works in the institution in order to achieve individual/social goal(s) by playing one or more roles which describe what actions it can do. Each role can be associated to some requirements that the agents playing such role(s) should fulfil in order to be a member of the institution.

Computational institutions consider three main roles:

- the *legislative* role, which consists of making laws;
- the *judicial* role, which consists of deciding whether there is a violation;
- the *executive* role, which consists of detecting violations and enforcing norms by applying the proper sanctions.

So, unlike normative systems and electronic institutions, considered in Section 2, within computational institutions a normative agent is an agent that plays one of the above roles. Moreover, unlike normative roles presented in [13], computational institutions distinguish the normative roles (legislative, judicial and executive) from the roles played by non-normative agents. In case the institution implements the separation of roles, in order to ensure objectivity, an agent can be assigned only one of the normative roles (as in any "well-formed" political structure).

Also, since every institution is created in order to achieve some goals, every agent must be able to perform its task correctly. For this purpose, the institution should establish some conventions for the interaction between agents. According to [14], conventions play a key role in the social process. They represent a behavioural constraint, striking a balance between individual freedom on the one hand, and the goal of the agent society on the other.

Within computational institutions, normative agents should ensure that all conventions are followed by creating suitable norms. Of course, normative agents should also enforce all norms necessary for the achievement of the institutional goal.

A computational institution, thus, can be defined by the n-ple:

$$\langle A, R, Req, N, G, aL, aJ, aE, S, Act \rangle$$

where

- A is the set of the agents participating to the institution;
- R is the set of the roles that agents can play;
- Req is the set of the requirements related to the roles R that the institution defines: each agent playing a given role is expected to satisfy the corresponding requirements;
- N is the set of the norms ruling institution execution;
- G is the institution goal (shared between all institution members);
- aL are the legislative agents;
- aJ are the judicial agents;
- aE are the executive agents;
- S is the set of the sanctions;
- Act is the set of the activities that need to be performed for the institution goal to be achieved. Such activities include also communication actions.

Given our model, the computational institutions architecture can be represented as composed of the following elements:

- an institutional goal;
- a set of agents, which works in the institution in order to achieve individual and institutional goals by playing one or more roles. They describe what actions agents can do and can be associated to some requirements that the agents playing such role(s) should fulfil in order to be a member of the institution. Computational institutions consider three main roles:
  - the legislative role, which consists of making laws;
  - the judicial role, which consists of deciding whether there is a violation;
  - the executive role, which consists of detecting violations and enforcing norms by applying the proper sanctions.
- a set of norms, whose violation implies the application of sanctions.

In order to help the reader in understanding the architecture of computational institutions, let us consider the case of *virtual enterprises* (VE henceforth) [15]. A VE is a temporary aggregation of autonomous and usually heterogeneous enterprises, aimed at achieving a common goal, and whose light-weight structure is well-suited to face the frequent changes and openness of business scenarios in a flexible and adaptable way. As an aggregation of enterprises, a VE requires suitable norms and sanctions, possibly negotiated in its set-up phase, so as to govern the mutual dependencies and coordinate the individual enterprises, as well as the definition of the roles needed to represent the tasks to be performed in order to achieve the VE's goal.

So, a VE can be interpreted as a computational institution, where the following elements are present:

- the VE goal;
- the set of the VE agents that cooperate in the VE. VE agents can play three kinds of role: client, VE initiator, and VE partner. Each VE agent must satisfy certain requirements, according to its role, in order to be admitted to participate to the VE;
- the set of the norms and sanctions ruling the VE, which are established either in the (initial) negotiation phase, or by some other higher- level entity, such as the Government, State, etc.;
- the legislative agent, which is the VE initiator or client;
- the judicial and executive agents, which are the competent bodies.

A more detailed example will be discussed in Section 5.

The advantages of using computational institutions are both the chance to define the requirements that agents should fulfil in order to be members of the institution, and the separation of executive, judicial and legislative powers, which—if it is implemented—enables to distinguish the different roles. Moreover, by abstracting from technical details, computational institutions can be seen as a general framework for virtual institutions.

So far, we discussed the definition of computational institution and its composing elements based on a legal analysis of human institutions. With respect to the social aspects of computational institutions, we should examine the activities performed by agents in order to achieve their goals.

According to the research studies in the field of human (cooperative) activities, mainly in Activity Theory [16, 17], non-trivial human activities are always mediated by some kind of artifacts, that enable and mediate interaction, ruling/governing the resulting global and "social" behaviour [18]. In fact, artifacts are widespread in human society: the language can be considered an artifact, as well as the writing, blackboards, maps, post-its, traffic signs such as semaphores, electoral cards or the signature on a document.

Based on this background, *coordination artifacts* were recently introduced as a conceptual and engineering framework for MAS and agent societies [4, 18]: our goal is to exploit coordination artifacts also for the engineering of computational institutions in MAS. So, in next Sections we explore this aspect, discussing in particular how two infrastructural abstractions—namely, coordination artifacts and ACCs—can be exploited for modelling and engineering computational institutions as MAS.

4   Coordination Artifacts for Computational Institutions

A coordination artifact [4, 18] is a conceptual and run-time abstraction aimed at entailing a form of mediation among the agents that use it, and embedding and effectively enacting some coordination policy (i.e. suitable laws and norms). Accordingly, from our viewpoint, coordination artifacts feature both a *constructive* and a *normative* nature, as they take care respectively of creating/composing social activities, and of ruling/governing them.

From a "norm-oriented" viewpoint, the *encapsulation, malleability, inspectability* and *controllability* properties of coordination artifacts are particularly relevant, since they correspond to desired properties of computational institutions.

Encapsulation means that a coordination artifact encapsulates a coordination service [19], allowing user agents to abstract from the actual service implementation. In the context of computational institutions, this translates in the chance for user agents to abstract from how normative agents actually rule/supervise the institutional activity (and possibly punish any "illegal" behaviour). Malleability, in its turn, represents the ability of a coordination artifact to be changed dynamically, following the intrinsic dynamism and unpredictability of MAS—so that coordination laws can be adapted and modified at run time. This aspect is common also to computational institutions, where norms have sometimes to be adapted dynamically to cope with change of organisations. Analogously, inspectability/controllability of the coordination artifact structure enable agents to use/control the artifact correctly; indeed, a worthy feature of computational institution is precisely the inspectability of its dynamic state, i.e., of what happens during the institution run-time. This property makes it possible to inspect/access any stored information about interaction histories and events occurred within an institution, for instance for normative purposes like incorrect behaviour detection and violation detection.

TuCSoN [20] is an example of agent coordination infrastructure supporting a notion of coordination artifact called *tuple centre* [21]. Tuple centres are programmable tuple spaces, which agents access by writing, reading, and consuming tuples—that is, ordered collections of heterogeneous information chunks—via simple communication operations (*out*, *rd*, *in*), which access tuples associatively. While the behaviour of a tuple space in response to communication events is fixed, the behaviour of a tuple centre can be programmed by defining a set of specification tuples expressed in the ReSpecT language [22], which define how a tuple centre should react to incoming/outgoing communication events. As a result, tuple centres can be seen as general-purpose customisable coordination artifacts, whose behaviour can be dynamically specified, forged and adapted so as to automate the co-ordination stage among agents [18].

Topologically, tuple centres are collected in TuCSoN coordination nodes, spread over the network: each node constitutes an organisation context. In order to access/use the tuple centres of an organisation context, an agent must first negotiate and enter an *Agent Coordination Context* (ACC henceforth, [23]), which defines the agent's presence and position inside the organisation in terms of actions allowed on tuple centres by virtue of the agent's role(s). An ACC is meant both to model the environment where the agent interacts, and to enable/rule the interactions between the agent and the environment, by defining the space of the admissible agent interactions [24].

As discussed above, the set of norms comprises regulative and constitutive norms. Since regulative norms aim at governing activities by expressing the obligation, the permission, or the prohibition to perform an action, they can be naturally managed by ACCs. On the other hand, constitutive norms may be embedded into coordination artifacts, e.g. by defining a suitable tuple or by programming the tuple centre so as to react to selected events. The corresponding specification tuples could be inserted in the tuple centres by the legislative agent.

Accordingly, while tuple centres can be used to model the social aspect of computational institutions, embedding the corresponding norms, ACCs can be exploited to model the presence of an agent in a computational institution with respect to organisation, access control, and relationships between agents and institution. So:

- in order to be member of a computational institution, an agent must first obtain an ACC, which defines its role in the institution. Then the agent exploits its ACC to perform actions (coordination primitives), that is, to access the tuple centres of the institution, according the constraints enforced by the specific ACC configuration;
- to exit the institution, the agent simply quits the ACC, thus ending its working session

Multiple ACCs can be held by an agent simultaneously, one for each institutions where the agent is actively playing.

Summing up, coordination artifacts appears to be suitable tools for building computational institutions, possibly in conjunction with other abstractions—such as ACCs—for the management of roles, requirements and regulative norms. According to that, next section discusses a simple example, showing how to define a computational institution on top of the TuCSoN infrastructure artifacts.

5 Example: Public Competitive Tender

In this section, we show how a simple *public competitive tender* could be seen as a computational institution, and also how it could be implemented upon TuCSoN coordination artifacts. Public competitive tenders are onerous contracts stipulated between one or more economic operators, called *bidders*, and one or more *awarding administrations*, whose subject is the execution of a work or the supply of a product or service. Among the various kinds of procedures usually adopted for competitive tenders, we consider here only the so-called "open procedure", i.e., the procedure adopted when any economic operator can participate to the tender as a bidder.

In the first step, the awarding administration publishes the announcement of the competitive tender; then, the examining commission is set up, according to the criteria defined in the announcement, which also states the acceptance criteria for the bidders' offers. Usually, the most common criteria for acceptance are either the *most advantageous offer* (evaluating altogether quality, price, feature, usage cost, terms of delivery, etc.) or simply the *lowest price*. When all the (valid) bids have been examined, the examining commission eventually announces the winner.

Public competitive tenders can be represented as computational institutions according to the definition introduced in Section 3, where:

- A is the set of the agents involved in competitive tenders;
- R is the set of roles occurring in a competitive tender as defined above, that is the awarding administration, the economic operators, the members of the examining commission;
- Req is the set of the requirements stated in the tender announcement, concerning skills and abilities required from the economic operators, such as, for instance, economic skills, financial abilities, technical or professional skills, etc.;
- N is the set of all the norms ruling the competitive tender according to the laws/directives in force;
- G is the institution goal, which in this case is to stipulate a contract between the awarding administration and the winner economic operator;
- aL are the legislative agents which issue the law/directive (e.g. the European Union);
- aJ are the judicial agents (e.g. judges, tribunals, etc.);
- aE are the executive agents, charged of enforcing the norms by applying sanctions (e.g. the police or some public officer);
- S is the set of the sanctions, usually listed in the norms stated by the legislative agent, to be applied in case of violations—for instance, exclusion from the current competitive tender, and possibly from further tenders;
- Act is the set of activities to be performed inside the procedure, such as emitting the announcement, setting up the examining commission, evaluating the offers, etc.

Mapping such a computational institution onto TuCSoN coordination artifacts amounts at adopting tuple centres to capture the institution's social aspects, and ACCs to model agent individual issues with respect to the organisation. So, a tuple centre could be charged of governing interaction among the tender's agents, according to the tender's procedure; moreover, suitable ACCs should be introduced for each of the different tender's roles/agents. Then, a suitable behaviour specification should be defined in order to enforce the norms related to agent interaction, and possibly also some norms related to regulative aspects; however, how much of the burden of norm enforcing should be charged onto specific normative agent(s), and how much should be embedded into the programmable coordination artifacts, is an open design dimension.

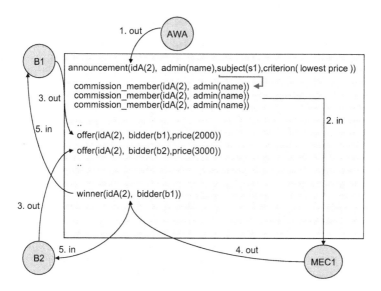

Fig. 1. Mapping a computational institution onto TuCSoN tuple centres: the public tender example

In particular, the "open procedure" described above may be expressed by introducing three agent roles (the awarding administration, *AWA*; the member of examining commission, *MEC*; and the bidder, *B*) along with the related interaction protocols in terms of exchanged tuples, and by representing the procedure phases, too, as suitable tuples.

Fig.1 shows a competitive tender in which the administration name publishes the announcement, and two bidder agents, *B1* and *B2*, participate to the tender. Of course, some commission will decide the winner. So, suitable ACCs should be introduced for the awarding administration role, the member of the examining commission role and the bidder role. Then, for instance, the procedure could take place as follows:

1. The agent playing the role of the awarding administration, *AWA*, publishes the announcement by inserting the announcement/4 tuple :

    announcement(idA(*ID*),admin(*Admin*),subject(*S*),criterion(*C*))

    where *ID* is the announcement's unique identifier, *Admin* is the awarding administration name, *S* is the subject of the contract, and *C* is the criterion (most advantageous offer or lowest price) to be used for this tender. In response, the tuple centre's supposed behaviour is to trigger the automatic insertion of a commission_member/2 tuple for each required member of the examining commission. i.e. for each *MEC* agent[1]:

---

[1] Their number is supposed to be a constitutive norm, expressed as a suitable tuple, too (not shown).

```
commission_member(idA(ID),admin(Admin))
```

This is possible by programming the tuple centre, with a suitable reaction.

2. The agents playing as bidders express their intention to bid for this tender by inserting an `offer/3` tuple such as

```
offer(idA(ID),bidder(Bidder),price(Price))
```

where *Bidder* is, rather obviously, the bidder agent's identifier, and *Price* is the offered price.

3. When the offer deadline expires, *MEC* agents (properly coordinating themselves via some interaction protocol enforced by the tuple centre rules) gather all the offers, and select the winner according to the criterion specified in the announcement. As a result, a `winner/2` tuple is emitted to publish the winner's name (see Fig.1).

Within an institutional context, the ACC can be interpreted / exploited as a legal artifact defining the kinds of interaction service(s) granted to the agent by the infrastructure—and, conversely, what kinds of actions the agent can be expected to execute given its role(s). Roughly speaking, the ACC could represent a contract between the agent and the institution releasing it. Such a contract is a description of the relationships between the agent and the institution, in particular of the policy enacted by the ACC in order to rule agent actions and interaction protocols.

In the following, we will briefly illustrate an example of ACC contracts for our case study (for a more detailed explanation of the ACC structure, we forward the interested reader to [24]).

Table 1 shows the ACC contracts for the different roles involved in the public competitive tender. Each contract contains the description of the relationships established between the agent and the institution, encoded in the Prolog language in the form of a logic theory. The information includes the name of the institution releasing the ACC (`institution(ID)`) and the roles actively played by the agent (`role(ID,SocietyID)`). Most importantly, the contract contains the policy that the ACC uses to establish if an agent action can be executed or not. This policy is obtained by composing the individual role policies, which are expressed[2] in the form of Prolog rules like the following:

```
can_do(CurrentState,Action,NextState)  :- Conditions.
```

This rule means that *Action* can be executed in the role state *CurrentState* if *Conditions* hold, and—in that case—next role state is *NextState*.[3] The concept of role state is used as a way to easily express interaction protocols: any Prolog term—also structured, partially specified—can be used to denote the role state. By default, the starting state is denoted by the `init` atom. Finally, *Action* denotes an agent action expressed in terms of coordination primitives.

---

[2] Inside the tuple centre of the gateway admitting the agent.

[3] *Conditions* can contain also builtin predicates useful to describe context-aware (with respect to local time, space and identity/positions of the agents) policies.

Table 1. ACC contracts for the awarding administration role (first chunk), the commission member role (second chunk) and the bidder role (third chunk)

```
0 institution(public_competitive_tender).
1 role(awarding_administration, buy).
2 can_do(init, out(announcement(_)), init).
0 institution(public_competitive_tender).
1 role(member_of_the_commission, buy).
2 can_do(init, rd(announcement(_)), publish_announcement).
3 can_do(publish_announcement, rd(offer(_)), award_bidder).
4 can_do(award_bidder, out(winner(_)), init).
0 institution(public_competitive_tender).
1 role(bidder, buy).
2 can_do(init, rd(announcement(_)), read_announcement).
3 can_do(read_announcement, out(offer(_)), bid).
4 can_do(bid, rd(winner(_)), init).
```

In particular, Table 1 shows the ACC policy for

- the awarding administration (first chunk), which enforces the publication of the announcement (line 2).
- the members of the commission (second chunk), which enforces an interaction protocol composed of three different role states (represented by the Prolog terms init, award_bidder, publish_announcement),which correspond to different protocol stages (initialisation, the publication of the announcement, and bidder awarding). The policy constraints the member of the commission to read the announcement (line 2), read the offers (line 3), award the agent which made the best offer and announce the winner (line 4).
- the bidders (last chunk), which specifies an interaction protocol composed of three states (init, read_announcement, bid), which correspond to different protocol stages (initialisation, announcement read, bidding and result retrieving). The policy constraints a bidder to read the announcement (line 2), make a bid (line 3) and read the winner (line 4).

On the other hand, constitutive rules may define the tuple templates used in the institution, as follows:

```
const_norm(announcement(ID,Admin,Subject,criterion([...]))).
const_norm(commission_member(ID,Admin)).
const_norm(offer(ID,Bidder,Price)).
const_norm(winner(ID,Bidder)).
```

Let us now consider a violation scenario: in Fig.2, the tender criterion (published in the announcement) is the lowest price, but the commission communicates that the winner is an agent whose offer is not the lowest. The executive agent monitoring the tender should then insert a tuple sanction/2 describing the agent involved in the violation, along with the type of sanction. The judicial agent will finally insert the tuple related to the correct winner. For the sake of simplicity, in this example the executive and the judicial agents take care of

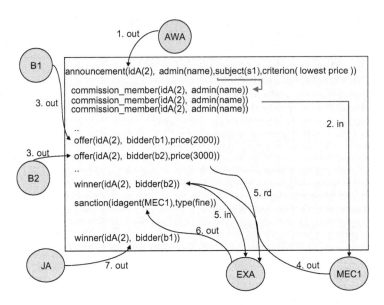

Fig. 2. Violation scenario

detecting violation and inserting the winner and sanction tuples in the tuple centre. In order to exploit the tuple centre programmability these tasks can be automatically performed by programming the tuple centre with proper reactions.

6   Related Work and Conclusion

In this paper we analysed the concept of norm both in the legal and coordination field. Although several analogies exist, there are different nuances of meaning: for instance, coordination policies rule only agent coordination, while norms are typical of the institutional goal, and therefore their violation entails sanctions [2].

This general concept of norm is common to all virtual institutions examined so far, that is computational institutions, electronic institutions and normative systems. Some differences comes out on the distinction between constitutive norms and regulative norms. Indeed, while agents and roles are intended basically in the same way, normative rules in electronic institutions only include regulative norms. Constitutive norms, on the other hand, exist in Boella and Van der Torre's normative system framework. Furthermore, electronic institutions define concepts such as *dialogic framework*, *scene* and *performative structure* that are particularly suited to capture the issues related to the communication languages and protocols, and that have no counterpart in computational institutions.

With respect to the management of roles within norm-regulated MAS, a similar approach can be found in the OperA framework [25], which exploits social contracts essentially for two functions:

– the enactment of roles, that is, social contracts describe the responsibilities and the capabilities of the agent within the society;

- the verification of the outcome of the system, since social contracts are translated into formal expressions and therefore ensure that compliance can be verified.

In short, the social contract provides a 'window' to the agent, through which other agents know what to expect and how to interact with the first agent.

The ACC, instead, models the environment where an agent can interact and the agent-environment interaction by defining the space of the admissible agent interaction. Even if the negotiation of an ACC specifies a sort of "contract" between the agent and the MAS, the ACC model goes far beyond. First, an ACC is a design and run-time abstraction which makes it possible to realise a wide range of conceptual frameworks. An example is the RBAC-MAS framework, rooted in role-based access control approaches, which exploits the notion of ACC as its basic brick [26]. TuCSoN ACCs are a particular instance of ACCs, whose action model is specialised to operate on tuple centres.

Summing up, on the one side ACCs resemble a social contract as they make it possible to represent the role(s) that an agent is playing inside an organisation, its responsibilities, permissions, interactive behaviour (protocols, conversations), what kind of interaction service the infrastructure promised to the agent, and, conversely, what kind of actions an agent was expected to execute depending on his role(s) [24]. On the other hand, the ACC abstraction can be further used to model both forms of dynamic access control to environment resources and the quality of interaction. Finally, unlike social contracts, an approach based on a runtime abstraction like ACC also allows that the compliance to be enforced a priori, not just verified a posteriori.

Of course, several other test cases need to be mapped as computational institutions to validate this approach. Moreover, some key aspects deserve a deeper investigation: in particular, further work is needed to better explore the issues related to mapping computational institutions onto TuCSoN coordination artifacts, with special regard to the critical issue of suitably mapping the (different kinds of) norms.

References

1. Searle, J.R.: The construction of social reality. New York: The Free Press (1995)
2. Sartor, G.: Legal Reasoning: a Cognitive Approach to the Law. Springer (2005)
3. Peczenik, A.: On Law and Reason. Kluwer (1989)
4. Omicini, A., Ricci, A., Viroli, M., Castelfranchi, C., Tummolini, L.: Coordination artifacts: Environment-based coordination for intelligent agents. In Jennings, N.R., Sierra, C., Sonenberg, L., Tambe, M., eds.: 3rd international Joint Conference on Autonomous Agents and Multiagent Systems (AAMAS 2004). Volume 1. ACM, New York, USA (2004) 286–293
5. Etzioni, A.: Modern Organisations. Prentice-Hall (1964)
6. Esteva, M., Rodriguez-Aguilar, J.A., Sierra, P., Arcos, J.L.: On the formal specification of electronic institutions. In Dignum, F., Sierra, C., eds.: Agent Mediated Electronic Commerce: The European AgentLink Perspective. Volume 1991 of LNAI. Springer (2001) 126–147

7. Vasconcelos, W.W.: Logic-based electronic institutions. In Leite, J.A., Omicini, A., Sterling, L., Torroni, P., eds.: Declarative Agent Languages and Technologies. Volume 2990 of LNCS. Springer (2004) 221–242
8. Noriega, P., Sierra, C.: Electronic institutions: Future trends and challenges. In Klusch, M., Ossowski, S., Shehory, O., eds.: Cooperative Information Agents VI. Volume 2446 of LNAI. Springer (2002) 14–17 6th International Workshop (CIA 2002), Madrid, Spain, 18–20 September 2002. Proceedings.
9. Broersen, J., Dastani, M., Hulstijn, J., van der Torre, L.W.N.: Goal generation in the BOID architecture. Cognitive Science Quarterly **2**(3-4) (2002) 428–447
10. Boella, G., van der Torre, L.W.N.: Regulative and constitutive norms in normative multiagent systems. In: 9th International Conference on the Principles of Knowledge Representation and Reasoning (KR 2004). (2004) 255–266
11. Boella, G., van der Torre, L.W.: Attributing mental attitudes to normative systems. In Rosenschein, J.S., Wooldridge, M.J., Sandholm, T., Yokoo, M., eds.: 2nd International Joint Conference on Autonomous Agents and Multiagent Systems (AAMAS 2003), ACM Press (2003) 942–943 Poster.
12. Castelfranchi, C., Dignum, F., Jonker, C.M., Treur, J.: Deliberative normative agents: Principles and architecture. In Jennings, N.R., Lespérance, Y., eds.: Intelligent Agents VI. Agent Theories, Architectures, and Languages. Volume 1757 of LNAI. Springer (2000) 364–378 6th International Workshop (ATAL'99), Orlando, FL, USA, 15–17 July 1999. Proceedings.
13. Lopez y Lopez, F., Luck, M.: Towards a model of the dynamics of normative multi-agent systems. In: International Workshop on Regulated Agent-Based Social Systems: Theories and Applications (RASTA 2002). (2002) 175–193
14. Wooldridge, M.: An Introduction to Multiagent Systems. John Wiley & Sons. Chichester, England (2002)
15. Petersen, S.A., Divitini, M., Matskin, M.: An agent-based approach to modelling virtual enterprises. International Journal of Production Planning & Control **12**(3) (2001) 224–233
16. Pea, R., Brown, J.S., Heath, C., eds.: Perspectives on Activity Theory. Cambridge University Press (1999)
17. Nardi, B.A.: Context and Consciousness: Activity Theory and Human-Computer Interaction. MIT Press (1996)
18. Ricci, A., Omicini, A., Denti, E.: Activity Theory as a framework for MAS coordination. In Petta, P., Tolksdorf, R., Zambonelli, F., eds.: Engineering Societies in the Agents World III. Volume 2577 of LNCS. Springer (2003) 96–110 3rd International Workshop (ESAW 2002), Madrid, Spain, 16–17 September 2002. Revised Papers.
19. Viroli, M., Omicini, A.: Coordination as a service: Ontological and formal foundation. Electronic Notes in Theoretical Computer Science **68**(3) (2003) 457–482 1st International Workshop "Foundations of Coordination Languages and Software Architecture" (FOCLASA 2002), Brno, Czech Republic, 24 August 2002. Proceedings.
20. Omicini, A., Zambonelli, F.: Coordination for Internet application development. Autonomous Agents and Multi-Agent Systems **2**(3) (1999) 251–269 Special Issue: Coordination Mechanisms for Web Agents.
21. Omicini, A., Denti, E.: From tuple spaces to tuple centres. Science of Computer Programming **41**(3) (2001) 277–294
22. Omicini, A., Denti, E.: Formal ReSpecT. Electronic Notes in Theoretical Computer Science **48** (2001) 179–196 Declarative Programming – Selected Papers from AGP 2000, La Habana, Cuba, 4–6 December 2000.

23. Omicini, A.: Towards a notion of agent coordination context. In Marinescu, D.C., Lee, C., eds.: Process Coordination and Ubiquitous Computing. CRC Press (2002) 187–200
24. Ricci, A., Viroli, M., Omicini, A.: Agent coordination context: From theory to practice. In Trappl, R., ed.: Cybernetics and Systems 2004. Volume 2., Vienna, Austria, Austrian Society for Cybernetic Studies (2004) 618–623 17th European Meeting on Cybernetics and Systems Research (EMCSR 2004), Vienna, Austria, 13–16 April 2004. Proceedings.
25. Dignum, V.: A Model for Organizational Interaction: Based on Agents, Founded in Logic. PhD thesis, Tekst. - Proefschrift Universiteit Utrecht (2003)
26. Omicini, A., Ricci, A., Viroli, M.: An algebraic approach for modelling organisation, roles and contexts in MAS. Applicable Algebra in Engineering, Communication and Computing 16(2-3) (2005) 151–178 Special Issue: Process Algebras and Multi-Agent Systems.

An Event Driven Approach to Norms in Artificial Institutions*

Francesco Viganò[1], Nicoletta Fornara[1], and Marco Colombetti[1,2]

[1] Università della Svizzera italiana, via G. Buffi 13, 6900 Lugano, Switzerland
{francesco.vigano, nicoletta.fornara,
marco.colombetti}@lu.unisi.ch
[2] Politecnico di Milano, piazza Leonardo Da Vinci 32, Milano, Italy
marco.colombetti@polimi.it

Abstract. The notion of artificial institution is crucial for the specification of open and dynamic interaction frameworks where heterogeneous and autonomous agents can interact to face problems in various fields. In our view the specification of artificial institutions requires a clear standard definition of some basic concepts: the notion of ontology, authorizations, conventions, and the normative component. In this paper we propose an event driven approach to the definition of norms that is mainly based on the manipulation of commitments. We will discuss the crucial differences between the notion of authorization and permission and how the notion of permissions, obligations, and prohibitions can be expressed in our model. We will investigate the connections among the specification of different artificial institutions, in particular how an institution can enrich or further regulate the entities defined in another one. Finally we will briefly present the specification of the Dutch Auction Institution and of the Auction House Institution in order to exemplify the model presented in this paper.

1 Introduction

In the literature, the term *institution* is used with different meanings. Following organization theories, an institution can be seen as an established organization (especially of a public character) with a code of law, like for example a hospital. Drawing inspiration from economics, in multiagent systems the term *electronic institution* is commonly used to refer to a specific organization or to an abstract pattern that regulates the interaction among agents [6, 21]. In particular, institutions are viewed as means for regulating agent behavior in open and dynamic interaction systems , that is, systems where heterogeneous and autonomous agents enter and leave dynamically. In such systems norms play a crucial role because they: (i) regulate the behavior of agents, and (ii) create expectations on the behavior of other agents.

In [17], the term institution is used to refer to a set of concepts that exist only thanks to the common agreement of a community of agents, like for example in the case of ownership. Drawing inspiration from Searle's analysis of social reality, in [9] we have

---

* Supported by Swiss National Science Foundation project 200021-100260, "An Open Interaction Framework for Communicative Agents".

O. Boissier et al. (Eds.): ANIREM and OOOP 2005, LNCS 3913, pp. 142–154, 2006.

introduced the concept of an *artificial institution* as a set of shared concepts and rules that regulate agent interactions. Artificial institutions are abstract specifications defined to obtain open interaction systems where agents can perform actions whose effects are not only limited to the state of the interaction system, but also affect human reality. For example, when an agent participates to an auction and offers an amount of money for an product on sale, if it is declared to be the winner, that product will be delivered to the address of its user, whose bank account will be charged of the negotiated amount of money. We envisage that our framework is suitable for modeling and analyzing e-business and e-government applications.

In [9] we have investigated the relation existing between agent communication and institutional reality, in particular on how agents can modify such reality. Our tenet is that agent communication changes the institutional reality existing among agents, by creating commitments between agents as in [8, 4] and also by creating new institutional states of affairs [9]. One of the most interesting aspects of our research is that we model the context where agent interactions take place and the semantics of communicative acts by means of the very same concepts. In particular, in [9] we have defined a model of institutional reality which can also be employed to describe commitments as institutional entities defined by an institution, that is, the Basic Institution.

Another important advantage of our approach is the coherence between the semantics of communicative acts and the normative component, that is, the set of norms and deontic concepts that model what agents should or should not do when their interactions are regulated by a specific institution. In fact, both communicative acts and norms are defined in terms of operations on institutional reality, in particular on social commitments, a concept widely used to define the semantics of communicative acts [19].

This paper is organized as follows. In Section 2 our view of the main components necessary for the specification of artificial institutions is presented. Among those components norms play a crucial role; our event driven model of norms based on the manipulation of commitments is discussed in Section 3. In Section 4 the connections among the specifications of different artificial institutions are investigated and in Section 5 our model is clarified through an example. Finally in Section 6 we draw some conclusions and delineate some directions for future work.

2   Artificial Institutions

To allow designers to program agents which are able to carry out institutional actions on behalf of their users in different environments, a clear and standard definition of what are the fundamental concepts of an artificial institution is needed. In our view, the specification of an artificial institution consists of the following components [9]:

- the *core ontology*, that is, the definitions of the institutional concepts introduced by the institution and of the institutional actions that operate on them;
- a set of *authorizations* specifying what agents are authorized to perform the institutional actions;
- a set of *conventions* for the concrete performance of institutional actions;
- a set of *norms* that impose obligations, prohibitions and permissions for the agents that interact within the institution.

To specify artificial institutions we adopt an operational semantics and an object-oriented style of specification, like that of the Unified Modeling Language (UML) [2] and Object Constraint Language (OCL) [16]. An advantage of this approach is the fact that it employs concepts that are close to the intuition and knowledge of practitioners. We believe the model we have developed can be easily understood by software engineers who design and implement open multiagent systems. Moreover, our model does not dictate how the system should be implemented, so that the specification of an artificial institution might be implemented on different platforms and with different languages (not necessarily object oriented), which is a fundamental requirement of open systems.

2.1   The Core Ontology

We assume that each institution defines an ontology describing the entities that constitute the context shared by the interacting agents and potentially affected by their communicative acts. In particular, the interaction system is modeled by a set of entities, represented through UML classes, which may have both *natural* and *institutional* attributes. While natural attributes are assumed to represent physical properties, like the size of a book, institutional attributes, like the price of a product on sale, exist only thanks to the common agreement of the agents participating to the institution. An ontology also provides a set of *institutional actions* that allow agents to change institutional attributes.

We define institutional actions by specifying:

- an action name followed by a possibly empty list of parameters: $iaction(param)$;
- a possibly empty set of (ontological) *preconditions*, which specify the values that certain institutional attributes must have;
- a nonempty set of *postconditions*, which specify the values of certain institutional attributes after a successful performance of the action.

Preconditions and effects of institutional actions are expressed through OCL formulae.

2.2   Authorizations and Conventions

Given that institutional actions modify institutional attributes, agents cannot perform such actions by exploiting causal links occurring in the natural world, like the movement of a robotic arm. Instead, we assume that all institutional actions are performed by means of a single type of instrumental actions, namely exchanging messages, thanks to the *counts-as* relation which binds the exchange of a message to the performance of an institutional action.

In order to enable counts-as relations, a set of conventions specifying what kind of message corresponds to every specific institutional action is needed. To specify what kind of message implements an institutional action we define conventions in the following form:

$$ExchMsg(msg\_type, sender, receivers, content) =_{conv} iaction(param)$$

By itself, a convention is not sufficient to guarantee the successful performance of an institutional action by the exchange of the appropriate message: indeed, some additional conditions must be satisfied. Firstly, an agent must be authorized to perform an institutional action. In the specification of an interaction system authorizations are expressed in term of roles, which are usually defined relative to an institutional entity. For example the role of participants and auctioneer are defined relative to the auction entity (see Section 5), and only the auctioneer can open an auction. Moreover an authorization typically holds if certain conditions about the state of the system, expressed by suitable Boolean expressions, are satisfied. For example, it may be established that an auction is validly opened only if there are at least two participants. Therefore, we abstractly define the authorization to perform a specific institutional action (with given parameters) associating it to a role defined in the context of a specific institutional entity (ientity) as follows:

$$Auth(ientity.role, iaction(param), conditions)$$

Secondly, messages realizing institutional actions should be received by all agents that are affected by the performance of the act; for example all the participants of an auction must receive the message that opens it. Finally, ontological preconditions of institutional actions should be satisfied; for instance, an auction cannot be closed if it has not been opened yet.

If all these conditions are satisfied, the exchange of a message conventionally bound to an institutional action counts as the successful performance of such action and its institutional effects take place. In [9] we have discussed how agents can perform all types of institutional actions by means of a single message type, that is, *declare*.

3   The Normative Component

In open systems, norms have been analyzed and used from two different points of view: the design of autonomous agents [13, 7] and the design of interaction systems [20, 21]. From the second perspective norms have been exploited to indicate desirable path for the evolution of the system from an external point of view and to verify if agents are correctly behaving. In doing so, norms play an important role in a multiagent system, in that they make an agent's behavior at least partially predictable and allow agents to coordinate and plan their actions according to the expected behavior of the others, as studied in [15, 14]. But if we do not assume that norms are constraints encoded in each agent as in [15] and [14], norms are not sufficient to prevent undesirable behavior. In fact, in an open multiagent system by themselves norms are not able to banish violations, because the sincerity and benevolence of agents are not guaranteed. In this respect, our point of view is close to [7, 20, 21], where no assumptions are made about the internal structure of agents.

In our framework norms play a fundamental role, because they regulate the execution of institutional actions by an authorized agent and indicate the desired behavior imposing which actions should or should not be performed. We represent agent obligations and prohibitions as commitments that are manipulated by norms, which are treated as event-driven rules. Therefore, before presenting our conceptualization of norms, we need to introduce our model of commitment and how we describe events occurring in a multiagent system.

3.1 Commitments

In this paper we give only a short description of our model of commitment, which is the fundamental entity of what we call the *Basic Institution* [9, 4].

We regard a commitment as an institutional entity characterized by a *debtor*, a *creditor*, a *content*, and a *state*. Commitments are represented with the following notation:

Comm(*state, debtor, creditor, content*)

A commitment undergoes the life cycle described in [8] by reacting either to institutional actions performed by agents or to domain-dependent events, which modify the truth value of the *temporal propositions* (for a detailed treatment see [4]), which can be *undefined*, *true*, or *false*. In [4] we have defined how the truth value of a temporal proposition is calculated. When the content of a commitment is no longer *undefined*, as a consequence of the occurrence of a domain event, the state of that commitment is automatically set to *fulfilled* if the content has become *true*, otherwise it is set to *violated*.

In our framework every agent is authorized to create a commitment by performing the *makeCommitment* institutional action, whose successful performance creates an *unset* commitment. The debtor of an *unset* commitment may refuse it by executing *setCancel*, or it may undertake the proposed commitment by executing *setPending*. We represent a refused commitment by means of the *cancelled* state, whereas an accepted commitment is depicted with the *pending* state. The creditor of *pending* or *unset* commitment can always set it to *cancelled*. Here we report the specification of another institutional action, used in the example of Section 5, *makePendingComm*, which creates a *pending* commitment and whose execution coincides with the sequential performance of *makeCommitment* and *setPending*.

name : **makePendingComm**(*debtor, creditor, content*)
pre :   not *Comm.allInstances* → *exists*(*c*|*c.debtor* = *debtor*
            and c.creditor = *creditor and c.content* = *content*)
post :   *Comm.allInstances* → *exists*(*c*|*c.state* = **pending** *and*
            c.debtor = *debtor and c.creditor* = *creditor and c.content* = *content*)

3.2 Events

As we will see, norms are event-driven rules that, when are fired by events happening in the system, modify commitments affecting the agents having a certain role. Inspired by UML notation for signals[1], here we propose to model type of events as stereotyped classes [2] having attributes that provide information about the state transition that caused them. In our formalization we have singled out three main categories of events:

- a *TimeEvent*, that occurs when the system reaches a certain instant of time;
- a *ChangeEvent*, that happens when an institutional entity changes in some way. This kind of event type can be specialized further:

---

[1] UML models four kinds of events: *signals, calls, passing of time* and *change in state*.

- an *InstitutionalPropertyChange*, registered when an attribute has changed its value;
- an *InstitutionalRelationChange*, occurring when a new relation is *created* or an existing one between the institutional entity and another one is *dropped*;
- an *InstitutionalStateChange*, occurring when an entity modifies its type in a given taxonomy (e.g., when an auction from open becomes closed);
- an *ActionEvent*, that happens when an agent perform an action (an interesting type of this kind of events is *ExchMsg* (see Section 2.2), which represents the act of sending a message).

The definition of event types allows us to describe *event templates*, that is, event types with some restrictions on certain attributes that describe a set of possible event occurrences. Event templates are used in the *on* section of a norm to specify what kind of domain dependent events makes a norm fire.

In our experience, the specification of event templates in the definition of norms can be exploited to obtain an efficient implementation of our framework. In fact, norms should observe events occurring in the system avoiding time consuming operation to detect such changes (a similar problem is also treated in [21]). For this reason, to implement our framework we propose to apply the *observer pattern* [11], which means that objects where certain kinds of events may happen are requested to notify their *observers*, that is, those objects interested in such events, whenever an event occurs. According to the observer pattern, when a norm is interested in observing a certain kind of events, it should register at the institutional entity where they may occur. In order to reduce the number of notifications a norm receives, norms register also an event template describing what kind of events they are interested in. When an event matches an event template, the institutional entity will notify the observer that has registered it by communicating the occurred event.

3.3 Norms

We regard norms as event-driven rules that create or cancel commitments affecting a set of agents that enact a specified role within the institution. From our point of view, commitments are not a specialization of norms as in [7] and norms are not themselves a special kind of commitments as in [3] and [18]. We perceive norms as rules that manipulate commitments of the agents engaged in an interaction. In fact, norms are associated to roles rather than to individual agents, and strictly speaking they cannot be fulfilled or violated: what can be fulfilled or violated is not a norm, but rather a commitment created by the application of a norm. Obviously, when a commitment created by a norm is violated, also that norm can be considered violated, but this fact is not directly recorded in the system.

At an abstract level, a norm is part of the definition of an artificial institution; its instances then regulate and are bounded by the organization that reifies the institution. When an agent fills a role in an institution, we assume that it accepts that norms create commitments binding the agent to a pseudo-agent representing the institution, which we call an *institutional agent*. Such agent allows us to keep trace of commitments created by a certain instance of institution, which also means that commitments created by norms of an institution can be canceled only by norms defined by the same institution; this is because only the creditor of a pending commitment can set it to cancelled [9]. Furthermore, if two commitments are in conflict, an agent can decide which is more important with respect to its own policy (see [13]) by reasoning about which institutional agents have created such commitments.

A norm is defined within an institution and observes an entity of that institution by registering an event template to be notified whenever an event matching the template occurs. Typically, interesting event types are not only communicative acts like in [20], but also the filling of a role by an agent, a value change of an institutional attribute, the reaching of certain instants of time, and so on. When an event matches the given descriptor, the corresponding norm is fired, its variable e is filled with the event, and the norm is activated. If certain contextual conditions, expressed through an OCL formula, are met, the activated norm is applied to a collection of *liable agents*, which are described by an OCL selection expression; in general, the collection of liable agents corresponds to the set of agents that play a given role in the institution. For every liable agent, the norm executes a sequence of institutional actions which create or cancel commitments of the agent toward the institutional agent. The general structure of a norm can be described as follows:

within *context_name*: *ientity*
on e: *event_template*
if *contextual conditions* **then**
    foreach *agent* **in** *liable agent selection expression*
    do $\{commitmentActionDescription(agent, inst\_agent, parameters)\}^+$

A crucial property of our approach is the possibility to verify at runtime if agents are compliant with a given system of norms by identifying whether they have fulfilled all commitments created by norms. Furthermore, by creating a new commitment whenever a norm is applied, we can compute how many times a norm has been violated or fulfilled by counting how many commitments instantiated by that norm are violated or fulfilled. This is important because we consider that a normative system should allow one to detect not only the presence of violations, but also differentiate when and how often they occur. For example, because sanctions may depend on how often an agent have violated a specific norm. Furthermore, the analysis of violations, the conditions that have produced them, and their frequency may provide useful information for the design and improvement of artificial institutions.

Using our formalization of norms, institutions can regulate in an uniform way both the communication protocol and protocol-independent normative aspects, like for instance the fulfillment of agreements made during the interaction. Norms can be used to specify protocols, because they can dictate that in certain circumstances an agent ought to send a given type of message, or react to a message in a specific way. At the same time, norms can forbid the execution of institutional actions, in particular communicative acts, even if they are authorized. Furthermore, in correspondence of events that conclude the interaction process, norms can instantiate commitments to noncommunicative actions, like the payment of the purchased goods at the price negotiated during the interaction (see section 5 and [9, 22]).

3.4   Obligations, Permissions, Prohibitions and Authorizations

In our framework commitments are used to represent all deontic relationships between agents, including as a special case the deontic relationships undertaken by the debtor through communicative acts [9]. In particular, commitments toward institutional agents are used to represent *obligations* and *prohibitions*. In general, we perceive obligations and prohibitions as commitments undertaken by an agent enacting a role within an institution, toward the institution itself; more precisely, obligations are commitments to perform an action of a given type, and prohibitions are commitments not to perform an action of a given type. Furthermore, we interpret the absence of positive or negative commitments to the execution of an action of a given type as *permissions*.

Usually in the agent literature authorization is not distinguished from permission or the former encompasses the latter [5]. For example, in [20] and [6] agent interaction are specified through finite state machines, which represent acts which are both authorized and permitted. Furthermore, in [6, 20] the authors introduce *governor agents*, which do not allow agents to perform communicative acts that are not acceptable according with the current protocol. Similarly, in [13] and [21] norms are used to specify authorizations, which are not distinguished from permissions.

Coherently with the concept of institutionalized power of [12, 1], we distinguish between the notions of authorization and permission. The main difference between authorization and permission resides in the effects of the action. Whereas the former represents a necessary condition for the execution of institutional action, permission represents the need to regulate the performance of authorized actions, but it cannot prevent the effects deriving from the performance of a forbidden act. According to [1] an unauthorized act is performed but invalid, while in our approach is not even performed. Instead, what is successfully performed is the act of exchanging a message, which does not count as the performance of the corresponding institutional action.

4   Connections Among Different Artificial Institutions

We envision that when a designer starts to specify a new artificial institution, there is at his or her disposal a library of previously defined institutions that can be used to create new ones. To obtain a modular and incremental specification of new institutions, we are investigating what relations hold among artificial institutions.

When a new institution is defined by the composition of existing institutions, it can only specify new properties which refer to them but it cannot alter previous specifications. This is because institutional facts exist only thanks to common agreement, and agents involved by the former institution might not participate in the second, and thus might not access it. To preserve agents' common agreement, the new institution must regulate further aspects not regarded by others institutions and cannot be employed as an alternative or substitute of them. Drawing inspiration from UML, we have named this kind of relationship *usage relation*, which means that a *client* institution introduces several features which refer to properties defined by a *supplier* institution. In particular, a client institution may:

- define new institutional attributes relative to entities defined in a supplier institution;
- create norms concerning the performance of institutional actions described by a supplier institution; however, to keep the supplier institutions unaffected, the set of agents liable to such norms must consist of the agents enacting a role in the client institution.

The possibility of creating a new institution from preexisting institutions brings to the foreground our distinction between authorizations and permissions (i.e., the absence of prohibitions). In fact, the supplier institution may authorize the agents enacting a given role to perform a type of institutional action, whose execution is then constrained by local norms in the client institution. In this case, the agent has the necessary institutional power, but it is not permitted to perform that action by the second institution. If it executes such action, its effects take place, but the agent violates a commitment created by a norm.

5   An Example: The Dutch Auction and the Auction House

In this section we will present two specification of *artificial institutions* to exemplify how norms are specified in our framework. This allows us to show how different institutions interact and to clarify the distinction between authorizations and permissions. To this purpose, we shall present our formalizations of the Dutch Auction and of the Auction House holding auctions regulated by the former institution. Due to space limitations, we focus our attention only on those aspects involved in fixing the price of the product on sale.

5.1   The Dutch Auction Institution

During a Dutch Auction an auctioneer tries to fix the price of a product. An agent taking part in a Dutch Auction can fill the role of *participant, auctioneer* or *transaction agent*, the agent that attends to the exchange of money and goods when a price has been accepted. During an auction we assume that a participant cannot be the auctioneer or the transaction agent, while an auctioneer might also fill the role of transaction agent.

After a period of time reserved to the registration of participants, the interaction starts when the *start time* has elapsed and the auctioneer has declared the auction open. Then, the price of the product on sale is initialized, usually higher than the expected final result. When a new price is declared, during the validity of such price, the auctioneer declares as the *winner* the first participant that accepts the *current price*, and then closes the auction. Otherwise, after the time of validity has elapsed, the auctioneer should declare a new *current price*, lower than the previous one, or close the auction.

The ontology of the Dutch Auction is described by the class diagram reported in Figure 1, where institutional entities are assigned to packages representing what institution defines them. Furthermore, concepts like *Agent, Product*, together with the *owner* role are imported from external ontologies. It is important to observe that the *current price* is defined relative to the Product, which means that the Dutch Auction ontology enriches the definition of such an entity by adding a new institutional attribute recognized by the agents involved in the current interaction.

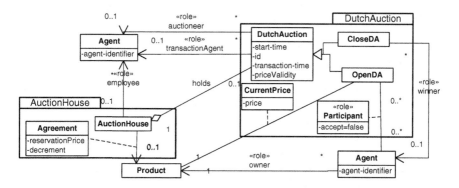

Fig. 1. The Dutch Auction and Auction House Ontologies

The Dutch Auction ontology also defines a set of institutional actions that allow agents to operate on such institutional entities. In particular, an agent may change the current price of a Dutch Auction by performing the *setCurPrice* institutional action. We assume that an agent may change the current price of a Dutch Auction only if the auction is open and the previous price is higher than the new one, which becomes the current price of the auction.

$name$: **setCurPrice**(a_id, p)
pre : $OpenDA.allInstances \rightarrow exists(id = a\_id \text{ and } currentPrice.price > p)$
$post$: $OpenDA.allInstances \rightarrow exists(id = a\_id \text{ and } currentPrice.price = p)$

The Dutch Auction defines a set of authorizations for the performance of institutional actions. Some of these authorizations are conditional: for example an auctioneer is authorized to open an auction only if its *start time* has elapsed and if there are at least two agents registered as participants. Here we report only the authorization that allows the auctioneer of a given auction to perform the *setCurPrice* institutional action.

Auth$(DutchAuction.allInstances \rightarrow select(id = auction\_id).auctioneer,$
    $setCurPrice(auction\_id, price), true)$

The behavior of agents that have joined an interaction system regulated by the Dutch Auction Institution is constrained by a normative system, which prescribes what agents should or should not do in correspondence to relevant institutional events. Likewise [9], we have defined a set of norms that regulate both the communicative acts performed by agents and the final exchange of good and money between the *transaction agent* and the *winner* of the auction (see [22]). The main advantage of our formalization with respect to the one specified by FIPA [10] is that, due to the explicit representation of norms as rules that modify agent commitments, it is possible to model in an uniform way the interaction protocols and the other rules that regulate the interaction framework. Furthermore, when an interaction terminates successfully, agents are explicitly committed by suitable norms to carry out the economic transaction.

5.2   The Auction House Institution

As reported in Figure 1, the Auction House is an institution constituted by a set of *employee* agents, holding several auctions and regulating the commercial relation with the *owner* of the product on sale. The Auction House defines only one role, *employee*, which is the role that an agent should hold in order to fill both the roles of auctioneer and transaction agent.

In order to obtain simpler and shorter OCL expressions, in this paper we will assume that an Auction House runs at most one Dutch Auction. When an agent decides to sell a product trough an auction, it reaches an *agreement* with the Auction House concerning the minimum price at which the product may be sold. Such an institutional fact does not require the agreement of the participants: in fact, participants are not even assumed to know about the existence of a reservation price (not to mention its actual current value). We regard reservation price as an institutional attribute associated to the product and representing a private agreement established between the Auction House and the *owner* of the product on sale.

A norm of the Auction House is related to the *agreement* stipulated between the owner of the good and the auction house and is activated when an employee becomes the auctioneer. This norm commits the auctioneer to not declare a price lower than agreed reservation price.

within h: $AuctionHouse$
on e: $InstitutionalRelationChange(h.dutchAuction, auctioneer, \text{created})$
if $true$ **then**
    foreach $agent$ **in** $h.employee \rightarrow select(em \mid e.involved \rightarrow contains(em))$
    do makePendingComm$(agent, DutchInstAgent(not\ setCurPrice($
        $h.dutchAuction.id, ?p\ [?p < h.agreement.reservationPrice]),$
        $< \text{now}, \text{now} + time\_of(e1 : InstitutionalStateChange($
        $h.dutchAuction, OpenDA, ClosedDA)) >, \forall))$

This norm is activated when an employee fills the role of auctioneer and constrains its behavior to not declare a current price lower than the reservation price, although any price would be legal from the point of view of the Dutch Auction. In fact, the Dutch Auction authorizes the auctioneer to set a new current price, imposing through the ontological preconditions of the *setCurPrice* that it should be lower than the previous one, but not further constrains are imposed.

This example shows clearly that authorizations and permissions may differ when they are relative to different sources. In fact, when a designer wants to force an agent to not perform an institutional action in correspondence of a certain state, he or she can: (i) define a new norm that creates a prohibition to not perform such action; (ii) remove the authorization to perform such act. When a designer specifies a new institution, he or she may arbitrarily choose one of these options to limit agent actions. Instead, when new institutions are defined by using previously defined institutions, agent behaviors can be conditioned only through norms, which prescribe prohibited and permitted actions.

6   Conclusions

In this paper we have presented a model for the specification of artificial institutions which clarify what are the basic concepts that must be specified in order to obtain an institution. We have focused on the conceptualization of norms as event-driven rules that modify agent commitments. The main advantage of our approach is that it employs concepts and a notation that are close to the intuition and knowledge of practitioners, and it is compatible with state-of-art software implementation techniques, in particular with *events programming*. Furthermore, we have discussed the fundamental role played by norms, which allow us to express obligations and prohibitions in terms of commitments. Indeed, norms can represent in a unified way both interaction protocols and other normative aspects. Finally we have shown, through an example, how an interaction system can be specified in terms of norms defined by different artificial institutions. In particular, we have discussed how a designer may define a new interaction framework by using several artificial institutions and what connections might exist between them.

Several research questions are still open, and will be tackled in our future work. We will investigate the development of methods for discovering inconsistencies among different artificial institutions. In particular, we are interested in verifying during the specification phase whether norms may create obligations to perform unauthorized actions, or under what conditions two norms may generate conflicting commitments.

References

1. A. Artikis, M. Sergot, and J. Pitt. Animated Specifications of Computational Societies. In C. Castelfranchi and W. L. Johnson, editor, *Proceedings of the 1st International Joint Conference on Autonomous Agents and Multi-Agent Systems (AAMAS 2002)*, pages 535–542, Bologna, Italy, 2002. ACM Press.
2. G. Booch, J. Rumbaugh, and I. Jacobson. *The Unified Modeling Language User Guide.* Addison-Wesley, Reading, Massachusetts, USA, 1 edition, 1999.
3. C. Castelfranchi. Commitments: From Individual Intentions to Groups and Organizations. In V. Lesser, editor, *Proceedings of the 1st International Conference on Multi-Agent Systems*, pages 528–535, San Francisco, USA, 1995. AAAI-Press and MIT Press.
4. M. Colombetti, N. Fornara, and M. Verdicchio. A Social Approach to Communication in Multiagent Systems. In J. A. Leite, A. Omicini, L. Sterling, and P. Torroni, editors, *Declarative Agent Languages and Technologies*, volume 2990 of *LNAI*, pages 191–220. Springer, 2004.
5. F. Dignum. Autonomous Agents with Norms. *Artificial Intelligence and Law*, 7(1):69–79, 1999.
6. M. Esteva, J. A. Rodríguez-Aguilar, B. Rosell, and J. L. Arcos. AMELI: An Agent-based Middleware for Electronic Institutions. In N. R. Jennings, C. Sierra, L. Sonenberg, and M. Tambe, editors, *Proceedings of the 3rd International Joint Conference on Autonomous Agents and Multi-Agent Systems (AAMAS 2004)*, pages 236–243, New York, USA, 2004. ACM Press.
7. F. López y López and M. Luck and M. d'Inverno. Normative Agent Reasoning in Dynamic Societies. In N. R. Jennings, C. Sierra, L. Sonenberg, and M. Tambe, editors, *Proceedings of the 3rd International Joint Conference on Autonomous Agents and Multi-Agent Systems (AAMAS 2004)*, pages 535–542, New York, USA, 2004. ACM Press.

8. N. Fornara and M. Colombetti. A Commitment-Based Approach to Agent Communication. *Applied Artificial Intelligence an International Journal*, 18(9–10):853–866, 2004.

9. N. Fornara, F. Viganò, and M. Colombetti. Agent Communication and Institutional Reality. In van Eijk et al. [19], pages 1–17.

10. Foundation for Intelligent Physical Agents. FIPA Dutch Auction Interaction Protocol Specification. http://www.fipa.org, 2001.

11. E. Gamma, R. Helm, R. Johnson, and J. Vlissides. *Design Patterns*. Addison Wesley, 1995.

12. A. Jones and M. J. Sergot. A formal characterisation of institutionalised power. *Journal of the IGPL*, 4(3):429–445, 1996.

13. L. Kagal and T. Finin. Modeling Conversation Policies using Permissions and Obligations. In van Eijk et al. [19], pages 123–133.

14. M. Barbuceanu and T. Gray and S. Mankovski. Coordinating with Obligations. In K. P. Sycara and M. Wooldridge, editors, *Proceedings of the 2nd International Conference on Autonomous Agents (Agents'98)*, pages 62–69, New York, 1998. ACM Press.

15. Y. Moses and M. Tennenholtz. Artificial social systems. *Computers and AI*, 14(6):533–562, 1995.

16. Object Management Group. UML 2.0 OCL Specification. http://www.omg.org/, 2003.

17. J. R. Searle. *The construction of social reality*. Free Press, New York, 1995.

18. M. P. Singh. An ontology for commitments in multiagent systems: Toward a unification of normative concepts. *Artificial Intelligence and Law*, 7:97–113, 1999.

19. R. van Eijk, M. P. Huget, and F. Dignum, editors. *Agent Communication*, volume 3396 of *LNAI*. Springer Verlag, 2005.

20. W. W. Vasconcelos. Norm Verification and Analysis of Electronic Institutions. In *Proceedings of the Workshop on Declarative Agent Languages and Technologies (DALT), 3rd International Joint Conference on Autonomous Agents and Multi-Agent Systems (AAMAS 2004)*, 2004.

21. J. Vázquez Salceda, H. Aldewereld, and F. Dignum. Implementing Norms in Multiagent Systems. In I. G. Lindemann, J. Denzinger, I. J. Timm, and R. Unland, editors, *Multiagent System Technologies: Second German Conference (MATES 2004)*, volume 3187 of *LNAI*, pages 313–327, Berlin, Germany, 2004. Springer Verlag.

22. F. Viganò, N. Fornara, and M. Colombetti. An Operational Approach to Norms in Artificial Institutions. Technical Report 2, Institute for Communication Technologies, Università della Svizzera Italiana, 2005.

Part III

Modelling Normative Designs

Designing Normative Behaviour
Via Landmarks*

Huib Aldewereld, Davide Grossi, Javier Vázquez-Salceda, and Frank Dignum

Institute of Information and Computing Sciences
Utrecht University, The Netherlands
{huib, davide, javier, dignum}@cs.uu.nl

Abstract. In highly regulated environments, where a set of norms defines accepted behaviour, protocols provide a way to reduce complexity by giving direct, step by step guidelines for behaviour, as long as the protocols comply with the norms. In this work we propose a formal framework to design a protocol from a normative specification. In order to be able to connect (descriptive) norms with (operational) protocols, an intermediate level is created by the use of landmarks.

1 Introduction

In the last years there has been an explosion of new approaches, both theoretical and practical, focusing on normative specifications as a flexible way to structure, restrict and/or impose behaviour in multiagent systems (MASs).In particular, recent developments focus on norm languages, agent-mediated electronic institutions, contracts, protocols and policies. Our work focuses on a normative approach based on the use of norms in electronic institutions (eInstitutions). Norms are high-level specifications of acceptable behaviour within a given context. Definitions of norms range from very philosophical, in deontic logic, to precise specifications of protocols in agent-mediated eInstitutions.

One of the questions that arises is how to properly connect the norm specification with the behaviour of the agents. Norms are usually defined in some form of deontic logic [19], in order to express accepted (legal) behaviour through *obligations*, *permissions* and *prohibitions*. However, it is hard to directly connect this kind of norms with the practice as:

1. Norms in law are formulated in a very abstract way, i.e., the norms are expressed in terms of concepts that are kept vague and ambiguous on purpose.
2. Norms expressed in deontic logic are *declarative*, i.e., they have no *operational* semantics (they express *what* is acceptable, but not *how* to achieve it).
3. As Wooldridge and Ciancarini explain in [24], in those formalisms and agent theories based in *possible worlds*, there is usually no precise connection between the abstract accessibility relations used to characterise an agent's state

---

* The research was supported by the Netherlands Organisation for Scientific Research (NWO) under project number 634.000.017.

O. Boissier et al. (Eds.): ANIREM and OOOP 2005, LNCS 3913, pp. 157–169, 2006.

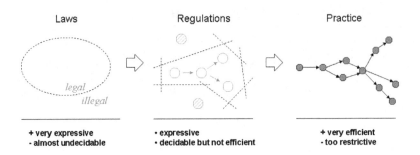

Fig. 1. Comparison between Laws, Regulations and Practice

and any computational model. This makes it difficult to go directly from a
formal specification to an implementation in a computational system.

All these three issues together create a gap between the normative dimension
of agent-mediated institutions and their procedural one (first introduced in [8]).
Some of our previous work has focused on reducing this gap from different perspectives. In [15, 16] formal tools have been proposed to link abstract normative
specifications to more concrete ones (issue 1). In [10, 12, 13] the expressiveness of
norms (issue 2) is extended by means of some variations of deontic logic that include conditional and temporal aspects [4, 9]. However, by introducing some sort
of temporal or dynamic logic operators, the resulting specification becomes more
expressive but computationally too expensive to be used at run-time by agents.
We have also explored some of the operational aspects of norms, by focusing on
how norms should be operationally implemented in multiagent systems (MAS)
from an institutional perspective [21, 22], including the ontological aspects of
norm implementation [3, 5, 15]. Here we try to bring our previous work further,
tackling in part issue 3 and proposing a formal approach to describe an explicit
bridge between institutional norms and protocols.

Our approach is inspired by how the gap is bridged in human institutions.
Human laws express in a very abstract way wanted (legal) and unwanted (illegal) states of affairs. Although laws are very expressive, they do not express
how to achieve a given state of affairs, and therefore they are very hard to use
in practice to, e.g., guide each decision point in a process. In practice more efficient representations are needed, such as protocols or guidelines. In rule-based
legal systems (those based in Roman-Germanic law), *regulations* add an intermediate level between laws and practice, by giving some high-level specifications
on some constraints about how things can or cannot be done. These high-level
descriptions are therefore interpretations of the law that add some operational
constraints to be met by the practice (see figure 1). Using this idea, we introduce
an intermediate level between institutional norm specifications and institutional
protocols based on *landmarks*.

In this paper we consider norms as specifying deontic constraints at a level that
abstracts from the procedural aspects of institutions which are instead involved
in the design of the protocols of the institution [8]. Additionally, we view norms

as specifying (abstract) constraints which have an intrinsic *temporal* flavour [11]. In particular, we are interested in two types of norms: 1) Norms of the form *"it ought to be the case that ρ is the case before δ happens"*, which will be represented by formulas such as $O(\rho \leq \delta)$; and 2) Norms of the form *"it ought never to be the case that ρ"*, which will be represented by formulas $F\rho$.

Throughout this paper we will use as an example a simplification of the information sharing problem between Police forces that belong to either a) different geographical regions, or to b) different levels of national security (standard police, secret services, military forces), with national and/or international regulations that highly constrain the amount of information that can be shared between the forces. In our simplified version of the problem, let us suppose that police officers from two different regions have an individual investigation towards a suspect. However, both regions are forced by law to protect their investigation and, therefore, they cannot always ask the other about this suspect because that could compromise their investigation. The problem can be summarised in the following norm:

> "Police regions are obliged to confirm the knowledge of other police regions about suspects (without leaking that information) before exchanging information on this suspect."

From this norm the following issues arise: 1) How can such a norm be linked to a norm-abiding protocol? 2) Can this link be formally described? These are, in a nutshell, the motivating questions of the present paper.

We claim that landmarks can provide a viable bridge between norms and protocols. If norms specify abstract constraints on a temporal structure, then from this normative/temporal specification a landmark pattern can be extracted which can be used as a *yardstick* to evaluate the norm compliance of concrete protocols. In order to tackle the problem, our approach consists of three steps: 1) formalising a conception of institutional norms (tuned on the ideas just presented); 2) extracting landmark patterns (from such a formalisation); and 3) relating landmark patterns to protocols.

The remainder of this paper is organised as follows. In the next section we discuss the framework for using norms, expressed in CTL, to obtain the landmarks which we use to design a protocol. Then in section 3 we show a concrete example using this formal framework. We end the paper with some conclusions.

2   From Norms to Protocols Via Landmarks: A Framework

2.1   Landmarks

The notion of landmarks has obtained much attention in recent work on multiagent systems. In [18] landmarks are used in order to specify conversation protocols between agents at an abstract level. They are represented as states and they are structured in a partial order describing, essentially, the respective order in which each landmark should be reached. In [12] and [23] landmarks are used with similar purposes in order to provide abstract specifications of organisational interaction in general. In that work, landmarks are formalised as state descriptions, and therefore as sets of states (in a modal logic setting). Analogously, these state descriptions are then partially ordered in directed graphs to form landmark structures which are called *landmark patterns*.

No matter how landmarks are represented – as states, or sets of states – their relevance in protocol specification is dictated by the simple observation that several different agents' actions can bring about the same outcome. Once the outcomes of actions are organised in a structured description (i.e. a landmark pattern), it becomes possible to represent families of protocols abstracting from the actual transitions by which each protocol is constituted. Intuitively, a landmark pattern then represents the important steps that any protocol should contain, and the order in which those steps should be performed: "which steps should be performed and in which order".

In this work, we intend to borrow the notion of landmarks and apply it to the domain of eInstitutions. However, to apply the landmark approach to eInstitutions a key refinement is necessary. In domains such as the one concerning information exchange between Police regions, such positive constraints are not always enough. In fact, institutional regulations also express explicit limitation aspects by means of norms of a prohibitive type. Therefore, in the present work we also introduce a notion of *negative landmarks*. Intuitively, negative landmarks mark the states that should not be reached by any protocol. By means of them, it becomes then possible to extend a landmark pattern description to incorporate a reference to "which steps should not be performed".

The formal definition of a landmark pattern we propose is the following one.

Definition 1 (Landmark pattern). *A landmark pattern is a structure $\mathfrak{L} = \langle L^+, L^-, \leq \rangle$ where L^+ and L^- are finite sets of landmarks and $\leq$ is a partial order on L^+.*

It is instructive to notice that landmarks will be treated just as distinct elements of a structure (the landmark pattern). In fact, we are not interested in representing the content of a landmark, but just that a landmark exists and is related in a specific way with other landmarks. Nevertheless, as we will see in Section 2.4, landmarks will be extracted on the basis of CTL expressions.

Protocols are treated as state-transition systems, that is, structures composed of states and labelled transitions expressing how one can change between states. This means that actions in protocols are expressed as state-transitions, changing the state of the world/protocol.

Definition 2 (Protocol). *A protocol is a structure $\mathfrak{P} = \langle S, \{R_\alpha\}_{\alpha \in \mathcal{A}} \rangle$ where: S is a non-empty finite set of states containing s_0 (the starting state of the protocol) and such that $S_f \subseteq S$ with S_f a finite non-empty set (the set of final states of the protocol), and $\{R_\alpha\}_{\alpha \in \mathcal{A}}$ is a family of relations indexed by a non-empty set of transition labels $\mathcal{A}$.*

The set $\mathcal{A}$ is inductively defined from a set A of atomic labels as follows: 1) $A \subset \mathcal{A}$; 2) if $\alpha, \beta \in \mathcal{A}$ then $\alpha; \beta$ and $\alpha \cup \beta \in \mathcal{A}$. Composite labels $\alpha; \beta$ and $\alpha \cup \beta$

denote transitions obtained via the relational algebra operations of, respectively, sequencing and choice. That is, labels of the form $\alpha; \beta$ denote the transitions obtained performing first an α-transition and then a β-transition: $(s_1, s_3) \in R_{\alpha;\beta}$ iff exists $s_2 \in S$ s.t. $(s_1, s_2) \in R_\alpha$ and $(s_2, s_3) \in R_\beta$. Analogously, labels of the form $\alpha \cup \beta$ denote the transitions obtained performing either an α-transition or a β-transition: $(s_1, s_2) \in R_{\alpha \cup \beta}$ iff $(s_1, s_2) \in R_\alpha$ or $(s_1, s_2) \in R_\beta$[1].

We will show how to connect these two definitions and how to exploit the notion of landmark pattern as a useful tool in order to build an intermediate step between the norms specifying the deontic constraints ranging on the institutions and the actual protocols operating the institution itself.

2.2 Computational Tree Logic

In this section we provide a brief sketch of computational tree logic (CTL), referring to [6, 7, 14] for more detailed discussions.

Well-formed formulas of the language $\mathcal{L}_{\mathrm{CTL}}$ consist of propositional elements combined with $\neg$, $\wedge$ and the temporal operators $E(\varphi U \psi)$ and $A(\varphi U \psi)$, with the following informal reading: $E(\varphi U \psi)$ means that there is a future for which eventually, at some point m the condition ψ will hold, while φ holds from now until then; $A(\varphi U \psi)$ means that for all futures, eventually, at some point m the condition ψ will hold, while φ holds from now until then. Other CTL-operators we use are introduced as abbreviations: $EF\varphi \equiv_{def} E(\top U \varphi)$ and $AG\varphi \equiv_{def} \neg EF \neg \varphi$. With the following informal meaning: $EF\varphi$ means that there exists a future in which φ will eventually hold; $AG\varphi$ means instead that for all possible futures φ holds globally. Standard propositional abbreviations are also assumed.

A CTL model $\mathcal{M} = (S, \mathcal{R}, \pi)$, consists of a non-empty set S of states, an accessibility relation $\mathcal{R}$, and an interpretation function π for propositional atoms. A full path σ in $\mathcal{M}$ is a sequence $\sigma = s_0, s_1, s_2, \ldots$ such that for every $i \geq 0$, s_i is an element of S and $s_i \mathcal{R} s_{i+1}$, and if σ is finite with s_n its final state, then there is no state s_{n+1} in S such that $s_n \mathcal{R} s_{n+1}$. We say that the full path σ starts at s if and only if $s_0 = s$. We denote the state s_i of a full path $\sigma = s_0, s_1, s_2, \ldots$ in $\mathcal{M}$ by σ_i. The validity, $\mathcal{M}, s \models \varphi$, of a CTL-formula φ in a world s of a model $\mathcal{M} = (S, \mathcal{R}, \pi)$ is defined as (the propositional connectives are interpreted as usual):

$$\mathcal{M}, s \models E(\varphi U \psi) \Leftrightarrow \exists \sigma \text{ in } \mathcal{M} \text{ with } \sigma_0 = s, \text{ and } \exists n \text{ such that:}$$
$$(1)\ \mathcal{M}, \sigma_n \models \psi \text{ and}$$
$$(2)\ \forall i \text{ with } 0 \leq i \leq n \text{ it holds that } \mathcal{M}, \sigma_i \models \varphi$$
$$\mathcal{M}, s \models A(\varphi U \psi) \Leftrightarrow \forall \sigma \text{ in } \mathcal{M} \text{ such that } \sigma_0 = s, \text{ it holds that } \exists n \text{ such that}$$
$$(1)\ \mathcal{M}, \sigma_n \models \psi \text{ and}$$
$$(2)\ \forall i \text{ with } 0 \leq i \leq n \text{ it holds that } \mathcal{M}, \sigma_i \models \varphi$$

Validity on a CTL model $\mathcal{M}$ is defined as validity in all states of the model. If φ is valid on a CTL model $\mathcal{M}$, we say that $\mathcal{M}$ is a model for φ. General validity of a formula φ is defined as validity on all CTL models. The logic CTL is the set of all general validities of $\mathcal{L}_{\mathrm{CTL}}$ over the class of CTL models.

---

[1] Notice that $\mathfrak{P}$ is then nothing but a frame for propositional dynamic logic [17].

2.3   A CTL Reduction of Deontic Logic

In this work, we represent norms making use of the CTL reduction approach of deontic logic investigated in [4, 9, 11]. The language $\mathcal{L}_{CTL}$ is expanded by adding a violation constant of the form $Viol^2$ to the set of propositional atoms. Semantically, the atom $Viol$ works like all other atomic propositions and it intuitively denotes the fact that "a violation (of the relevant regulation) occurs".

Definition 3 (Semantics of $O(\rho \leq \delta)$). *Let $\mathcal{M}$ be a CTL model, s a state, and σ a full path starting at s. The modal semantics for formulas $O(\rho \leq \delta)$ is then defined as follows:*

$$\mathcal{M}, s \models O(\rho \leq \delta) \Leftrightarrow \forall \sigma \text{ with } \sigma_0 = s, \forall j :$$
$$\text{if } \forall i, 0 \leq i \leq j : \mathcal{M}, \sigma_i \models \neg \rho$$
$$\text{then } \mathcal{M}, \sigma_j \models \delta \to Viol.$$

This captures the following intuitive reading: if at some future point δ occurs, and until then ρ has not yet been achieved, a violation occurs at that point. Another way to express this is that what norms do is specify which temporal substructures (i.e. which CTL paths) are norm abiding, i.e., do not contain a violation state. It is easy to see that this semantic constraint corresponds to the semantics of the following CTL-formula: $\neg E(\neg \rho U(\delta \wedge \neg Viol))$. Intuitively, there is no path where a state σ_j exists satisfying δ and $\neg Viol$ and such that $\neg \rho$ holds in all the states up to σ_j. This yields the following CTL reduction of $O(\rho \leq \delta)$ expressions:

$$O(\rho \leq \delta) \equiv \neg E(\neg \rho U(\delta \wedge \neg Viol)).$$

More complex reductions are extensively discussed in [4, 9].

With respect to prohibitive norms we define the following CTL reduction.

Definition 4 (Semantics of $F\rho$). *Let $\mathcal{M}$ be a CTL model, s a state, and σ a full path starting at s. The modal semantics for formulas $F\rho$ is then defined as follows:*

$$\mathcal{M}, s \models F\rho \Leftrightarrow \forall \sigma \text{ with } \sigma_0 = s, \forall i : \mathcal{M}, \sigma_i \models \rho \to Viol.$$

Intuitively, the semantics just says that in all future paths it is globally true that ρ implies a violation. Readers acquainted with deontic logic will recognise that this semantics reflects a straightforward transposition of the Andersonian reduction of deontic logic [2] in a CTL modal setting[3]. Notice also that this semantics consists in an unconditioned version of the semantics presented in

---

[2] For reasoning in a multiagent context we may provide violation constants of the form $Viol(a)$ where $a \in Ag$, and Ag a finite set of agent identifiers.

[3] Anderson's reduction consists of interpreting a deontic operator in terms of an alethic one in combination with a violation constant: $O\phi := \Box(\neg \phi \to Viol)$. Such reduction strategy has the advantage of enabling deontic notions in a simple and intuitive way. However, it suffers the typical shortcomings lying in the use of classical material implication. For a discussion of these issues see [19].

Definition 3. Indeed, a CTL characterisation of this reduction is the following one:

$$F\rho \equiv AG(\rho \to Viol).$$

This is easily proven considering the equivalences between the AG and EF operators stated in the previous section: $AG(\rho \to Viol) \equiv \neg E(\top U(\rho \to Viol))$.

2.4   From Norms to Landmark Patterns

Given the semantics of norms presented in the previous section, the operation of extracting landmark patterns from normative specifications amounts to considering the temporal structure characterising the CTL paths in which no violation ever occurs. Technically, this means to explore the CTL models which satisfy the set of norms at issue together with the assertion $AG\neg Viol$ (for all paths, it holds globally that $\neg Viol$). Please note that a general and automated manner for extracting landmarks from a large set of norms is still future work. In this section we give an example to show the intuitions of the idea.

Let us consider the simple case in which the only norms are $O(\rho \leq \delta)$ and $F\psi$. It is easy to see that the following semantic constraint is obtained:

$$\forall \sigma \text{ with } \sigma_0 = s, \forall j : \text{ either } \mathcal{M}, \sigma_j \models \neg\delta \text{ and not } \mathcal{M}, \sigma_j \models \psi$$
$$\text{or } \exists i, 0 \leq i \leq j : \mathcal{M}, \sigma_i \models \rho \text{ and not } \mathcal{M}, \sigma_j \models \psi.$$

As we would intuitively expect, ψ never occurs and either the condition δ also never occurs, or, if it occurs at a certain state, then ρ is the case in some preceding state. In other words, among the paths that abide by $F\psi$, there are two types of paths which abide by $O(\rho \leq \delta)$: the ones in which the condition δ never occurs, and the ones in which the condition does occur after the required state ρ has been reached. Given that we want our protocols to be not just norm-abiding (*safety*), but also goal directed (*liveness*)[4], a trivial landmark pattern for $O(\rho \leq \delta)$ and $F\psi$ would then be the structure $\mathfrak{L} = \langle L^+, L^-, \leq \rangle$ where $L^+ = \{l_1^+, l_2^+\}$, $L^- = \{l_1^-\}$ and $\leq = \{(l_1^+, l_2^+)\}$ and $l_1^+ = \rho$, $l_2^+ = \delta$, $l_1^- = \psi$; this is expressed in figure 2.

This way of understanding the relation between norms and landmark patterns presupposes the idea that, from one set of norms, many landmark patterns can actually be extracted which are equivalent as far as that set of norms is concerned. Trivially, another landmark pattern for the simple example above can be obtained strengthening the positive landmarks or weakening the negative one.

2.5   From Landmark Patterns to Protocols

Given the landmark structure, we design a protocol which abides by the norms of the domain. In this process the landmarks are considered to be sub-goals that protocols need to fulfil. The idea is then that certain protocol states can be linked to the landmark states that were obtained from the norms. For the

---

[4] The point is that a "do nothing" protocol is usually norm-compliant. The liveness issue has been discussed in [1].

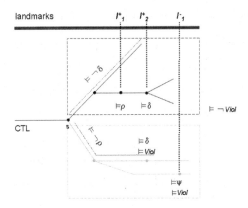

Fig. 2. From norms to landmarks

protocol to be norm-compliant, the linked states of the protocol should satisfy the relational constraints that are included in the landmark structure.

Technically, we have to define a formal relation between definitions 1 and 2.

Definition 5 ($\mathfrak{P}$ compliance with $\mathfrak{L}$). *Given a landmark pattern $\mathfrak{L} = \langle L^+, L^-, \leq \rangle$ and a protocol $\mathfrak{P} = \langle S, \{R_\alpha\}_{\alpha \in \mathcal{A}} \rangle$, we say that $\mathfrak{P}$ complies with $\mathfrak{L}$ if it is possible to define a relation $\mathcal{R} \subseteq L^+ \cup L^- \times S$ such that:*

1. *the restriction $L^+{\restriction}\mathcal{R}$ of the domain of $\mathcal{R}$ to L^+ is non-empty and such that: if $(l, s) \in L^+{\restriction}\mathcal{R}$, then there is an $\alpha \in \mathcal{A}$ such that $(s_0, s) \in R_\alpha$; and there is at least a pair $(l_i, s_i) \in L^+{\restriction}\mathcal{R}$ where landmark $l_i \in L^+$ and $s_i \in S_f$.*
2. *the restriction $L^-{\restriction}\mathcal{R}$ of the domain of $\mathcal{R}$ to L^- is either empty, or such that if $(l, s) \in L^-{\restriction}\mathcal{R}$, then there is no $\alpha \in \mathcal{A}$ such that $(s_0, s) \in R_\alpha$.*
3. *there is no state $s \in S$ such that $(l_i, s), (l_j, s) \in \mathcal{R}$ with $l_i \in L^+$ and $l_j \in L^-$.*

Condition 1 can be strengthened in order to force an embedding of the landmark pattern on the protocol, we say that $\mathfrak{P}$ is linearly compliant with $\mathfrak{L}$:

- *the restriction $L^+{\restriction}\mathcal{R}$ of the domain of $\mathcal{R}$ to L^+ defines an embedding $f : \mathfrak{L} \longrightarrow \mathfrak{P}$. That is to say, that f is a mapping from L^+ to S such that, for all $l_1, l_2 \in L^+$: $l_1 \leq l_2$ iff there exists an $\alpha \in \mathcal{A}$, s.t. $f(l_1)R_\alpha f(l_2)$; and there is at least a pair $(l_i, s_i) \in L^+{\restriction}\mathcal{R}$ where landmark $l_i \in L^+$ and $s_i \in S_f$.*

Condition 1 says that positive landmarks are related to states in the protocol such that those states are always reachable in the protocol from the starting state and that at least one landmark is related to one of the protocol's final states[5]; condition 2 states that $\mathfrak{P}$ does not contain states which count as negative landmarks and if it contains them they are innocuous since they are not reachable from the starting point; condition 3 states that a state cannot be at the same time linked to a positive and a negative landmark. In case $\mathfrak{P}$ is linearly

---

[5] This is a way of capturing the liveness condition we touched upon in Section 2.4.

compliant with $\mathfrak{L}$, the set of positive landmarks is actually mapped on (and not just related to) the protocols. Intuitively, in order for a protocol to embed a landmark pattern, the protocol should behave linearly with respect to the pattern, avoiding branches which require a multiplication of the landmark corresponding states. The example analysed in the following section displays such a protocol.

3   Landmarks in Practice

In this section we show how the theory, explained in previous sections, can be used to guide the behaviour of normative multiagent systems. To do so let us return to the example. Let it be the case that the police in region A has an investigation towards a suspect X that operates in region A. A, however, suspects that X is operating in region B as well, and therefore A assumes that B might have an investigation towards X as well. Moreover, as A suspects that X has connections to corrupt police officers it is imperative that A does not simply asks B "Do you know anything about X?", since that would expose that X is a suspect in an investigation of A, and thereby jeopardising his investigation.

To ensure the safety of A's investigation, A has to abide to the norms holding for this domain. That would mean that A should be aware of whom he is talking to (if A does not confirm that he asks his questions to B it would jeopardise his investigations even more) and that he has to make certain that B knows about X before asking for information about X. Also, by regulation, police regions are not allowed to ask or exchange personal details about persons not being suspected of a criminal offence. The norms that are applicable to this domain are:

1. The identity of police officers should be known to both parties before they begin interacting.
2. Police regions are obliged to confirm the knowledge of other police regions about suspects (without leaking that information) before exchanging information on this suspect.
3. Sharing information about persons who are not under suspicion (of a crime) is forbidden.

By means of the logical formalism described in 2.2 and 2.3 we can translate these norms into the following formulas (we use P_1 and P_2 as variables for police regions, and Y as variable for a person):

1. $O(authenticated(P_1, P_2) \leq interacted(P_1, P_2))$
2. $O(confirmed\_know(P_1, P_2, suspect(Y)) \leq exchanged\_info(P_1, P_2, Y))$
3. $F(exchanged\_info(P_1, P_2, non\_suspect(Y)))$

From these formal norms we can derive, by use of the process described in section 2.4, the positive and negative landmarks and the landmark pattern. From the first norm we obtain the positive landmarks $l_1^+ = authenticated(P_1, P_2)$ and $l_2^+ = interacted(P_1, P_2)$, and the sub-pattern $(l_1^+, l_2^+) \in \leq$. The landmarks we derive from the second norm are $l_3^+ = confirmed\_know(P_1, P_2, suspect(Y))$ and $l_4^+ = exchanged\_info(P_1, P_2, Y)$, and the sub-pattern $(l_3^+, l_4^+) \in \leq$. Finally we obtain a negative landmark $l_1^- = exchanged\_info(P_1, P_2, non\_suspect(Y))$ from the third norm. When combined this forms the following landmark structure:

$$\mathfrak{L} = \langle \{l_1^+, l_2^+, l_3^+, l_4^+\}, \{l_1^-\}, \{(l_1^+, l_2^+), (l_3^+, l_4^+)\}\rangle$$

As described in section 2.5 we use this landmark structure to guide the behaviour of the multiagent system used to assist the officers in regions A and B. The protocol that we obtain from the landmark structure given above is basically made of three separate parts. The first part is a protocol for determining the identity of the different parties involved. This can be anything from the exchange of identity-papers (or, in the case of agents, digital certificates hashed/encoded by some cryptographic key), to something as complex as a cryptography-based authentication protocol for determining identities.

1. A sends B its certificate signed by A's private key ($s_0 \rightarrowtail s_1$).
2. B sends A its certificate signed by B's private key ($s_1 \rightarrowtail s_2$).

After obtaining the certificate from the other party, A needs to decide whether he wants to continue (in case he is convinced of the identity of B), or that he wants to halt the protocol (steps 3.1 ($s_2 \rightarrowtail s_{3.1}$) and 3.2 ($s_2 \rightarrowtail s_{3.2}$)); we are now in landmark l_1^+.

The part of the protocol that A and B execute when A decides to go forth is, in itself, a complex protocol, taken from [20], that needs to be executed so that A knows that B already knows about X and vice versa, i.e., the protocol is used such that both parties prove their knowledge about X to the other party. Note that starting this part of the protocol is considered *interacting*, and we therefore reached landmark l_2^+.

4. Region A chooses an Information Block (IB) $I_A \in KB_A$ of which they want to prove their knowledge to region B, and of which they want to test B's possession ($s_{3.1} \rightarrowtail s_4$).
5. A computes $I_{A*} \subseteq KB_A$ and generates a random challenge C_A such that it discriminates within I_{A*} ($s_4 \rightarrowtail s_5$).
6. A sends B the message $\{H_1 = hash(pad(I_A, \{N\})), C_A\}$ ($s_5 \rightarrowtail s_6$).
7. B computes $I_{B*} \subseteq KB_B$ ($s_6 \rightarrowtail s_7$).
8. B does one of the following:
   (1) B generates a random challenge C_B such that it discriminates within I_{B*}, and sends A the message $\{C_B\}$ ($s_7 \rightarrowtail s_{8.1}$).
   (2) B sends A the message $\{halt\}$ and the protocol is halted ($s_7 \rightarrowtail s_{8.2}$).
9. A sends B the message $\{H_{2_A} = hash(pad(I_A, \{N, A, C_B\}))\}$ ($s_{8.1} \rightarrowtail s_9$).
10. B verifies whether the received H_{2_A} equals any $hash(pad(I_{B_i}, \{N, A, C_B\}))$, where $I_{B_i} \in I_{B*}$ (locally computed). If they are equal, B concludes that I_A equals the matching I_{B_i}, and thereby verifies that A knows the matching I_{B_i} (which is called I_B from here on) ($s_9 \rightarrowtail s_{10}$).
11. If B is willing to prove his knowledge of I_B to A, B sends A the message $\{H_{2_B} = hash(pad(I_B, \{N, B, C_A\}))\}$ ($s_{10} \rightarrowtail s_{11}$).
12. A verifies whether the received H_{2_B} is equal to $hash(pad(I_A, \{N, B, C_A\}))$ (locally computed). If they are equal, A concludes that I_A equals I_B, and thereby verifies that B knows the matching I_A ($s_{11} \rightarrowtail s_{12}$).

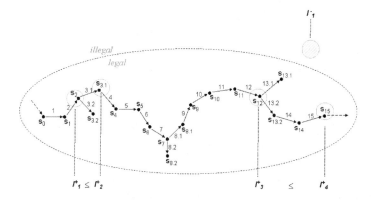

Fig. 3. From landmarks to protocol

Again, at the end A needs to decide whether he wants to go through or not, depending on whether B succeeded in proving to A that he knows about A (step 13.1 ($s_{12} \rightarrowtail s_{13.1}$) and 13.2 ($s_{12} \rightarrowtail s_{13.2}$)). Note that B has a similar decision point at step 8. By now we have arrived landmark l_3^+.

The final part (to get from l_3^+ to l_4^+) can then be as simple as:

14. A tells B everything he knows about X ($s_{13.2} \rightarrowtail s_1 4$).
15. B tells A everything he knows about X ($s_1 4 \rightarrowtail s_{15}$).

More complex interaction and information exchange protocols can be used instead if desired, though.

Given the protocol specification above we obtain the following formal protocol structure (as specified in definition 2):

$$\mathfrak{P} = \langle \{s_0, s_1, s_2, s_{3.1}, s_{3.2}, \dots, s_{15}\}, \{R_i\}_{i \in \mathcal{A}} \rangle$$

where $\mathcal{A}$ is the set $\{1, 2, 3.1, 3.2, \dots, 14, 15\}$ closed under ; and $\cup$ operations. Figure 3 depicts this protocol and its compliance with the landmark pattern. Compliance of $\mathfrak{P}$ is guaranteed, on the basis of definition 5, by the following relation between landmarks and states in the protocols:

$$\mathcal{R} = \{(l_1^+, s_2), (l_2^+, s_{3.1}), (l_3^+, s_{12}), (l_4^+, s_{15})\}.$$

Please note that a) $(l_1^+, l_2^+) \in \leq$ iff $(s_2, s_{3.1}) \in R_{3.1}$, and $(l_3^+, l_4^+) \in \leq$ iff $(s_{12}, s_{15}) \in R_{13.2;14;15}$; b) there is no $s \in \{s_0, \dots, s_{15}\}$ such that $(l_1^-, s) \in \mathcal{R}$; and c) that landmark l_4^+ is associated to one of the final states of the protocol.

4   Conclusions

In this paper we proposed a formal framework to design agent protocols from a normative specification. As norms are declarative in nature, they cannot be directly connected to a protocol (operational in nature). In order to tackle the problem, we introduced landmarks as an intermediate level. Landmarks reduce the complexity of normative reasoning by capturing a) the important states of affairs, as defined in the norms, and b) the operational constraints between those states. This information can then be used to design a norm-compliant protocol.

Although we only examined a small set of norms in this paper, we feel confident that this approach can be used for larger and more complex domains as well. Note, however, that large sets of complex norms can lead to a CTL-model with violations occurring along all paths. This does not indicate a flaw in the model or the technique used, but merely indicates that no norm-compliant protocol can be extracted for such a domain.

Norm compliance has also been studied in [1], where the main focus was on checking the norm compliance of a given protocol against the norms by means of a formal framework. Here instead, we introduce the idea of extracting landmarks from the norms to guide the protocol design. We also foresee landmarks as a way for agents to evaluate norm compliance of protocols on-line, i.e. at runtime.

One of the lines we want to explore is how agents may use landmarks to dynamically create or adapt protocols at run-time: given a protocol and the landmarks, agents may reason about acceptable variations of the protocol that are *legal* and that allow them to fulfil their interests or to cope with an unexpected situation not foreseen in the protocol. Given some landmarks, agents may even negotiate the protocol to use. Another line to explore is the impact of landmarks in norm enforcement: on-line checking the execution of protocols by making sure that the systems does not pass through any negative landmarks.

References

1. H. Aldewereld, J. Vázquez-Salceda, F. Dignum, and J.-J.Ch. Meyer. Proving norm compliancy of protocols in electronic institutions. Technical Report UU-CS-2005-010, Institute of Information and Computing Sciences, Utrecht University, 2005.
2. A.R. Anderson. A reduction of deontic logic to alethic modal logic. *Mind*, 22:100–103, 1958.
3. G. Boella and L. Lesmo. Deliberative normative agents. In C. Dellarocas and R. Conte, editors, *Workshop on Norms and Institutions in Multi-Agent Systems*, pages 15–25. ACM-AAAI, ACM Press, 2000.
4. J. Broersen, F. Dignum, V. Dignum, and J.-J. Ch. Meyer. Designing a Deontic Logic of Deadlines. In *7th Int. Workshop on Deontic Logic in Computer Science (DEON'04)*, Portugal, May 2004.
5. C. Castelfranchi, F. Dignum, C. Jonker, and J. Treur. Deliberative Normative Agents: Principles and architecture. In *Proc. of the 6th Int. Workshop on Agent Theories, Architectures, and Languages (ATAL-99)*, 1999.
6. E.M. Clarke, E.A. Emerson, and A.P. Sistla. Automatic verification of finite-state concurrent systems using temporal logic specifications. *ACM Transactions on Programming Languages and Systems*, 8(2), 1986.
7. E.M. Clarke, O. Grumberg, and D. Long. Verification tools for finite-state concurrent systems. In *A decade of concurrency*, volume 803 of *Lecture Notes in Computer Science*, pages 124–175. Springer, 1993.

8. F. Dignum. Abstract norms and electronic institutions. In *Proceedings of the International Workshop on Regulated Agent-Based Social Systems: Theories and Applications (RASTA '02), Bologna*, pages 93–104, 2002.

9. F. Dignum, J. Broersen, V. Dignum, and J.-J. Ch. Meyer. Meeting the Deadline: Why, When and How. In *3rd Goddard Workshop on Formal Approaches to Agent-Based Systems (FAABS)*, Maryland, April 2004.

10. F. Dignum, D. Kinny, and L. Sonenberg. From Desires, Obligations and Norms to Goals. *Cognitive Science Quarterly*, 2(3-4):407–430, 2002.

11. F. Dignum and R. Kuiper. Combining dynamic deontic logic and temporal logic for the specification of deadlines. In R. Sprague Jr., editor, *Proc. of 13th HICSS*, 1997.

12. V. Dignum. *A Model for Organizational Interaction*. SIKS Dissertation Series, 2003.

13. V. Dignum, J.-J.Ch. Meyer, F. Dignum, and H. Weigand. Formal Specification of Interaction in Agent Societies. In *2nd Goddard Workshop on Formal Approaches to Agent-Based Systems (FAABS)*, Maryland, Oct. 2002.

14. E.A. Emerson. Temporal and modal logic. In J. van Leeuwen, editor, *Handbook of Theoretical Computer Science, volume B: Formal Models and Semantics*, chapter 14, pages 996–1072. Elsevier Science, 1990.

15. D. Grossi, H. Aldewereld, J. Vázquez-Salceda, and F. Dignum. Ontological aspects of the implementation of norms in agent-based electronic institutions. Accepted for the 1st International Symposium on Normative Multiagent Systems (NorMAS2005), 2005.

16. D. Grossi and F. Dignum. From abstract to concrete norms in agent institutions. In M. G. Hinchey, J. L. Rash, W. F. Truszkowski, and et al., editors, *Formal Approaches to Agent-Based Systems: Third International Workshop, FAABS 2004*, Lecture Notes in Computer Science, pages 12–29. Springer-Verlag, April 2004.

17. D. Harel. Dynamic logic. In D. Gabbay and F. Guenthner, editors, *Handbook of Philosophical Logic: Volume II: Extensions of Classical Logic*, pages 497–604. Reidel, Dordrecht, 1984.

18. Sanjeev Kumar, Marcus J. Huber, Philip R. Cohen, and David McGee. Toward a formalism for conversation protocols using joint intention theory. *Computational Intelligence*, 18(2):174–228, 2002.

19. J.-J. Ch. Meyer and R.J. Wieringa. *Deontic Logic in Computer Science: Normative Systems Specification*. John Wiley and sons, 1991.

20. W. Teepe. New protocols for proving knowledge of arbitrary secrets while not giving them away. In Sieuwert van Otterloo, Peter McBurney, Wiebe van der Hoek, and Michael Wooldridge, editors, *Proceedings of the 1st Knowledge and Games Workshop*, pages 99–116, Liverpool, July 2004.

21. J. Vázquez-Salceda, H. Aldewereld, and F. Dignum. Implementing norms in multiagent systems. In G. Lindemann, J. Denzinger, I.J. Timm, and R. Unland, editors, *Multiagent System Technologies*, LNAI 3187, pages 313–327. Springer-Verlag, 2004.

22. J. Vázquez-Salceda, H. Aldewereld, and F. Dignum. Norms in multiagent systems: some implementation guidelines. In *Second European Workshop on Multi-Agent Systems (EUMAS'04)*, Barcelona, December 2004.

23. J. Vázquez-Salceda, V. Dignum, and F. Dignum. Organizing multiagent systems. Technical report, Institute of Information and Computing Sciences, Utrecht University, 2004.

24. M. Wooldridge and P. Ciancarini. Agent-oriented software engineering. In S. K. Chang, editor, *Handbook of Software Engineering and Knowledge Engineering*, volume 1, pages 507–522. World Scientific Publishing Co., 2002.

Design by Contract
Deontic Design Language for Multiagent Systems

Christophe Garion[1] and Leendert van der Torre[2]

[1] SUPAERO
10 avenue Édouard Belin
31055 Toulouse
France
garion@supaero.fr
[2] University of Luxembourg
Luxembourg
leendert@vandertorre.com

Abstract. Design by contract is a well known theory that views software construction as based on contracts between clients (callers) and suppliers (routines), relying on mutual obligations and benefits made explicit by assertions. However, there is a gap between this theory and software engineering concepts and tools. For example, dealing with contract violations is realized by exception handlers, whereas it has been observed in the area of deontic logic in computer science that violations and exceptions are distinct concepts that should not be confused. To bridge this gap, we propose a software design language based on temporal deontic logic. Moreover, we show how preferences over the possible outcomes of a supplier can be added. We also discuss the relation between the normative stance toward systems implicit in the design by contract approach and the intentional or BDI stance popular in agent theory.

1 Introduction

Design by contract [1, 2, 3] is a well known software design methodology that views software construction as based on contracts between clients (callers) and suppliers (routines), relying on mutual obligations and benefits made explicit by assertions. It has been developed in the context of object oriented programming, it is the basis of the programming language Eiffel, and it is well suited to design component-based and agent systems. However, there is still a gap between this methodology and formal tools supporting it. For example, dealing with contract violations is realized by exception handlers, whereas it is well known in the area of deontic logic in computer science [4, 5] that violations and exceptions are distinct concepts that should not be confused. Formal tool support for design by contract is therefore a promising new application of deontic logic in computer science [6]. In this paper we study how extensions of deontic logic can be used as a design language to support design by contract. We address the following four research questions.

1. Which kind of deontic logic can be used as a design language to support design by contract?

O. Boissier et al. (Eds.): ANIREM and OOOP 2005, LNCS 3913, pp. 170–182, 2006.

2. How can we add preferences over possible outcomes of a routine?
3. What kind of properties can be formalized by such a design logic?
4. How does this approach based on deontic logic compare to the BDI approach, dominant in agent oriented software engineering?

The motivation of our work is the formal support for agent based systems. Recently several agent languages and architectures have been proposed which are based on obligations and other normative concepts instead (or in addition to) knowledge and goals (KBS), or beliefs, desires and intentions (BDI). In artificial intelligence the best known of these normative approaches is probably the IMPACT system developed by Subrahmanian and colleagues [7]. In this approach, wrappers built around legacy systems are based on obligations. We are interested in particular in designing component based agent systems such as agents based on the BOID architecture [8]. Notice that this paper does not address pure logical aspect. We do not define a specific logic for reasoning about such notions, but we use existing formalisms to model design by contract and preferences about possible outcomes of a routine.

The layout of this paper is as follows. In Section 2 we discuss design by contract, the deontic design language and contract violations. In Section 3 we introduce preferences over outcomes. In section 4 we compare this approach based on deontic logic to the KBS/BDI approach.

2 Design by Contract

We explain design by contract by an example program in the Eiffel programming language. The explanation of design by contract as well as the example have been taken from [9]. For further details on design by contract, see [1, 2, 3].

2.1 Conditional Obligations

Design By Contract views software construction as based on contracts between clients (callers) and suppliers (routines), relying on mutual obligations and benefits made explicit by *assertions*. These assertions play a central part in the Eiffel method for building reliable object-oriented software. They serve to make explicit the assumptions on which programmers rely when they write software elements that they believe are correct. In particular, writing assertions amounts to spelling out the terms of the *contract* which governs the relationship between a routine and its callers. The precondition binds the callers; the postcondition binds the routine.

The Eiffel class in the left column of Figure 1 illustrates assertions (ignore for now the right column). An account has a balance (an integer) and an owner (a person). The only routines – **is** ... **do** ... **end** sequences – accessible from the outside are increasing the balance (deposit) and decreasing the balance (withdraw). Assertions play the following roles in this example.

Routine preconditions express the requirements that clients must satisfy when they call a routine. For example the designer of *ACCOUNT* may wish to permit a withdrawal operation only if it keeps the account's balance at or above the minimum. Preconditions are introduced by the keyword **require**.

```
class ACCOUNT
feature
 balance: INTEGER
 owner: PERSON
 min_balance: INTEGER is 1000
 deposit(sum:INTEGER) is
  require
   sum >= 0                              -- Ocr(sum >= 0)
  do
   add(sum)
   ensure balance = old balance + sum   -- Orc(balance = old balance + sum)
  end
 withdraw(sum:integer) is
  require
   sum >= 0                              -- Ocr(sum >= 0)
   sum <= balance - min_balance         -- Ocr(sum <= balance - min_balance)
  do
   add(-sum)
  ensure
   balance = old balance - sum          -- Orc(balance = old balance - sum)
  end
feature [NONE]
 add(sum:INTEGER) is
  do
   balance:=balance+sum
  end
invariant
 balance >= min_balance                 -- Or(balance >= min_balance)
end -- class ACCOUNT
```

Fig. 1. Class $ACCOUNT$

Routine postconditions, introduced by the keyword **ensure**, express conditions that the routine (the supplier) guarantees on return, if the precondition was satisfied on entry.

A class invariant must be satisfied by every instance of the class whenever the instance is externally accessible: after creation, and after any call to an exported routine of the class. The invariant appears in a clause introduce by the keyword **invariant**, and represents a general consistency constraint imposed on all routines of the class.

2.2 Deontic Design Language

We are interested in a deontic design language to support specification and verification based on design by contract. The deontic design language is therefore a kind of specification and verification language.

Syntactically, assertions are boolean expressions. To formalize the assertions in our design language, we use a deontic logic based on directed obligations, as used in electronic commerce and in artificial intelligence and law [10, 11, 12, 13]. A modal formula $O_{a,b}(\phi)$ for a, b in the set of objects (or components, or agents) is read as "object a is obliged toward object b to see to it that ϕ holds". We write c and r for the caller and for the routine, such that the assertions in the program can be expressed as the logical formulae given in the right column in Figure 1. Summarizing:

Require $\phi = O_{c,r}(\phi)$: caller c is obliged toward routine r to see to ϕ.
Ensure $\phi = O_{r,c}(\phi)$: routine r is obliged toward caller c to see to ϕ.
Invariant $\phi = O_r(\phi)$: routine r is obliged to see to ϕ.

To use the obligations above in a deontic design language, we have to add temporal information. First, we have to formalize "**old** *expression*" as it occurs for example in line 12 of class $ACCOUNT$. This expression is only valid in a routine postcondition, and denotes the value the expression has on routine entry. Consequently, we have to distinguish between expressions true at entry of the routine and at exit of it. More generally, we have to reason how the assertions change over time. For example, the require obligation only holds on entrance, the **ensure** obligation holds on exit, and the invariant obligation holds as long as the object exists. The obligations only hold conditionally. For example, if the preconditions do not hold, than the routine is not obliged to see to it that the ensure expression holds. Finally, the conditional obligations come into force once the object is created, and cease to exist when the object is destructed.

We therefore combine the logic of directed obligations with linear time logic (LTL), well known in specification and verification [14]. There are many alternative temporal logics which we could use as well. For example, in [15] deontic logic is extended with computational tree logic in $BDIO_{CTL}$, and in [16] it is extended with alternating time logic (ATL). Semantics and proof theory are straightforward, see for example [15].

Definition 1 (Syntax O_{LTL}). *Given a finite set A of objects (or components, or agents) and a countable set P of primitive proposition names. The admissible formulae of O_{LTL} are recursively defined by:*

1 Each primitive proposition in P is a formula.
2 If α and β are formulae, then so are $\alpha \wedge \beta$ and $\neg \alpha$.
3 If α is a formula and $a, b \in A$, then $O_{a,b}(\alpha)$ is a formula as well.
4 If α and β are formulae, then $X\alpha$ and $\alpha U \beta$ are formulae as well.

We assume the following standard abbreviations:

disjunction	$\alpha \vee \beta \equiv_{def} \neg(\neg \alpha \wedge \neg \beta)$
implication	$\alpha \rightarrow \beta \equiv_{def} \neg \alpha \vee \beta$
globally α	$\Diamond(\alpha) \equiv_{def} \top U \alpha$
future α	$\Box(\alpha) \equiv_{def} \neg\Diamond(\neg\alpha)$
permission	$P_{a,b}(\alpha) \equiv_{def} \neg O_{a,b}(\neg\alpha)$
prohibition	$F_{a,b}(\alpha) \equiv_{def} \neg P_{a,b}(\alpha)$
obligation	$O_a(\alpha) \equiv_{def} O_{a,a}(\alpha)$

We now illustrate how to use the logic to reason about assertions. We assume the following propositions: create(c) holds when object c is created, destruct(c) holds when object c is destructed, call(c_1,c_2,f) holds when object c_1 calls routine f in object c_2. We assume that if a routine in an object is called, there is an earlier moment in time at which the object is created. However, since our operators only consider the future, this property cannot be formalized. We assume that propositions can deal with integers, a well known issue in specification and verification, see [14] for further details. Finally, we assume that the time steps of the temporal model are calls to routines. The first routine and the invariant in the class account in Figure 1 can now be formalized as:

call(c_1,c_2,deposit(sum:INTEGER)) $\rightarrow O_{c_1,c_2}$(sum ≥ 0)
(call(c_1,c_2,deposit(sum:INTEGER))) $\wedge$(sum $>= 0$) $\wedge$ (balance = b)) $\rightarrow XO_{c_2,c_1}$(balance = b + sum)
create(c) $\rightarrow$ (O_c(balance $\geq$ min_balance) U destruct(c))

These formulas can be read as follows. If there is a call of c_1 to c_2 to deposit a sum, then c_1 is obliged towards c_2 that this sum is not negative. If there is such a call, the sum is not negative and the balance is b, then there is an obligation of c_2 towards c_1 that the new balance is b increased with the deposited sum. Once an object is created and until it is destructed, it is obligatory that the balance is at least the minimal balance.

2.3   Contract Violations

Whenever there is a contract, the risk exists that someone will break it. This is where exceptions come in the design by contract theory. Exceptions – contract violations – may arise from several causes. One is an assertion violation, if run-time assertion monitoring is selected. Another is a signal triggered by the hardware or operating system to indicate an abnormal condition such as arithmetic overflow, or an attempt to create a new object when there is not enough memory available. Unless a routine has been specified to handle exceptions, it will **fail** if an exception arises during its execution. This in turn provides one more source of exceptions: a routine that fails triggers an exception in its caller.

A routine may, however, handle an exception through a **rescue** clause. An example using the exception mechanism is the routine *attempt_deposit* that tries to add *sum* to *balance*:

```
attempt_deposit(sum:INTEGER) is
 local
  failures: INTEGER
 require
  sum >= 0;                      -- Ocr(sum >= 0)
 do
  if failures < 50 then
   add(sum);
   successful := True
  else
   successful := False
 rescue
  failures := failures + 1;
  retry
 ensure
  balance = old balance + sum    -- Orc(balance = old balance + sum)
 end
```

The actual addition is performed by an external, low-level routine *add*; once started, however, *add* may abruptly fail, triggering an exception. Routine *attempt_deposit* tries the deposit at most 50 times; before returning to its caller, it sets a boolean attribute *successful* to *True* or *False* depending on the outcome. This example illustrates the simplicity of the mechanism: the **rescue** clause never attempts to achieve the routine's original intent; this is the sole responsibility of the body (the **do** clause). The only role of the **rescue** clause is to clean up the objects involved, and then either to fail or to retry.

The principle is that *a routine must either succeed or fail*: it either fulfills its contract, or not; in the latter case it must notify its caller by triggering an exception. The optional **rescue** clause attempts to "patch things up" by bringing the current object to a stable state (one satisfying the class invariant). Then it can terminate in either of two ways: either the **rescue** clause may execute a **retry** instruction, which causes the routine to restart its execution from the beginning, attempting again to fulfil its contract, usually through another strategy (this assumes that the instructions of the **rescue** clause, before the retry, have attempted to correct the cause of the exception), either the **rescue** clause does not end with a **retry** and the routine fails; it returns to its caller, immediately triggering an exception (the caller's **rescue** clause will be executed according to the same rules).

In our design language, the exception can be formalized as a violation, and the exception handler gives rise to a so-called contrary-to-duty obligation, a kind of obligation comes in force only in sub-ideal situations. The formalization of contrary-to-duty obligations has been the subject of many debates in deontic logic due to its role in many of the notorious deontic paradoxes such as the Chisholm and Forrester paradox; we do not go into the details here.

For example, there is a violation if the postcondition does not hold, i.e., we do not have balance = old balance + sum. In case of violation, a retry means that the obligation persists until the next time moment. We extend the language with the proposition *retry*. Now, the fact that a retry implies that the postcondition holds again for the next moment can be characterized as follows: $O_{c_1,c_2}(\phi) \wedge \neg\phi \wedge retry \rightarrow XO_{c_1,c_2}(\phi)$. This formula can be read as follows. If c_1 is obliged towards c_2 that ϕ, ϕ is not the case and retry is true, then in the next state there is again such an obligation for c_1 towards c_2.

3 Contracts for Agents

In this section we adapt the design by contract theory to deal with the autonomy of agents, and we extend the deontic design language with preferences.

3.1 Preferences over Outcomes

In this paper we are in particular interested in contracts with agent routines [17]. We assume as usual that the distinction between agents and components or objects is that agents are autonomous. In this paper we interpret this autonomy in the sense that agent routines can select among various outputs satisfying the caller's condition. We illustrate our notion of autonomy by adapting the class `Account`, which is often used to illustrate design by contract and other object-oriented techniques, such that a call to a routine may result in several outcomes. An account now consists of a set of bank notes, and when depositing we have to specify not only the amount but also how the amount is distributed over the notes. Moreover, when withdrawing money, the routine can choose how to return it. For example, when returning euro 100 the routine can either return one euro 100 note, two euro 50 notes, five euro 20 notes, etc.

Considering now such an autonomous routine, both routine and caller have preferences over outcomes. The routine specifies which outcomes it tries to achieve, and the caller has preferences over outcomes too, and uses them to evaluate whether the routine has satisfactorily fulfilled the contract. In some cases the preferences of both caller and routine coincide. For example, concerning the level of precision, both caller and routine may prefer more precise outcomes over less precise ones. However, this is not always the case. For example, a routine may prefer fast global results over slow detailed results.

In the running example, it may seem unnatural to define preferences over outcomes – it is therefore also not a good example to illustrate the use of autonomy for agents. However, many examples discussed in the agent literature can naturally be described in this way. That is, the autonomy of agents can often be described by their ability to decide for themselves which answer to return from a set of alternatives. For example, an agent component for hotel search in a web-based booking application has to choose among a huge set of answers. This agent component can be specified by a contract as defined in section 2. The preconditions may be the location of the hotel, the arrival and departure dates of the customer. An informal postcondition for the hotel search component can be "the component will produce a set of hotels satisfying the precondition". However, among this set of hotels, the caller of the routine may choose only the cheapest hotels. Or the agent component may prefer not to have all the hotels satisfying the preconditions, but to obtain the result in less than one second to economize resources. When these criteria are taken into account in the agent component's preconditions, then the component would not longer be autonomous. However, this is clearly not how it works in practice. The reason that such web services are autonomous is that the number of possible answers is very large, and it is changing all the time. Obliging the caller to foresee all possible answers is unrealistic.

We do not want to claim that all kinds of autonomy – or all kinds of agents - can be modelled using preferences over outcomes. For example, another kind of autonomy is the ability of agents to violate norms. It is not clear how to specify this kind of autonomy using preferences over outcomes. However, this kind of norm autonomy can already be specified in the deontic design language introduced in the previous section, because agents can violate the obligations.

3.2 Quality of Outcomes

In the design by contract theory, such preferences have not been incorporated yet. The reason is that this theory has been developed for passive objects and components. However, such preferences have been studied in cases where the routines are more autonomous, such as service level architectures, agent theory and artificial intelligence. We therefore propose to extend the contracts between caller and routine such that the contract specifies the preferences of the routine as well as the preferences of the caller.

In our deontic design language, we have to combine the deontic notion of obligation with conditional preferences studied in practical reasoning and decision theory. We use a preference order on the possible answers given by the component. For instance, consider the withdraw routine of the Account class. Suppose that the routine can return euro 100 notes, euro 50 notes and euro 20 notes. The routine may prefer to deliver as many euro 100 notes as possible, thereafter as many euro 20 notes as possible and finally as many euro 50 notes as possible. Using 20, 50 and 100 as propositional variables with the obvious meaning, the preference order over outcomes for the routine will be (these outcomes are mutually exclusive): $100 \wedge \neg 50 \wedge \neg 20 <_r \neg 100 \wedge \neg 50 \wedge 20 <_r \neg 100 \wedge 50 \wedge \neg 20$.

Those preferences are given *ceteris paribus* [18], i.e., the routine prefers delivering as many euro 100 notes as possible to delivering as many euro 50 notes as possible all else being equal. Notice that the previous preference order over outcomes can be *conditional*. The conditions are some properties of the input of the component, as properties of the outcomes are used in the preference order. For instance, the routine may use this order only if the sum to be withdrawn is more than 200 euros. In the contrary case, the routine may prefer to deliver as many euro 50 notes as possible. Like in the CP-net formalism [19], the preference specification of the `withdraw` routine can now be represented by *a conditional preference table*:

200+	$100 \land \neg 50 \land \neg 20 <_r \neg 100 \land \neg 50 \land 20 <_r \neg 100 \land 50 \land \neg 20$
¬ 200+	$\neg 100 \land 50 \land \neg 20 <_r \neg 100 \land \neg 50 \land 20 <_r 100 \land \neg 50 \land \neg 20$

The caller of the routine may also specify some preference order over the outcomes. For instance, a user of the `withdraw` routine may specify that he/she prefers to have as many euro 20 notes as possible, then to have as many euro 50 notes as possible and finally to have as many euro 100 notes as possible: $\neg 100 \land \neg 50 \land 20 <_c \neg 100 \land 50 \land \neg 20 <_c 100 \land \neg 50 \land \neg 20$.

In a preference specification, the caller of the routine may use an "aspiration level" to specify under which level the answer of the component is no more acceptable. For instance, let us resume the previous preference specification for the caller of `withdraw`. The caller may want to precise that in this specification, he/she will consider that the quality is not satisfactory if the `withdraw` routine delivers as many euro 100 notes as possible. This specification does not interfere with the primary preference specification and the caller may be able to change the acceptability level. For instance, he/she may now want to consider only $\neg 100 \land \neg 50 \land 20$ as a satisfactory quality. We will use a marker $\ll_c$ in the caller preference specification to indicate where the least acceptable outcome is for the caller. This can be viewed as a *quality* specification for the caller of the routine. As previously, we can use conditional preference tables to represent the caller preferences. A complete preference specification of routine `withdraw` is:

200+	$100 \land \neg 50 \land \neg 20 <_r \neg 100 \land \neg 50 \land 20 <_r \neg 100 \land 50 \land \neg 20$
¬ 200+	$\neg 100 \land 50 \land \neg 20 <_r \neg 100 \land \neg 50 \land 20 <_r 100 \land \neg 50 \land \neg 20$

⊤	$\neg 100 \land \neg 50 \land 20 <_c \neg 100 \land 50 \land \neg 20 \ll_c 100 \land \neg 50 \land \neg 20$

3.3 Deontic Design Language

We now extend the syntax of O_{LTL} to OP_{LTL} which takes into account the preference specification. The crucial question here is how time and preferences interact. Can we reason about the change of preferences in time (external dynamics), or can we reason about preferences among propositions at distinct moments in time (internal dynamics)? It is tempting to define temporal preference logics along these lines, but they seem to be too complex to be used in practice. We therefore encode in our logic preferences separately from the temporal reasoning over obligations. The preferences specify desired behavior, but the preferences themselves cannot change. This may seem very limited at first sight, though it should be observed that it is in line with standard models in decision theory, where typically a utility function is assumed to be fixed over time.

The preference relations $<_{a,b}$ are indexed by two objects. The first one represents the object asking for a specification and the second one represents the object on which the preference specification is made. For instance $<_{withdraw,withdraw}$ represents a preference specification on the `withdraw` routine emitted by the routine itself. $<_{c,withdraw}$ represents a preference specification on the `withdraw` routine emitted by another agent or routine C.

Definition 2 (Syntax OP$_{LTL}$). *Given a finite set A of objects (or components, or agents) and a countable set P of primitive proposition names. The admissible formulae of OP$_{LTL}$ are recursively defined by:*

1 If Φ is a formula of O_{LTL}, then Φ is a formula of OP$_{LTL}$.
2 If $\alpha, \beta_1, \ldots \beta_m$ are propositional formulae and $a, b \in A$, then the following formula is a formula of OP$_{LTL}$.

$$\alpha : \beta_1 <_{a,b} \cdots <_{a,b} \beta_i \ll_{a,b} \beta_j <_{a,b} \cdots <_{a,b} \beta_m$$

The semantics of the O$_{LTL}$ part of OP$_{LTL}$ is straightforward, see for instance [15]. The preference specification semantics is given by CP-net semantics, see [19]. Notice that, as shown in [19], we can use indifference between outcomes in the preference specification without losing interesting properties of CP-nets.

3.4 Contract Violations

Now, as a routine contract can provide a level of acceptability in the preference specification expressed by the caller of a routine, we have to define what happens if this acceptability level is not verified by the routine's outcome. For instance, if the `withdraw` routine specified in the previous section delivers as many euro 100 notes as possible, the user specification is violated. We must integrate the acceptability notion into the contract we defined previously. Let us consider a routine r, its preconditions $O_{cr}(\phi)$ and a preference specification $<_{c,r}$ and its associated quality level represented by $\beta_1 <_{c,r} \ldots \beta_j \ll_{c,r} \cdots <_{c,r} \beta_m$. There are two possibilities:

- either the violation of the acceptability level is unacceptable for the caller and in this case we can express it as a postcondition for the component. This will be called as a **strong** acceptability level. We can integrate the acceptability level in the contract by specifying $\phi \rightarrow X O_{rc}(\beta_1 \vee \ldots \vee \beta_j)$.
- either the violation of the acceptability level is acceptable for the caller. For instance, a caller may consider that what is important for him/her is that the component produces an outcome verifying the postcondition. The quality specification he/she produces is a bonus for his/her use of the application. In this case, we cannot express the acceptability level as a postcondition, because the violation of the postcondition will induce strong consequences on the component. We denote such acceptability level specification as **weak** acceptability specification. It can be integrated in the contract by the following formula: $\phi \rightarrow X(\neg(\beta_1 \vee \ldots \vee \beta_j) \rightarrow unsatisfied(c))$. The meaning of *unsatisfied* is the following: if the quality is not enough for the caller, then he/she has a right which he/she can execute or leave.

In the case of a strong acceptability specification, there are still good reasons to differentiate the satisfactory quality and "classical" postconditions. The acceptability specification can evolve: the user can change his/her mind, there is not only one user, ..., so the acceptability specification is not a real postcondition which will be verified by all "executions" of the component.

In a real-world application, several components are combined in order to build the whole application. Those components will have contracts as preference specification. We can use the CP-net formalism to represent the information flow among components and to represent the quality specification of a component as preference relations conditioned by the outcome of the previous component. For instance, consider a web-based booking system. This system is composed of two components: a component C_p which searches plane tickets and a component C_h which searches hotel rooms. A user of the system can specify that he/she wants first to find a plane ticket before finding an hotel. For instance, the first component may prefer fast travels. C_h may then prefer cheap hotels if the outcomes of C_p are fast travels (because they are more expensive), and comfortable hotels if the travel is not fast (because the traveller may want to have rest). A CP-net graph formalising this specification is:

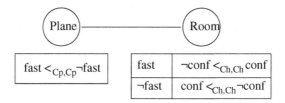

Using the CP-net machinery, we can deduce that the preference specification for the global component is: fast$\wedge\neg$conf $<_{Cp+Ch,Cp+Ch}$ fast$\wedge$conf $<_{Cp+Ch,Cp+Ch}$ $\neg$fast $\wedge$ conf $<_{Cp+Ch,Cp+Ch}$ $\neg$fast$\wedge\neg$conf. An important subject for further research is how to formally derive global acceptance level from each component's acceptability level, or the implication of using a cyclic graph representing the components "communications". Some references about cyclic CP-nets are given in [19].

4   The Normative Stance

In this section we compare the normative stance, a phrase due to Jan Broersen [20] and implicit in design by contract, with the intentional or BDI stance popular in agent oriented software engineering. The following table summarizes the comparison between the intentional stance and the normative stance:

Stance	intentional stance	normative stance
Concepts	BDI	OP, rights, responsibility
from	folk psychology	ethics, law, sociology
Computer	human = angry, selfish, …	God, master/slave, servant
Class of systems	decision making	decision making
Realization	specification and verification	components
Implementation	programming	objects, operation
specification	BDI$_{\text{CTL}}$	temporal deontic logic

First, the intentional stance is rooted in the philosophical work of Dennett, whereas such grounding does not seem to exist for the normative stance (though there are candidates, such as [21]). The concepts from the intentional stance come from folk psychology. The normative stance borrows concepts from ethics, law or sociology. Other examples of this normative stance we mentioned in the introduction are the IMPACT system [7] and the BOID architecture [8].

Second, the success of the intentional stance is that people like to talk about their computer as a human which has beliefs and desires, which may be selfish, or which can become angry. The implicit assumption of design by contract is that designers find it useful to understand software construction in terms of contracts, or, more generally, in terms of obligations. The success of design by contract may be explained by the fact that "social contract" is well established in social sciences [22]. We may call this the normative stance towards computer systems. The success is due to the fact that humans either consider the computer as their master, which has to be obeyed, or as their slave, which has to obey orders.

Third, the intentional stance has been advocated for agent systems, which are for example autonomous and proactive. It has been used as a high level specification language, as well as low level programming language. We believe the normative stance can be used in a wider setting. In the examples we used it also for low level objects. However, it is particularly useful if we use a higher abstraction level in terms of components or agents.

5   Concluding Remarks

In this paper we study how extensions of deontic logic can support design. We propose a deontic design language, that is a kind of specification language whose primary operator is an "obligation" operator (see Section 4). First, we ask which kind of deontic logic can be used as a design language to support design by contract We show how directed modal operators are capable of formalizing contracts between clients (callers) and suppliers (routines), relying on mutual obligations and benefits made explicit by assertions. These formalisms have been developed and studied in electronic commerce and artificial intelligence and law. Moreover, we show how temporal operators can be used to formalize dynamic behavior such as contract violations.

Second, we introduce preferences over outcomes of a routine. This is a necessary extensions of the design by contract approach when the components is autonomous in the sense that it can return several outputs, such as autonomous agents or autonomous services. We illustrate how the preferences can be used to specify the desired quality of a contract. We show how the preferences can be specified with ceteris paribus or CP nets. In further research we study qualities of service level contracts that refer to multiple routine calls, such as average response times.

Third, we ask what kind of properties should be formalized by such a design logic. This is summarized in the following table:

social contract	assertions	directed obligations
violation	exception	violations
repair	exception handling	contrary-to-duty reasoning
contract form	interface	?
testing and debugging	?	?

In this paper, we do not consider contract forms and contracts for testing and debugging. The contract form of a class, also called its "*short form*", serves as its interface documentation. It is obtained from the full text by removing all non-exported features and all implementation information such as **do** clauses of routines, but keeping interface information and in particular assertions. The use of these elements in our deontic design language, for example to *combine* assertions, is subject of further research.

Fourth, we ask how this approach based on deontic logic compares to the BDI approach, dominant in agent based software engineering. Whereas the BDI approach is based on an attribution of mental attitudes to computer systems, design by contract is based on an attribution of deontic attitudes to systems. We suggest that the normative stance has a wider scope of applicability than the intentional stance, though this has to be verified in practice. In further research we study the relation with commitments in Shoham's Agent Oriented Programming (AOP) [17], and with rely/guarantee reasoning [23].

The formalism developed here may seem too "formal" to be used in real applications. It would be interesting to develop practical tools taking our approach into account, in order to offer a support for deontic software engineering. We may for instance extend CP-nets tools.

Another topic for further research is the introduction of other elements of contracts in our formalism. Contracts typically consist not only of regulative norms (obligations), but also of constitutive norms (counts-as conditionals) [24]. How to introduce them in design by contract, and in particular in our deontic design language OP_{LTL}?

References

1. Meyer, B.: Design by contract. In Mandrioli, D., Meyer, B., eds.: Advances in Object-Oriented Software Engineering. Prentice-Hall, New York, London (1991) 1–50
2. Meyer, B.: Applying design by contract. IEEE COMPUTER **25(10)** (1992) 40–51
3. Meyer, B.: Systematic concurrent object-oriented programming. Communication of the ACM **36(9)** (1993) 56–80
4. Meyer, J., Wieringa, R.: Deontic Logic in Computer Science: Normative System Specification. John Wiley and Sons (1993)
5. von Wright, G.: Deontic logic. Mind **60** (1951) 1–15
6. Wieringa, R., Meyer, J.: Applications of deontic logic in computer science: A concise overview. In: Deontic Logic in Computer Science. John Wiley & Sons, Chichester, England (1993) 17–40
7. Eiter, T., Subrahmanian, V., Pick, G.: Heterogeneous active agents, I: Semantics. Artificial Intelligence **108** (1999) 179–255
8. Broersen, J., Dastani, M., Hulstijn, J., van der Torre, L.: Goal generation in the BOID architecture. Cognitive Science Quarterly **2(3-4)** (2002) 428–447
9. Meyer, B.: Invitation to Eiffel. Technical Report TR-EI-67/IV, Interactive Software Engineering (1987)
10. Dignum, F.: Autonomous agents with norms. Artificial Intelligence and Law **7(1)** (1999) 69–79
11. Krogh, C., Herrestad, H.: Hohfeld in cyberspace and other applications of normative reasoning in agent technology. Artificial Intelligence and Law **7(1)** (1999) 81–96
12. Singh, M.P.: An ontology for commitments in multiagent systems: toward a unification of normative concepts. Artificial Intelligence and Law **7** (1999) 97–113
13. Tan, Y., Thoen, W.: Modeling directed obligations and permissions in trade contracts. In: Proceedings of the Thirty-First Annual Hawaian International Conference on System Sciences. (1998)

14. Manna, Z., Pnueli, A.: The Temporal Logic of Reactive and Concurrent Systems. Springer-Verlag, Heidelberg, Germany (1992)
15. Broersen, J., Dastani, M., van der Torre, L.: $BDIO_{CTL}$: Properties of obligation in agent specification languages. In: Proceedings of IJCAI'03. (2003) 1389–1390
16. Jamroga, W., van der Hoek, W., Wooldridge, M.: On obligations and abilities. In: Deontic logic in computer science. Volume 3065 of LNAI. (2004) 165–181
17. Shoham, Y.: Agent-oriented programming. Artificial Intelligence **60** (1993) 51–92
18. Boutilier, C., Brafman, R., Hoos, H., Poole, D.: Reasoning with conditional ceteris paribus preference statement. In Laskey, K., Prade, H., eds.: Proceedings of the Fifteenth Conference on Uncertainty in Artificial Intelligence, Morgan Kaufmann (1999) 71–80
19. Boutilier, C., Brafman, R.I., Domshlak, C., Hoos, H., Poole, D.: CP-nets: a tool for representing and reasoning with conditional *ceteris paribus* preference statements. Journal of Artificial Intelligence Research (JAIR) **21** (2005) 135–191
20. Broersen, J.: Modal Action Logics for Reasoning about Reactive Systems. PhD thesis, Vrije Universiteit Amsterdam (2003)
21. Brandom, R.: Making it explicit. Harvard University Press, Cambridge, MA (1994)
22. Rousseau, J.: The social contract. (1762) http://www.constitution.org/jjr/socon.htm.
23. Stark, E.W.: A proof technique for rely/guarantee properties. In: Foundations of Software Technology and Theoretical Computer Science. Volume 206 of Lecture Notes in Computer Science. (1985) 369–391
24. Boella, G., van der Torre, L.: Contracts as legal institutions in organizations of autonomous agents. In: Proceedings of the Third International Joint Conference on Autonomous Agents and Multi Agent Systems (AAMAS'04). (2004) 948–955

Informed Deliberation During Norm-Governed Practical Reasoning

Martin J. Kollingbaum and Timothy J. Norman

Department of Computing Science
University of Aberdeen
Aberdeen, AB24 3UE, UK
{mkolling, tnorman}@csd.abdn.ac.uk

Abstract. A norm-governed agent takes social norms into account in its practical reasoning. Such norms characterise its role within a specific organisational context. By adopting a role, the agent commits to fulfil and adhere to the social norms associated with that role. These commitments require the agent to act in a way that does not violate any of its prohibitions or obligations. In adopting different sets of norms, an agent may experience conflicts between these norms as well as inconsistencies between possible actions for fulfilling its obligations and its currently adopted set of norms. In order to resolve such problems, it must be informed about conflicts and inconsistencies. The NoA architecture for norm-governed agents implements a computationally efficient mechanism for identifying and indicating such problems – possible candidates for action are assigned a specific label that contains cross-referenced information of actions and norms. As actions are indicated as problematic and not simply filtered out, the agent can still choose to either act according to its norms or against them. The labelling mechanism presented in this paper is therefore a critical step towards enabling an agent to reason about norm violations – the agent becomes norm-autonomous.

1 Introduction

Norm-governed agents are able to reason about rules and regulations established in an organisational context. With that, their practical reasoning is not only based on what they believe, desire and intend, but what they are actually obliged, permitted or forbidden to do in a specific social context. Norms are essential for the creation of organisational structures, because they characterise the rights and duties of individuals taking on specific organisational roles. Agents in such roles must be norm-governed - they must be able to take their current normative position into account in their decision-making [14]. To provide an agent with abilities to reason about norms, a set of issues must be investigated:

- How are norms and actions represented?
- How do norms influence the practical reasoning of the agent?
- How do agents resolve conflicts between norms they currently hold and deal with inconsistencies between their actions and their norms?

O. Boissier et al. (Eds.): ANIREM and OOOP 2005, LNCS 3913, pp. 183–197, 2006.

A specific model and architecture for norm-governed practical reasoning has been developed in the form of the NoA architecture [12]. NoA is a reactive planning architecture in the tradition of concrete implementations of practical reasoning systems [10] with extensions that allow the reasoning about norms. Specific care has been taken to make NoA agents *norm-autonomous* [5] – a NoA agent can decide whether to honour its obligations and prohibitions. This requires that the agent, in its attempt to fulfill obligations, does not simply filter out options for action that are inconsistent with its current set of norms, but that the complete set of options for action are taken into account during deliberation. NoA agents use a labelling mechanism to characterise options for action as either consistent or inconsistent with their current set of norms. In this paper, we use concepts introduced in [14] and [12] and investigate in more detail the concept of "informed" deliberation. For this purpose, an enriched form of a label for candidate actions is introduced that guides or "informs" the deliberation of a norm-governed agent. In its deliberation, the agent can use this label to reason about consistency of a possible option for action – whether an action is norm-compliant or not. In case of inconsistencies, it will be beneficial for the agent to become informed about the reasons of such an inconsistency – which norms are responsible for the inconsistency of an action? Are all options inconsistent, or is there still a possibility to remain norm-compliant? Can the normative authority, which issued such norms, be convinced to revoke existing prohibitions or obligations or at least temporarily grant a permission that overrides a prohibition? Which violation of a norm results in the least damage to the agent's reputation? To support the agent in resolving inconsistency, the labelling mechanism described in this paper holds cross-referenced information between possible candidates for action of the agent and its currently held set of norms.

2   Norm-Governed Agents

Norm-governed agents are able to reason about norms and take them into account in their practical reasoning. Such an agent must be socially aware – it must be able to (a) adopt norms such as obligations, permissions and prohibitions as they are established within a community of agents, (b) process them correctly and (c) anticipate the possible interactions between the effects of its actions and its norms. The NoA system [12, 14] comprises an abstract model of norm-governed agency and a concrete agent architecture for the implementation of norm-governed agents. In the development of this model and architecture, a set of design decisions were made: (a) practical reasoning is based on reactive planning, with a set of pre-specified plan procedures representing the agent's behavioural repertoire, (b) obligations are the principal motivators for the agent to act, (c) plan procedures are declared with explicit effect specifications – this allows the agent to reason about the effects of its actions, whether they are consistent with its currently held norms and (d) a clear distinction is made between the agent achieving a state of affairs or performing an action (see [16]). This distinction is reflected in the NoA norm and plan specifications, with norms refering to an *activity* that is either the achievement of a state or the performance of an action. Norms are central to the NoA model of norm-governed practical reasoning. In this model, the norms held by the agent are its obligations, permissions and prohibitions:

- Obligations are the principal *social* motivators within NoA — they motivate the agent to either achieve a state of affairs or to perform an action. Based on such a motivation, a norm-governed agent may select an appropriate plan for execution. Obligations can be viewed as analogous (although not identical) to goals (or desires) within traditional Belief-Desire-Intention agent architectures such as Jason [1].[1] The analogy lies in the fact that, as with goals (or desires), it may not be the case that the agent will instantiate and select a plan (i.e. adopt an intention) to satisfy an obligation; this will depend on other social constraints on the agent's activities along with its capabilities (encoded in its available plans) and the current circumstances it finds itself in (that leads to the generation of a set of instantiated plan options).
- Prohibitions require the agent to not achieve a state of affairs or perform an action – the agent is forbidden to pursue a specific activity. Prohibitions are not motivators for the agent, but explicitly restrict the choices of activities the agent can ideally employ.
- Permissions explicitly allow the achievement of a state of affairs or the performance of an action.

In the following, we present a detailed specification of the NoA model of norm-governed agency.

2.1   The Abstract Model

The NoA model of norm-governed agency maintains a set of $BELIEFS$ as a representation of the current state of the world, the set $PLANS$ containing the plan specifications, the set $NORMS$ representing the adopted set of norms, and the set $ROLES$ comprising all those roles the agent has adopted. Each role is characterised by a set of norms – when the agent adopts a role it adopts all the norms annotated to this role as well. All norm specifications over all the adopted roles comprise the set $NORMS$. An agent joins an organisation and adopts (one or more) roles within this organisation by signing a contract with members (representatives) of the organisation. Each role $r \in ROLES$ is specified in a contract $c \in CONTRACTS$. To allow a unique identification of elements within these sets, the concept of an identifier is introduced. These concepts are plans, norms, roles, agents and contracts:

---

[1] In the research reported here, we do not discuss the distinctions between desires (internal motivators) and obligations (social motivators), but focus exclusively on the way that norms are interpreted; this is clearly a topic for future investigation, but see, for example, Castelfranchi [3] for some insights into this issue.

Definition 1. *The set $I^{NORMS} = \{n_1, ..., n_n\}$ describes a finite set of norm identifiers. The set $I^{Plans} = \{p_1, ..., p_n\}$ describes a finite set of plan identifiers. The set $I^{Roles} = \{r_1, ..., r_n\}$ describes a finite set of role identifiers. The set $I^{Agents} = \{a_1, ..., a_n\}$ describes a set of agent identifiers. The set $I^{Contracts} = \{c_1, ..., c_n\}$ describes a finite set of contract identifiers. $IDENTIFIERS = I^{Roles} \cup I^{Agents} \cup I^{Plans} \cup I^{Contracts}$ is the set of all identifiers, where I^{Roles}, I^{Agents}, I^{Plans} and $I^{Contracts}$ are mutually disjunct.*

In the context of NoA, the norm-governed agent is described as pursuing either a state-oriented or action-oriented *activity* [16]. Norm declarations, therefore, contain a so-called *activity specification*:

Definition 2. *An activity A determines either the achievement of a state of affairs, called state-oriented activity, or the performance of an action, called action-oriented activity. The expression achieve(p) expresses the achievement of a state of affairs p. The expression perform(σ) expresses the performance of action σ, where σ describes the signature of a pre-specified plan procedure formulated in the NoA language. An agent can be allowed, forbidden or required to achieve or **not** achieve a state of affairs (or its negation):*

- *"achieve a state of affairs p": $achieve(p)$*
- *"achieve a state of affairs $\neg p$": $achieve(\neg p)$*
- *"not achieve a state of affairs p": $\neg achieve(p)$*
- *"not achieve a state of affairs $\neg p$": $\neg achieve(\neg p)$*

*An agent may also be obliged, forbidden or allowed to perform or to **not** perform an action:*

- *"perform action σ": $perform(\sigma)$*
- *"not perform action σ": $\neg perform(\sigma)$*

Norm specifications, comprising the set $NORMS$ and expressing either an obligation, permission or prohibitions, contain such activity specifications expressing that a state or action is either *obliged, permitted* or *prohibited*. A label is introduced to identify a norm specification as either an obligation, permission or prohibition.

Definition 3. *The set $L^{Norms} = \{obligation, permission, prohibition\}$ is the set of labels used to identify obligations, permissions and prohibitions[2].*

A norm specification can then be defined in the following way:

Definition 4. *A norm specification, expressing an obligation, permission, prohibition is a tuple $\langle n, i^{Roles}, A, a, e \rangle$, where*

- *$n \in L^{NORMS}$*
- *$i^{Roles} \in I^{Roles}$ is a role identifier for a norm addressee*

---

[2] A label "sanction" exists as syntactic sugar, as it is an obligation for an agent in the role of a so-called "authority" to pursue certain activities that represent such sanctions (see [13] for more details).

– *A is the activity specification*
– *a is the activation condition*
– *e is the expiration condition*

With such a definition in place, norms can be specified in NoA. Norms are declared according to the possibilities of expressing a specific activity. For example, according to this definition of a norm specification, an obligation can express that a norm addressee is obliged to *see to it* that a specific state of affairs is achieved (or not achieved) or that it is obliged to **not** *see to it* that a specific state of affairs is achieved (or not achieved).

Norms in NoA are conditional entities — they are *relevant* to an agent under specific circumstances only. Our model of norm-governed agents includes a concept of explicit norm activation and deactivation: norms carry two conditions, an activation condition and an expiration condition. These two conditions allow an exact specification of circumstances under which a norm becomes active and, therefore, relevant to the agent, and when it expires. A separate expiration condition allows a more precise specification of the circumstances when a norm is actually active:

– As soon as the activation condition holds, a norm is activated and becomes relevant to the agent.
– It continues to be activated, even if the activation condition ceases to hold.
– A norm is transferred from an activated into a deactivated state only if the expiration condition holds.

With that, the two conditions test two events — the occurrence of a state of affairs that activates the norm and the occurrence of a state of affairs that deactivates the norm.

NoA is a reactive planning system. Characteristic for a reactive planning system is the provision of pre-specified plan procedures at design time as the behavioural repertoire of an agent. A NoA agent adopts a set of such plans as its set *PLANS*. Obligations can motivate either the achievement of a state of affairs or the performance of an action. Plan procedures in NoA service both cases. If a *state-oriented* activity is required, plans are selected according to their *effects* – NoA introduces explicitly specified effects into plan declarations. If an *action-oriented* activity is required, plans are selected directly according to their signature. An abstract definition of a plan is given in the following:

Definition 5. *A plan is defined as a tuple $P = \langle \sigma, precondition, effects, body \rangle$, where:*

– *σ is the signature of the plan specification, with $\sigma = \langle I^{Plans}, \{par_1, .., par_n\} \rangle$ comprising a plan identifier and a set of parameters,*
– precondition *comprises an expression over predicates and operators $\wedge, \vee, \neg$; if the set $BELIEFS$ reflects a state of affairs that evaluates the precondition to true, the plan becomes activated,*
– effects *comprises a list of terms expressing possible effects occurring during the execution of the plan body,*
– body *comprises an executable specification of the plan.*

2.2   Activation, Selection and Execution

The concept of *activation* is essential in NoA. As described before, norm and plan declarations contain conditions that determine under what circumstances norms are activated (and instantiated in the course of this activation) and, therefore, *relevant* to the agent and when plans are activated and, therefore, instantiated and available as potential options for execution. The currently activated norms determine the agents current *normative position*. The currently activated plans determine its current potential behavioural repertoire. Two sets express the current activation state of an agent: (a) the set $INSTNORMS$, representing the set of activated and instantiated norms and (b) the set $INSTPLANS$, representing the set of activated and instantiated plans.

Definition 6. *The set* $INSTNORM$ = $INSTOBL$ ∪ $INSTFOR$ ∪ $INSTPER$ *is the set of currently activated and, therefore, instantiated norms. Subsets of the set* $INSTNORMS$ *are* $INSTOBL, INSTFOR$ *and* $INSTPER$, *which are the sets of currently instantiated obligations, prohibitions and permissions.*

The sets $INSTNORMS$ and $INSTPLANS$ are permanently changing according to changes in the set of beliefs of the agent. Therefore, at any time, a specific set of norms is activated and and a set of plans instantiated. A subset of these activated norms are the currently activated obligations of the agent, $INSTOBL$. Each obligation $o \in INSTOBL$ motivates the agent to act – either to achieve a state of affairs or to perform an action. The agent has to select options or *candidates* for action from the set of currently instantiated plans, $INSTPLANS$. The set $CANDIDATES$ is formed, containing all those plan instantiations that are candidates for obligations in the set $INSTOBL$.

Traditionally, agents based on reactive planning architectures have to select one specific candidate for execution from this set (which is described here as the set $CANDIDATES$) – in a process of deliberation, the agent has to apply specific strategies for this selection. Norm-governed agent have to take norms into account in their practical reasoning. With the introduction of norm-awareness into an agent architecture, the agent is enabled to reason about the *consistency* of its actions in terms of norms – certain actions, which are possible candidates for fulfilling an obligation are maybe forbidden. One way of dealing with such *inconsistent* candidates would be to simply filter them out – but with such a strategy the agent becomes completely benevolent and is not norm-autonomous. Norm-autonomy is essential to NoA agents – the agent can decide whether to honour its obligations and prohibition. Therefore, before the agent decides which candidate from the set $CANDIDATES$ will be executed, it has to investigate the consistency of these options. For this, NoA introduces a labelling mechanism that identifies each candidate as either consistent or inconsistent with the set $INSTNORMS$.

2.3   Investigating Norm Consistency

In essence, two problems have to be investigated: (a) *Possible Conflicts* between permissions and prohibitions and (b) *Possible Inconsistencies* between candidate plans and norms. Permissions and prohibitions *configure* the normative position of an agent, either restricting or expanding the set of possible actions (plans) the agent can employ without causing norm violation. In terms of inconsistency, obligations may motivate the creation of a set $CANDIDATES$, where *none*, *some* or *all* plan instantiations contained in this set are prohibited because either the execution of the plan itself is prohibited or because the plan produces at least one (side-)effect that is prohibited. Conflicts between permissions and prohibitions have to be resolved so that the consistency of candidates in the set $CANDIDATES$ can be investigated. For this purpose, NoA puts forward conflict resolution strategies that are discussed in detail in [12, 14].

For a definition of consistent execution of plans in NoA, it is necessary to observe the relationship between candidates – plan instantiations – and norms. The set $INSTNORMS$ expresses that either the achievement of certain states of affairs or the performance of certain actions (plan instantiations) is either allowed, forbidden or obliged:

Definition 7. *The set S_O describes those states of affairs obliged by currently active obligations contained in the set $INSTOBL$, whereas the set T_O describes actions obliged by currently active obligations contained in the set $INSTOBL$. Similarly, the sets S_F and S_P and the sets T_F and T_P describe states of affairs prohibited / permitted and actions prohibited / permitted by currently active norms.*

According to definition 10, a plan instantiation in the set $INSTPLANS$ is a consistent candidate for a specific obligation $o \in INSTOBL$, if this plan instantiation is (a) not a currently forbidden action, (b) none of its effects are forbidden states of affairs and (c) none of its effects *counteracts* any obligation in the set $INSTOBL$. To allow the investigation of possible effects of an instantiated plan $p \in INSTPLANS$, a function $effects(p)$ is introduced:

Definition 8. *For a plan instantiation $p \in INSTPLANS$, the function $effects(p)$ provides the set of fully instantiated effect specifications:*

$$effects(p) = \{\ e \mid e \text{ is an effect of plan instantiation } p \in INSTPLANS\}$$

A second function is needed that allows us to refer to states of affairs that are the negation of states expressed by plan effects. The function producing this set is called $neg\_effects(p)$.

Definition 9. *For a plan instantiation $p \in INSTPLANS$, the function $neg\_effects(p)$ describes a set that contains a negated version for each element e of the set described by $effects(p)$:*

$$neg\_effects(p) = \{\ n \mid e \in effects(p) \land n = \neg e\}$$

With these definitions in place, a norm-consistent execution of a plan can be expressed in the following way:

Definition 10. *The execution of a plan instantiation $p \in INSTPLANS$, with $p \notin T_F$ (p is not a currently forbidden action), is consistent with the current set of active norms, $INSTNORMS$, of an agent, if none of the effects of p is currently forbidden and none of the effects of p counteracts any currently active obligation:*

$$consistent(p, T_F, S_F, S_O) \text{ iff } p \notin T_F$$
$$and\ S_F \cap effects(p) = \emptyset$$
$$and\ S_O \cap neg\_effects(p) = \emptyset$$

An investigation into the consistency in NoA takes place according to this definition of consistent execution of a plan instantiation. The result of such an investigation will be the set of prohibitions that either forbid the candidate to be executed directly or that forbid the candidate's effects to occur as states of affairs, and the set of obligations that are counteracted by the effects of the candidate. In NoA, this information is accumulated in the consistency label for candidates:

Definition 11. *A label, expressing consistency / inconsistency of a plan instantiation $c \in CANDIDATES$, is a tuple*

$$L = \langle c, MOTIVATORS, PROHIBITORS \rangle,$$

where

- $c \in CANDIDATES$ *is the labelled candidate for a set of motivating obligations*
- $MOTIVATORS = \{\ o^c\ |\ o^c \in INSTOBL \wedge c \in CANDIDATES \wedge effects(c) \cap S_O \notin \emptyset\ \} \cup \{\ o^c\ |\ o^c \in INSTOBL \wedge c \in CANDIDATES \wedge c \in T_O\ \}$ *is the set of obligations that motivated the addition of this candidate to the the set $CANDIDATES$, because (a) one of its effects achieves the state of affairs demanded by this obligation or (b) it is the action demanded by these obligations*
- $PROHIBITORS = \{\ f^c\ |\ f^c \in INSTFOR \wedge c \in CANDIDATES \wedge c \in T_F\} \cup \{\ f^c\ |\ f^c \in INSTFOR \wedge c \in CANDIDATES \wedge effects(c) \cap S_F \notin \emptyset\} \cup \{\ o^c\ |\ o^c \in INSTOBL \wedge c \in CANDIDATES \wedge neg\_effects(c) \cap S_O \notin \emptyset\}$ *is the set of conflicting prohibitions or obligations*

From this labelling, the agent can derive the consistency of its current normative position. For a candidate $c \in CANDIDATES$, a label expresses consistency, if the set of $PROHIBITORS$ is empty:

- Label expressing *consistency*: $\langle\ c, MOTIVATORS, \{\}\ \rangle$

A partitioning of the set $CANDIDATES$ emerges into *consistent* and *inconsistent* candidates. By translating the set $CANDIDATES$ into a *labelled* set $CANDIDATES^L$, this partitioning occurs, where each element is annotated with a label L expressing consistency or inconsistency.

Via characterising the consistency of candidate plans, we can define the consistency of an obligation. To be able to address the subset of candidates that are options for a specific obligation, the function $options(o)$, with $o \in INSTOBL$, is defined:

Definition 12. *For a specific instantiated obligation $o \in INSTOBL$, the function options(o) describes a subset of elements from the set $CANDIDATES$, where each element of this subset is a candidate for obligation o:*

$$options(o) = \{ \; c^o \; | \; c^o \in CANDIDATES \; \wedge \; o \in$$
$$INSTOBL \wedge is\_candidate(c^o, o)\}$$

For a specific obligation $o \in INSTNORMS$, a specific subset of the set $CANDIDATES^L$ represents the set $options(o)$ of possible candidates. There are three possible configurations for this set: (a) all elements in $options(o)$ are labelled consistent, (b) at least one element in $options(o)$ is labelled consistent or (c) all elements are labelled inconsistent. According to these three possibilities, we introduce three so-called *consistency levels* for a specific obligation:

- *Strong Consistency.* An obligation is strongly consistent if all $options(o) \subseteq CANDIDATES^L$ are labelled as consistent:

  $strong\_consistent(o, S_F, S_O, T_F)$ *iff*
  $$\forall p \in options(o). \; consistent(p, T_F, S_F, S_O)$$

- *Weak Consistency.* An obligation is weakly consistent if at least one candidate in the set $options(o)$ is labelled as consistent:

  $weak\_consistent(o, S_F, S_P, S_O, T_F)$ *iff*
  $$\exists p \in options(o) \; s.t. consistent(p, T_F, S_F, S_P, S_O)$$

- *Inconsistency.* An obligation is inconsistent if no candidate in the set $options(o)$ is labelled as consistent:

  $$inconsistent(o, S_F, S_O, T_F) \; iff \; \forall p \in options(o). \; \neg consistent(p, T_F, S_F, S_O)$$

For a NoA agent, this norm-annotated set of candidates, $CANDIDATES^L$, is the input into the subsequent deliberation process to find a single plan for execution for each obligation in the set $INSTOBL$. According to the concept of *norm-autonomy* [5], norm-inconsistent options for action are not simply filtered out but remain – albeit inconsistent – options for the agent's deliberation. During deliberation, the agent can then decide whether to honour its obligations and prohibitions by only selecting norm-consistent options or to act against its currently held norms. NoA agents are, therefore, norm-autonomous.

3   Informed Deliberation

Informed Deliberation is the mechanism within NoA for dealing with consistency between the agent's actions and its currently held set of norms. For the agent to be able to deliberate about its actions, it needs information about a partitioning of the set $CANDIDATES$ of applicable actions into allowed and forbiddent actions. Such a partitioning must be "complete" – if the normative situation for specific candidates is not decided because of conflicts in the set of norms, then these conflicts have to be resolved. In the context of NoA, specific conflict resolution strategies are proposed (see [12]). The following strategies are under investigation in the context of the NoA model: (a) Arbitrary decision, (b) Recency, (c) Seniority, (d) Cautiousness, (e) Boldness, (f) Social power and (g) negotiation with the norm issuer. These are conflict resolution strategies that can be employed during the agent's deliberation. It helps the agent to achieve a complete partitioning of its candidate set into allowed and forbidden plans. The strategy "*arbitrary decision*" can be utilised as the simplest form of conflict resolution as it does not take into account any information about the conflict situation itself. If the agent chooses "*recency*" or "*seniority*", then a form of time stamp is required that records the activation time of a norm. With that, a ranking according to activation time can be established and selections according to "*recency*" or "*seniority*" can take place. The agent is pursuing a "*cautious*" strategy, if prohibitions always overrule permissions and it is pursuing a "*bold*" strategy, if permissions always overrule prohibitions.

An agent can also "*renegotiate*" specific norms and reach agreements to either revoke prohibitions or receive additional permissions that override prohibitions.

A conflict resolution strategy according to "*social power*" would utilise relationships of dependency and influence between roles. Such relationships can be used to determine, if a norm is "more powerful" to override a conflicting norm. If the issuer of norms, acting in a position of power, issues multiple conflicting norms, the agent, despite being able to detect such conflicts, will not be able to resolve the conflict according to "*social power*" as all conflicting norms are issued by the same source. The agent may claim that this source is inconsistent itself and require it to resolve these conflicts and to reissue a set of norms without conflicts. Such a situation can be regarded as a *distributed conflict resolution strategy*.

Finally, the agent may not be able to remove prohibitions on its actions. If these actions are necessary for the fulfilment of its obligations, it may decide to act against existing prohibitions. In such a case, it may investigate the *consequences* or *sanctions* for such a violation – according to a rational reasoning, the agent may decide to choose an action that incurs a minimum of costs in terms of sanctions. This would require the enhancement of the NoA labelling mechanism to capture such costs.

The consistency label of candidates is used in NoA to indicate the consistency of specific candidate plans – candidate plans for execution are simply identified as either consistent or inconsistent. In the following discussion, the information conveyed by the label in the form of the set *PROHIBITORS* is taken into account in a more detailed fashion. The goal is to give an agent means to *remove* inconsistencies so that it can pursue its intended activities. The agent has to change its consistency level.

The normative situation within a society can be quite complex. An agent can take on different roles and, with that, adopt different sets of – possibly conflicting – norms. NoA employs a model of norm specifications with conditions that determine under what circumstances norms are "active" and, therefore, "relevant" to the agent. Inconsistencies between norms and actions are, therefore, apparent only if specific circumstances activate inconsistent norms and actions.

3.1 Example

For example, let us assume that an agent holds a set $INSTNORMS = \{\, p_1, p_2 \,\}$ with two plans p_1 and p_2 as its current (instantiated) capabilities. We assume that these plans will produce the following states of affairs as their effects during execution:

- plan p_1 : $\mathit{effects}(p_1) = \{\, s, t \,\}$
- plan p_2 : $\mathit{effects}(p_2) = \{\, s \,\}$

We also assume that the agent adopts two roles, $ROLES = \{\, r_1, r_2 \,\}$ and, consequently, two sets of norms annotated to these roles. If we use specific syntactic forms to express norm specifications according to Definition 4 (see [14, 12] for details), then we can describe the two role-related norm sets in the following way:

- role r_1 : $\{\, obligation(r_1, achieve(s), \phi, \psi), prohibition(r_1, perform(p_2), \phi, \psi) \,\}$
- role r_2 : $\{\, prohibition(r_2, achieve(t), \phi, \psi) \,\}$

According to Definition 4, norm specifications are characterised by a reference to a role, an activity specification and two conditions, the activation and expiration condition (denoted here as ϕ and ψ). For the following discussion, we assume that these two norm sets are issued by two different normative authorities, authority A_x and A_y. With that, the agent's set $INSTNORMS$, comprising these two role-related norm sets, contains norms issued by different normative authorities.

This agent is motivated by its obligation $obligation(r_1, achieve(s), \phi, \psi)$ to achieve this state of affairs. Consequently, it forms the set $CANDIDATES$. Plan p_1 as well as p_2 produce s as one of their effects and, therefore, comprise the set $CANDIDATES$:

- $CANDIDATES = \{\, p_1, p_2 \,\}$

The investigation of consistency yields following problems: candidate p_1 is inconsistent with the prohibition to achieve state t, as $t \in \mathit{effects}(p_1)$ and candidate p_2 is inconsistent with the prohibition to perform action p_2. A set of labels emerges, characterising these inconsistencies (see Definition 11):

$$L_{p_1} = \langle p_1, \{obligation(r_1, achieve(s), \phi, \psi)\}, \{prohibition(r_2, achieve(t), \phi, \psi)\}\rangle$$

$$L_{p_2} = \langle p_2, \{obligation(r_1, achieve(s), \phi, \psi)\}, \{prohibition(r_2, perform(p_2), \phi, \psi)\}\rangle$$

In both labels, the set $MOTIVATORS$ (see Definition 11) contains the one motivating obligation. In both cases, the set $PROHIBITORS$ is not empty but contains the corresponding conflicting prohibitions. The motivating obligations responsible for forming this set $CANDIDATES$ is at a level of *inconsistency*.

In this situation, the agent has two options:

- although the agent is in a state of inconsistency, it acts by selecting one of the candidates for execution.
- the agent tries to *improve* the level of consistency for its obligation, so that at least one of the candidates becomes a consistent option

3.2   Improving the Level of Consistency

As outlined before, the consistency of candidate plans defines the consistency of an obligation. For a specific obligation $o \in INSTNORMS$, a specific subset of the set $CANDIDATES^L$ represents the set $options(o)$ of possible candidates for this obligation. This set can have one of the three following states: (a) all candidates are consistent, (b) at least one of them is consistent or (c) none of them is consistent. According to the consistency situation of $options(o)$, the obligation o is then either *strongly consistent*, *weakly consistent* or *inconsistent*. An obligation can be fulfilled without violating other norms, if it is at least weakly consistent. A change of such a consistency level may take place because of the activation of new permissions and prohibitions. Permissions allow actions to occur whereas prohibitions declare certain actions as forbidden.

In the previous example, the set $MOTIVATORS$ for the two candidates p_1, p_2 contains one obligation to achieve a state of affairs s:

$$obligation(r_1, achieve(s), \phi, \psi)$$

According to the labelling outlined in the example, none of the candidate plans for this obligation are consistent – a prohibition exists for both candidates in the set $CANDIDATES$. The agent is regarded as operating at a "level of inconsistency" in terms of this obligation.

If the agent decides to fulfill this obligation in a norm-consistent way, then it must try to *upgrade* the level of consistency of this obligation. This would mean to free – maybe temporarily – at least one of the candidate plans from its *prohibitors*. This can take place by engaging with the authority that issued the prohibitors in a dialogue and reach an agreement that can be the following:

– the authority revokes the prohibiting norms
– the authority issues a permission that temporarily overrides the existing prohibition (see [14, 12] for details about precedence and overriding between norms and appropriate conflict resolution strategies)

If the authority issues a (temporary) permission, then a situation of conflict occurs with the existing norms contained in the set $PROHIBITORS$ of at least one of the candidates for this obligation. In this case, such a conflict is intentional – during the dialogue with the authority, the agent negotiates the release of such a permission, using knowledge about the possible classes of conflict (as outlined above) between norms. After receiving such a permission, the agent relies on its set of conflict resolution strategies to achieve the correct overriding between norms.

Let us assume that the agent could convince the authority to issue following permission:

$$permission(r_1, achieve(t), \phi, \psi)$$

In our example, the agent has adopted two roles, r_1 and r_2. Let us assume that the agent receives this permission for its role r_1. As this permission allows the achievement of state t that is forbidden by the existing prohibition, a *conflict* occurs. The agent can employ a conflict resolution strategy – for example, one of those outlined in [12] – to make the permission the dominant norm. With that, the agent allows the prohibitor for candidate plan p_1 to be overridden – this candidate becomes a consistent choice. Candidate p_2 is still inconsistent, therefore the agent can fulfill this obligation at a level of *weak consistency*.

In the example above, two different normative authorities are introduced, A_x and A_y. The agent has to decide which authority to contact for relaxing its normative situation. It also has to decide, for which action the prohibition should be either revoked or relaxed. The information contained in the label assigned to each candidate in the set $CANDIDATES$ can be used in this decision process. It gives a clear indication about all the norms that create the current state of inconsistency. If additional information about relationships of power and influence between authorities is made available, these power relationships within organisations can be used to find an authority at a superior level in this hierarchy that has the power to override decisions of subordinates and upgrade the agent's level of consistency. A conflict resolution strategy according to *social power* would require a substantial extension of the role model within NoA to express relationships of dependency and influence between roles. Such relationships can be used to determine, if a norm is "more powerful" to override a conflicting norm. The indication of such role-relationships within the NoA labelling mechanism will be investigated in future work.

As the NoA architecture uses mechanisms to perform plan and norm activations efficiently (using a Rete network implementation [9]), information contained in labels is maintained whenever plan and norms are activated or deactivated. It represents, therefore, an efficient form of informing the deliberation of the agent.

4   Related Work

Research into norm-governed reasoning and the concept of norm-autonomy, as described in this paper, is influenced by related work, especially [4, 6, 7] and [5]. The model of norm-governed agency also takes influences from the work by Jones and Sergot [11] and by Pacheco and Carmo [17]. They describe the modelling of complex organisations and organisational behaviour based on normative concepts. The design of the NoA architecture takes influences from various sources, most prominently the BDI model of agency [18], but also from classical planners regarding the declaration of plans and from production systems regarding plan activation, selection and execution. NoA is a reactive planning architecture [8, 10], where the behaviour of an agent is determined by pre-specified plans. NoA differs from these classic models and systems: (a) a clear distinction is made between agents achieving a state of affairs or performing an action, reflected in norm and plan specifications, (b) plan procedures contain explicit effect specifications to allow a norm-governed practical reasoning, and (c) NoA employs a detailed model of conflict resolution and inconsistencies between actions and norms and inform the deliberation of the agent about possible inconsistencies to make the agent norm-autonomous. In terms of designing a normative architecture, Broersen et al. [2] describe the BOID architecture. Conflict resolution strategies are presented as overruling orders between the concepts "belief", "obligation", "intention" and "desire". NoA takes, in contrast to BOID, a practical approach towards modelling norm-governed agency and provides a design for a specific architecture for norm-governed agents. But similar problems, as conflicts between norms and precedence relationships between them, are also discussed in the context of NoA. NoA, as a practical reasoning system based on reactive planning mechanisms, puts forward a set of conflict resolution strategies. Similarly, Lopez et al. [15] discuss how agents decide whether or not to adopt norms, taking into account issues of consistency.

5   Conclusion

A norm-governed agent must be able to anticipate whether its actions are violating any norms that are associated with its role in a specific organisational context. The NoA model of norm-governed practical reasoning introduces a labelling mechanism to focus the deliberation of the agent on such violations. The deliberation of the agent is informed about inconsistencies between potential candidate actions it could deploy to fulfill its obligations and its currently held set of norms. Instead of simply filtering out inconsistent candidates for action, a label is attached to each candidate action containing a rich set of information, cross-referencing options for action (plans) with motivating obligations and possible norms that are inconsistent with such an action. With that, an agent may attempt to comply with a specific norm, but still violate others. By informing and focussing the deliberation of the agent on such cases of inconsistencies, the agent can use certain resolution strategies such as, for example, engaging in a dialogue with a normative authority to reach an agreement about "relaxing" its social constraints. Or it can decide to simply violate a norm. The mechanisms within NoA to identify such violations is an important step in enabling an agent to reason about norm violations.

References

1. R. Bordini and J. Huebner. *Jason: A Java-based AgentSpeak Interpreter used with Saci for Multi-Agent Distribution over the Net, Manual,* 2004.
2. J. Broersen, M. Dastani, J. Hulstijn, Z. Huang, and L. van der Torre. The BOID architecture: Conflicts between Beliefs, Obligations, Intentions and Desires. In *Proceedings of Autonomous Agents 2001,* pages 9–16, 2001.
3. C. Castelfranchi. Modelling Social Action for AI Agents. *Artificial Intelligence,* 103:157–182, 1998.
4. C Castelfranchi, F. Dignum, C. Jonker, and J. Treur. *Deliberate normative Agents: Principles and Architecture,* volume Intelligent Agents VI LNAI 1757 of *Lecture Notes in Artificial Intelligence,* pages 364–378. Springer-Verlag, 2000.
5. R. Conte, R. Falcone, and G. Sartor. Agents and Norms: How to fill the Gap? *Artificial Intelligence and Law,* 7(1), March 1999.

6. F. Dignum. Autonomous Agents with Norms. *Artificial Intelligence and Law*, 7:69–79, 1999.
7. F. Dignum, D. Kinny, and L. Sonenberg. From Desires, Obligations and Norms to Goals. *Cognitive Science Quarterly*, 2(3–4):407–430, 2002.
8. R.J Firby. An Investigation into Reactive Planning in Complex Domains. In *Proceedings of the National Conference on Artificial Intellgence (AAAI)*, pages 809–815, 1987.
9. C.L. Forgy. Rete: A Fast Algorithm for the Many Pattern / Many Object Pattern Match Problem. *Artificial Intelligence*, 19:17–37, 1982.
10. M.P. Georgeff and A. Lansky. Reactive Reasoning and Planning. In *Proceedings AAAI-87*, pages 677–682, Seattle, WA, 1987.
11. A.J.I. Jones and M. Sergot. A Formal Characterisation of Institutionalised Power. *Journal of the IGPL*, 4(3):429–445, 1996.
12. M.J. Kollingbaum. *Norm-governed Practical Reasoning Agents*. PhD thesis, University of Aberdeen, 2005.
13. M.J. Kollingbaum and T.J. Norman. Supervised Interaction - creating a Web of Trust for Contracting Agents in Electronic Environments. In C. Castelfranchi and W. Johnson, editors, *First International Joint Conference on Autonomous Agents and Multi-Agent Systems AAMAS 2002*, pages 272–279. ACM Press, 2002.
14. M.J. Kollingbaum and T.J. Norman. Strategies for Resolving Norm Conflict in Practical Reasoning. In *ECAI Workshop CEAS 2004*, 2004.
15. F. Lopez y Lopez, M. Luck, and M. dInverno. Constraining autonomy through norms. In *In Proceedings of the First International Joint Conference on Autonomous Agents and Multi-agent Systems*, pages 647–681, 2002.
16. T.J. Norman and C.A. Reed. Delegation and Responsibility. In C. Castelfranchi and Y. Lesperance, editors, *Intelligent Agents VII, LNAI 1986*, volume 1986 of *Lecture Notes in Artificial Intelligence*, pages 136–149. Springer-Verlag, 2001.
17. O. Pacheco and J. Carmo. A Role Based Model for the Normative Specification of Organized Collective Agency and Agents Interaction. *Autonomous Agents and Multi-Agent Systems*, 6(2):145–184, 2001.
18. M. Wooldridge. *Reasoning about Rational Agents*. MIT Press, 2000.

Organizations in Artificial Social Systems

Guido Boella[1] and Leendert van der Torre[2]

[1] Dipartimento di Informatica - Università di Torino- Italy
guido@di.unito.it
[2] University of Luxembourg
leendert@vandertorre.com

Abstract. In this paper we introduce organizations and roles in Shoham and Tennenholtz' artificial social systems, using a normative system. We model how real agents determine the behavior of organizations by playing roles in the organization, and how the organization controls the behavior of agents playing a role in it. We consider the design of an organization in terms of roles and the assignment of agents to roles, and the evolution of organizations. We do not present a complete formalization of the computational problems, but we illustrate our approach by examples.

1 Introduction

The basic idea of the artificial social systems approach of Shoham and Tennenholtz [12, 13] is to add a mechanism, called a social law, that will minimize the need for both centralized control and on-line resolution of conflicts. A social law is defined as a set of *restrictions* on the agents' activities which allow them enough freedom on the one hand, but at the same time constrain them so that they will not interfere with each other. Several variants have been introduced to reason about the design and emergence of social laws. Shoham and Tennenholtz use game theoretic approach and inherit the advantages and drawbacks of game theory. On the one hand they work in a well understood framework, agent interactions can be defined precisely and computational problems can be defined in a precise way, but on the other hand due to the used abstractions it is difficult to differentiate agents and to simulate complex systems.

Several extensions have been proposed to this game-theoretic approach to artificial social systems. Shoham and Tennenholtz [12] introduce off-line design of *useful* social laws for artificial agent societies, and Fitoussi and Tennenholtz [7] distinguish two criteria to choose social laws called *minimal* and *simple* social laws. Shoham and Tennenholtz [13] study the emergence of *rational* social laws in repeated games instead of their off-line design. Briggs and Cook [6] introduce so-called *flexible* social laws that can be violated if an agent cannot obey the law [1]. Moreover, Tennenholtz [14] introduces *stable* social laws as a kind of qualitative equilibrium, in the sense that agents can deviate from the law, but they do not want to do so when the other agents follow it. This approach deals with bridging social laws with conflict resolution. Brafman and Tennenholtz [5] study efficient learning equilibria in repeated games. Boella and van der Torre [3] introduce *enforceable* social laws by extending artificial social systems with a control system – called a normative system – that represents the (consequences of) social laws.

O. Boissier et al. (Eds.): ANIREM and OOOP 2005, LNCS 3913, pp. 198–210, 2006.

There is a significant body of literature on the role of organizations in multi-agent systems going back to the beginnings of the field in the late 70's [9]. Despite the popularity of the game theoretic approach to artificial social systems as initiated by Shoham and Tennenholtz, as far as we know organizational concepts have not yet been introduced in them. However, the use of organizations could be useful to explain the interaction of social laws and other social concepts such as roles and norms. Moreover, organizations allow to describe the system at different levels of abstraction. Finally, the introduction of organizational concepts leads to new interesting computational problems which can be defined and studied using the game-theoretic framework, such as an organizational design problem (decompose the organization into a set of roles such that the organizational goals are achieved if the roles' goals are achieved), a role assignment problem (assign real agents to roles such that goals of roles and thus goals of organization are achieved), etc. We are therefore interested in the following research questions in this paper:

1. How can organizations and roles be defined in artificial social systems?
2. How do role playing agents determine the behavior of an organization?
3. How does the organization use real agents playing roles in organization to enforce social laws (so-called defender agents)?
4. How can we define an organizational design problem in artificial social systems?
5. How can we define a role assignment problem in artificial social systems?
6. How can we model the evolution of organizations in artificial social systems?

To answer these questions, we use a model of artificial social systems and enforceable social laws developed in [3, 4] as an extension of Tennenholtz' stable social laws. The normative system is represented by a socially constructed agent. Roughly, a social law is in force when it can be extended to a stable social law. Design of social laws can be formalized as updating the utility function of the normative system. In this paper the organization is modeled as the normative system, i.e., a a control system, and we extend the model of artificial social systems with another class of socially constructed agents called roles.

This extension with a normative system of the game-theoretic approach to artificial social systems builds on work in normative multiagent systems. This work formalizes norms as a kind of soft constraint, jut like other approaches, but it also considers what happens when a norm is violated (and how this can be repaired), permissions and rights and their relations to obligations, how norms change in time, the negotiation of new norms, decision making in normative systems, the interaction among normative systems, norms as a coordination mechanism, etc. Moreover, as Searle [10] argues, a distinction can be made between two types of rules, a distinction which also holds for formal rules like those composing normative systems:

> "Some rules regulate antecedently existing forms of behaviour. For example, the rules of polite table behaviour regulate eating, but eating exists independently of these rules. Some rules, on the other hand, do not merely regulate an antecedently existing activity called playing chess; they, as it were, create the possibility of or define that activity. The activity of playing chess is constituted by action in accordance with these rules. The institutions of marriage, money,

and promising are like the institutions of baseball and chess in that they are systems of such constitutive rules or conventions" ([10], p. 131).

For Searle, institutional facts like marriage, money and private property emerge from an independent ontology of "brute" physical facts through constitutive rules of the form "such and such an X counts as Y in context C" where X is any object satisfying certain conditions and Y is a label that qualifies X as being something of an entirely new sort. E.g., "X counts as a presiding official in a wedding ceremony", "this bit of paper counts as a five euro bill" and "this piece of land counts as somebody's private property".

In this paper we consider how the behavior of an organization is determined by the behavior of role playing agents. We therefore consider how real agents enforce control in artificial social systems. To be able to reason about roles when no agent has been assigned to it yet, we distinguish between the possible behaviors of the role and the possible behaviors of the real agent. In a fully specified organization, the behavior of the organization is determined by the behavior of the roles, and the behavior of the role is determined by the behavior of the real agents. We formalize how role playing agents determine the behavior of a organization using the constitutive norms of the normative systems. The relations between the behaviors is represented by a counts-as relation among strategies, such that a strategy of a real agent can count as a strategy of a role, and a strategy of a role can count as a strategy of the organization. These counts-as rules are abstractions of constitutive norms defining the organization.

As an illustrating example of the kind of analysis which can be done in our extension of the game-theoretic approach to artificial social systems, consider some real agents and an organization controlling their behavior. The behavior of the socially constructed organization is determined by the real agents in the system, for example by a policeman. Moreover, the behavior of the policeman is also controlled by the normative system, so to get system stability, we may have an infinite set of agents each controlling one another. So there is a police-policeman controlling the policeman, a police-police-policeman controlling the police-policeman, etc. In reality there is no infinite set of agents. Instead it is assumed that at some point the agents are trusted, due to the bounded reasoning of agents, or we have two policemen, each controlling the other and thus breaking the infinite sequence. For example, assume that we have four agents $\{a_1, a_2, p_1, p_2\}$ and the usual kind of prisoner's dilemma for $\{a_1, a_2\}$. Then we have two policemen $\{p_1, p_2\}$, where p_1 can punish a_1 if he defects, and p_2 can punish a_2 if he defects. Moreover, p_1 can punish p_2 if a_2 defects but p_2 does not punish him, and p_2 can punish p_1 if a_1 defects but p_1 does not punish him. Our game theory can be used to analyze under which conditions this solution works.

The layout of this paper is as follows. In Section 2 we discuss artificial social systems and stable social laws as introduced by Tennenholtz and colleagues, and we introduce our extension with explicit normative system and enforceable social laws. In Section 3 we discuss how role playing agents determine the behavior of the organization, and how the organization controls agents playing a role in it. In Section 4 we discuss the (top-down) design of organizations, in Section 5 the assignment of roles, and in Section 6 we discuss the evolution of organizations in artificial social systems.

2   Artificial Social Systems and Social Laws

Shoham and Tennenholtz [12] introduce social laws in a setting without utilities. They define also *rational* social laws [13] as social laws that improve a social game variable. A game or multi-agent encounter is a set of agents with for each agent a set of strategies and a utility function defined on each possible combination of strategies. We extend artificial social systems with a control system, called a normative system, to model enforceable social laws. Following Boella and Lesmo [2], the normative system is represented by a socially constructed agent called the normative agent or agent 0. In [3], the normative system is represented by the set of control strategies of agent 0, but not by a utility function.

Definition 1. *A normative* game *(or a* normative multi-agent encounter*) is a tuple* $\langle N, R, S, T, U_1, U_2 \rangle$, *where* $N = \{0, 1, 2\}$ *is a set of agents,* R, S *and* T *are the sets of strategies available to agents 0, 1 and 2 respectively, and* $U_1 : R \times S \times T \to \mathbb{R}$ *and* $U_2 : R \times S \times T \to \mathbb{R}$ *are real-valued utility functions for agents 1 and 2, respectively.*

We use here as game variable the maximin value, following Tennenholtz [14]. This represents safety level decisions, see Tennenholtz' paper for a motivation.

Definition 2. *Let* R, S *and* T *be the sets of strategies available to agent 0, 1 and 2, respectively, and let* U_i *be the utility function of agent i. Define* $U_1(R, s, T) = \min_{r \in R, t \in T} U_1(r, s, t)$ *for* $s \in S$, *and* $U_2(R, S, t) = \min_{r \in S, s \in S} U_2(r, s, t)$ *for* $t \in T$. *The* maximin value *for agent 1 (respectively 2) is defined by* $\max_{s \in S} U_1(R, s, T)$ *(respectively* $\max_{t \in T} U_2(R, S, t)$). *A strategy of agent i leading to the corresponding maximin value is called a* maximin strategy *for agent i.*

A social law is useful with respect to an efficiency parameter q if each agent can choose a strategy that guarantees it a payoff of at least q.

Definition 3. *Given a normative game* $g = \langle N, R, S, T, U_1, U_2 \rangle$ *and an efficiency parameter* q, *we define a social law to be a restriction of* S *to* $\overline{S} \subseteq S$, *and of* $\overline{T} \subseteq T$. *The social law is* useful *if the following holds: there exists* $s \in \overline{S}$ *such that* $U_1(R, s, \overline{T}) \geq q$, *and there exists* $t \in \overline{T}$ *such that* $U_2(R, \overline{S}, t) \geq q$.

A social law is quasi-stable if an agent does not profit from violating the law, as long as the other agent conforms to the social law (i.e., selects strategies allowed by the law).

Definition 4. *Given a normative game* $g = \langle N, R, S, T, U_1, U_2 \rangle$, *and an efficiency parameter* q, *a* quasi-stable social law *is a useful social law (with respect to* q) *which restricts* S *to* $\overline{S}$ *and* T *to* $\overline{T}$, *and satisfies the following: there is no* $s' \in S \setminus \overline{S}$ *which satisfies* $U_1(R, s', \overline{T}) > \max_{s \in \overline{S}} U_1(R, s, \overline{T})$, *and there is no* $t' \in T \setminus \overline{T}$ *which satisfies* $U_2(R, \overline{S}, t') > \max_{t \in \overline{T}} U_2(R, \overline{S}, t)$.

When the set of strategies R of agent 0 is a singleton, then our definitions reduce to those of Tennenholtz [14]. With the extension of agent 0 representing the control system we define enforceable social laws as quasi-stable social laws in normative games where the strategies of agent 0 may have been restricted [3].

Definition 5. *Given a normative game $g = \langle N, R, S, T, U_1, U_2 \rangle$, and an efficiency parameter e, a social law (i.e., a restriction of S to $\overline{S} \subseteq S$, and of $\overline{T} \subseteq T$) is enforceable if there is a restriction of R to $\overline{R} \subseteq R$ such that $\overline{S}, \overline{T}$ is quasi-stable in the normative game $g = \langle N, \overline{R}, S, T, U_1, U_2 \rangle$.*

In [4] we extend normative games with a utility function of agent 0, to represent the enforced norms. Since agent 0 is a socially constructed agent, in the sense of Searle [11], its utility function can be updated. In particular, the enforcement of a social law by $\overline{R} \subseteq R$ is represented by giving $\overline{R}$ strategies a high utility, and $R \setminus \overline{R}$ strategies a low utility. Moreover, we vary the utility of agent 0 depending on the strategies played by the other agents, and by considering incremental updates of the utility function to represent the evolution of artificial social systems. Formally, we extend a normative game with a utility function $U_0 : R \times S \times T \Rightarrow \mathbb{R}$, we define $U_0(r, S, T) = \min_{s \in S, t \in T} U_0(r, s, t)$ for $r \in R$, and we define useful and quasi-stable social laws in the obvious way. Enforced social laws are defined as follows.

Definition 6. *Given a normative game $g = \langle N, R, S, T, U_0, U_1, U_2 \rangle$, and an efficiency parameter e, a social law (i.e., a restriction of S to $\overline{S} \subseteq S$, and of $\overline{T} \subseteq T$) is enforced if there is a unique restriction of R to $\overline{R} \subseteq R$ such that $\overline{R}, \overline{S}, \overline{T}$ is quasi-stable.*

The game in Table 1 illustrates that the computational problem to find quasi-stable laws corresponds in extended normative games to the identification of enforced social laws. The table should be read as follows. Strategies are represented by literals, i.e., atomic propositions or their negations. Each table represents the sub-game given a strategy of agent 0, represented by $\neg n$ and n, respectively. Agent 1 is playing columns and agent 2 is playing rows. The values in the tables represent the utilities of agent 0 (in italics), 1 and 2.

Table 1. What is the enforced social law?

$\neg n$	p	$\neg p$		n	p	$\neg p$
q	3,3,3	0,4,1		q	3,3,3	1,2,1
$\neg q$	0,1,4	1,2,2		$\neg q$	1,1,2	0,2,2

Agent 0 can play strategy $\neg n$ or n, agent 1 can play strategy p or $\neg p$, agent 2 can play strategy q or $\neg q$. When the normative system plays $\neg n$, the sub-game of agent 1 and 2 is a classical prisoner's dilemma. Intuitively, the strategy $\neg n$ corresponds to the state before the social law is introduced, and n corresponds to the introduction of a control system that sanctions an agent for deviating from p, q. For example, the utility of agent 1 in $\neg p, q, n$ (2) is lower than its utility in $\neg p, q, \neg n$ (4) due to this sanction.

When the normative system plays n, the agents are always worse off compared to the normative agent playing $\neg n$, all else being equal. Nevertheless, due to the dynamics of the game, the overall outcome is better for both agents. For example, in the sub-game defined by strategy $\neg n$, the only Nash equilibrium is $2, 2$. Now suppose we set the efficiency parameter to 3, which means that all agents will be better off. If the normative system plays n, then the sub-game has a Nash equilibrium which is the (Pareto optimal) $3, 3$. This explains why the agents accept the possibility to be sanctioned.

3   Role Playing Agents Enforcing Social Laws

The behavior of the organization is determined by real agents. We formalize this intuition in our game theoretic setting such that in a fully specified organization, the organization can play only one strategy. Likewise, if a role is assigned to an agent, then the role can play only the unique strategy determined by the agent playing the role. However, if the organization has not been fully specified yet, or the role has not yet been assigned to agents, then the behavior of the socially constructed agents is not deterministic.

3.1   Organized Games

To define that role playing agents determine the behavior of an organization, we assume that there is a set of counts as conditionals defined on strategies of agents, which decrease the set of strategies socially constructed agents can play. At first sight, it may seem strange that we relate the behaviors of agents with counts-as conditionals. Normally, at a much more detailed level of analysis, counts-as conditionals are used to say that a piece of paper counts as money, or that going through a particular kind of ceremony counts as marrying two people. In general, counts-as conditionals are used to create institutional acts, such as money, marriage, property, liability, etc. However, at our level of abstraction, this implies that the behavior of the organization is defined by counts-as conditionals. We do not claim that our notion of counts-as conditionals covers all possible notions of counts-as conditionals, but it is sufficient for our purposes.

The basic idea of an organizational structure with counts-as conditionals is as follows. First, an organizational structure is a relation $Org \subseteq 2^N \times N$ that relates a set of agents to an agent, such that $(A, i) \in Org$ means that set of agents A directly determines the behavior of agent i. The relation $\{(a, b) \mid \exists (A, b) \in Org, a \in A\}$ reflects a hierarchy on agents and is therefore anti-reflexive, anti-symmetric and anti-transitive. Moreover, for each $(A, i) \in Org$, a counts-as conditional from a set of agents A to agent i is a function from the set of strategies played by the agents A to a function on the strategies of agent i: $counts\text{-}as : \times_{k \in A} S_k \rightarrow (S_i \rightarrow S_i)$. Applying the counts-as conditional to a game results in a new game, defined by $U_j(s_1, \ldots, s_i, \ldots, s_n) = U_j(s_1, \ldots, counts\text{-}as(s_A)(s_i), \ldots, s_n)$. Applying all counts-as conditionals is formalized by applying all these rules from the bottom of the organizational structure to the top. The counts-as conditionals have to satisfy the following properties, which intuitively represents that the agents can no longer distinguish between the strategies within an equivalence class of agent i.

1. The strategies of the agents A determine an equivalence relation on the set of strategies of agent i. For all $(A, i) \in Org$ with associated $counts\text{-}as$, and for any set of strategies S_1 and S_2 of the agents A, the reflexive, symmetric and transitive closures on $counts\text{-}as(S_1)$ and on $counts\text{-}as(S_2)$ are the same equivalence relation. If A determines the behavior of agent i, then it is a universal relation.
2. For each equivalence class, all strategies of the equivalence class are mapped onto the same strategy. For all $(A, i) \in Org$ with associated $counts\text{-}as$, and all set of strategies S of the agents A, if $(s_1, s_2), (s_2, s_3) \in counts\text{-}as(S)$, then $s_2 = s_3$.
3. If there are two sets of agents that together determine the behavior of agent i, then the order of applying the counts-as rules to a game is irrelevant (to simplify the

procedure). For all $(A, i), (B, i) \in Org$ with associated *counts-as*$_1$ and *counts-as*$_2$, we have *counts-as*$_1(S_A) \circ$ *counts-as*$(S_B) =$ *counts-as*$_1(S_B) \circ$ *counts-as*(S_A).

Definition 7. *An* organized game *(or an* organizational multi-agent encounter*) is a tuple* $\langle N, S_0, \ldots, U_0, \ldots, Org, counts\text{-}as \rangle$, *where* $N = \{0, 1, 2, \ldots\}$ *is a set of n agents,* S_i *is the set of strategies available to agent i, and* $U_i : S_0 \times \times S_{n-1} \rightarrow \mathbb{R}$ *is the utility function for agent i, and* Org *and counts-as are as defined above.*

An organized game can be reduced to a normal game using the procedure described above. Thus, from the bottom of the organizational structure to the top, we apply the counts-as rules. We call the bottom of the organizational structure the real agents, and all the other agents socially constructed agents. Moreover, if the top of the organizational structure is unique, then we refer to it as the organization. If there are more socially constructed agents in between the real agents and the organization, then we call the socially constructed agents just above the real agents the roles, and the other socially constructed agents we call functional areas.

3.2   Illustration of Organized Games

We illustrate the counts-as conditionals first by extending the running example with a *defender* or police agent enforcing the control system. Assume a police agent 3 playing either the strategy to work w or not to work $\neg w$. We assume he is lazy and gives utility 10 to not working and utility 0 to working. The organizational structure is such that the behavior of the policeman determines the behavior of the organization, $Org(3, 0)$. There are no roles or functional areas. Moreover, assume that the associated counts-as conditional is that w counts as n, and $\neg w$ counts as $\neg n$. Thus, we have *counts-as*$(w)(x) = n$ and *counts-as*$(\neg w)(x) = \neg n$ for $x \in \{n, \neg n\}$.

If we reduce the game using the counts-as rules, the game in Table 2 results. The cells of the table have been extended with the utility of agent 3. The left table contains the utilities when agent 3 does not work and the right table represents the utilities when agent 3 does work. Since the utilities of agent 0 for all its strategies have become the same due to the counts-as rules, we only represent one of its strategies.

Table 2. p, q is not an enforced social law

$\neg w$	p	$\neg p$		w	p	$\neg p$
q	3,3,3,10	0,4,1,10		q	3,3,3,0	1,2,1,0
$\neg q$	0,1,4,10	1,2,2,10		$\neg q$	1,1,2,0	0,2,2,0

In this game the norm will not be enforced, because the policeman is lazy and will play $\neg w$ whatever the other agents play. From a role assignment perspective, assigning agent 3 to enforce the social law of the organization was not a smart choice. Moreover, the example illustrates that the organization should also contain mechanisms to motivate the agents playing a role in it. There two issues are discusses in further sections.

We now illustrate how the mechanism used to define the behavior of the organization can be used to define the behavior of roles and role playing agents. We assume that there is an additional socially constructed agent for the police role, as an abstraction from the real agent playing the police role. Assume that there is a role 4 which can play strategy police in role r and no police in role $\neg r$ respectively. We define this socially constructed role by giving utility 10 to r and utility 0 to $\neg r$. The organizational structure is such that the behavior of the police role determines the behavior of the organization, $Org(4, 0)$, and we no longer assume $Org(3, 0)$. Moreover, assume that the associated counts-as conditional is that r counts as n, and $\neg r$ counts as $\neg n$. Thus, we have $\textit{counts-as}(r)(x) = n$ and $\textit{counts-as}(\neg r)(x) = \neg n$ for $x \in \{n, \neg n\}$.

If we reduce the game using the counts-as rules, the game in Table 3 results. This figure can be read as follows. The cells of the table have been extended with the utility of role 4 (in italics, since it is a socially constructed agent). The left table contains the utilities when role 4 is not being played and the right table represents the utilities when agent 4 is being played. Agent 3 does not influence the game so we have not represented its utilities. In the case of an ideal police role, p, q is an enforced social law.

Table 3. p, q is an enforced social law (enforced by r)

$\neg r$	p	$\neg p$		r	p	$\neg p$
q	3,3,3,?,0	0,4,1,?,0		q	3,3,3,?,10	1,2,1,?,10
$\neg q$	0,1,4,?,0	1,2,2,?,0		$\neg q$	1,1,2,?,10	0,2,2,?,10

Moreover, assume that agent 3 is assigned to the role 4. The organizational structure is such that the behavior of the police role determines the behavior of the organization as before, $Org(4, 0)$, and now we also have that the behavior of the police agent determines the behavior of the police role, $Org(3, 4)$. Moreover, assume that the associated counts-as conditional is that as before r counts as n, and $\neg r$ counts as $\neg n$, but now also w counts as r, and $\neg w$ counts as $\neg r$. Thus, we have as before $\textit{counts-as}(r)(x) = n$ and $\textit{counts-as}(\neg r)(x) = n$ for $x \in \{n, \neg n\}$, and now also $\textit{counts-as}(w)(x) = r$ and $\textit{counts-as}(\neg w)(x) = \neg r$ for $x \in \{n, \neg n\}$. If we reduce the game using the counts-as rules, the game in Table 4 results.

Table 4. p, q is not an enforced social law

$\neg w$	p	$\neg p$		w	p	$\neg p$
q	3,3,3,10,0	0,4,1,10,0		q	3,3,3,0,10	1,2,1,0,10
$\neg q$	0,1,4,10,0	1,2,2,10,0		$\neg q$	1,1,2,0,10	0,2,2,0,10

This figure can be read as follows. The cells of the table have been extended with the utility of role 4. The left table contains the utilities when role 4 does not being played and the right table represents the utilities when agent 4 is being played. As before in Table 2, with a lazy policeman, p, q is not an enforced social law.

4 Organizational Design Problem

We now consider the construction of socially constructed agents. The design problem consists of various sub-problems: we have to design the utility function of the organization (or normative system), the socially constructed agents such as functional areas and roles with their utility functions, and the organizational structure with the counts-as norms. While doing this, we have to ensure that the organizational goals are achieved. In the previous examples, for example, when we assigned the ideal police role the social law was enforced, but when we assigned a lazy police agent to the police role, the social law was no longer enforced. Likewise, if we would assign another role such as a secretary, probably the social social law would not be enforced either.

We now consider the example in the introduction, where, to get system stability, we may have an infinite set of agents each controlling one another. So there may be a police-policeman controlling the policeman, a police-police-policeman controlling the police-policeman, etc. In real life there is no infinite set of agents, for example because at each step of recursion control become easier (it is easier to check a policeman or a judge than a mafia boss), sanctions are easier to apply (just remove earning), and the controller is more motivated to stick to the rules since its power depends on the reputation of the institution he works in (no fun to be a policeman of a corrupted police: no one listen to you). Here we consider the possibility that police agents control each other.

So we consider an organization, agent 0, with four real agents, 1, 2, 3, 4. For simplicity we do not consider roles or functional areas. Agent 1 and 2 play the same prisoner's dilemma as before. The behavior of the socially constructed organization is determined by policemen 3 and 4. Agent 3 can play w_1 or $\neg w_1$, and agent 4 can play w_2 or $\neg w_2$. Moreover, the behavior of the policeman is also controlled by the normative system, in the sense that the two policemen are controlling each other. Consider the utility functions in Table 5, where we assume that the behavior of the organization is deterministic (i.e., determined by the two policemen).

Table 5. p, q is an enforced social law

$\neg w_1, \neg w_2$	p	$\neg p$
q	3,3,3,5,5	0,4,1,5,5
$\neg q$	0,1,4,5,5	1,2,2,5,5

w_1, w_2	p	$\neg p$
q	3,3,3,3,3	1,2,1,3,3
$\neg q$	1,1,2,3,3	0,2,2,3,3

	w_1	$\neg w_1$
w_2	?,?,?,3,3	?,?,?,0,10
$\neg w_2$	?,?,?,10,0	?,?,?,5,5

This table should be read as follows. The first two tables are the same as before, besides the fact that they do not depend on w but on w_1 and w_2, that is, whether both the agent 3 and agent 4 work. Both agents prefer not to work over working; we did not represent the case in which only one of them works in these tables. The third table details the utilities of the two policemen. When one of them works but the other does not, then the working agent gets a high utility and the one not working a low one. This represents that the one not working is sanctioned by the other one. To keep things simple, the utilities of the policemen do not depend on the strategies of the two other agents.

If we consider only the last table, then we see that this is again a prisoner's dilemma. The two policemen would prefer not to work, but the only stable outcome is that they work. The reason is that if they do not work, they may be punished by the other police agent. This is independent of the strategies of the other agents. Consequently, we have w_1 and w_2, and therefore the prisoner's dilemma for the first two agents is evaded too. Summarizing, p, q is again an enforceable social law.

It is instructing to consider the case in which agent 1 and 2 play $\neg p$ and $\neg q$, but agent 3 and 4 do not punish them, and they do not punish each other. Before our formal analysis, intuition might tell us that this should also be an equilibrium. However, it is not the case, because agent 3 and agent 4 cannot cooperate. Remarkably, the prisoner's dilemma for agent 3 and 4 has led to this solution, which shows that although the prisoner's dilemma may indicate a social problem in general, in some particular cases like the one under consideration, the prisoner's dilemma may be used to solve a social problem.

One may object to our analysis that agent 1 and 2 have increased their utilities by introducing a social law, so why don't agent 3 and 4 also create a social law to increase their utilities? The answer is, of course, that an artificial social system must be designed such that defender agents like our policemen cannot change the normative system. Agent 1 and 2 would suffer from such a new social law, and they should have the power to block it.

We have a huge freedom in designing organizations in this framework, and it is therefore at this point not clear how to define the organizational design problem as a computational problem. We leave this for further research.

5   Role Assignment Problem

The role assignment problem is to find a set of real agents such that the real agents determine the behavior of the roles, and enforce the social law. In other words, in the role assignment function a game is given, and we are looking for an organizational structure with counts-as conditionals.

At this moment, it may be useful to take a further look into our roles: what are they precisely? When there is no agent playing the role, then the role describes the ideal behavior of a role playing agent. If there is an agent playing the role, then the role describes the actual role playing agent.

From this interpretation follows that there can be only one agent playing a particular role. If there are for example two policemen, as in our running example, then we have to introduce two roles. This illustrates that roles in our setting are what is sometimes called a role instance.

6   Evolution of Organizations

We may further extend the example by introducing another role and another agent who has the power to change the normative system. This is well known from political science, in particular from the separation of powers in the Trias Politica.

The social law design problem in this setting is, given a normative game, to define a new utility function for the normative system [4]. The principle that we like to maintain as much as possible from the existing social laws can be represented by the use of the principle of minimal change. Table 6 represents the evolution of an artificial social

Table 6. Iterated design

$\neg n_1, \neg n_2$	p_1	p_2	$\neg p_1, \neg p_2$
q_1	0,3,3	0,4,1	0,6,0
q_2	0,1,4	0,2,2	0,0,0
$\neg q_1, \neg q_2$	0,0,6	0,0,0	0,0,0

n_1	p_1	p_2	$\neg p_1, \neg p_2$
q_1	1,3,3	1,4,1	1,0,0
q_2	1,1,4	1,2,2	1,0,0
$\neg q_1, \neg q_2$	1,0,0 1,0,0		1,0,0

n_2	p_1	p_2	$\neg p_1, \neg p_2$
q_1	3,3,3	3,1,1	3,0,0
q_2	3,1,1	3,0,0	3,0,0
$\neg q_1, \neg q_2$	3,0,0	3,0,0	3,0,0

system by an incremental increase of the utility of agent 0 to the efficiency parameter of the new social law.

The first table represents that the normative system does not impose a control system, the second table represents that there is a sanction for playing $\neg p_1, \neg p_2$ or $\neg q_1, \neg q_2$, and the third table represents that there is an additional sanction for playing something else than p_1 and q_1. The first social law is $\overline{S} = \{p_1, p_2\}, \overline{T} = \{q_1, q_2\}$ based on control system $\overline{R} = \{n_1, n_2\}$, and the second social law is $\overline{S} = \{p_1\}, \overline{T} = \{q_1\}$ based on control system $\overline{R} = \{n_2\}$.

7 Related Research

There is a lot of related research in organizational science, in multiagent systems, in normative multiagent systems, and in game theory. For example, evolutionary game theory can be used as an inspiration to make the ideas in this paper more precise. However, as ar as we know, these game theories have not been reduced to artificial social systems setting we have considered in this paper.

There are also many systems where the issues discussed in this paper can be used to study the interaction among agents. For example, it can be used in the development of electronic institutions where self-interest agents (from different organizations) form virtual organizations (coalitions) to solve a users problem [8].

8 Concluding Remarks

Enforceable social laws are a bridge between two important theories of social systems. On the one hand artificial social systems based on social laws, and on the other hand normative multiagent systems based on norms and deontic logic. In this paper we illustrate how organizations and roles, which were already defined in normative multiagent systems, can be defined in artificial social systems. Moreover, we illustrated how the game theory used in artificial social systems can be used to analyze the interaction among role playing agents in an organization. The use of organizations could be useful to explain the interaction of social laws and other social concepts such as roles and norms. Moreover, organizations allow to describe the system at different levels of abstraction. Finally, the introduction of organizational concepts leads to new interesting computational problems which can be defined and studied using the game-theoretic framework, such as an organizational design problem (decompose the organization into a set of roles such that the organizational goals are achieved if the roles' goals are achieved), a role assignment problem (assign real agents to roles such that goals of roles and thus goals of organization are achieved), etc.

Organizations, functional ares and roles are defined as agents in artificial social systems. The advantage is that we do not extend the ontology of the games we play, and we can use the same game theory as used in other artificial social systems. Role playing agents determine the behavior of an organization using counts-as rules, which transform a game into another game. The resulting game is again a standard game which can be used to determine quasi-stable and enforceable social laws. An organized game with organizational hierarchy and counts-as conditionals can be used to define new computational problems. The organization uses real agents playing a role in the organization by controlling their behavior too. We can define the control of such defender agents by using the game dynamics. In particular we have illustrated that we can use a prisoner's dilemma to ensure that agents do not cooperate to evade the control of the normative system.

Two kinds of organizational design problems are given. The first organizational design problem is given a game including the roles, find counts-as rules to associate roles to the organization such that its behavior is determined by the roles, and there is stable social law such that organizational goals are achieved. The second organizational problem is to create roles (with appropriate utilities) such that the first problem can be solved. The role assignment problem can simply be defined as associating the roles with the agents, such that the agents determine the behavior of the roles, and the organization goals are achieved. The evolution of organizations can be modeled by updating the utilities of the organization. Here additional principles can be accepted, such as minimal change criteria.

In future work, we intend to further formalize the various notions introduced in this paper, study the complexity of the decision problems, and test the model on some examples. We are also interested in further extensions of our model, for example for other organizational structures, or systems in which all powers of the Trias Politica are formalized.

References

1. E. Alonso. Rights and argumentation in open multi-agent systems. *Artificial Intelligence Review*, 21(1):3–24, 2004.
2. G. Boella and L. Lesmo. A game theoretic approach to norms. *Cognitive Science Quarterly*, 2(3-4):492–512, 2002.
3. G. Boella and L. van der Torre. Enforceable social laws. In *Procs. of AAMAS'05*, pages 682–689, New York (NJ), 2005. ACM Press.
4. G. Boella and L. van der Torre. The evolution of artificial social systems. In *Procs. of IJCAI'05*, pages 1655–1556. Professional Book Center, 2005.
5. R. Brafman and M. Tennenholtz. Efficient learning equilibrium. *Artificial Intelligence*, 159(1-2):27–47, 2004.
6. W. Briggs and D. Cook. Flexible social laws. In *Procs. of IJCAI'95*, pages 688–693, 1995.
7. D. Fitoussi and M. Tennenholtz. Choosing social laws for multi-agent systems: Minimality and simplicity. *Artificial Intelligence*, 119(1-2):61–101, 2000.

8. T. J. Norman, A. Preece, S. Chalmers, N. R. Jennings, M. Luck, V. D. Dang, T. D. Nguyen, V. Deora, J. Shao, A. Gray, and N. Fiddian. Conoise: Agent-based formation of virtual organisations. In *Procs. of 23rd SGAI International Conference on Innovative Techniques and Applications of AI*, pages 353–366, Cambridge, UK, 2003.
9. W.G. Ouchi. A conceptual framework for the design of organizational control mechanisms. *Management Science*, 25(9):833–848, 1979.
10. J.R. Searle. *Speech Acts: an Essay in the Philosophy of Language*. Cambridge University Press, Cambridge (UK), 1969.
11. J.R. Searle. *The Construction of Social Reality*. The Free Press, New York, 1995.
12. Y. Shoham and M. Tennenholtz. On social laws for artificial agent societies: off-line design. *Artificial Intelligence*, 73(12):231–252, 1995.
13. Y. Shoham and M. Tennenholtz. On the emergence of social conventions: Modeling, analysis and simulations. *Artificial Intelligence*, 94(1–2):139–166, 1997.
14. M. Tennenholtz. On stable social laws and qualitative equilibria. *Artificial Intelligence*, 102(1):1–20, 1998.

Part IV

Evaluation and Regulation

Exploring Congruence Between Organizational Structure and Task Performance: A Simulation Approach

Frank Dignum[1], Virginia Dignum[1], and Liz Sonenberg[2]

[1] ICS, Utrecht University, The Netherlands
{dignum, virginia}@cs.uu.nl
[2] DIS, University of Melbourne, Australia
l.sonenberg@unimelb.edu.au

Abstract. Reorganization of the structure of an organization is a crucial issue in multi-agent systems that operate in an open, dynamic environment. Ideally, autonomous agents must be able to evaluate and decide the most appropriate organization given the environment conditions. That is, there is a need for dynamic reorganization of coordination structures. In this paper, we describe how simulation studies could help to determine whether and how reorganization should take place, and present a simulation scenario that can be used to evaluate the congruence, or fit, between organizational structure and task performance. Preliminary results using a simulation environment illustrate how one can explore triggers for reorganization and compare strategies.

1 Introduction

Establishing an organizational structure that specifies how agents in a system should work together helps the achievement of effective coordination in Multi-Agent Systems (MAS) [1]. An organization-oriented MAS starts from the social dimension of the system, and is described in terms of organizational concepts such as roles (or functions, or positions), groups (or communities), tasks (or activities) and interaction protocols (or dialogue structure). The structure of an agent organization significantly influences its performance characteristics – in different environments and on different tasks [16].

Environments in which MAS function are not static. Their characteristics can change, ranging from new communication channels to tasks that are no longer useful or are new. In such a changing environment, agents can disappear, be created or they can migrate. In addition, organizational objectives can change, or operational behavior can evolve. Models for MAS must therefore not only cater for adaptive agents [17] but also be able to describe organizations that can adapt dynamically to changes in the environment or to accommodate changes in the organizational objective(s) [7]. We are interested in mechanisms for an organization to evaluate its own own "health" (i.e. success and other utility parameters) and to action to preserve or recover it, by performing suitable integration and reconfiguration actions.

O. Boissier et al. (Eds.): ANIREM and OOOP 2005, LNCS 3913, pp. 213–230, 2006.

Many applications require a set of agents that are individually autonomous (in the sense that each cognitive agent determines its actions based on its own state and the state of the environment, without explicit external command), but corporately structured. As such, there is a growing recognition that a combination of structure and autonomy is often necessary. More realistic models for the simulation of organizations should also be based on cognitive agents. In fact, greater cognitive realism in social simulations may make significant differences in terms of organizational performance. [21] presents a study showing that different combinations of social structure and individual cognition level influence organizational performance. In this work we do not address these key issues of the interplay between individual autonomy and the pursuit of organizational goals. Rather we focus on the organizational level, in particular on aspects of how and why organizations should seek to restructure.

In [7], we discussed different types and motivations for reorganization and the consequences for MAS models of enabling dynamic reorganization at different complexity levels. We also described an abstract framework for classifying reorganization and discussed how simulations could be used to discover some properties of the reorganization process. Here we build on that framework, to draw from a discussion of related literature from the study of adaptivity in human organizations, to make more precise some elements of that framework, and also to present some initial illustrations of working with a simulation [8] to tease out relevant characteristics of organizational adaptation.

The paper is structured as follows. In section 2 we discuss our assumptions of the organizational frameworks. Organizational change is discussed in section 3 and motivations for the use of simulations to study reorganization are presented in section 4. Section 5 introduces the VILLA simulation tool. The use of VILLA for the exploration of reorganization strategies is discussed in section 6. Conclusions are presented in section 7.

2   An Organizational Framework

Both in the MAS literature as well as in management literature there are many ways to describe organizational structures focussing on different aspects. For the purpose of this paper, we assume a basic organizational model containing roles, agents and interactions [7].

- The *Organizational structure* consists of a set of roles, their relationships and pre-defined (abstract) interaction patterns. The organizational structure must reflect and implement the global objectives of the organization. *Roles* are characterized by their capabilities, objectives and norms. Role objectives are determined by the global aims of the organization and determine possible dependencies between different roles. Roles are related to other roles by *dependency relations*. Desired *interaction patterns* between roles can be specified.
- An *Agent* participates in the organization (system) by playing one or more roles. Role enactment is achieved either by allocation by the system devel-

opers that determine which available agent is the most adequate for a task, or is decided by the agents themselves. In both cases, analysis techniques are needed to compare and evaluate different role allocations [19]. The set of agents that at a given moment is active in an organization, is called the *population*. An agent population achieves the animation of organizational structures.

- The *Interaction* between different agents realizes the organizational objectives. Activities in a society are the composition of multiple, distinct and possibly concurrent interactions, involving different agents, playing different roles. Actual interactions form the *behavior* of the organization.

Even though not all MAS models recognize these concepts explicitly , we feel that by raising these concepts to the status of first-class modelling entities [18], we allow for the specification of open systems, and can describe both emergent and designed organizations. Similar modelling approaches have been advocated in [6, 13, 23].

2.1 Organizational Utility

One of the main reasons for having organizations, is to achieve stability. Nevertheless, environment changes and natural system evolution (e.g. population changes), require the adaptation of organizational structures. Reorganization is the answer to change in the environment or the organizational goals. As reorganization is contrary to stability, the question is then: under which conditions is it better to reorganize, knowing that stability will be (momentarily) diminished, and when to maintain stability, even if that means loss of response success. In order to answer this question, it is necessary to define the *utility* of an organization. Reorganization is therefore desirable if it leads to increased utility of the system. That is, the reorganized instance should perform better in some sense than the original situation.

Given the assumption of agent autonomy, utility must be able to be evaluated differently from the perspectives of the organization and of the agents. Here we focus on the organizational level:

Organizational Utility. We define the utility of an organization based on organization properties:

- *Goal Success*: how well are global objectives met.
- *Interaction success*: how often do interactions result in the desired aim.
- *Role success*: how often do enacting agents realize role goals.
- *Structure success*: how well are global objectives achieved in an organizational structure.
- *Adaptation costs*: how difficult is it to adapt this organization to a change in the environment.

The factors indicated above are not very precise yet. The research and simulations reported in this paper are exactly intended to find some indications on how these factors can be made more precise and how they should be combined. For example, *Goal Success* can be defined if the goal is defined quantitatively for a fixed period. E.g. "sell 100 computers each month". The goal success of an organization can then be defined as the ratio of the actual number of computers sold and the target set. However, one might right away question whether it would not be better to take an average over at least 12 months to measure the success. Just like in human organizations, the temporal aspect in measuring the success of an organization is very important. Using long time spans creates a stable utility number, but is maybe too rigid. A very short time span has as consequence that the utility changes quickly as well (one bad month has a direct effect on the utility). This might again lead to overreaction of the organization on the environment.

It is worth noting that the organizational utility depends also on the *cost* of a possible reorganization. That is, any function to measure organization utility must take in account both the success of a given structure, and the cost of any change needed to achieve that structure from the current situation [14].

Given the above very general and rather vague observations, the only (general) statement that can be made at this point is that a given combination of structure and population is said to be successful if the overall success (given a certain measuring system for all factors) of the organization is higher in that situation than for others.

3   Organizational Change

In early work on reorganization, restructuring was only possible off-line. I.e. if different organizational structures were tried one had to change the structure by hand in between runs of the software. During the actual runs, the structure was fixed. Currently, most dynamic approaches to reorganization are concerned with the change of the *behavior* of the organization. That is reorganization affects the current population of agents in the system, both at the social (i.e. interactions and relationships) [2], as well as individual level [15]. Existing implementations of organizational adaptation include approaches based on load balancing or dynamic task allocation. The later is often the case in organizational self-design in emergent systems that, for example, include composition and decomposition primitives that allow for dynamic variation of the organizational *structure* (macro-architecture) while the system population (micro-architecture) remains the same [20]. Another common approach is dynamic participation, in which agent interaction with the organization is modelled as the enactment of some roles, and adaptation occurs as agent move in and out of those roles [3, 6, 14, 22]. However, few of these systems allow agents to change the problem-solving framework of the system itself [1]. Basically, reorganization is a response to two different stimuli: a reaction to (local) changes in the environment, or as the means to implement modified overall intentions or strategies. Based on the above considerations, we have separated out in [7, 8] the following reorganization aspects[1]:

---

[1] Elsewhere we will seek to make more precise these categorizations, but for now we leave them as informally presented.

Behavioral change: Change at the behavior level, that is, the organizational structure remains the same, but the behavior of agents enacting organizational roles changes. Examples are when agents join or leave the society, when they change between existing roles, or when their characteristics change (e,g. more or less consumption or production of some resources). It does not affect future enactments and therefore there is no need for organizational memory.

Structural change: Aims at accommodating long-term changes, such as new situations or objectives. Structural change influences the behavior of the current but also of future society instantiations. Examples of structural change are adding, deleting or modifying structural elements (e.g. roles, dependencies, norms, ontologies, communication primitives) Change at social level implies a need for society level learning. That is, by keeping an organizational memory, the society itself can reflect on the difference between desired and actual behavior and decide on social level changes (roles, norms, etc.).

Another dimension of the reorganization problem, concerns the ways the reorganization decision is taken, i.e. who has the authority to take a decision to reorganize, and how the decision is conveyed and implemented. For example, in distributed decision-making situations it may be that all roles are collectively responsible for a change decision, whereas in other situations (for example, those typified by military structures as C3 [23] - Command, Control and Communications - different roles may have authority to effect changes at different levels). Furthermore, reorganization decisions can be evaluated in terms of timing (reactive or proactive) and intention (defensive or offensive) [12]. Together, these considerations form the 5 W's of reorganization, as follows:

What - the aspects of an organization that are to be reorganized.
- Behavior: change of the individual characteristics of the current population, as a response to environment changes
- Structure: change of the global characteristics of the organization, as a response to change of intent or strategy

Who - authority to take reorganization decisions, how are decisions taken:
- Directive, role-based decision making
- Collaborative, consensus-based decision making

When - the timing, when should the reorganization occur:
- Proactive, preparing in advance for an unpredictable future change
- Reactive, making adjustments after an event has occurred

Why - The strategic reasons for reorganization
- Offensive, aiming at gaining competitive advantage
- Defensive, aiming at organizational survival

Whether - the threshold for reorganization, when is the fit so bad that reorganization is likely to be beneficial
- High threshold, stability is seen as more desirable than flexibility
- Low threshold, flexibility is seen as more desirable than stability

4   Towards a Useful Simulation for Reorganization

In the previous sections we have outlined a number of aspects and ideas that play
a role in the reorganization of MAS. In this section we wish to explain how we
see the use of simulations to substantiate the theory. To motivate the discussion
we draw on some recent research in the investigation of organizational restructuring in human organizations [5, 10] to assist in identifying aspects of organizational
structuring that need to be made explicit in the design of organizational adaptation. Our interest in drawing on research in human organizations is twofold: first
we look to draw on general organizational principles that may apply to artificial as
well as human organizations; second, we are ultimately interested in being able to
build hybrid human-agent networks, and so staying within the bounds of organizational properties that have some analogue in human behavior seems desirable.

In human settings, organizational performance has been demonstrated empir-
ically to be associated with the degree of congruence (or 'fit') between organizational structure and properties of the task or environment [9]². Accordingly,
it is to an organizations advantage to monitor the fit between its structure and
mission, and to alter its structure when a misfit is identified. There is empirical evidence that high performing organizations can discern when environmental
forces have changed the state of congruence (i.e., the goodness of fit), thus driving
changes in the strategies (e.g., communication patterns, back-up behaviors) that
they employ [11]. Rarely, however, do human organizations make changes to their
organizational structures (i.e., asset allocation, team member roles and responsibilities) in order to facilitate congruence and some, at least, of the explanation
for this relates to the characteristics of human behavior which is not necessarily
replicated in artificial organizations. However, we believe there are aspects of human organizational adaptation from which lessons can be drawn for the design
of mechanisms for the adaptivity of artificial organizations. In particular we are
interested to understand what can be identified from human organizational behavior about the triggers for reorganization, and strategies for implementation.
We are especially interested to explicate the kinds of knowledge that need to be
considered when making reorganization decisions.

The research that is of most direct value to the above goals has been performed
in military settings. Especially interesting is the extensive empirical work of the
Aptima group www.aptima.com on organizational adaptation in military settings.
They have manipulated experimental conditions to explore degradation of organizational performance in a fine-grained way - monitoring the nature and quantity
of communication, and perceived workload of individuals, as well as measures of
task performance [5, 10]. They were seeking to identify how organizations coped
with incongruence, and in particular sought to identify the conditions that might
be salient enough to cause organizations to alter not only their strategies, but also
their structures. Their data pointed toward a set of indicators that have the potential to yield diagnostic information regarding congruence early in a mission

---

² Unfortunately the theory is described in rather vague and verbose terms and thus
  is not readily used for our purposes

scenario, including: performance measures (composite variables such as mission tasks processed, latency, and accuracy), team coordination processes (e.g. communication patterns), and workload levels (e.g. subjective assessments).

Now let us turn to consider the implications of these observations for the design of simulation settings in which (artificial) organizational redesign can be investigated. Here, we must point out that a theory on reorganization brings together a number of aspects on different levels of the MAS that cannot be studied all in the same simulation. Therefore we have to divide the process into a number of steps, each building on the previous one. The main complicating factor is that we assume that the behavior of an agent in a MAS does not only depend on its own internal state and the state of the environment, but that it also depends on the organizational structure of the MAS in which it operates. Importantly, we cannot assume the organization to be just another part of the environment, because it cannot be changed in the same way as other parts of the environment by a single agent (we recognize that this is not a very strict distinction, but the important part is that the organization does have a special status when we take into account explicit reorganizations). We will now describe the different steps in the development of the theory in turn.

1. Identify the factors that determine the need for reorganization
The first step in the exploration of the reorganization process is thus to find out exactly what is the influence of the organization form on the behavior of the MAS in a certain environment. In order to make this more precise we have to indicate which are the elements of the organizational form that we consider.

Without claiming completeness, we consider the following aspects to be the most important ones[3]:

- The type of goal of the organization. Is it a very simple, unrestrictive goal or a hard to achieve, very limiting goal. Is the goal quantifiable or is it a qualitatively one?
- Which are the roles to be distinguished? I.e. how are the organizational goals divided over roles. In the extreme cases all agents play the same role or all agents play a different role.
- Related to the previous point is how the roles are instantiated to agents. How many agents play the same role.?
- The interaction between the agents playing roles. This concerns both the interaction patterns (communication protocols) as well as role dependencies (does a role have power over resources, task allocation, etc. and can thus steer other roles).

Given a certain environment and agents with fixed capabilities we can use simulations with differently organized MAS to find out which of the organizations performs "best" in such an environment. In such a way it will be possible to make a match between organizational form and type of environment. The

---

[3] As noted above, we do not consider yet the important interplay between organizational form, agent cognitive capability and organizational performance cf. [21].

research question here is thus "Which type of organization structure performs best given a certain environment and organizational objectives?"

2. How should the reorganization be performed?

The next step in the exploration process is about the actual reorganization itself. In this step we want to find out how an organization should be reorganized from one form to another to best suit an environment that changed (drastically). So, in this step we actually explore the possibilities for reorganization given in the previous section. Aspects that will be important here are how quick an organization can react to a changing environment and how big are the "costs" of the reorganization. If a certain mechanism takes too much time the MAS might not recover in time to survive. On the other hand, the costs of a reorganization can be so big that it is better to quit the organization and start all over from scratch. The aim of this step is thus to evaluate the different possibilities for changing into a more adequate structure given a change of environment characteristics.

3. Who initiates the reorganization and based on which triggers?

In the previous we assumed that all agents within the organization somehow will know that the environment changed and a certain type of reorganization has to be performed. In the last step we will look at cases where certain agents will discover that the environment changes and the reorganization has to be initiated through communication. This is a very typical scenario for crisis management in which teams of agents have to react to changing circumstances that are detected by one or more members of the team. Especially in this last step we will look at the reasoning and communication capabilities of the agents in the MAS and the influence this has on the reorganization possibilities.

In summary: Exploration of organizational adaptation requires not only that we have an explicit representation Ω of the set of available organization types, ω, and some measure of organizational utility, but we also need to represent:

1. organizational performance (with respect to a goal, and measured over time);
2. a set Γ of change indicators γ, i.e. potential triggers for changing organizational structure, these will relate to observable suboptimal or degraded organizational performance, and are likely highly context dependent, cf [5];
3. a mapping $\mu : \omega \rightarrow \omega\prime$ between organization types that provides a recipe for reorganization; and
4. a cost function $f(\omega, \omega\prime)$ that computes the cost of implementing the reorganization.

Then organizational adaptation should occur when the performance falls below some acceptable level, and/or some trigger condition is activated. The trigger condition likely takes into account a performance trajectory over time, as part of the context, and not just an instantaneous snapshot. The choice of structure for the new organization should take into account the expected increase in organizational utility, and discount for the cost of change.

Ultimately we would seek to encode such dynamism explicitly as part of organizational definition. For now, we seek to simulate various alternate conditions and understand the tradeoffs between structure and performance, given different environmental conditions. In the next section we discuss an initial attempt to develop a simulation tool that on the one hand is simple enough to be controllable and interpretable, and on the other hand is complex enough to allow rich parameter variation and the exhibition of interesting behaviors.

5 Discovering Conditions for Reorganization

As described in the previous section, the aim of our research is to develop a simulation tool that enables the study of the effects of reorganization strategies on the performance of societies consisting of multiple agents. We are interested in investigating both the properties of systems that exhibit reorganization possibilities and the degree of complexity necessary to build agents that are able to reason about social reorganization. In order to simulate real-life organizations it is first necessary to find out which are the most important parameters and measurements. I.e. part of the first step in the development process discussed in the previous section. For this purpose we have developed a simulation environment, VILLA, representing a simple organization. The VILLA environment is described in more detail in section 5.1.

5.1 The VILLA Simulation Environment

The simulation environment, VILLA, was designed to meet the following requirements: (1) be simple enough to enable empirical evaluation of the results, but (2) be complex enough to emulate situations where reorganization really matters. The basic requirement was thus that in VILLA an organization should be described in which different roles with different capabilities play a role. It should be possible for agents to switch roles. Furthermore, the organization should have a global goal that was (at least partly) independent from the goals of the agents. We found that the society as we will shortly describe is one of the most simple organizational structures that complies to the above requirements. VILLA has been fully described in [8]. For the ease of understanding the remainder of this paper, we will describe here the main features of VILLA. VILLA simulates a society inhabited by number of Creatures, divided into three groups: the Gatherers, the Hunters, and the Others. The unique goal of the society is to survive (one or more Creatures stay alive). All Creatures must eat in order to survive. When Creatures don't eat, their health decreases, until their health is 0 and they die. Gatherers and Hunters are responsible to keep the food stack supplied. Gatherers and Hunters should eat more than Others to allow for the effort of collecting food. Furthermore, the health of Gatherers and Hunters determines how much food they can collect. That is, the healthier a Hunter or Gatherer is the more food it can collect. However, food collection is not always guaranteed and Gatherers or Hunters may only sporadically be successful. The probability of success of Gatherers is higher than that of Hunters. On the other hand, when successful, Hunters can collect more food than Gatherers. Gatherers find food on their own but Hunters must hunt in groups (two or more). Therefore,

Hunters must be able to move in order to find other Hunters with whom they can hunt. The hunting capability increases with the size of the group. Other Creatures can be seen as the elderly and children of the society, they only eat and are not in state of contributing to the food collection effort. Concentrating on the food aspect makes it possible to restrict the environmental variables that influence the performance of the society. The VILLA simulation game consists of a fixed number of runs. During each run, Gatherers and Hunters will gather food, and as many Creatures will eat as the food stack allows. Each run consists of a number of 'ticks'. Each agent can use each tick either to act or to reason (not both simultaneously). Each of the agents occupies a cell in a large grid (that represents the natural environment of the Creatures).

The definition of VILLA implements Ω, the explicit representation of organization types discussed in section 4 and assuming the role-based model described in section 2[4]. Formally, a VILLA simulation can be defined through the following tuple:

$Villa\_SIM = (E, T, S, Villa)$, where:

- $E \in Int$, is the number of runs
- $T \in Int$, is the number of ticks per run
- $S \subset Int \times Int$, is the size of the grid
- $Villa = (C, G, H, FS, F_0, m_E, M_E, S, R)$ describes the actual society

The elements of the tuple $Villa = (C, G, H, FS, F_0, m_E, M_E, S, R)$ are described as follows:

- $C = \{c : c = (\{health, foodintake\}, \{eat\}, \{O_c(eat|food > 0)\})\}$,
  are the creatures (i.e the set of agents fulfilling the creature role c). For each creature we keep track of its health and food-intake. All creatures have eating as their objective. Finally, the obligation indicates that all creatures must eat if there is food available.
- $G = \{g : g = (\{gatherpower, gatherprobability\}, \{gather\},$
  $\{t < E, O_g(gather(g, t))\}\}\}$,
  is the subset of Gatherers (i.e the set of agents fulfilling the gatherer role g). Their objectives are to eat and to gather. The obligation indicates that gatherers are obliged to gather food in each run.
- $H = \{h : h = (\{huntpower, huntprobability, position\},$
  $\{hunt, observe, move\}, \{t < E, O_h(hunt \vee move))\}\}$,
  is the subset of Hunters (i.e the set of agents fulfilling the hunter role h). Their objectives are to eat, to hunt, but also they want to observe and to move around. The obligation indicates that hunters are obliged to either hunt or move in each run.
- $G \subseteq C, H \subseteq C, H \cap G = \oslash$ Gatherers and Hunters are both creatures and thus inherit properties, objectives and norms from the creature role and no agent can be both Gatherer and Hunter at the same time.
- $FS = \{food\}$, is the food stack, describing the amount of food available at any moment
- $F_0 \in Int$, is the value of the initial food stack

---

[4] In VILLA roles are defined as $Role = \{Properties, Objectives, Norms\}$

- $m_E \in Int, m_E \leq |C|$, minimal number of creatures at time E
- $M_E \in Int$, maximal amount of food at time E
- $R = \{r1, r2, r3, ..., r12\}$ are the society rules

The society rules use the properties and objectives of the roles as functions for the individual creatures.

r1 $\forall c \in C, \forall i \leq E, eat(c, i) \rightarrow food(i) = food(i-1) - foodintake(c)$ i.e. the food stack decreases with the amount that is eaten.

r2 $\forall g \in G, \forall i \leq E$,
$gather(g, i) \rightarrow food(i) = food(i-1) + gatherpower(g, t) \times gatherprobability(g, t)$ i.e. the food stack increases with the amount the gatherers have gathered, which is related to their power and the probability that they find food.

r3 $p = \{h_1, ..., h_n\} \leftrightarrow \forall h_x, h_y \in p, adjacent-position(h_x, h_y)$ A group of hunters is defined as hunters occupying adjacent positions on the grid.

r4 $\forall p \in 2^H, \forall i \leq E$,
$p = \{h_1, ..., h_n\} \wedge hunt(p, i) \rightarrow food(i) = food(i-1) + \Sigma_{i=1}^{n}((huntpower(h_i, t) \times huntprobability(h_i, t)))$ A group of hunters brings in the sum of what all the individual hunters might bring in (once they are part of the group).

r5 $\forall c \in C, (food(i) \neq 0) \rightarrow eat(c, i)$ Each creature eats at each cycle iff there is food available.

r6 $\forall c \in C, noteat(c, i) \rightarrow health(c, i) = health(c, i-1) - 1$ if a creature does not eat, its health decreases.

r7 $\forall c \in C, health(c, i) = 0 \rightarrow dead(c)$ if the health of a creature gets down to 0 it dies.

r8 $\forall g \in G, \forall i \leq E, gatherpower(g, i) = f(health(g, i))$, i.e. gatherpower is a function of health

r9 $\forall h \in H, \forall i \leq E, huntpower(h, i) = f(health(h, i))$, i.e. huntpower is a function of health

r10 $\forall h \in H, \forall i \leq E, move(h, i) \rightarrow position(h, i) \neq position(h, i-1)$ when a hunter moves it changes position.

r11 $\forall c \in C, dead(c) \rightarrow |C| = |C| - 1$ if a creature dies the the number of creatures diminishes with 1.

r12 $success(Villa) \leftrightarrow |C| \geq m_E \wedge food \leq M_E$ A particular configuration of VILLA is successful if enough creatures are left in the end and not too much food is stocked (the latter to ensure a fair division of the food).

Informally, the goal of VILLA can be described as to have as many as possible creatures surviving at as low possible cost. In each run, all Creatures eat, as long as there is enough food; Gatherers and Hunters try to catch some food to replenish the common food stack. Furthermore, Hunters need to move around the field in order to get together with other hunters and therefore be able to hunt. All other agents (Gatherers and Others) either gather food and/or eat in their own block. Rule r12 describes the success factors of VILLA. At this stage, we only consider *goal success* (cf. section 2.1) as a measure of success, which in VILLA is strongly related to *role success*. Due to the simplicity of interactions in VILLA, we do not consider yet *interaction success*. *Structure success* will be the object of the extension of VILLA discussed in section 6, where we will look at the appropriateness of different reorganization strategies. We have implemented the VILLA simulation game using the RePast simulation environment [4]. VILLA is a very simple organization, and can hardly be taken as a representation of realistic situation. However, we have found it useful to start with a simple artificial organization in order to keep the complexity in hand and as such be able to identify conditions for reorganization, as described in the next section 5.2. In the next steps of this project, we will move into more realistic situations.

5.2   Using Simulation in the Identification of Reorganization Conditions

As discussed before, the first step in the exploration of the reorganization process is to find out what is the influence of the organization form on the behavior of the MAS in a certain environment. In order to make this more precise, we have to indicate which elements of the organizational form we need to consider. The representation in VILLA of the aspects presented in section 4:

- **Organizational Goal**: survival.
- **Organizational Roles**: Gatherers, Hunters and Others.
- **Agents**: in each simulation, different numbers of agents can play VILLA roles. At this stage of development, agents are not cognitive entities, but are limited to reproduce the behavior described in the role specification
- **Interaction**: Interaction occurs through sharing of resources (the food stack and the area of movement)

We have simulated different organizational settings (varying the amount of initial food, food collection probabilities, the number of agents per role, and the capabilities of roles) in order to find out which of the organizations performs "best" in that environment. Assuming the amount of initial food and the food collection probabilities as a representation of the 'hardship' of a certain environment, the aim of the simulation is to find out which type of population is the most appropriate for each environment. The availability of such a match between environment characteristics and successful organizational types, makes dynamic adaptation possible by giving agents the heuristics to determine which is the best structure for given environment conditions. For this effect, VILLA was run using the version without reorganization. Basically the experiment consisted of running many simulations, each with the same initial environment setup, but with variable organization setups: role combinations (only one type, different types,...), number of agents per role, and role capabilities (catch power, eating power,...).

Society Typologies. Society typology (types of roles and numbers of agents per role) can be seen as a simple way to describe an organization structure, abstracting from interaction forms and role dependencies. Our first study was to analyze the influence of agent distribution to the success of a society. For this effect, we simulated several societies where reorganization was not available, fixing the all society parameters except for the number of agents per role, which

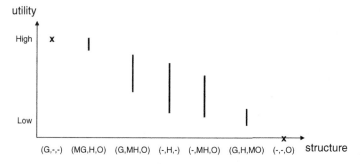

Fig. 1. Success of different society typologies. *Legend: typologies are given as (Gatherer, Hunter, Other). An M before the role indicates a majority of that type.*

was different for each simulation. Figure 1 gives an overview of the results of simulations with different configurations, for simulations with a length of 500 runs and a total of 117 agents. The large difference in utility of the different settings involving Hunters, can be attributed to the fact that Hunters must hunt in groups and are therefore dependent on the chance of finding other Hunters. Gatherers are the stable factor on collecting food, even if by design their catch power is lower than that of Gatherers. Actually, the simulation tool demonstrates that in societies with only Gatherers the chances of survival depend on the initial food stack and on the gather probability. More realistic settings, with still a high chance of survival, are those where there is a majority of Gatherers. It can also be seen that Others are mainly a "burden" for the society since they only eat. Their function is their capability to assume other roles, during society reorganization, as will be discussed in the next section. The simulations showed that a society could reach an equilibrium with the existence of all three roles.

Environment Conditions. Besides its typology, the success of a society depends on the conditions of the environment. In VILLA, the hardship of an environment is represented by a low probability of collecting food. Easy, friendly environments have high food collection probabilities. Furthermore, large environments make it more difficult for Hunters to find each other and as such, the ratio between number of Hunters and grid size can also be interpreted as an indication of the difficulty of an environment. We have performed a large number of simulations, varying on the size of the grid, the number of agents and the food collection probabilities. In these simulations the society typology was fixed (7 Gatherers, 6 Hunters and 4 Others). Due to lack of space, we will not describe these simulations in detail. In general, given this setting, environments where gather probability is higher than 15% result in healthier societies, independently of the capabilities of the Hunters and the size of the grid. It should be evident that given a fixed society typology, a larger grid will make it more difficult for Hunters to contribute to food collection, as it will be more difficult for them to form groups. Figure 2 shows an example of a healthy society on a grid of 60x60 that becomes bad on a grid of 120x120.

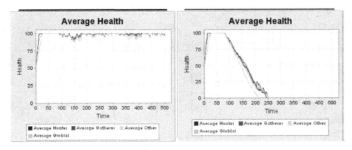

Fig. 2. Average health of typology (10,6,4). Left: 60x60 grid. Right: 120x120 grid.

5.3 Discussion

The success of societies where no reorganization can occur is, as can be expected, highly dependent on the initial settings (environment conditions and typology). An important factor for mixed societies (containing all different roles) to survive is the likelihood that Hunters will effectively be able to contribute to the food collection effort, which is dependent on their chances of forming groups. In the current version of VILLA, initial position of the agents and the movements of Hunters are randomly determined. A more realistic version should include the possibility for Hunters to actively search for partners, and possibly to learn from their earlier efforts. Translating this back to the general case means that successful interactions are crucial for the success of an organization. In VILLA, failing interactions (Hunters that cannot find the other Hunters) even cause the organization to fail completely.

The above experiments have enabled us to start to understand the conditions that indicate the need for reorganization of a society. By studying the results of many different simulations, several aspects have been identified that can be taken as candidate conditions for reorganization. In particular, we have studied food stack value, average food in a certain period of time, health of Others, and average health. In general, the food stack decreases drastically at the beginning of the simulation. To define it as a trigger for reorganization is useful because the reorganization process will be done early and the society will have time to adapt to the change. The same can be said from the use of the average of food stack as a parameter for reorganization. Food stack average also decreases strongly, even if less drastically. The food stack could be compared to taking the value of an organizations stock as a measure of its utility value. It also reacts quick to the environment, but is prone to volatile (quick changing) environmental changes. In addition, we have used the overall average health and the average health of Others as possible triggers for reorganization. Finally, we have observed that measures for utility, or success, of an organization should not consider only one point in time, but look at the situation during a time interval. That is why average health seems to be more relevant as trigger for reorganization than the current value of the food stack. So, in general derived measures that take longer periods of time in consideration are better measures for an organizations success than quick reacting measures such as stock or food stack.

As a side effect, the analysis of reorganization conditions lead us to understand that the status of the society should not be evaluated too soon after a reorganization trial. That is, it is necessary to allow for the reorganization to take effect before another trial is performed. This has been achieved by introducing a new parameter defining the delay of reorganization, which specifies a time interval that the simulator will wait to apply the reorganization rule again.

6 Simulating Reorganization

Our objective is to use the VILLA environment to understand and implement different reorganization strategies. Based on the experiments described in the previous section, we have come up with a set of *change indicators* (cf. section 4) to be used as triggers for reorganization: amount of food in the stack, average food stack, average overall health, average Hunter health, average Gatherer health, and average Other health. So far, we have only considered the role-based decision making case (cf. section 3), in which one role has the capabilities to evaluate the current situation, and the power to order others to effectuate changes demeaned necessary. To this effect, a new role is introduced, the society Head, that evaluates the overall state of the society, and decides on possible changes for the next run. VILLA implements the reorganization strategies discussed before as follows:

- **Behavioral change**: the Head can change the food intake and food collection power of creatures. Society typology remains fixed.
- **Structural change**: the village Head can order Others to enact the role of either Gatherer or Hunter, and as such change the society typology.

The simulation environment enables the user to indicate which reorganization strategy to be chosen, which condition the Head should use to determine the utility of the society at a given moment, and the reorganization action that the Head must take. The user can also indicate the length of the simulation.

6.1 Using VILLA to Determine Congruence

We are currently setting up the empirical experimentation that will allow for the rigorous evaluation of the different reorganization strategies described above, and how they compare to the situation where no reorganization occurs. Initial statistical results are available, but lack of time has prevented us to present here the complete experiment. The current experiment concerns the comparison of different reorganization strategies, given a fixed initial setting. We have performed 30 simulations (10 without reorganization, 10 following a behavioral adaptation strategy and 10 following a structural adaptation strategy). Initial environment conditions and society typology were the same in all 30 simulations, as follows: $Villa = \{C, G, H, FS, 200, 200, 1, 0, \infty, 60 \times 60, Rules\}$, where:

- $C = \{c_1, ..., c_{25} : c = (\{100, 2.0\}, \{eat\}, ...)\}$
- $G = \{g_1, ..., g_{10} : g = (\{100, 4.0, 20, 9\%\}, \{eat, gather\}, ...)\}$
- $H = \{h_1, ..., h_8 : h = (\{100, 4.0, 30, 15\%\}, \{eat, gather, observe, move\}, ...)\}$

The change indicator that triggers reorganization (both in the structural as in the behavioral case) is: $\gamma = (AverageHealth \leq 75)$. Reorganization attempts have a delay of 4 runs (that is, during 4 runs after a change no other reorganization attempt will happen). The mapping μ between organizations types, that provides the recipe for reorganization (cf. section 4) is for the behavioral case: γ then $g \in G : gatherpower(g) = gatherpower(g) + 3$; and, for the structural case: if γ then $\exists c \in C : c \notin G \wedge c \notin H \rightarrow G = G \cup \{c\}$

The comparison of the simulations is depicted in figure 3, where the three sets of simulations are organized from worse to best performance. Both reorganization

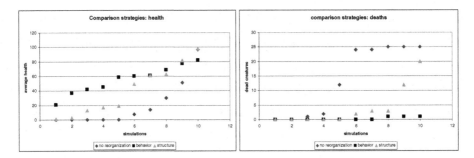

Fig. 3. Comparison of reorganization strategies

strategies are, as expected, better than no reorganization. This as to do with the initial setting. In this setting, where Gatherers alone are not able to collect enough food to feed the whole group, a society without reorganization can only survive if Hunters manage to form groups and thus contribute to the food stack. This was also the case in the four best simulations without reorganization. From the results, it also appears that behavioral reorganization performs better than structural reorganization. However, this is for some part the consequence of the fact that no limit was set to how much food a Gatherer can collect and thus *gatherpower* can increase for ever, which is of course a not very realistic situation. In the case of a structural reorganization, the number of new Gatherers is fixed by the number of available Others, and thus finite. Our next step is to introduce a limit to the amount of food that can be collected by a Gatherer. A final remark concerns the cost of reorganization. As discussed in section 4, the exploration of organizational adaptation, requires the definition of a function $f(\omega, \omega\prime)$ that computes the cost of implementing the reorganization. So far, our experiments have not considered the cost of reorganization. This is again a reason for the less realistic results obtained and is an issue we are now implementing.

7   Conclusions

Reorganization of an organization is a crucial issue in multi-agent systems that operate in an open, dynamic environment. In this paper, we presented a classification of reorganization types which considers two layers of reorganization:

behavioral and structural. We further described how simulations can help to determine whether and how reorganization should take place. We presented current work on the development of a simulation tool, VILLA, that is used to evaluate the different reorganization forms. The aim of VILLA is to understand triggers for reorganization and evaluate different strategies and not to enable the dynamic adaptation of organization. As such, triggers and strategies are setup by the user. The specific scenario of VILLA was chosen due to its simple yet rich structure as discussed in section 5.1. We are not specially interested in the anthropological or ecological issues of the scenario. Our current research on the development of a simulation tool for reorganization experimentation will enable to identify conditions and requirements for change, ways to incorporate changes in (running) systems, how to determine when and what change is needed, and how to communicate about changes. Another important future research direction (following the simulation work), is the development of conceptual formal models that enable the specification of dynamic reorganization of agent societies. Furthermore, we also plan to simulate decentralized decision-making reorganization strategies.

Acknowledgements

We gratefully acknowledge the help we got with the implementation of the VILLA environment which has been done by Adriano Melo and Vasco Furtado at the University of Fortaleza in Brazil.

References

1. K. S. Barber and C. E. Martin. Dynamic reorganization of decision-making groups. In *Proceedings of the 5th Autonomous Agents*, pages 513–520. ACM Press, 2001.
2. K. Carley and L. Gasser. Computational organization theory. In G. Weiss, editor, *Multiagent Systems: A Modern Approach to Distributed Artificial Intelligence*, pages 299–330. The MIT Press, 1999.
3. Lawrence Cavedon and Liz Sonenberg. On social commitments, roles and preferred goals. In *Proceedings of the 1998 International Conference on MultiAgent Systems (ICMAS98)*, pages 80–87, July 1998.
4. N. Collier. Repast: An extensible framework for agent simulation. In *http:repast.sourceforge.net*, 2003.
5. F J Diedrich, E E Entin, S G Hutchins, S P Hocevar, B Rubineau, and J MacMillan. When do organizations need to change (part i)? coping with incongruence. In *Proc. of Command and Control Research and Technology Symposium*, 2003.
6. V. Dignum. *A Model for Organizational Interaction: based on Agents, founded in Logic*. Utrecht University, 2004. PhD Thesis.
7. V. Dignum, F. Dignum, and L. Sonenberg. Towards dynamic organization of agent societies. In G. Vouros, editor, *Workshop on Coordination in Emergent Agent Societies, ECAI 2004*, pages 70–78, 2004.
8. Virginia Dignum, Frank Dignum, Vasco Furtado, Adriano Melo, and Liz Sonenberg. Towards a Simulation Tool for Evaluating Dynamic Reorganization of Agents Societies. In *Proc. of WS. on Socially Inspired Computing, AISB Convention*, 2005.

9. L Donaldson. *The Contingency Theory of Organizations.* Sage, 2001.
10. E E Entin, F J Diedrich, D L Kleinman, W G Kemple, S G Hocevar, B Rubineau, and D Serfaty. When do organizations need to change (part ii)? incongruence in action. In *Command and Control Research and Technology Symposium*, 2003.
11. E E Entin and D Serfaty. Adaptive team coordination. *Journal of Human Factors*, 41:321–325, 1999.
12. J. Evans. Strategic flexibility for high technology manoeuvres: A conceptual framework. *Journal of Management Studies*, 28(1):6989, 1991.
13. J. Ferber and O. Gutknecht. A meta-model for the analysis and design of organizations in multi-agent systems. In *Proceedings of the 3rd International Conference on Multi Agent Systems*, pages 128–135. IEEE Computer Society, 1998.
14. N. Glasser and P. Morignot. The reorganization of societies of autonomous agents. In *MAAMAW*, pages 98–111, 1997.
15. M. Hannebauer. *Autonomous Dynamic Reconfiguration in Multi-Agent Systems*, volume 2427 of *LNAI*. Springer-Verlag, 2002.
16. Bryan Horling and Victor Lesser. A Survey of Multi-Agent Organizational Paradigms. Computer Science Technical Report 04-45, University of Massachusetts, May 2004.
17. N. R. Jennings, K. Sycara, and M. Wooldridge. A roadmap of agent research and development. *JAAMAS*, 1(1):7–38, 1998.
18. S. Miles, M. Joy, and M. Luck. Towards a methodology for coordination mechanism selection in open systems. In P. Petta, R.Tolksdorf, and F. Zambonelli, editors, *Engineering Societies in the Agents World III*, LNAI 2577. Springer-Verlag, 2003.
19. R. Nair, M. Tambe, and S. Marsella. Role allocation and reallocation in multiagent teams: Towards a practical analysis. In *AAMAS 2003*, pages 552–559. ACM, 2003.
20. Y. So and E. Durfee. An organizational self-design model for organizational change. In *AAAI-93 Workshop on AI and Theories of Groups and Organizations: Conceptual and Empirical Research*, pages 8–15, 1993.
21. R. Sun and I. Naveh. Simulating organizational decision-making usinga cognitively realistic model. *Journal of Artificial Societies and Social Simulation*, 7(3), 2004.
22. M. Tambe. Towards flexible teamwork. *Journal of Artificial Intelligence Research*, (7):83–124, 1997.
23. G. Tidhar and L. Sonenberg. Engineering organization-oriented systems. In H. Hexmoor, editor, *Proc. of Workshop on Autonomy, Delegation and Control: From Inter-Agent to Organizations and Institutions*, AAMAS, 2003.

Verifying Norm Compliancy of Protocols*

Huib Aldewereld, Javier Vázquez-Salceda, Frank Dignum,
and John-Jules Ch. Meyer

Institute of Information and Computing Sciences
Utrecht University
{huib, javier, dignum, jj}@cs.uu.nl

Abstract. There is a wide agreement on the use of norms in order to specify the expected behaviour of agents in open MAS. However, in highly regulated domains, where norms dictate what can and cannot be done, it can be hard to determine whether a desired goal can actually be achieved without violating the norms. To help the agents in this process, agents can make use of predefined (knowledge-based) protocols, which are designed to help reach a goal without violating any of the norms. But how can we guarantee that these protocols are actually norm-compliant? Can these protocols really realise results without violating the norms? In this paper we introduce a formal method, based on program verification, for checking the norm compliance of (knowledge-based) protocols.

1   Introduction

Agents in open multiagent systems are sometimes as diverse as humans, as heterogeneous agents may behave in different ways in trying to complete their specified tasks. As some of this behaviour might not be desired, one needs mechanisms to constrain the behaviour of the agents joining the system by defining what is right and wrong. By doing so one can guarantee a safe and regulated environment for the agents to work in.

An Electronic Institution (eInstitution) is such an environment, where the expected behaviour of the agents joining the institution is described by means of an explicit specification of *norms* [9] [24]. As in human institutions, norms in eInstitutions are stated in such a form that allows them to regulate a wide range of situations over time without the need for modification. To achieve this stability, the formulation of norms abstracts from a variety of concrete aspects [11] [24]; i.e., norms are expressed in terms of concepts that are kept vague and ambiguous on purpose [13].

Because of their abstract nature, norms tend to be hard to understand and, as in real life, adhering to the norms that regulate the institution of which you are a part can be, at the least, a bit challenging. In highly regulated systems agents might become overly cautious, trying not to violate any of the norms. This can seriously reduce their efficiency and even influence the outcome and success of their goals. In order to help agents act in such an environment and increase their efficiency as well as their chance of success

---

* The research was supported by the Netherlands Organisation for Scientific Research (NWO) under project number 634.000.017.

O. Boissier et al. (Eds.): ANIREM and OOOP 2005, LNCS 3913, pp. 231–245, 2006.

one can specify *norm-compliant protocols* for the tasks that are to be accomplished in the institution.

A norm-compliant protocol is a guideline that makes sure that, when followed, one does not violate any of the norms, and as such it provides a quick and efficient manner to do the tasks one is assigned, since one does not need to review the norms and check norm compliance whenever one is planning to perform an action. In order to guarantee this the protocol should be checked for norm compliance, which means that one should check that no norms are violated by the protocol during its execution in all situations, i.e. the norm compliance of the protocol should not depend on the state of the world. Therefore, the protocol should provide a violation-free path to achieve the agent's goals. As long as the protocol is followed *to the letter* the agent should stay out of harm's way.

In this paper we present a formal method for checking the norm compliance of protocols based on temporal logic, using an approach used in concurrent programming [14]. We have chosen this approach over traditional techniques for verifying (sequential) programs, because verification methods for concurrent programs and temporal logics allow us to see whether norms are violated in intermediate steps as well, where traditional techniques are only for checking the input and output of a program. The formalism of [14] is, however, limited to checking properties and assertions for concurrent programs, not for checking norm compliance. Therefore we enhanced the formalism with the means to express norms and violations and prove the non-violating of these norms by the protocol. Some of the additions to the formalism from [14] are mentioned in the following sections.

The novelty of the approach presented in this paper lies in merging known techniques for verifying concurrent programs with deontic logics, in order to create a formalism for verifying the norm compliancy of protocols in highly normative domains; a problem which, to our knowledge, has not been handled in literature before. We would like to stess that we are not trying to invent a new version of a deontic formalism to represent and reason with norms; instead we propose a formalism that uses (static) representations of norms, expressed in one of the existing formats, and checks whether a protocol specified for a highly regulated domain adheres to the constraints that are layed down by these norms. While deontic reasoning is interesting in itself, the approach we are discussing in this paper is aimed at verifying protocols which can be used by agents in normative systems such that the agent does not have to reason about the norms of the system at run-time, thus reducing the complexity of the system.

The outline of this paper is as follows. We start by a discussion of the work done in the field of norms and agents. Then, in §3, we present the formal framework and explain some of the difficulties one will encounter when formalising protocols and norms. In §4 we show how the formalism works on an example protocol taken from the medical domain. We end this paper with some conclusions and propose some future work.

The example problem that we are going to use throughout this paper is a real-life protocol that describes which steps should be taken by a doctor to determine whether he can extract the organs of a donor or not (for the use of transplantation). This protocol is run after the patient has deceased, and specifies that a doctor needs to check whether the patient satisfies all of the listed criteria and none of the contra-indications of becoming a donor. If this first test is succesful, the doctor needs to check whether the patient

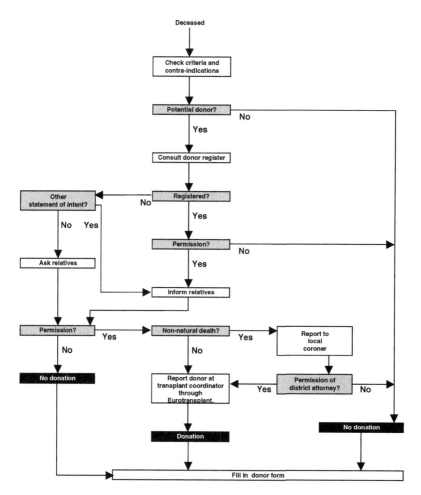

Fig. 1. Protocol for organ donation

is registered in the Donor Register (a special register which contains the approval or disaproval of people to become a post-mortal donor), and whether this registration permits the doctor to extract the organs for donation. If no such registration exists, other routes need to be taken to check whether the patient would have approved to donating his organs (by checking for the existance of an statement of intent giving this approval, or by consulting the relatives of the patient). Only if the permission for donation can be obtained (through any of these routes), and if the patient has not died from a non-natural death is the removal of the organs allowed.

A simplified version of this protocol is included in figure 1. We are using this real-life protocol because of the complexity of the norms applicable to the domain. We feel that if the formalism is able to express and handle such norms, it can be applied to all sorts of normative domains. Also, although it is not feasible to have agents performing the tasks mentioned in this example protocol, protocols that are designed for use by agents are of similar structure and complexity. And even though this protocol is knowledge-based[1], the method we present in this paper can be applied to other sorts of protocols as well.

2   Related Work

In those situations where agents might deviate from expected behaviour to fulfil their own goals, a multi-agent system needs mechanisms to defend and recommend right and wrong behaviour, along with safe environments to support those mechanisms. As we mentioned in §1, in eInstitutions expected behaviour is defined by means of *norms*. But providing agents with a set of norms is not enough; an eInstitution should also ensure *norm compliance*.

In the literature, there are two approaches for norm compliance from the individual agent perspective:

- agents that always obey norms [3] [20]
- agents that autonomously decide to obey norms [2] [5] [7] [16] [15] [24].

The former ensures norm compliance by default and it is used in those domains where total control of the agent behaviour is needed, but issues on the conflict between the agent goals and the norms should be solved. The latter allows the design of dynamic systems where agents are able to join a society while satisfying their own goals. The conflict between the agents' goals and the norms controlling their behaviour is handled explicitly in the reasoning process of the agent. In [15], *autonomous norm compliance* is divided in two separate processes: a) a process to deliberate about whether to comply with a norm (the *norm deliberation process*), and b) a process to update the goals and intentions of agents accordingly (the *norm compliance process*).

In those systems where autonomous norm compliance is allowed from the agent perspective, there is a need to enforce to some extent the compliance of norms from the social perspective. In [15] there is no direct enforcement on norm compliance, but *influenced* norm compliance, where behaviour of other agents against the non-compliance of a norm influences the decision of each agent. In [23] a more direct approach is taken: the agent platform hosting the eInstitution provides time-efficient services to help a special type of agent (the *Police Agents*) to enforce proper behaviour. As Police Agents cannot see or control the internal mental states and the reasoning process of the other agents, norm enforcement is based on the detection of *violation situations* in terms of (public) messages and (visible) actions.

The use of protocols to ease agent interaction (as discussed in §1) adds an extra level between the norms and the agent behaviour. In this case norm compliance is divided into two different levels:

- *norm compliance of the protocol*: to ensure that a given protocol adheres to the norms defined in a context. If the protocol is norm-compliant, following the protocol ensures that the agent(s) will not violate the norms.

---

[1] Knowledge-based protocols depend on the knowledge of the agent to decide which action is to be performed next, which results in a change of knowledge. The goal of such protocols is to determine whether something is known by the agent at the end of the protocol's execution.

– *protocol compliance by the agent*: to check that the behaviour of an agent complies with the expected behaviour defined by the protocol [25].

The former is the focus of this paper (see §3.3 and §4), as it is usually overlooked in other works. The latter (protocol compliance) has been studied both in theoretical and practical approaches. In [25] a formal framework for commitment protocols is presented. Verification in this case is an external process and therefore it cannot use the internal knowledge of the agents, only the (observable) behaviour. In [8] protocol compliance is handled by means of interaction scripts that are explicitly accepted by the agents through *interaction contracts*. Each contract includes the interacting agents, the roles they are playing, the contract clauses and the protocol. Verification of protocol compliance is an optional clause in the contract that, if included, specifies who and how will verify the interaction and the actions to take if the protocol is not followed. In [9] interaction protocols are structured in a *performative structure*. Although agents can decide not to follow the protocol (there is no direct control of the agent platform over the agents' beliefs and desires), there is an intermediate actor, the *governor*, that filters any non-allowed message that the agent tries to send to the eInstitution and is not allowed. Therefore protocol compliance is ensured by filtering those messages that, for a given state of the interaction, are not included in the protocol as possible messages to be uttered. However, in none of these works there is a method to ensure that the protocols are norm-compliant.

3   Our Approach

In this section we will set out the steps of the verification process necessary for checking the norm compliance of protocols. While discussing these steps we will also focus on some interesting aspects and problems that one can encounter.

3.1   Formalising the Protocol

First, we start with formalising the protocol that we want to check. Since protocols are very similar to programs we have based our protocol checking formalism on the formal verification methods designed for parallel programs taken from [14]. This program verification method uses first-order linear-time temporal logic (LTL) to express how programs change the world over time, and uses this logic to prove that certain specified properties of a program hold (e.g., deadlock freedom, mutual exclusion, termination, etc.). In this paper we will not go into an elaborate syntactical and semantical definition of the language used and will only give the informal interpretations of the operators. The proper definitions of the operators can be found in [1].

The protocol we want to verify is translated into a program using a syntax containing among others variable assignments, **if** – **then** – **else** – **fi** and **while** – **do** – **od** statements, with the conditions of these statements being formulas of a classical first-order predicate logic $\mathscr{L}_P$. For ease of reference all statements are labelled, with the labels being unique throughout a program, i.e., no two labels occurring in a program are equal. Using this we can formalise the example-protocol from figure 1 as follows (we only include the part of the protocol necessary for the proof we provide in §4, the complete version can be found in [1]):

$\Pi=$ **Initial R**;

    π_0: $\langle$check_criteria_&_contra-indications$\rangle$;
    π_1: **if** *know_criteria(d,y)$\wedge$know_no_contra-indication(d,y)*
        then π_2: *know_potential_donor(d,y)*:=TRUE
        else π_3: *know_not_potential_donor(d,y)*:=TRUE
        fi;
    π_4: **if** *know_potential_donor(d,y)*
        then π_5: $\langle$consult_donor_register$\rangle$
        fi;
          $\vdots$
    π_{33}: $\langle$fill_donor_form$\rangle$;
    π_e: **stop**

This formal program is a representation of the top three boxes of the protocol shown in figure 1 and describes the steps taken by the doctor. These steps are; 1) the doctor first checks whether the patient satisfies the conditions and none of the contra-indications for becoming an organ donor (formalised in π_0), then 2) using the results of these tests the doctor determines whether the patient is a suitable donor (formalised in π_1 to π_3). In the case that the patient does not satisfy the criteria or shows one of the contra-indications, the doctor knows that the patient is not a potential donor, thereby terminating the protocol (shown in π_3[2]). However, if the patient does satisfy the criteria and does not show any of the contra-indications, the doctor determines that the patient is a potential donor (see π_2), and then 3) continues to check whether the patient has registered his permission (or prohibition) for extracting organs for transplantation (formalised in π_4 and π_5).

Note that the result of the actions like check_criteria_&_contra-indications is dependent on the domain, i.e. if the patient satisfies the criteria and none of the contra-indications, the result of the action in π_0 would be that the doctor knows this, thus *know_criteria(d, y)* $\wedge$ *know_no_contra-indication(d, y)*.

The logic used for verifying protocols consists of a classical first-order predicate logic $\mathscr{L}_P$ which is extended with $\bigcirc$ (*next-state*), $\square$ (*always*) and **atnext** (*first time*) operators to obtain a first-order linear-time temporal predicate logic $\mathscr{L}_{TP}$. Using these operators we can also derive the $\Diamond$ (*sometime*) and **until** operators. To reason about events in the past, $\mathscr{L}_{TP}$ is extended with past-time operators, which are discussed in the next section (for formal semantics of $\mathscr{L}_{TP}$ see [14] and [1]). The logic $\mathscr{L}_{TP}$ is then expanded to $\mathscr{L}_{TP_\Pi}$ by adding the set of propositional variables at λ (which means that action labelled λ is next to be executed), to link the protocol state to a state in the temporal model of the logic. Therefore, although the protocol has actions, the logic, instead, only uses the labels of the actions.

In order to prove that a protocol is norm-compliant in all situations that might arise we need to check the protocol in various different models and see whether the norm compliance holds. For instance, a protocol for obtaining donor organs needs to be checked in models where the donor is male and in models where the donor is female to determine that the protocol does not violate a norm about no discrimination between donors based on sex, race, etc. Only if the protocol generates the desired and expected result in both situations, we can say that the protocol does not violate that norm.

---

[2] The fact that *know_not_potential_donor(d, y)* becomes true means in this protocol that all of the next steps are skipped, and the protocol terminates by specifying that no permission can be obtained.

Since time is defined as semi-finite (it starts at the start of the protocol), protocols cannot use information about previous runs and next runs (unless explicitly modelled). If protocols Π_1 and Π_2 are run one after another (i.e., $\Pi_1; \Pi_2$), Π_1 cannot use information from or about Π_2 and Π_2 cannot use information from or about Π_1; they are considered as separate runs. This means that the value of program variables, truth values of predicates and states and information gathered is restricted to the runtime of the protocol. Propositions and predicates *can* change their truth values during a protocol run, however, but only because of actions taken in the protocol.

3.2 Formalising the Norms

The norms that apply to the domain in which we are checking the protocol are then translated into a high-level formal language, which should provide enough room for the formal representation of the norms to keep their abstract nature. We have used a formalism similar to the one used in [23]. In order to be able to use these high-level formalised norms in the checking of the protocols we needed to extend the first-order language specified above with deontic concepts, O_x, P_x, F_x, to express x being obliged, permitted or prohibited some action, respectively. To give meaning to these deontic operators we introduced special predicates to denote when violations occur. To handle the temporal aspects of norms, such as deadlines, we used ideas from [4], [6] and [8] and adapted these to be used with the first-order temporal logic as specified above. Furthermore we have extended our language with $DO_x \lambda$ (*x is going to do λ next*) to reason about actions and $\Diamond\varphi$ (*past operator*) and $\ominus\varphi$ (*previous-state operator*) to reason about the events that have happened (such as actions that have been done: $DONE_x \alpha \equiv \odot DO_x \alpha$).

The deontic operators discussed above are introduced as abbreviations of complex temporal formulas. Definition 1 shows the temporal translations of obligations in our formalism (based on [8]).

Definition 1 (Obligations)

$$O_x(DO_x \alpha < \delta) \equiv \Diamond\delta \wedge \big[(\neg\delta \wedge \neg viol(x, DO_x \alpha, \delta) \wedge \neg DONE_x \alpha) \text{ until}$$
$$((DO_x \alpha \wedge \bigcirc(\Box\neg viol(x, DO_x \alpha, \delta))) \vee$$
$$(\neg DO_x \alpha \wedge \bigcirc(\delta \wedge viol(x, DO_x \alpha, \delta))))\big]$$

This definition intuitively expressing that a) a deadline always occurs at sometime, b) until that moment no violations can occur because of the norm, and c) either the action is done before the deadline and no violations occur ever because of this norm, or the deadline passes while the action has not yet been done and a violation occurs. Similar temporal translations are made for permissions and prohibitions (not included here due to space constrains, see [1] for these definitions).

Norms applicable to the example mentioned in §1 are, for instance, obliging doctors to talk to relatives for obtaining permission before extracting organs from a donor, prohibiting the extraction of organs without the approval of the district attorney in case of suspicion of a non-natural death , etc[3]. In §4 we prove that the protocol abides to the norm that doctors are obliged to pronounce dead of a patient before removing an organ.

---

[3] A full set of norms is available in [1].

Permissions and Non-permissions. In theoretical deontic studies, such as [17], [21] permissions are normally modelled as $P_x(DO_x\,\alpha) \equiv DO_x\,\alpha \rightarrow \neg viol(x, \alpha)$, which says that being permitted to do α means that doing α leads to non-violation. Moreover, permissions are, in classic deontic studies, normally defined as being equivalent to $\neg F_x(DO_x\,\alpha)$ and $\neg O_x(\neg DO_x\,\alpha)$. The problem with this definition, which is also discussed in deontic studies (cf. [18]), is that it makes the existence of permissive norms nonessential when trying to determine whether violations occur. From observations of the legal domain, and as already proposed in [18], it follows, however, that permissions can be considered as exceptions to a general prohibition. The fact that an article in a law provides a certain set of people in a certain situation with the permission to do α means that in other situations these people, or other people at all times, are prohibited to do α. Some lawbooks even express this explicitly by means of an article that something is forbidden unless stated otherwise within that lawbook. We model this relation between permissions by a technique similar to *negation as failure*, as used in logic programming [22]; the inability to derive that you are permitted to do α means that you are forbidden to do α:

$$\sim P_x(DO_x\,\alpha) \rightarrow F_x(DO_x\,\alpha)$$

Of course, we could have opted for a relation in the other direction, i.e., $\sim F_x(DO_x\,\alpha) \rightarrow P_x(DO_x\,\alpha)$ which means that if something is not explicitly forbidden it is permitted. The choice between whether to use the first or the second relation entirely depends on the nature of the norms one is trying to formalise, i.e., the choice is dependent on the character of the legal system, thus whether it is permissive in nature or restrictive (see [19] for a discussion on the character of legal systems).

Now, since we add the $\sim P_x(DO_x\,\alpha) \rightarrow F_x(DO_x\,\alpha)$ rule to our system to model that permissions are exceptions to general prohibitions (where this general prohibition might only follow from the characteristic nature of the law), we get into trouble if we don't assume that permissions follow from obligations (i.e., $O_x(DO_x\,\alpha) \rightarrow P_x(DO_x\,\alpha)$). This assumption is an axiom in most deontic systems, but we are reluctant to insert it because we feel that in the real world this might not necessarily hold. It is, however, true that a normative system is supposed to uphold this principle, i.e., normative systems should be designed such that obligations to do α can actually be fulfilled, but this is actually the ideal situation. When designing a normative system (thus, when laws are postulated) it should be taken into account that obligations can be fulfilled. However, it is not necessarily the case that this condition is always met in normative systems (due to mistakes in designing the system). In the case presented in §4, however, we can safely assume that this assumption has not been violated by the law-maker.

Linking Levels. A problem that arises because of the high-level of abstraction for the formalisation of norms is the mapping between the concepts in the norms and the actions specified by the protocols. In order for the norms to range over a wide variety of situations, and in order to function for a long duration without the need of modification, norms tend to abstract from a variety of concrete aspects, such as time, role, etc. Therefore, in order to check whether certain concrete actions and situations contained in the protocol violate a norm we need to map these concrete actions and situations to the abstract actions and situations described by the norms. The mappings that we can provide are generally considered to be one-way mappings, that is, a concrete action a

in a protocol can be considered to be an instance of an abstract action α mentioned in the norms, but since there are many more actions conceivable that can be considered instances of α, we cannot say that a and α are equivalent; we can only say that a is an instance of α, or that doing a *counts as* doing α ($DO_x a \rightsquigarrow DO_x \alpha$). Although this mapping problem seems to follow from our high-level formal language, it is also present when using formalisms with a lower abstraction level (although implicit). The explicit mapping that we need to make between the protocols and norms now is in such a case taken care of when formalising the norms (by means of choosing the appropriate concrete concepts in the formalisation of the norms). In this paper we use a simplified version of the *counts as* as defined in [10] and [12].

3.3   Verifying Protocols

The next step of the process is the actual verification of the protocol. The formalism that we have chosen allows us to specify properties that are verified by means of automated reasoning. This means that we check the protocol in all sorts of different situations (that apply to the protocol and norms) in order to check whether all situations guarantee the norm compliance that we require.

In order to check the protocol on norm compliance we specify a *safety* property that has to be derivable from the protocol. This safety property is an invariant, a formula that should hold during the entire execution of the protocol. We define the safety property for checking protocols as follows:

Definition 2 (Safety Property of Protocols)

$$\text{start}_{\Pi} \wedge \Box Norms \rightarrow \Box\neg violation$$

Where $\text{start}_{\Pi} \equiv \text{at } \alpha_0$ (*the protocol is at its start label*), *Norms* being the conjunction of all applicable norms, and *violation* $\equiv \bigvee_{x,\alpha,\delta} viol(x, \alpha, \delta)$ (*violation is the disjunction of all viol-formulas that occur in Norms*). This safety property of protocols is defined as the global invariance of $\neg violation$ for the protocol Π under the condition that *Norms* always holds, i.e., if $\Box Norms$ holds upon the start of running Π, then $\neg violation$ will hold in all states of the run.

To prove that a protocol satisfies this property we introduce the following rule:

Theorem 1 (Invariance Rule). *The following rule is valid:*

$$\frac{\begin{array}{c} \text{start}_{\Pi} \wedge \Box Norms \rightarrow \neg violation \\ \neg violation \text{ invof } \mathcal{M}_{\Pi} \end{array}}{\text{start}_{\Pi} \wedge \Box Norms \rightarrow \Box\neg violation}$$

Where C invof $\alpha \equiv \text{at } \alpha \wedge C \rightarrow \bigcirc C$ (*C is an invariant of α*) and C invof $\mathcal{M} \equiv C$ invof $\alpha_1 \wedge \ldots \wedge C$ invof α_m (*C is an invariant of every $\alpha \in \mathcal{M}$*), and $\mathcal{M}_{\Pi}$ is the set of all labels in the program except for the label of stop, the end-statement. A proof of this theorem can be found in [14]. This rule is also very close to the intuition one might have about protocols being norm-compliant, namely if there are no steps in the protocol that violate any norm, the protocol will not violate any of the norms as a whole (if no violation existed when the protocol started running).

Of course, this is not the only property that a protocol needs to satisfy. Because law is generally applicable to a single context, one who is not participating in the activities of that context is not regulated by these laws; the laws mean nothing to someone not trying to do anything regulated by that particular set of laws. For instance, traffic laws have no influence on those who do not participate in traffic situations; if someone sits at home all times, these laws will never be violated. The problem is that laws regulating a specific domain assume that you are trying to do something or otherwise participate in that domain, and only regulates these actions and participations.

While all protocols that satisfy the aforementioned safety property are compliant to the norms, we would actually like to be able to say a bit more about the protocols we are trying to verify. Since protocols that do satisfy the safety protocol, and thereby the norm compliance, that merely consist of actions that are not regulated by the applicable norms, are not that interesting to the agents interacting in the eInstitutions (e.g., although "**while** True **do** skip **od**" does satisfy almost all violation invariances, it is not very interesting from an interaction or institution's point of view). Therefore, we need to define another property that allows us to determine whether a protocol is, next to being norm-compliant, also trying to achieve something interesting. Norm-compliant protocols that are actually relevant to the domain not only satisfy the violation invariance property, but also a liveness property. These sorts of properties specify that a protocol/program will, at sometime, reach a certain (interesting) state. We can use this to check whether the protocol achieves a specified goal at the end of its run:

Definition 3 (Liveness Property of Protocols)

$$\text{start}_\Pi \wedge \Box Norms \rightarrow \Diamond(\text{at } \alpha_e \wedge goal)$$

Where at α_e is the stop-statement of Π and $goal$ is the goal that the protocol should reach. In our example this is a complex declarative statement specifying that when the conditions hold (i.e., the donation should ideally take place), the agent/doctor running the protocol will know that the donation can take place, and when one of the conditions for the donation fails, the agent/doctor knows that the donation cannot take place.

4 Practice

Now that we have seen a description of the approach we are using to verify the norm compliance, we show in this section how this approach is to be used. We show this by using the example protocol mentioned above in figure 1. To ensure the norm compliance of this protocol we need to check whether the safety and liveness properties, as specified before, are satisfied. Although it is possible to give a fully formal proof we will only show the first steps due to space limitations. In this proof we assume that y denotes the patient with respect to whom the protocol is run, d denotes the doctor running the protocol and d' is a doctor-variable (denoting a unspecified doctor).

For the invariance proof, i.e. proving that $\neg violation$ is an invariant of the protocol, we make use of the invariance rule as mentioned in theorem 1. We assume that $\text{start}_\Pi \wedge \Box Norms \rightarrow \neg violation$ holds (1) and will try to prove that $\neg violation$ is an invariance of every following step of the protocol, thereby deriving that $\neg violation$ is an invariant of the protocol. We can make this assumption because we are not interested in the situations where this assumption does not hold, such as the situation in which the protocol is started when a violation has already occurred, since starting the protocol in such a situation would say nothing about the norm compliance of the protocol, only that it cannot "repair" the situation it started in.

Note that we only need to check the actions taken by the protocol, since the "control points" used in the protocol (i.e. protocol labels referring to conditions of **if**-clauses) are trivially norm-compliant since they do not change the value of any *viol*-predicate (actually, the action that is thereafter chosen shows whether the decision made at the control point was correct). This is expressed in step (3).

(1) $start_\Pi \land \Box Norms \rightarrow \neg violation$	assumption
(2) $start_\Pi \rightarrow (at\, \pi_0 \land intended(organ\_removal))$	definition of $start_\Pi$
(3) $\neg violation$ invof $\mathcal{M}_\Pi \setminus \{\pi_0, \pi_5, \pi_7, \pi_9, \pi_{14}, \pi_{16}, \pi_{21}, \pi_{23}, \pi_{24}, \pi_{26}, \pi_{33}\}$	Trivial

Next we prove that step π_0 of the protocol (checking whether the patient satisfies the criteria and none of the contra-indications for being a donor) is norm-compliant. The only norm in the law concerning this actions is the fact that doctors are supposed to check whether a patient is brain death before removing any organs, of which the translation is seen in step (5). In order to use this deontic expression for determining whether violations occur, we need to "expand" the norm in (5) to its temporal counterpart by using the definition 1 seen earlier, as seen in (6). Now, since we can derive from the structure of the protocol that $DO_{d'}\, remove\_organ(d', y)$ has not yet occurred, or is occurring now (7), we can derive that the value of V_1 will not be changed by $DO_d\, certify\_dead(d, y)$, shown in (8) and (10). Finally, after connecting the abstract norm level to the protocol level using (4) to derive (11), remembering the fact that obligations imply permissions (12) (and therefore do not lead to violations by acting upon the obligation)[4], and adding the fact that no other norms were applicable and thereby cannot be violated (13), we can conclude that $\neg violation$ is an invariant of π_0, see (15).

(4) $at\, \pi_0 \rightsquigarrow DO_d\, certify\_dead(d,y)$	
(5) $O_d(DO_d\, certify\_dead(d,y) < DO_{d'}\, remove\_organ(d',y))$	Art. 14
(6) $\Diamond DO_{d'}\, remove\_organ(d',y) \land \big[(\neg DO_{d'}\, remove\_organ(d',y) \land \neg V_1 \land \neg DONE_d\, certify\_dead(d,y))$ until $((DO_d\, certify\_dead(d,y) \land \bigcirc \Box \neg V_1) \lor$ $(\neg DO_d\, certify\_dead(d,y) \land \bigcirc (DO_{d'}\, remove\_organ(d',y) \land V_1)))\big]$ $V_1 = viol(d, DO_d\, certify\_dead(d,y), DO_{d'}\, remove\_organ(d',y))$	(5)
(7) $\neg \Diamond DO_{d'}\, remove\_organ(d',y)$	(Π)
(8) $DO_d\, certify\_dead(d,y) \land \neg violation \rightarrow \bigcirc \Box \neg V_1$	(6),(7)
(9) $\bigcirc \Box \varphi \rightarrow \bigcirc \varphi$	(taut)
(10) $DO_d\, certify\_dead(d,y) \land \neg violation \rightarrow \bigcirc \neg V_1$	(8),(9)
(11) $at\, \pi_0 \land \neg violation \rightarrow \bigcirc \neg V_1$	(4),(10)
(12) $P_d(DO_d\, certify\_dead(d,y) < DO_{d'}\, remove\_organ(d',y))$	(5)
(13) $at\, \pi_0 \land \neg violation \rightarrow \bigcirc \neg viol(d, \alpha, \delta)$ for all viol-predicates other than V_1	(VC)
(14) $at\, \pi_0 \land \neg violation \rightarrow \bigcirc \neg violation$	(11),(13)
(15) $\neg violation$ invof π_0	(14)

---

[4] Remember that not being able to derive this permission would have meant that there existed a prohibition on this action, see §3.2.

And so, after checking the norm compliance of π_0 we continue with checking whether the next actions (starting with π_5 and so on, see the formalised protocol in §3.1 and the full proof in [1]) do not violate the norms. After deriving that $\neg violation$ is an invariant of all the protocol steps we can derive, by theorem 1, that the protocol does not violate any of the norms, see (111).

$$\vdots$$

(110) $\neg violation$ invof π_{33}
　　　No norms concerning filling in donor form (VC)
(111) $\neg violation$ invof $\mathcal{M}_\Pi$ $(1),(3),(15),...,(110)$

In a similar fashion we can prove that a liveness property as specified in definition 3 holds for Π. Where

at α_e $\equiv$ at π_e

goal $\equiv$ $criteria(y) \wedge \neg contra\text{-}indication(y) \wedge (statement\_permission(y) \vee other\_statement(z,y) \vee relative\_permission(y)) \wedge$

　　　　　$(\neg non\text{-}natural\_dead(y) \vee DA\_permission(p,remove\_organs))$

　　　　　$\rightarrow know\_permission(d,remove\_organ(y))$

　　$\wedge \neg (criteria(y) \wedge \neg contra\text{-}indication(y) \wedge (statement\_permission(y) \vee other\_statement(z,y) \vee relative\_permission(y)) \wedge$

　　　　　$(\neg non\text{-}natural\_dead(y) \vee DA\_permission(p,remove\_organs)))$

　　　　　$\rightarrow know\_no\_permission(d,remove\_organ(y))$

This *goal* represents that the protocol is supposed to make sure that the agent obtains the knowledge whether it has the permission for the organ transplantation or not, after ending the protocol run. By proving these safety and liveness properties we show that Π is not only norm-compliant, but also that Π actually achieves the goal for which it is designed (that is, to determine whether you are allowed to extract the patients organs for transplantation).

5 Evaluation

While proving the liveness of the example protocol, shown partially in the previous section, it became even more evident that the attempt to represent a domain for verifying the norm compliance of a protocol (i.e. trying to "flesh out" the meaning of the concepts used in the domain) is a very important aspect of the approach presented in this paper. Without the formal meaning of the concepts in the domain, the verification cannot take place and with the wrong meaning the verification could lead to incorrect results. In a sense, the approach discussed in this paper is actually about defining the logical context of these concepts, and therein very similar to the legal domain where legality/illegality of certain events/actions is determined by the interpretation of the details of an investigation.

At the end of the verification process described in this paper, a list of assumptions under which the protocol can be proven correct has been composed and it is not only the proof itself, but, perhaps even more, this list of assumptions that is the interesting result of the verification process. This list of assumptions is what actually makes the verification of norm compliance different from other protocol verification techniques as well as concurrent program verification methods, as it is this list of assumptions that defines the correctness of the proof. These latter approaches are only useable when all is crystal clear and neatly specified, but this is a situation that cannot occur when handling norms. The approach presented in this paper shows that for proving normative protocols such a list of assumptions is necessary in order to be able to say anything about the norm compliance of a protocol.

6   Conclusions and Future Work

In this paper we discussed a formal approach on norm compliance of protocols based on the verification of programs. We give a view of how these techniques can be used, after some adaptation and extension, to verify that a (knowledge-based) protocol is norm-compliant. We also show, as an example, how norm compliance of a knowledge-based protocol (actually used in the medical domain) can be proven. Moreover we have shown that it is actually the assumptions that one has to make when trying to proof the norm compliance of a protocol that are the most interesting result of the presented work, as one can never fully handle the abstractness of norms when trying to proving norm compliance.

Please note that norm compliance of the protocols used by the agents is only a step towards the implementation of norms in MAS. Protocols are guidelines and agents are, therefore, not necessarily constrained to follow the protocol. A more direct enforcement is needed instead. Norms can be enforced either by the use of violation detection and sanctioning these violations [23], or by directly constraining the agents such that they can only do actions that do not violate norms.

Currently our formal method is suited for verification of single sequential protocols. We plan to extend our $\mathscr{L}_{TP_{\Pi}}$ language to prove norm compliance of parallel protocols (such as interaction protocols). We also plan to extend the $\mathscr{L}_{TP}$ language with operators from epistemic logic in order to improve expressiveness of knowledge and beliefs of agents following a protocol. Moreover, we are very interested in seeing how this extended approach can, for instance, be used for the checking of security and authentication protocols.

The framework discussed in this paper uses a theorem proving method to verify the norm compliance of protocols. This is known to be labour-intensive. We are currently considering the use of model-checking, instead.

References

1. H. Aldewereld, J. Vázquez-Salceda, F. Dignum, and J.-J.Ch. Meyer. Proving norm compliancy of protocols in electronic institutions. Technical Report UU-CS-2005-010, Institute of Information and Computing Sciences, Utrecht University, 2005.
2. G. Boella and L. Lesmo. Deliberative normative agents. In C. Dellarocas and R. Conte, editors, *Workshop on Norms and Institutions in Multi-Agent Systems*, pages 15–25. ACM-AAAI, ACM Press, 2000.

3. M. Boman. Norms in artificial decission making. *Artificial Intelligence and Law*, 7(1):17–35, 1999.

4. J. Broersen, F. Dignum, V. Dignum, and J.-J. Ch. Meyer. Designing a Deontic Logic of Deadlines. In *7th Int. Workshop on Deontic Logic in Computer Science (DEON'04)*, Portugal, May 2004.

5. C. Castelfranchi, F. Dignum, C. Jonker, and J. Treur. Deliberative Normative Agents: Principles and architecture. In *Proc. of the 6th Int. Workshop on Agent Theories, Architectures, and Languages (ATAL-99)*, 1999.

6. F. Dignum, J. Broersen, V. Dignum, and J.-J. Ch. Meyer. Meeting the Deadline: Why, When and How. In *3rd Goddard Workshop on Formal Approaches to Agent-Based Systems (FAABS)*, Maryland, April 2004.

7. F. Dignum, D. Morley, and E.A. Sonenberg. Towards socially sophisticated BDI agents. In *DEXA Workshop*, pages 1134–1140, 2000.

8. V. Dignum. *A Model for Organizational Interaction: based on Agents, founded in Logic*. SIKS Dissertation Series 2004-1. SIKS, 2004. PhD Thesis.

9. M. Estava. *Electronic Institutions: from specification to development*. PhD thesis, Universitat Politèchnica de Catalunya, 2003.

10. D. Grossi, H. Aldewereld, J. Vázquez-Salceda, and F. Dignum. Ontological aspects of the implementation of norms in agent-based electronic institutions. Accepted for the 1st International Symposium on Normative Multiagent Systems (NorMAS2005), 2005.

11. D. Grossi and F. Dignum. From abstract to concrete norms in agent institutions. In M. G. Hinchey, J. L. Rash, W. F. Truszkowski, and et al., editors, *Formal Approaches to Agent-Based Systems: Third International Workshop, FAABS 2004*, Lecture Notes in Computer Science, pages 12–29. Springer-Verlag, April 2004.

12. D. Grossi, F. Dignum, and J-J. Ch. Meyer. Contextual taxonomies. In J. Leite and P. Toroni, editors, *Proceedings of CLIMA V Workshop, Lisbon, September*, pages 2–17, 2004.

13. H. L. A. Hart. *The Concept of Law*. Clarendon Press, Oxford, 1961.

14. Fred Kröger. *Temporal Logic of Programs*, volume 8 of *EACTS monographs on theoretical computer science*. Springer-Verlag, 1987.

15. F. López y Lopez. *Social Power and NormsL Impact on Agent Behaviour*. PhD thesis, Faculty of Engineering and Applied Science, Univ. of Southampton, 1997.

16. F. López y Lopez, M. Luck, and M. d'Inverno. A framework for norm-based inter-agent dependence. In *Proceedings of The Third Mexican International Conference on Computer Science*, pages 31–40. SMCC-INEGI, 2001.

17. J.-J. Ch. Meyer and R.J. Wieringa. Deontic logic: A concise overview. In *Deontic Logic in Computer Science: Normative System Specification*, pages 3–16. John Wiley & Sons Ltd., Chichester, UK, 1994.

18. L. Royakkers and F. Dignum. Giving permission implies giving choice. In E. Schweighofer, editor, *8th International Conference and Workshop on Database and Expert Systems Applications*. Toulouse, France, 1997.

19. M.J. Sergot, F. Sadri, R.A. Kowalski, and F. Kriwaczek. The british nationality act as a logic program. *Communications of the ACM*, 29(5):370–386, May 1986.

20. Y. Shoham and M. Tennenholtz. On social laws for artificial agent societies: Off-line design. *Artificial Intelligence*, 73(1-2):231–252, 1995.

21. A. Soeteman. *Logic in Law: Remarks on logic and rationality in normative reasoning, especially in law*. Kluwer Academic Publishers, 1989.

22. M.H. van Emden and R.A. Kowalski. The semantics of predicate logic as a programming language. *Journal of the ACM (JACM)*, 23(4):733–742, October 1976.

23. J. Vázquez-Salceda, H. Aldewereld, and F. Dignum. Implementing norms in multiagent systems. In G. Lindemann, J. Denzinger, I.J. Timm, and R. Unland, editors, *Multiagent System Technologies*, LNAI 3187, pages 313–327. Springer-Verlag, 2004.
24. J. Vázquez-Salceda and F. Dignum. Modelling electronic organizations. In V. Marik, J. Muller, and M. Pechoucek, editors, *Multi-Agent Systems and Applications III*, LNAI 2691, pages 584–593. Springer-Verlag, 2003.
25. Mahadevan Venkatraman and Munindar P. Singh. Verifying compliance with commitment protocols. *Autonomous Agents and Multi-Agent Systems*, 2(3):217–236, 1999.

A Rule Language for Modelling and Monitoring Social Expectations in Multi-agent Systems

Stephen Cranefield

Department of Information Science, University of Otago
PO Box 56, Dunedin, New Zealand
scranefield@infoscience.otago.ac.nz

Abstract. This paper proposes a rule language for defining social expectations based on a metric interval temporal logic with past and future modalities and a current-time binding operator. An algorithm for run-time monitoring compliance of rules in this language based on formula progression is also presented.

1 Introduction

The study of *electronic institutions*—explicit declarative models of the rules governing particular open systems of autonomous agents—has gained much recent attention [1]. An institution provides a social model of a multi-agent system in which agents agree (by the act of joining the society) or are required to conform to particular norms of behaviour and role and empowerment structures. However, in an open system it is not sufficient to simply formally or semi-formally define an institution and hope that agents will follow its rules. As in human society, the successful functioning of an institution requires that all (or at least most) members will conform. There is therefore a need for mechanisms that prevent or at least discourage anti-social behaviour. Possible approaches to maintaining social order include designing the rules of interaction so that rational agents will have no benefit from breaking them, the formal verification of agents' code to prove they will behave as expected—something that is not possible in an open system, and the implementation of infrastructure supporting social constructs such as trust and reputation. When it is not possible to ensure compliance by design or verification, it is necessary to have a means of determining when agents fulfil or violate the norms of their society, whatever use is then made of the resulting information.

There has been a significant amount of recent research on statically verifying properties of institutions as well as interpreting institutions to manage or guide agent interaction (examples include several papers in the DALT'04 workshop [2] as well as earlier work such as that by Huget et al. [3] and Cliffe and Padget [4]). However, there has been less attention paid to mechanisms for run-time compliance checking, i.e. monitoring events in a running agent system, determining the future expectations of agents' behaviour according to norms of the institution, and checking if these are fulfilled or violated. This paper focuses on that issue.

Verdicchio and Colombetti [5, 6] have developed a formal model of social commitment with its semantics based on a propositional branching time logic with future and past-time modal operators ($CTL^{\pm}$), but with an axiomatic account of events and

O. Boissier et al. (Eds.): ANIREM and OOOP 2005, LNCS 3913, pp. 246–258, 2006.

commitments expressed using predicate logic and CTL$^{\pm}$ operators together. This paper presents the results of an investigation into how implication formulae of the style used by Verdicchio and Colombetti can be formally characterised and, with appropriate syntax restrictions, be used for practical reasoning by agents at run time. An important requirement for this purpose is the ability to reason efficiently about how event occurrences relate to specific points or intervals in time. We have therefore developed a logic named hyMITL$^{\pm}$ that combines CTL$^{\pm}$ with Metric Interval Temporal Logic (MITL) [7], as well as features of hybrid logics [8]. We present a subset of hyMITL$^{\pm}$ that provides a rule language for defining social expectations and show how the technique of formula progression from the planning system TLPlan [9] can be used to monitor social expectations until they are fulfilled or violated.

The structure of the paper is as follows. Sections 2 and 3 define the syntax and semantics of hyMITL$^{\pm}$, respectively, with the rule language presented in Section 4 and an example of its use in Section 5. Section 6 gives details of the compliance-monitoring algorithm. Finally some related work is discussed in Section 7 and Section 8 concludes the paper.

2   Syntax of hyMITL$^{\pm}$

Formulae of hyMITL$^{\pm}$ are defined by the following grammar:

$$\phi ::= p \mid \neg\phi \mid \phi \wedge \phi \mid \forall x.\phi_x \mid \mathsf{X}^{+}\phi \mid \mathsf{X}^{-}\phi \mid$$
$$\phi \mathsf{U}_I^{+}\phi \mid \phi \mathsf{U}_I^{-}\phi \mid \mathsf{A}\phi \mid \mathsf{E}\phi \mid \downarrow^{u}x.\phi_x \mid I$$
$$I ::= (-\infty,+\infty) \mid [b,b] \mid [b,b) \mid (b,b] \mid (b,b)$$
$$b ::= a \mid +d \mid -d$$

where:

- p is an atomic formula from a first order language L.
- ϕ_x denotes a formula ϕ in which variable x is free (i.e. not bound by $\forall$ or $\downarrow$).
- u is a unit selector on the $\downarrow$ binding operator, referring to the desired granularity of time (e.g. year or minute) for binding x to the current time. A value of now indicates maximum precision.
- a and d are terms, possibly containing variables, that denote (respectively) absolute points in time and durations[1].

We constrain the use of variables within interval bounds b: any such variables must be bound by an enclosing $\downarrow$ operator.

In this logic, the temporal operators X (the next/previous state) and U (until) can be applied in the future direction (when adorned with a superscript '+') or the past (indicated by a '−'). Following MITL [7], the two U operators are qualified by an interval I that can be open or closed at each end (depending on whether a round or

---

[1] We do not define a language for these terms in this paper, but note that Verdicchio and Colombetti [10] have proposed a suitable language, which has inspired the treatment here.

square bracket is used, respectively)[2]. The meaning of $\mathsf{X}^+\phi$ is that ϕ is true in the next state, and $\phi\,\mathsf{U}_I^+\psi$ asserts that ϕ will remain true from the current state for some (possibly empty) sequence of consecutive future states, followed by a state that is within the time interval I and for which ψ holds. X^- and U_I^- are defined similarly, but in the past direction.

The bounds of intervals can be specified either relatively or absolutely—a prefix of "+" or "−" indicates a relative time value. Relative times (except for values of plus or minus zero) must indicate the units used, and the language for expressing time points must define a syntax for this, e.g. "−3 hours". When qualifying U^-, the interval bounds are written in the reverse order from usual (e.g. $[-2\,\text{hours}, -3\,\text{hours}]$), to reflect the backwards-looking nature of this operator.

A and E are temporal path quantifiers. They assert that the formula that follows the operator applies to all, or respectively at least one, of the possible sequences of states passing through the current state.

The $\downarrow$ operator is the "binder" operator used in hybrid logics [8]. It binds a variable to a term denoting the current date/time, using the same syntax as absolute interval bounds. The optional unit selector u is a time unit constant from the date/time sublanguage and indicates that the variable should be bound to the time point resulting from rounding down the current date/time to a particular degree of precision, e.g. to the start of the current year, month or day.

The final type of formula is an interval formula. This is true if the timepoint associated with the current state is within the interval[3]. The usual abbreviations of predicate logic are defined for disjunction ($\vee$), implication ($\rightarrow$) and existential quantification ($\exists$). We also use the standard abbreviations for existential and universal quantification over states in a path: $\mathsf{F}_I^+\phi \equiv \text{true}\,\mathsf{U}_I^+\phi$ and $\mathsf{G}_I^+\phi \equiv \neg\mathsf{F}_I^+\neg\phi$, with similar definitions for F_I^- and G_I^-. We define future and past "weak until" operators in the following way[4]:

$$\phi\,\mathsf{W}_{[l,u]}^+\psi \;\equiv\; \downarrow^{\text{now}} t.(\mathsf{G}_{[t,u]}^+\phi \vee \phi\,\mathsf{U}_{[l,u]}^+\psi)$$

with similar definitions for intervals with open bounds and for W^-. Finally, if a temporal operator is qualified by the interval $(-\infty,+\infty)$, we allow this to be suppressed for brevity, and a $\downarrow$ operator with no superscript is an abbreviation for $\downarrow^{\text{now}}$.

3   Semantics of hyMITL$^\pm$

Let S be a set of states, each being a first-order model for the language L over the fixed domain D, and all having the same interpretation for the date/time sublanguage of L. We denote the image of date terms under this shared interpretation by *Date* and the image of the set of time unit constants by U.

---

[2] We do not choose to qualify X^- and X^+ by an interval. Although one version [11] of MITL qualifies its next-state operator in this way, the version used in TLPlan [12] does not, and the original definition of MITL [7] did not include this operator at all.

[3] This is a generalisation of the notion of a *nominal* in hybrid logics: a formula that names a point in a model and is true if the current point is the one named.

[4] A straightforward extension of the usual definition would give $\phi\,\mathsf{W}_I^+\psi \equiv \mathsf{G}_I^+\phi \vee \phi\,\mathsf{U}_I^+\psi$, which would be true if ϕ is true throughout a future interval I but not before then.

$\langle M, p, V \rangle \models \phi$ where ϕ is an atomic formula, iff $\langle p_0, V \rangle \models \phi$.

$\langle M, p, V \rangle \models \neg\phi$ iff $\langle M, p, V \rangle \not\models \phi$.

$\langle M, p, V \rangle \models \phi \wedge \psi$ iff $\langle M, p, V \rangle \models \phi$ and $\langle M, p, V \rangle \models \psi$.

$\langle M, p, V \rangle \models \forall x.\phi_x$ iff for all $d \in D$, $\langle M, p, V[d/x] \rangle \models \phi_x$.

$\langle M, p, V \rangle \models \mathsf{X}^+\phi$ iff $\langle M, p^1, V \rangle \models \phi$.

$\langle M, p, V \rangle \models \mathsf{X}^-\phi$ iff for some path q, $q^1 = p$ and $\langle M, q, V \rangle \models \phi$.

$\langle M, p, V \rangle \models \phi \mathsf{U}_I^+ \psi$ iff for some $n \geq 0$, $\langle M, p^n, V \rangle \models \psi$, $\tau(p^n) \in I^{M,V}$ and for all m s.t. $0 \leq m < n$, $\langle M, p^m, V \rangle \models \phi$.

$\langle M, p, V \rangle \models \phi \mathsf{U}_I^- \psi$ iff for some path q and for some n, $q^n = p$, $\langle M, q, V \rangle \models \psi$, $\tau(q) \in I^{M,V}$, and for all m s.t. $0 < m \leq n$, $\langle M, q^m, V \rangle \models \phi$.

$\langle M, p, V \rangle \models \mathsf{A}\phi$ iff for all $q \in Paths(p_0)$, $\langle M, q, V \rangle \models \phi$.

$\langle M, p, V \rangle \models \mathsf{E}\phi$ iff for some $q \in Paths(p_0)$, $\langle M, q, V \rangle \models \phi$.

$\langle M, p, V \rangle \models \downarrow^u x.\phi_x$ iff $\langle M, p, V[floor(\tau(p), u^M)/x] \rangle \models \phi_x$.

$\langle M, p, V \rangle \models I$ where I is an interval formula, iff $\tau(p) \in I^{M,V}$.

Fig. 1. The semantics of hyMITL$^\pm$

A hyMITL$^\pm$ model M is a tuple $\langle S, <, \tau, \prec, floor \rangle$ where $<$ is a a total order relation on *Date*, τ is a function mapping from S into *Date*, $\prec$ is a state predecessor relation in which every state has a unique predecessor and a non-empty set of successors and which is consistent with the ordering on dates: $\forall s_1, s_2 \in S, s_1 \prec s_2 \rightarrow \tau(s_1) \leq \tau(s_2)$, and *floor* is a function from *Date* $\times U$ to *Date* representing the notion of rounding down a time value to a particular level of granularity[5].

A *path* in a model is an infinite sequence of states with each pair of adjacent elements s_i and s_{i+1} satisfying $s_i \prec s_{i+1}$. Following the notation of Verdicchio and Colombetti we write p_i to denote element $i+1$ of a path p (with indices starting at 0), p^i for the subsequence of p beginning with state p_i, and we extend the date function τ to operate on paths: $\tau(p) = \tau(p_0)$. The set of all paths starting from state s is denoted *Paths(s)*.

Let V be a variable assignment mapping variables to elements of the domain D. The notation $V[d/x]$ represents a variable assignment that is identical to V, except with x mapping to d. For interval expressions I in our language we write $I^{M,V}$ (or just I^M for ground interval expressions) to denote the interval in *Date* formed by applying V and the interpretation of date constants and function symbols that is common in all states of M to the bounds of I. We define $(-\infty, +\infty)^{M,V} = Date$. The interpretation in D of a ground term t in the date/time sublanguage is denoted t^M.

---

[5] The *floor* function is subject to a number of semantic constraints that we do not discuss here.

The truth of a formula in a model M and for a path p in M is then defined as shown in Figure 1. Note that as states in our semantics are first order models for L, the truth of an atomic formula on a given path reduces to its truth in the initial state of that path.

4   The Rule Language

We now identify a subset of hyMITL$^\pm$ that is suitable for encoding social expectations in a form that can be used in run-time compliance monitoring. We define the language R to be the set of all formulae of the following form:

$$\mathsf{AG}^+ \forall_{1 \le i \le n} x_i.(\phi \to \psi)$$

for $n \ge 0$, where:

- ϕ and ψ are linear-time formulae, i.e. they do not contain A or E;
- $\mathit{free\_variables}(\phi) = \mathit{free\_variables}(\psi) = \{x_1, \ldots, x_n\}$;
- ϕ and ψ do not contain any occurrences of $\forall$, except when represented using the $\exists$ abbreviation as outlined in the following clause.
- Any occurrence of $\exists$ must be of the following restricted form[6]: $\exists x.(\alpha_x \wedge \beta_x)$ where x is free in α_x and β_x, and α_x is atomic.

The intent of the last restriction is that matching α_x to the current state should produce a finite set of variable bindings for x, each of which should leave β_x with no free variables. This cannot be expressed syntactically and remains the responsibility of the rule designer (although any insufficiently instantiated instances of β_x can be detected and discarded at run time).

Rules of this form are intended to be used in the following compliance-monitoring process:

Given a current state and the history of all prior states and their associated times, for each rule, match the left hand side (ϕ) against the current state and history, resulting in a set of instances of the right hand side (ψ). Add these instances to the set of current expectations, then check all expectations to see which are fulfilled or violated. Any expectations that cannot yet be evaluated because they involve future states will be 'progressed' to the next state when it is created by an event observation.

This process requires that the left hand side of a rule can be matched against the current state and history, leaving no residual formula involving future states. This is not a syntactic constraint—e.g. future modalities can legitimately appear in the left hand side of a rule: consider $\mathsf{F}_I^- (\alpha \wedge \mathsf{X}^+ \beta)$. However, this constraint can be checked at run time, with a rule application simply failing if its left hand side cannot be matched using the current state and history alone. The rule designer must also use his/her knowledge of the domain model to ensure that the left hand side can only have a finite (and preferably bounded) number of matches for any state and history.

The following section presents an example rule in this notation and then Section 6 describes the compliance-monitoring process in more detail.

---

[6] This is equivalent to TLPlan's bounded existential quantification [9].

$$\mathsf{AG}^+ (\mathrm{Done}(c, \text{ make\_payment}(c,p,amount,prod\_num)) \wedge [t, \ t+1\,\text{week}) \ \rightarrow$$

$$\downarrow^{\text{week}} \mathrm{w}.(\downarrow^{\text{week}} \mathrm{cw}.(\neg \mathsf{X}^- [\mathrm{cw}, \ -0] \ \rightarrow$$

$$\mathsf{F}^+_{[+0, \ \mathrm{cw}+1\,\text{week})} \mathrm{Done}(p, \text{ send\_report}(c, prod\_num, \mathrm{cw})))$$

$$\mathsf{W}^+_{[\mathrm{w}+1\,\text{week}, \ \mathrm{w}+53\,\text{weeks})}$$

$$\mathrm{Done}(c, \text{ cancel\_order}(c,p,prod\_num)))))$$

Fig. 2. A rule expressing the terms of service offered by agent p to agent c

5   Example

Consider the case of an agent that can provide weekly reports on a particular market for an annual fee. A potential customer is advised of a fee for the service and has one week to confirm the order and make payment. After this time the price is not valid and a new quote must be sought. Once payment is made, the service-providing agent is committed to sending a report to the customer once a week for 52 weeks or until the customer cancels the order. If the customer cancels the order before 52 weeks have passed, he or she may be eligible for a partial refund, but we do not model that here.

Figure 2 shows how the service-providing agent could encode its conditional commitment using our rule syntax (where p and c are the names of service provider and customer agents respectively, t is an expression representing the time the offer is made, and *amount* and *prod_id* are expressions representing the amount to be paid for the service and the service provider's identification number for this product). This rule could be sent from the provider to the customer as the content of a communicative act that explicitly asserts the commitment is being made. Alternatively, making this commitment may be an "institutional action" [6] that is inferred by both p and c to have occurred as a result of a particular dialogue between them having been completed.

The rule in Figure 2 states that if the current state is one in which c has just made payment for the service, and this state is within the one week period from the time the offer was made (time t) then weekly reports will be sent during the next 52 weeks (beginning the week after the payment is made) until p optionally cancels the order. The assertion that weekly reports will be sent (the left hand side of the W^+ operator) is encoded as the implication that if it is not the case that the previous state is in the closed interval from the start of the current week to the present time (i.e. the current state is the first since the start of the current week) then the report will be sent some time between now and the end of the week[7].

This rule assumes that the actions of making a payment, sending a report and cancelling an order can be observed by both agents as occurring at a unique well defined time. In practice, agents will not observe events simultaneously, and their clocks cannot be guaranteed to be perfectly synchronised. However, if these actions are implemented by sending messages, the sending time (as recorded by the sender and included in the message header) can be taken as the time the action occurs. Provided that the intervals in a commitment are of a significantly greater magnitude than the likely clock

---

[7] A tighter specification could identify a particular day of the week on which the report will be sent.

function *check_state*
inputs: A history of state/time pairs $h = \langle(s_0, t_0), \ldots, (s_n, t_n)\rangle$,
where s_n is the new state to be checked, a set of formulae
E_{n-1} representing expectations that could not be fully
evaluated in s_{n-1}, and a set of rules R.
outputs: A set of partially evaluated formulae E_n and a set of
notification assertions N
begin
    vars $E = progress\_formulae(E_{n-1}, h, n-1) \cup$
        $new\_expectations(h, R)$,
        $E_n = \varnothing, N = \varnothing$
    for each ϕ in E:
        var $\phi' = peval(\phi, h, n)$
        if $\phi' = $ true, $N = N \cup \{$fulfilled$(\phi)\}$
        else if $\phi' = $ false, $N = N \cup \{$violated$(\phi)\}$
        else if $worth\_progressing(\phi')$, $E_n = E_n \cup \{\phi'\}$
    return $\langle E_n, N\rangle$
end

Fig. 3. The main algorithm: *check_state*

slippage and message delivery delay, this approximation should be acceptable. The possibility of significantly inaccurate message times (either forged or caused by inaccurate clocks) is difficult to deal with; however, for ease of modelling, the attempted detection of such occurrences (if possible and required) is best handled by a separate mechanism.

6   The Compliance-Monitoring Process

The compliance monitoring process is performed by function *check_state* shown in Figure 3. This should be called by an agent when it has performed an action or observed some event that it (or the agent programmer) considers significant. The *check_state* function assumes that the agent has already created a new state name and asserted into its world model for that state any facts that it knows to hold (including facts expressing the occurrence of the actions and events that are considered to have triggered the transition to a new state). The function receives as arguments the history of states, the current unfulfilled expectations, and the set of rules defining the social expectations of the institution to which the agent currently belongs.

The function *progress_formulae* applies a modified version of the *progress* algorithm of Bacchus and Kabanza [12] to every unfulfilled expectation from the previous state, with that previous state's time stamp as an additional argument. This algorithm generates a formula expressing what needs to be true in the new state if the input expectation was required to be true in the previous state, but was not yet able to be evaluated there. For example, $progress(\mathsf{X}^+\phi, t) = \phi$, and if t is within the interval I, $progress(\phi\,\mathsf{U}_I^+\psi, t)$ has the following value:

$$\ulcorner progress(\psi, t)\urcorner \vee (\ulcorner progress(\phi, t)\urcorner \wedge \phi\,\mathsf{U}_{\ulcorner rtoa(I,t)\urcorner}^+\psi)$$

function *match* (non-deterministic)
inputs: A formula ϕ, a history of state/time pairs $h = \langle (s_0, t_0), \ldots, (s_n, t_n) \rangle$, and an index i for the current state
output: A variable binding or $\bot$ (failure)
begin
  if $(i < 0 \lor i > n)$ **fail**
  case ϕ is an atomic formula:
    choose any σ s.t. $Dom(\sigma) = vars(\phi)$ and $\langle s_i, \sigma \rangle \models \phi$
    return σ
  case $\phi = \neg\phi_1$:
    if *free_variables*$(\phi) = \varnothing$ and *match*(ϕ_1, h, i) fails, **return** $\{\}$
    else fail
  case $\phi = \phi_1 \land \phi_2$:
    choose $\sigma_1 = match(\phi_1, h, i)$ and $\sigma_2 = match(\phi_2\sigma_1, h, i)$
    return $\sigma_1 \cup \sigma_2$
  case $\phi = \exists x.(\phi_1 \land \phi_2)$:
    choose $\sigma_1 = match(\phi_1, h, i)$
    if *nonvar*$(x\sigma_1)$, **choose** $\sigma_2 = match(\phi_2\sigma_1, h, i)$ and **return** $\sigma_1\!\restriction_{dom(\sigma_1)\setminus\{x\}} \cup \sigma_2$
    else fail
  case $\phi = \mathsf{X}^+\phi_1$: **return** $match(\phi_1, h, i+1)$
  case $\phi = \mathsf{X}^-\phi_1$: **return** $match(\phi_1, h, i-1)$
  case $\phi = \phi_1 \mathsf{U}_I^+ \phi_2$:
    begin
      case $t_i > I$: **fail**
      case $t_i < I$: **choose** $\sigma = match(\phi_1, h, i)$
                return $match(\ulcorner\phi_1\sigma\urcorner \mathsf{U}_{\ulcorner rtoa(I, t_i)\urcorner}^+ \ulcorner\phi_2\sigma\urcorner, h, i+1)$
      case $t_i \in I$: **either choose** σ as for case $t_i < I$
                or choose $\sigma = match(\phi_2, h, i)$
    end
  case $\phi = \phi_1 \mathsf{U}_I^- \phi_2$:
    Mirror image of U_I^+ *case*
  case $\phi = \downarrow^u x.\phi_x$:
    return $match(\ulcorner\phi_x[\lfloor floor(t_i, u^M)\rfloor/x]\urcorner, h, i)$
  case $\phi = I$, where I is an interval formula:
    if $t_i \in I$ **return** $\{\}$ **else fail**
end

Fig. 4. The *match* function

where corner quotes ($\ulcorner$ and $\urcorner$) are used to indicate the parts of the formula that should be evaluated to generate subexpressions, and *rtoa* ("relative to absolute") is a function that takes an interval and the 'current' time and produces an equivalent interval with any relative bounds converted to absolute time points[8].

---

[8] As some units of relative time (such as month) have a length that depends on the current date, the *rtoa* function is used during progression instead of TLPlan's adjustment of relative intervals by the time difference between adjacent states.

The function *new_expectations* matches the left hand side of each rule to the state history, and for each resulting rule instantiation, adds the instantiated right hand side to the set of new expectations that this function returns. Any expectations that are not fully instantiated by this process (i.e. they have free variables) are discarded. The *match* function used in this process is shown in Figure 4. It is presented in the figure as a non-deterministic function that can either fail or return multiple variable bindings (one at a time). The notation $\llcorner t \lrcorner$ indicates a mapping from the semantic to the syntactic domain that chooses a term that names a given time point. This must be built into an implementation.

Once the new expectations have been computed, each formula in the combined set of old and new expectations is partially evaluated using the function *peval* shown in Figure 5. This uses the history to evaluate a formula as much as possible, resulting in true or false if the truth of the formula can be determined yet, and otherwise returning a formula equivalent to the original one (given the facts in the history states) but modified where possible to make progression and future evaluation easier. The *simplify* function removes double negations and simplifies formulae that have true and false as subformulae. In the U_I^+ case of the *match* function, when $t_i < I$, the *rtoa* function is used to convert any relative interval bounds to absolute ones. In the case for $\downarrow$ formulae, a time constant must be generated using the *floor* function that is part of the semantic domain.

The test *worth_progressing* can be used to discard expectations that could not be evaluated for reasons other than lack of future information, such as atomic formulae for which *peval* did not return true or false (if closed-world reasoning is not used within states) or formulae with past modalities that needed a longer history in order to be evaluated.

The use of the *peval* function means that the progression function does not need to handle atomic formulae (so it needs no state argument as in the original definition [12]), $\exists$, $\downarrow$ or interval formulae.

In the *match* and *peval* functions, comparisons and operations involving intervals are required. The semantics of hyMITL$^\pm$ assumed that there is a date/time sublanguage with a total order $<$ on time, and in the following we assume we have an implementation of that relation, extended in the obvious way to allow comparisons with $\pm\infty$. As both absolute and relative times can appear in interval bounds, we extend equality and the $<$ relation to apply to the combined set of absolute and relative times: for any absolute time t and relative time r, $t \neq r$, $t < r \equiv r > 0$ and $r < t \equiv r < 0$. We define membership of a point in an interval as follows:

$$t \in [l, u] \equiv ((l < t < u) \vee (l \text{ is a relative bound and } l = \pm 0)$$
$$\vee \ (l \text{ is an absolute bound and } l = t)$$
$$\vee \ (u \text{ is a relative bound and } u = \pm 0)$$
$$\vee \ (u \text{ is an absolute bound and } u = t))$$

with similar (but simpler) definitions for intervals with open ends.

A consequence of these definitions is that (e.g.) $\forall t \in Date, t \in [-1, +1]$. The intuition is that we are only interested in performing this test when considering t as the current time.

For a time point t and interval I with lower bound l we define:

$$t < I \equiv (t < l \vee (t = l \wedge l \notin I))$$

We define $t > I$ in similar way.

7   Related Work

Several other approaches to the modelling and run-time monitoring of social norms have been proposed recently.

The SOCS-SI system [13] performs run-time protocol compliance monitoring based on *social integrity constraints*: rules that express positive and negative expectations as the consequences of observed actions. Abductive inference is used to generate expectations during run time and these are monitored to determine their fulfilment or violation. The semantics do not include an underlying model of time. Instead explicit time variables are associated with the observation and expectation atoms in rules, and constraint logic programming constraints can be used to relate these time points.

Mallya et al. [14] proposed a language for representing social commitments that have a temporal nature. Their notation uses interval expressions representing universal or existential state quantification within these intervals, with semantics based on a timed version of CTL. They provided an analysis showing how to determine when a given commitment could be known to be fulfilled or violated.

Verdicchio and Colombetti [10] presented a rich language for making statements involving time, including interval expressions that are a generalisation of the work by Mallya et al. The language is defined axiomatically, and so would not support runtime use as efficiently as the approach proposed here, where metric time is built in to the semantics and evaluation mechanism. This work inspired the use of a date/time sublanguage in the present paper.

Farrell et al. [15] use event calculus to represent contracts by modelling the effects that actions have on the normative relations between agents. They have implemented a system to track the state of contracts expressed in this way.

García-Camino et al. [16] proposed a language that can express conditional permissions, prohibitions and obligations of agents, including temporal constraints, and described a mechanism for tracking the normative state of an institution by translating these rules into rules of the production system JESS. The JESS rules, when fired, assert facts representing new rules that will be added to the production system at a specific time point by an external process that monitors the time and the JESS working memory.

In other research, García-Camino et al. [17] developed a form of production system that uses constraint logic programming techniques to maintain the institutional state as a set of facts and constraints. Rules expressing norms can assert and retract facts and add constraints. In addition, a tuple space is used to store the instiutional state, allowing multiple agents to access it.

Endriss [18] discusses the use of *generalised model checking* for deciding whether a trace of an agent dialogue conforms to a protocol expressed in propositional linear temporal logic.

Case	Result
$\phi = I$ (an interval formula)	true if $0 \leq i \leq n \wedge t_i \in I$ false if $(0 \leq i \leq n \wedge t_i \notin I) \vee (i < 0 \wedge t_0 < I) \vee (i > n \wedge t_n > I)$ ϕ otherwise
$\phi = \phi_1 \, \mathsf{U}_I^+ \, \phi_2$	ϕ if $i < 0 \vee$ $(i > n \wedge t_n \leq I)$ false if $(i > n \wedge t_n > I) \vee$ $(0 \leq i \leq n \wedge t_i > I)$ *simplify(* $\ulcorner peval(\phi_2, h, i) \urcorner \vee$ $(\ulcorner peval(\phi_1, h, i) \urcorner \wedge$ if $0 \leq i \leq n \wedge t_i \in I$ $\mathsf{X}^+ \ulcorner peval(\phi_1 \, \mathsf{U}^+_{\ulcorner rtoa(I, t_i) \urcorner} \phi_2, h, i+1) \urcorner))$ *simplify(* $\ulcorner peval(\phi_1, h, i) \urcorner \wedge$ if $0 \leq i \leq n \wedge t_i < I$ $\mathsf{X}^+ \ulcorner peval(\phi_1 \, \mathsf{U}^+_{\ulcorner rtoa(I, t_i) \urcorner} \phi_2, h, i+1) \urcorner)$
$\phi = \phi_1 \, \mathsf{U}_I^- \, \phi_2$	*Mirror image of* U_I^+ *case*
Other formula types when $i < 0 \vee i > n$	ϕ
The following cases assume $0 \leq i \leq n$	
ϕ is atomic	true if $s_i \models \phi$ false if $s_i \not\models \phi$
$\phi = \neg \phi_1$	$simplify(\neg \ulcorner peval(\phi_1, h, i) \urcorner)$
$\phi = \phi_1 \wedge \phi_2$	$simplify(\ulcorner peval(\phi_1, h, i) \urcorner \wedge \ulcorner peval(\phi_2, h, i) \urcorner)$
$\phi = \exists x.(\phi_x \wedge \psi_x)$	false if $match(\phi_x, h, i)$ fails *simplify(* if $\Psi = \{\psi_x \sigma \mid \sigma = match(\phi_x, h, i) \wedge$ $\bigvee_{\psi \in \Psi} \ulcorner peval(\psi, h, i) \urcorner)$ $nonvar(x \sigma)\}$ is non-empty $\bot$ otherwise (an error condition)
$\phi = \mathsf{X}^+ \phi_1$	$simplify(\mathsf{X}^+ \ulcorner peval(\phi_1, h, i+1) \urcorner)$
$\phi = \mathsf{X}^- \phi_1$	$simplify(\mathsf{X}^- \ulcorner peval(\phi_1, h, i-1) \urcorner)$
$\phi = \downarrow^u x.\phi_x$	$simplify(\ulcorner peval(\ulcorner \phi_x [\llcorner floor(t_i, u^M) \lrcorner / x] \urcorner, h, i) \urcorner)$

Fig. 5. Function $peval(\phi, h, i)$, where $h = \langle (s_0, t_0), \ldots, (s_n, t_n) \rangle$

This paper presented an extension of the CTL$^\pm$ logic and defined first-order semantics for it. Verdicchio and Colombetti have recently provided their own first-order semantics for a multi-sorted version of CTL$^\pm$ [6].

8   Conclusion

This paper has defined a rule language for defining social expectations based on a branching time metric interval temporal logic and has presented an algorithm that can be used at run time in a multi-agent system to monitor when expectations are generated, fulfilled and violated—either for the system as a whole (if all events can be detected by a specialised monitoring agent) or within an individual agent wishing to monitor the expectations it has of other agents. A prototype implementation of the compliance monitoring procedure has been implemented using SWI Prolog. Most of the features described here have been implemented, although currently the system is not connected to an agent—it uses a static database of states and their facts.

Future work includes investigating the expressivity of the rule language for modelling complex scenarios, enhancing it with additional operators (e.g. bounded universal quantification) and applying it to interaction protocol verification—where the X^+ operator will have particular relevance. It is also intended to deploy and evaluate this approach in a distributed multi-agent application.

Acknowledgements

Thanks to Hans van Ditmarsch and Willem Labuschagne for their comments on a draft of this paper.

References

1. Cortés, U.: Electronic institutions and agents. AgentLink News **15** (2004) 14–15
2. Leite, J.A., Omicini, A., Torroni, P., Yolum, P., eds.: Proceedings of the Workshop on Declarative Agent Languages and Technologies (DALT 2004), Third International Joint Conference on Autonomous Agents and Multiagent Systems. (2004)
3. Huget, M.P., Esteva, M., Phelps, S., Sierra, C., Wooldridge, M.: Model checking electronic institutions. In: Proceedings of the Workshop on Model Checking and Artificial Intelligence (MoChArt-2002), 15th European Conference on Artificial Intelligence. (2002)
4. Cliffe, O., Padget, J.: A framework for checking agent interaction within institutions. In: Proceedings of the Workshop on Model Checking and Artificial Intelligence (MoChArt-2002), 15th European Conference on Artificial Intelligence. (2002)
5. Verdicchio, M., Colombetti, M.: A logical model of social commitment for agent communication. In: Proceedings of the 2nd International Joint Conference on Autonomous Agents and Multiagent Systems (AAMAS 2003), ACM Press (2003) 528–535
6. Verdicchio, M., Colombetti, M.: A commitment-based communicative act library. In: Proceedings of the 4nd International Joint Conference on Autonomous Agents and Multiagent Systems (AAMAS 2005), ACM Press (2005) 755–761
7. Alur, R., Feder, T., Henzinger, T.A.: The benefits of relaxing punctuality. Journal of the ACM **43** (1996) 116–146
8. Blackburn, P., de Rijke, M., Venema, Y.: Modal Logic. Cambridge University Press (2001)
9. Bacchus, F., Kabanza, F.: Using temporal logics to express search control knowledge for planning. Artificial Intelligence **116** (2000) 123–191
10. Verdicchio, M., Colombetti, M.: Dealing with time in content language expressions. In: Proceedings of the Workshop on Agent Communication, Third International Joint Conference on Autonomous Agents and Multiagent Systems. (2004) 90–104

11. Haslum, P.: Partial state progression: An extension to the Bacchus-Kabanza algorithm, with applications to prediction and MITL consistency. In: Proceedings of the Workshop on Planning via Model-Checking, Sixth International Conference on AI Planning and Scheduling. (2002) 64–71
12. Bacchus, F., Kabanza, F.: Planning for temporally extended goals. Annals of Mathematics and Artificial Intelligence **22** (1998) 5–27
13. Alberti, M., Chesani, F., Gavanelli, M., Lamma, E., Mello, P., Torroni, P.: Compliance verification of agent interaction: a logic-based software tool. In Trappl, R., ed.: Cybernetics and Systems 2004. Volume II., Austrian Society for Cybernetics Studies (2004) 570–575
14. Mallya, A.U., Yolum, P., Singh, M.P.: Resolving commitments among autonomous agents. In: Advances in Agent Communication. Volume 2922 of Lecture Notes in Computer Science., Springer (2004) 166–182
15. Farrell, A.D.H., Sergot, M.J., Sallé, M., Bartolini, C.: Using the event calculus for tracking the normative state of contracts. International Journal of Cooperative Information Systems **14** (2005) 99–129
16. García-Camino, A., Noriega, P., Rodríguez-Aguilar, J.A.: Implementing norms in electronic institutions. In: Proceedings of the 4nd International Joint Conference on Autonomous Agents and Multiagent Systems (AAMAS 2005), ACM Press (2005) 667–673
17. García-Camino, A., Rodríguez-Aguilar, J.A., Sierra, C., Vasconcelos, W.: A distributed architecture for norm-aware agent societies. In: Proceedings of the 3rd International Workshop on Declarative Agent Languages and Technologies (DALT 2005). (2005) http://www.doc.ic.ac.uk/~ue/DALT-2005/papers/24.pdf.
18. Endriss, U.: Temporal logics for representing agent communication protocols. In: Proceedings of the Workshop on Agent Communication, 4th International Joint Conference on Autonomous Agents and Multiagent Systems. (2005) 33–47

Author Index

Lecture Notes in Artificial Intelligence (LNAI)

Vol. 3849: I. Bloch, A. Petrosino, A.G.B. Tettamanzi (Eds.), Fuzzy Logic and Applications. XIV, 438 pages. 2006.

Vol. 3848: J.-F. Boulicaut, L. De Raedt, H. Mannila (Eds.), Constraint-Based Mining and Inductive Databases. X, 401 pages. 2006.

Vol. 3847: K.P. Jantke, A. Lunzer, N. Spyratos, Y. Tanaka (Eds.), Federation over the Web. X, 215 pages. 2006.

Vol. 3835: G. Sutcliffe, A. Voronkov (Eds.), Logic for Programming, Artificial Intelligence, and Reasoning. XIV, 744 pages. 2005.

Vol. 3830: D. Weyns, H. V.D. Parunak, F. Michel (Eds.), Environments for Multi-Agent Systems II. VIII, 291 pages. 2006.

Vol. 3817: M. Faundez-Zanuy, L. Janer, A. Esposito, A. Satue-Villar, J. Roure, V. Espinosa-Duro (Eds.), Nonlinear Analyses and Algorithms for Speech Processing. XII, 380 pages. 2006.

Vol. 3814: M. Maybury, O. Stock, W. Wahlster (Eds.), Intelligent Technologies for Interactive Entertainment. XV, 342 pages. 2005.

Vol. 3809: S. Zhang, R. Jarvis (Eds.), AI 2005: Advances in Artificial Intelligence. XXVII, 1344 pages. 2005.

Vol. 3808: C. Bento, A. Cardoso, G. Dias (Eds.), Progress in Artificial Intelligence. XVIII, 704 pages. 2005.

Vol. 3802: Y. Hao, J. Liu, Y.-P. Wang, Y.-m. Cheung, H. Yin, L. Jiao, J. Ma, Y.-C. Jiao (Eds.), Computational Intelligence and Security, Part II. XLII, 1166 pages. 2005.

Vol. 3801: Y. Hao, J. Liu, Y.-P. Wang, Y.-m. Cheung, H. Yin, L. Jiao, J. Ma, Y.-C. Jiao (Eds.), Computational Intelligence and Security, Part I. XLI, 1122 pages. 2005.

Vol. 3789: A. Gelbukh, Á. de Albornoz, H. Terashima-Marín (Eds.), MICAI 2005: Advances in Artificial Intelligence. XXVI, 1198 pages. 2005.

Vol. 3782: K.-D. Althoff, A. Dengel, R. Bergmann, M. Nick, T.R. Roth-Berghofer (Eds.), Professional Knowledge Management. XXIII, 739 pages. 2005.

Vol. 3763: H. Hong, D. Wang (Eds.), Automated Deduction in Geometry. X, 213 pages. 2006.

Vol. 3755: G.J. Williams, S.J. Simoff (Eds.), Data Mining. XI, 331 pages. 2006.

Vol. 3735: A. Hoffmann, H. Motoda, T. Scheffer (Eds.), Discovery Science. XVI, 400 pages. 2005.

Vol. 3734: S. Jain, H.U. Simon, E. Tomita (Eds.), Algorithmic Learning Theory. XII, 490 pages. 2005.

Vol. 3721: A.M. Jorge, L. Torgo, P.B. Brazdil, R. Camacho, J. Gama (Eds.), Knowledge Discovery in Databases: PKDD 2005. XXIII, 719 pages. 2005.

Vol. 3720: J. Gama, R. Camacho, P.B. Brazdil, A.M. Jorge, L. Torgo (Eds.), Machine Learning: ECML 2005. XXIII, 769 pages. 2005.

Vol. 3717: B. Gramlich (Ed.), Frontiers of Combining Systems. X, 321 pages. 2005.

Vol. 3702: B. Beckert (Ed.), Automated Reasoning with Analytic Tableaux and Related Methods. XIII, 343 pages. 2005.

Vol. 3698: U. Furbach (Ed.), KI 2005: Advances in Artificial Intelligence. XIII, 409 pages. 2005.

Vol. 3690: M. Pěchouček, P. Petta, L.Z. Varga (Eds.), Multi-Agent Systems and Applications IV. XVII, 667 pages. 2005.

Vol. 3684: R. Khosla, R.J. Howlett, L.C. Jain (Eds.), Knowledge-Based Intelligent Information and Engineering Systems, Part IV. LXXIX, 933 pages. 2005.

Vol. 3683: R. Khosla, R.J. Howlett, L.C. Jain (Eds.), Knowledge-Based Intelligent Information and Engineering Systems, Part III. LXXX, 1397 pages. 2005.

Vol. 3682: R. Khosla, R.J. Howlett, L.C. Jain (Eds.), Knowledge-Based Intelligent Information and Engineering Systems, Part II. LXXIX, 1371 pages. 2005.

Vol. 3681: R. Khosla, R.J. Howlett, L.C. Jain (Eds.), Knowledge-Based Intelligent Information and Engineering Systems, Part I. LXXX, 1319 pages. 2005.

Vol. 3673: S. Bandini, S. Manzoni (Eds.), AI*IA 2005: Advances in Artificial Intelligence. XIV, 614 pages. 2005.

Vol. 3662: C. Baral, G. Greco, N. Leone, G. Terracina (Eds.), Logic Programming and Nonmonotonic Reasoning. XIII, 454 pages. 2005.

Vol. 3661: T. Panayiotopoulos, J. Gratch, R. Aylett, D. Ballin, P. Olivier, T. Rist (Eds.), Intelligent Virtual Agents. XIII, 506 pages. 2005.

Vol. 3658: V. Matoušek, P. Mautner, T. Pavelka (Eds.), Text, Speech and Dialogue. XV, 460 pages. 2005.

Vol. 3651: R. Dale, K.-F. Wong, J. Su, O.Y. Kwong (Eds.), Natural Language Processing – IJCNLP 2005. XXI, 1031 pages. 2005.

Vol. 3642: D. Ślęzak, J. Yao, J.F. Peters, W. Ziarko, X. Hu (Eds.), Rough Sets, Fuzzy Sets, Data Mining, and Granular Computing, Part II. XXIII, 738 pages. 2005.

Vol. 3641: D. Ślęzak, G. Wang, M. Szczuka, I. Düntsch, Y. Yao (Eds.), Rough Sets, Fuzzy Sets, Data Mining, and Granular Computing, Part I. XXIV, 742 pages. 2005.

Vol. 3635: J.R. Winkler, M. Niranjan, N.D. Lawrence (Eds.), Deterministic and Statistical Methods in Machine Learning. VIII, 341 pages. 2005.

Vol. 3632: R. Nieuwenhuis (Ed.), Automated Deduction – CADE-20. XIII, 459 pages. 2005.

Vol. 3630: M.S. Capcarrère, A.A. Freitas, P.J. Bentley, C.G. Johnson, J. Timmis (Eds.), Advances in Artificial Life. XIX, 949 pages. 2005.

Vol. 3626: B. Ganter, G. Stumme, R. Wille (Eds.), Formal Concept Analysis. X, 349 pages. 2005.

Vol. 3625: S. Kramer, B. Pfahringer (Eds.), Inductive Logic Programming. XIII, 427 pages. 2005.

Vol. 3620: H. Muñoz-Ávila, F. Ricci (Eds.), Case-Based Reasoning Research and Development. XV, 654 pages. 2005.

Vol. 3614: L. Wang, Y. Jin (Eds.), Fuzzy Systems and Knowledge Discovery, Part II. XLI, 1314 pages. 2005.

Vol. 3613: L. Wang, Y. Jin (Eds.), Fuzzy Systems and Knowledge Discovery, Part I. XLI, 1334 pages. 2005.

Vol. 3607: J.-D. Zucker, L. Saitta (Eds.), Abstraction, Reformulation and Approximation. XII, 376 pages. 2005.